An Uninhibited Treasury of Erotic Poetry

An Uninhibited Treasury of Erotic Poetry

EDITED, WITH A RUNNING COMMENTARY, BY

Louis Untermeyer

toExcel
San Jose New York Lincoln Shanghai

An Uninhibited Treasury of Erotic Poetry

Published by toExcel
an imprint of iUniverse.com, Inc.

For information address:
iUniverse.com, Inc.
620 North 48th Street
Suite 201
Lincoln, NE 68504-3467
www.iuniverse.com

ISBN: 0-595-00654-X

Printed in the United States of America

Acknowledgments

ROBERT BAGG
for "Soft Answers," copyright © 1960 by Robert Bagg. Reprinted by permission.

JUDSON CREWS
for "Oh Beach Love Blossom," "Declaration at Forty," and "Love Poem." Copyright by Judson Crews and reprinted with his permission.

J. V. CUNNINGHAM
for "The Pick-Up" and "It Was in Vegas," originally printed in the *Partisan Review*, Fall, 1960, and reprinted by permission.

DOUBLEDAY & COMPANY
for "I Knew a Woman," copyright 1954 by Theodore Roethke, "The Sensualists," copyright © 1958 by Theodore Roethke, from *Words for the Wind*. Reprinted by permission of Doubleday & Company, Inc. "Lilith" and "In a Prominent Bar" from *Nude Descending a Staircase* by X. J. Kennedy. Copyright © 1961. Reprinted by permission of Doubleday & Company, Inc.

EYRE & SPOTTISWOODE
for "Sublimation" and "After You, Madam" from *Haste to the Wedding* by Alex Comfort. Copyright 1962.

CERISE FARALLON
for "The Serpent of God" and "Pride and Hesitation." Copyright 1962. Reprinted by permission.

HAMISH HAMILTON LTD.
for "Imperial Adam," "The Gateway," and "Chorale" from *Poems* by A. D. Hope. © 1960 by A. D. Hope. Reprinted by permission.

LOUIS UNTERMEYER

for translations and paraphrases from *The Greek Anthology*, Horace, Petronius, Heine, Verlaine, and the Sampler of German Love Sayings, most of them published here for the first time.

THE VIKING PRESS, INC.

for "Lightning" from *Collected Poems* by D. H. Lawrence. Copyright 1929 by Jonathan Cape and Harrison Smith, Inc.; 1957 by Frieda Lawrence Ravagli. Reprinted by permission of The Viking Press, Inc. "Imperial Adam," "The Gateway," and "Chorale" from *Poems* by A. D. Hope. Reprinted by permission of The Viking Press, Inc. All rights reserved.

Contents

x

A World of Wit

Ballads and Folk Songs

The Merry Muses

Nineteenth Century Romantics

The Modern World

*An
Uninhibited
Treasury
of
Erotic Poetry*

Introduction: Variations on the Theme of Love

The dictionaries define "erotic" variously as "having to do with sexual love . . . of or pertaining to desire . . . amatory . . ." but we must go back to the source to find the multiple meanings of the word. It stems naturally from Eros, the Greek god of love who, in his Roman incarnation, became Cupid. As a god he was, like many of his fellow Olympians, very human, romantic, restless, unruly, irresponsible and irresistible. He was also unpredictable, at times a sly mischief-maker, at other times a cruel tyrant, a rascal playing with dangerous arrows, and a beatific divinity, a dispenser as well as a healer of wounds.

Since "erotic" is derived from a capricious deity it follows that the erotic impulse is similarly wayward, being, true to its origin, both fervid and whimsical, faithful and wanton. No single definition can cover its manifestations, and its range of subjects is so broad that there are no limits to its expressiveness. This is especially true when the the poet makes himself a spokesman for the willful god. Much of his poetry may burn with mounting emotion and smolder with importunate pleadings, aggravating delays, passionate fulfillment or, alas too often, painful frustration. But a great portion of erotic verse is inspired by nothing more violent than banter—the constant play between men and women, arch teasing, light philandering, ardent protestations, all the oaths of fidelity and the casual deceptions which are the by-products of love. Freedom of range is matched by an equal freedom of speech. The language of love can be beautiful or bawdy, naively simple or boldly salacious, elegantly baroque or coarse and common as the vernacular, or, in certain moments, a wild mixture of all these.

In poetry one often finds the innocent and the sophisticated, the virtuous and the vulgar, side by side. Sometimes both extremes are encompassed by the same poet. The lusty sensuality in Robert Burns's *Merry Muses of Caledonia* is a realistic countermeasure (and

1

perhaps a peasant's corrective) to the bard's more familiar bucolic lyricism. Though some readers may object to the unashamed union of love and lust, the earthy celebration of carnal pleasure is no more pornographic than many of the passages in Shakespeare's noblest tragedies as well as in his rowdiest comedies. And while love is one of the noblest emotions, it is frequently depicted as a game; the Elizabethans as well as the eighteenth-century followers of Dryden delighted to present the purely (or impurely) sportive side.

The ever-varying phases of the pursuit of love, a game in which the pursued and the pursuer occasionally change places, are illustrated in this collection. If not all of it is to be taken seriously, it may be said that the wholly serious is seldom diverting, and diversion is one thing which is not absent from this book. One may trace a development of poetic traditions in the progress of the changing idioms shown here; but, although the arrangement, being chronological, may be a help to the student of mores, the historical aspect is incidental. While some of the pages, preserving pictures of the period, have a documentary importance, most of them are content to record the development of man's amatory nature, his response to its demands, even an awareness of its follies.

Here, then, are the infinite variations in the traditional battle between the sexes: the gallant approach, the tentative flirtation, the provocative badinage, the coy denial, the gradually permitted intimacy, the timid or breathless consent, and the finally shared extremity of passion. The accent is on the lively rather than the morbid, on the exalted or exasperating or ridiculous but always enjoyable—and highly readable—manifestations of love.

The history of literature is full of paradoxes of what has been considered fit for general conversation and preservation in print. The earthiness of Rabelais and the amorality of Boccaccio, relished on every level and by all classes during the fourteenth and fifteenth centuries, were bowdlerized and banned a few hundred years later. The early 1900's encouraged armies of censors and, since no one could agree on a satisfactory definition of pornography, the confusion as to its limits continued to increase. In his opening chapter in *The Erotic in Literature*, David Loth calls attention to the fact that Lawrence's *Lady Chatterley's Lover*, which gives details of the sexual act in crude four letter words, is sold widely, while John Cleland's *Memoirs of Fanny Hill*, an eighteenth century classic which does not contain a coarse word, is still considered so pornographic that it cannot be openly published.

2

The accepted candor of one generation tends to become the shocking obscenity of another—and vice versa. However, since the death of Mrs. Grundy, who presided over English morals in the person of Queen Victoria, language and literature have grown less rigid and more unrestricted than they have been for centuries. The seemingly unlimited resources of the modern novel and the ever-enlarging reach of contemporary cinema permit the respectable citizen to explore territories which, until recently, he was not allowed to survey. It is under these conditions that this collection has been completed. The conditions are not merely favorable but liberating. They have permitted this anthologist to roam freely and to fulfill his function as editor of literature rather than apprehensive critic of man's *mores*.

LOUIS UNTERMEYER

From the Bible

The Song of Songs

"The Song of Songs" is the most beautiful erotic poem ever written. It is also, in its context, the strangest. Enshrined in the Bible between the severe preaching of Ecclesiastes and the prophetic visions of Isaiah, it stands out as a magnificent incongruity, a set of irreligious and sensual love lyrics. Its origins and authorship as well as its purpose have been the subject of continual disputations; its very title has given rise to countless debates. The King James version calls it "The Song of Solomon"; other editions amplify it to "The Song of Songs, which is Solomon's." This presents a further problem. One implication is that Solomon was the author of the poem, which most scholars deny; another is that Solomon is its hero, the royal suitor in an episodic drama. It is, however, generally accepted that the name of Solomon was added at a later date in order to give the work a dignity and authority which would justify its inclusion in the Old Testament.

In any case, what are these warm, voluptuous chapters doing in Holy Writ? The ancient rabbis steadfastly maintained that the "Song" was a parable in which the ardent lover was God and the beloved was Israel. From the third to the eighth centuries, from Origen to the Venerable Bede, the early churchmen adopted the same method. They established another allegory and soberly declared that the lover was Christ, and the beloved was both the Church and the adoring Christian. In the same way the priests "explained" the secular and often carnal tales in the *Gesta Romanorum*, the most popular collection of the Middle Ages. The monks who related the lawless legends of the *Gesta* supplied pious and often ridiculously irrelevant morals, or "applications," but held the attention of their listeners by not skipping a detail of the delightfully wicked stories.

Modern commentators departed completely from the religious symbolism. They gave the "Song" a wide variety of readings. Some of them rearranged the chapters to effect a greater continuity, fur-

7

nished a sort of plot, distributed the lines among a set of leading characters assisted by a chorus of maidens, and turned the "Song" into a half-secular, half-sacred drama. Some saw it as a cycle of lyrics, a loose prothalamion, sung at a wedding ceremony; others insisted it was originally used as a ritual of a fertility cult dating from the fourth or fifth century B.C. and that it was absorbed into later civilizations because of its human appeal. Lastly, there are those who regard it as a collection of songs, a small but precious anthology embodying the eternal desire of a man for a woman and a woman for a man.

No matter how it may be interpreted, "The Song of Songs" is essentially a deeply affecting outpouring of love. Set against a pellucid oriental background, enriched with startling images and unforgettable phrases, it remains a glowing rhapsody, a poem which is passionate, exalted, and unsurpassed in beauty.

The Song of Songs

1

Let him kiss me with the kisses of his mouth:
For thy love is better than wine.
Because of the savor of thy good ointments
Thy name is as ointment poured forth;
Therefore do the virgins love thee.

Draw me. We will run after thee.

The king hath brought me into his chambers.
We will be glad and rejoice in thee,
We will remember thy love more than wine:
The upright love thee.

I am black, but comely,
O ye daughters of Jerusalem,
As the tents of Kedar,
As the curtains of Solomon.

Look not upon me, because I am black,
Because the sun hath looked upon me:
My mother's children were angry with me;
They made me the keeper of the vineyards;
But mine own vineyard have I not kept.

Tell me, O thou whom my soul loveth,
Where thou feedest,
Where thou makest thy flock to rest at noon:
For why should I be as one that turneth aside
By the flocks of thy companions?

"If thou know not, O thou fairest among women,
Go thy way forth by the footsteps of the flock,
And feed thy kids beside the shepherds' tents."

I have compared thee, O my love,
To a company of horses in Pharaoh's chariots.
Thy cheeks are comely with rows of jewels,
Thy neck with chains of gold.
We will make thee borders of gold
With studs of silver.

While the king sitteth at his table,
My spikenard sendeth forth the smell thereof.

A bundle of myrrh is my wellbeloved unto me;
He shall lie all night betwixt my breasts.
My beloved is unto me as a cluster of camphire
In the vineyards of En-gedi.

"Behold, thou art fair, my love;
Behold, thou art fair;
Thou hast doves' eyes.
Behold, thou art fair, my beloved, yea pleasant;
Also our bed is green.
The beams of our house are cedar,
And our rafters are fir."

2

I am the rose of Sharon,
And the lily of the valleys.
As the lily among thorns,
So is my love among the daughters.
As the apple tree among the trees of the wood,
So is my beloved among the sons.

I sat down under his shadow with great delight,
And his fruit was sweet to my taste.
He brought me to the banqueting house,
And his banner over me was love.

Stay me with flagons, comfort me with apples
For I am sick of love.

His left hand is under my head,
And his right doth embrace me.

I charge you, O ye daughters of Jerusalem,
By the roes, and by the hinds of the field,
That ye stir not up, nor awake my love,
Till he please.

The voice of my beloved!
Behold, he cometh leaping upon the mountains,
Skipping upon the hills.
My beloved is like a roe or a young hart.
Behold, he standeth behind our wall,
He looketh forth at the windows,
Showing himself through the lattice.
My beloved spake, and said unto me,
"Rise up, my love, my fair one, and come away.
For, lo, the winter is past.
The rain is over and gone;
The flowers appear on the earth;
The time of the singing of birds is come,
And the voice of the turtle is heard in our land;
The fig tree putteth forth her green figs,
And the vines with the tender grape give a good smell.
Arise, my love, my fair one, and come away.

"O my dove, that art in the clefts of the rock,
In the secret places of the stairs,
Let me see thy countenance,
Let me hear thy voice;
For sweet is thy voice,
And thy countenance is comely."

Take us the foxes,
The little foxes, that spoil the vines:
For our vines have tender grapes.

My beloved is mine, and I am his:
He feedeth among the lilies.
Until the day break, and the shadows flee away,
Turn, my beloved, and be thou like a roe
Or a young hart upon the mountains of Bether.

11

By night on my bed I sought him whom my soul loveth:
I sought him, but I found him not.

I will rise now,
And go about the city in the streets,
And in the broad ways I will seek him whom my soul loveth:
I sought him, but I found him not.
The watchmen that go about the city found me:
To whom I said, "Saw ye him whom my soul loveth?"

It was but a little that I passed from them,
But I found him whom my soul loveth:
I held him, and would not let him go,
Until I had brought him into my mother's house,
And into the chamber of her that conceived me.

I charge you, O ye daughters of Jerusalem,
By the roes, and by the hinds of the field,
That ye stir not up, nor awake my love,
Till he please.

Who is this that cometh out of the wilderness
Like pillars of smoke, perfumed with myrrh and frankincense,
With all powders of the merchant?
Behold his bed, which is Solomon's;
Threescore valiant men are about it, of the valiant of Israel.
They all hold swords, being expert in war:
Every man hath his sword upon his thigh
Because of fear in the night.

King Solomon made himself a chariot
Of the wood of Lebanon.
He made the pillars thereof of silver,
 The bottom thereof of gold,
The covering of it of purple,
The midst thereof being paved with love,
For the daughters of Jerusalem.

Go forth, O ye daughters of Zion,
And behold king Solomon

With the crown wherewith his mother crowned him in the
  day of his espousals,
And in the day of the gladness of his heart.

4

Behold, thou art fair, my love;
Behold, thou art fair;
 Thou hast doves' ees within thy locks:
Thy hair is as a flock of goats that appear from mount Gilead.

Thy teeth are like a flock of sheep that are even shorn,
Which came up from the washing;
Whereof every one bear twins,
And none is barren among them.
Thy lips are like a thread of scarlet,
And thy speech is comely;
Thy temples are like a piece of a pomegranate
Within thy locks;
Thy neck is like the tower of David
Builded for an armory,
Whereon there hang a thousand bucklers,
All shields of mighty men.
Thy two breasts are like two young roes that are twins,
Which feed among the lilies.

Until the day break, and the shadows flee away,
I will get me to the mountain of myrrh,
And to the hill of frankincense.

Thou art all fair, my love;
There is no spot in thee.
Come with me from Lebanon, my spouse,
With me from Lebanon:
Look from the top of Amana,
From the top of Shenir and Hermon,
 From the lions' dens,
From the mountains of the leopards.
Thou hast ravished my heart, my sister, my spouse;
Thou hast ravished my heart with one of thine eyes,
With one chain of thy neck.

How fair is thy love, my sister, my spouse!
How much better is thy love than wine!
And the smell of thine ointments than all spices!
Thy lips, O my spouse, drop as the honeycomb:
Honey and milk are under thy tongue;
And the smell of thy garments is like the smell of Lebanon.

A garden inclosed is my sister, my spouse;
A spring shut up, a fountain sealed.
Thy plants are an orchard of pomegranates,
With pleasant fruits; camphire, with spikenard,
Spikenard and saffron;
Calamus and cinnamon,
With all trees of frankincense;
Myrrh and aloes,
With all the chief spices:
A fountain of gardens,
A well of living waters,
And streams from Lebanon.

Awake, O north wind; and come, thou south;
Blow upon my garden,
That the spices thereof may flow out.
Let my beloved come into his garden,
And eat his pleasant fruits.

5

"I am come into my garden, my sister, my spouse:
I have gathered my myrrh with my spice;
I have eaten my honeycomb with my honey;
I have drunk my wine with my milk:
Eat, O friends;
Drink, yea, drink abundantly, O beloved."

I sleep, but my heart waketh:
It is the voice of my beloved that knocketh, saying,
"Open to me, my sister, my love, my dove, my undefiled:
For my head is filled with dew,
And my locks with the drops of the night."

I have put off my coat; how shall I put it on?
I have washed my feet; how shall I defile them?

My beloved put in his hand by the hole of the door,
And my bowels were moved for him.
I rose up to open to my beloved;
And my hands dropped with myrrh,
And my fingers with sweet-smelling myrrh,
Upon the handles of the lock.

I opened to my beloved;
But my beloved had withdrawn himself, and was gone;
My soul failed when he spake:
I sought him, but I could not find him;
I called him, but he gave me no answer.

The watchmen that went about the city found me,
They smote me, they wounded me;
The keepers of the walls took away my veil from me.
I charge you, O daughters of Jerusalem,
If ye find my beloved, that ye tell him,
That I am sick of love.

"What is thy beloved more than another beloved,
O thou fairest among women?
What is thy beloved more than another beloved,
That thou dost so charge us?"

My beloved is white and ruddy,
The chiefest among ten thousand.
His head is as the most fine gold;
His locks are bushy, and black as a raven;
His eyes are as the eyes of doves by the rivers of waters,
Washed with milk, and fitly set;
His cheeks are as a bed of spices,
As sweet flowers;
His lips like lilies, dropping sweet-smelling myrrh;
His hands are as gold rings set with the beryl;
His belly is as bright ivory overlaid with sapphires;
His legs are as pillars of marble,
Set upon sockets of fine gold;
His countenance is as Lebanon,
Excellent as the cedars;
His mouth is most sweet:

15

Yea, he is altogether lovely.
This is my beloved,
And this is my friend,
O daughters of Jerusalem.

6

"Whither is thy beloved gone,
O thou fairest among women?
Whither is thy beloved turned aside?
That we may seek him with thee."

My beloved is gone down into his garden,
To the beds of spices,
To feed in the gardens, and to gather lilies.
I am my beloved's, and my beloved is mine:
He feedeth among the lilies.

Thou art beautiful, O my love, as Tirzah,
Comely as Jerusalem,
Terrible as an army with banners.
Turn away thine eyes from me,
For they have overcome me:
Thy hair is as a flock of goats
That appear from Gilead.
Thy teeth are as a flock of sheep
Which go up from the washing,
Whereof every one beareth twins,
And there is not one barren among them.
As a piece of a pomegranate are thy temples
Within thy locks.

"There are threescore queens, and fourscore concubines,
And virgins without number.
My dove, my undefiled is but one;
She is the only one of her mother,
She is the choice one of her that bare her.
The daughters saw her, and blessed her;
Yea, the queens and the concubines, and they praised her."

"Who is she that looketh forth as the morning,
Fair as the moon, clear as the sun,
And terrible as an army with banners?"

I went down into the garden of nuts
To see the fruits of the valley,
And to see whether the vine flourished,
And the pomegranates budded.
Or ever I was aware,
My soul made me
Like the chariots of Ammi-nadib.

"Return, return, O Shulamite;
Return, return, that we may look upon thee."

What will ye see in the Shulamite?

"As it were the company of two armies."

7

How beautiful are thy feet with shoes,
O prince's daughter!
The joints of thy thighs are like jewels,
The work of the hands of a cunning workman.
Thy navel is like a round goblet,
Which wanteth not liquor;
Thy belly is like an heap of wheat
Set about with lilies;
Thy two breasts are like two young roes that are twins;
Thy neck is as a tower of ivory;
Thine eyes like the fishpools in Heshbon,
By the gate of Bath-rabbim;
Thy nose is as the tower of Lebanon
Which looketh toward Damascus;
Thine head upon thee is like Carmel,
And the hair of thine head like purple—
The king is held in the galleries.
How far and how pleasant art thou,
O love, for delights!

This thy stature is like to a palm tree,
And thy breasts to clusters of grapes.

I said "I will go up to the palm tree,
I will take hold of the boughs thereof."

Now also thy breasts shall be as clusters of the vine;
And the smell of thy nose like apples;
And the roof of thy mouth like the best wine for my beloved,
That goeth down sweetly,
Causing the lips of those that are asleep to speak.

I am my beloved's,
And his desire is toward me.

Come, my beloved,
Let us go forth into the field;
Let us lodge in the villages;
Let us get up early to the vineyards;
Let us see if the vine flourish,
Whether the tender grape appear,
And the pomegranates bud forth.
There will I give thee my loves.

The mandrakes give a smell,
And at our gates are all manner of pleasant fruits,
New and old, which I have laid up for thee,
O my beloved.

8

O that thou wert as my brother,
That sucked the breasts of my mother!
When I should find thee without, I would kiss thee;
Yea, I should not be despised.

I would lead thee, and bring thee into my mother's house,
Who would instruct me:
I would cause thee to drink of spiced wine,
Of the juice of my pomegranate.

His left hand should be under my head,
And his right hand should embrace me.

I charge you, O daughters of Jerusalem,
That ye stir not up, nor awake my love,
Until he please.

"Who is this that cometh up from the wilderness,
Leaning upon her beloved?"

I raised thee up under the apple tree:
There thy mother brought thee forth:
There she brought thee forth that bare thee.

Set me as a seal upon thine heart,
As a seal upon thine arm:
For love is strong as death;
Jealousy is cruel as the grave:
The coals thereof are coals of fire,
Which hath a most vehement flame.

Many waters cannot quench love,
Neither can the floods drown it:
If a man would give all the substance of his house for love,
It would utterly be contemned.

"We have a little sister,
And she hath no breasts:
What shall we do for our sister
In the day when she shall be spoken for?

"If she be a wall,
We will build upon her a palace of silver:
And if she be a door,
We will inclose her with boards of cedar."

I am a wall,
And my breasts like towers:
Then was I in his eyes as one that found favor.

Solomon had a vineyard at Baal-hamon;
He let out the vineyard unto keepers;
Every one for the fruit thereof
Was to bring a thousand pieces of silver.

My vineyard, which is mine, is before me:
Thou, O Solomon, must have a thousand,
And those that keep the fruit thereof two hundred.

Thou that dwellest in the gardens,
The companions hearken to thy voice:
Cause me to hear it.

Make haste, my beloved,
And be thou like to a roe or to a young hart
Upon the mountains of spices.

From Greece and Rome

The Greek Anthology

More than two thousand years ago, during the second century B. C., a Syrian named Meleager collected a series of Greek inscriptions, dedications, and short poems from tombstones, statues, walls, public buildings, and records of votive offerings. Some of the inscriptions dated back to the seventh century B.C.

Meleager, a poet, thus became the first anthologist, literally a flowergatherer (*anthos*: a flower, *legein*: to gather), and he termed his collection a "garland." There was an immediate response, and a number of other collections, variously classified as "wreaths" and "cycles," followed. The material that went into these anthologies consisted of poetic epigrams—short, simple, and pointed verses which packed devotion, satire and suggestiveness, morality, amorality and mockery in a few lines. More than four thousand of these terse poems were collected by assiduous editors; the vogue for them extended over one thousand years.

The origins of many of the individual epigrams in *The Greek Anthology*, the title by which we know selections from the ancient compilations, are uncertain. Meleager and his successors list such names as Sappho, Simonides, Callimachus, Rufinus, Antipater of Sidon, Plato, and Paulus Silentarius in their introductions, but who wrote which poem is often a scholar's conjecture. Nor have the various editions of *The Greek Anthology* revealed any authoritative arrangement. Some editors have attempted to impose an order upon the scattered pieces by dividing them into classes entitled Dedicatory, Didactic, Sepulchral, Satirical, Homosexual, Narrative, Literary, and Amatory. This, too, is a diverting editorial pastime, but it is little more.

The following forty-two selections are those in which the sensual and the cynical, the impassioned and the pragmatic, the lovesick sentimental and the bitterly disillusioned mingle without respect to chronology or authorship. All the adaptations are by the editor.

23

A Game of Dice

Playing one day with Rhodopé at dice,
I rolled the little bones and threw twelve twice.
Rhodopé looked and laughed: "O what delight
If you could only do as well at night."

Melissa

Her name, Melissa, means she is a bee;
    Her lips touch mine with honey, and her wings
Brush over all my body lovingly.
    But when she asks for money, how she stings!

Sweetest of All

Sweet in the heat of summer is cool water for one's thirst;
Sweet, after winter, is the air when the first bud has burst;
Sweet to the sailor is the sight of land that saw his growth;
But sweeter still two lovers when one mantle covers both.

The Artist as Cuckold

This portrait painter boasted twenty sons,
But never got a likeness—no, not once.

All-Knowing Lamp

You were a witness, lamp, you saw him kneel
And swear he would be faithful, heard him seal
His urgent kisses with a sacred vow.
Where is he now?

You know whose arms are raised for his embrace,
Whose lips in semi-darkness seek his face;
You know whose naked breast supports his brow
Where he lies now.

Infatuated

"Faithless again!" I cry, and she replies
With smiles and kisses . . . "I am sick of lies!
I scorn you! I will go away—today!"
"But kiss me first," she says. And so I stay.

Husbands and Wives

Husbands would never go whoring,
    They'd stay with the ones they adore
If wives were but half as alluring
    After the act as before.

To Venus

With wine and words of love and fervid vow
    He lulled me into bed. I closed my eyes,
A sleepy, stupid innocent . . . And now
    I dedicate the spoils of my surprise:
The silk that bound my breasts, my virgin zone,
    The cherished purity I could not keep . . .
Goddess, remember we were all alone,
    And he was strong—and I was half asleep.

25

Apple Offering

Here is an apple. Like your little breast
It has a tart-sweet flavor, savored best
After your lips' lascivious zest.

Now satisfy my hunger; give me what
Will cure my appetite. If you will not,
Then keep your apple—wait, and watch it rot.

Wasted Night

In the dark night where none could ever spy
We lay for hours, two lovely girls and I;
Warmly caressed by one, though I would rather
With double passion, have caressed the other;
But she, in jealousy, had turned away.
And so, through the long night, I groaned and lay
Unable to perform, unfit to play.

Tormenting Virgin

Naked and breast to breast we lie;
   She coaxes, kisses, teases;
Her parted lips are eager—I
   Press on . . . and then she freezes.

She turns her hips away, although
   My roving hand's unchided;
Her body's warm and lithe, but so
   Frustratingly divided.

Her upper half, all wanton, feigns
   Fulfillment with each lure;
But oh, her lower half remains
   Impenetrably pure.

26

To a History Professor

Although confused with details and a dunce,
What Paris did to Menelaus once
I can't forget. Moreover I can tell in
A few short words what every other day,
While you are teaching school and well away,
Some other Paris does to your fair Helen.

Lovesick

I long to be the wanton breeze
    That, blowing wayward everywhere,
Plucks at your loosened robe, and frees
    Your bosom beautiful and bare.

I long to be the rose you wear
    Between your little breasts, too sweet
For rude exploring hands, and there
    I'd give your heart an added beat.

I long to be the virgin zone,
    That zealous guardian, trim and tight;
I'd clasp you till the day was done
    And lie beside you all the night.

Venus Accoutered as Mars

Venus, what mood inspires you to don
Mars' own equipment; why put on
Whatever foolish armor comes to mind.
No warrior can resist your conquering charm;
Naked, without a weapon, you disarm
The god of war himself, and all mankind.

To Chloe

Some say you dye your hair. But I deny it.
Your hair *is* black, for that's the way you buy it.

Plea to Eros

Eros, pray discard your bow;
Eros, spare your arrows now.
On my body there's no part
But bears a scar for every dart.

~∙∙∙~

The Golden Spurs

I, Lysidus, equestrian, offer these
Two golden spurs, token of victories
With horses and with women. I renounce
All pleasure in my courses and my mounts,
Although no mare or filly could complain
Her rider cut her flanks or caused her pain.
And so I give to Venus these gold spurs
That once were my best trophies. Now they're hers.

~∙∙∙~

Didyma

My Didyma is dark, but I aspire
To keep her mine, dark body and dark soul.
Yes, it is true, Didyma's black as coal.
But what gives greater heat than coal on fire?

~∙∙∙~

Hoarded Grapes

When your grapes formed, you swore to save them;
Whey they grew round, you passed me by.
Yet anyone who asks can have them
Now that the grapes are shrunk and dry.

~∙∙∙~

Aphrodite Pandemos

This is the golden goddess; friend is she
To young and old, to bashful and to bold.
She gives herself with generosity
For love—if love's accompanied with gold.

Two Against One

I have abjured the flesh, and I
Can now at last the god of love defy.
But if the wine-god helps him, I am through.
What can one mortal do against those two!

〜∞〜

Foolish Proverb

Mockery murders love, they say, and she
    Laughed in my face last night and slammed her door.
I swore to stay away for life—but see,
    It's break of day, and here I am once more.

〜∞〜

Class Dismissed

Lifting my eyes from Hesiod's book
    I saw young Pyrrha pass and nod,
Linger, and give another look . . .
    Good-by to dull old Hesiod.

〜∞〜

Matter of Taste

Great Zeus, beset by love and lechery,
    Became a bull, a swan, a shower, a ram.
Such sports delight the gods; but as for me
    I pay my girl and stay the way I am.

〜∞〜

Double Gift

Accept this garland and this girl together.
Enjoy them both in bloom before they wither.

〜∞〜

The Easiest Way

Warm wine, warm baths, warm women, onetime ladies,
Will take you down the easiest way to Hades.

29

Faithless

I am the lamp that Flaccus gave his love
When first she swore fidelity. And now
Nightly beside her bed I witness how
Lightly she breaks her vow.
                              Despairing of
The faith of women and the way they lie,
Unhappily we burn, Flaccus and I.

~∽୨∊~

Long Pursuit

How long I pleaded I can never guess,
    Nor can I recollect the things we said.
Now, after months, you answer yes,
    And you are in my bed.

Yet, though stretched out and naked here you lie,
    You close your lips; you turn away; you weep.
Finally you consent . . . And I,
    Worn out with coaxing, sleep.

~∽୨∊~

Embarrassed Judge

Melita, Rhodópis, and young Rhodocleia
Three famous, unmatchable beauties, made me a
Judge of their glories. They let me behold
Their bodies unfettered with clothing, as bold
As Juno, Minerva, and Venus of old.

Rhodópis was like a rich, half-opened rose;
Melita was marble that flushes and glows;
No statue could ever surpass Rhodocleia
Whose soft dimpled buttocks were fashioned to be a
Delight and distraction. The three would embarrass
A man who would venture to choose, even Paris
Would feel too transported, would stare and say nothing . . . .
I gaped like a fool while they put on their clothing.

30

Dawn

Thou enemy of love, how slow you creep
Across the sky when she decides to sleep
With someone else. And oh, how fast you fly
When she is in my arms till night goes by.

Ageless

Now Charito is sixty. But her hair
Is dark; her ample bosom's firm and fair;
Her skin is like a young girl's, warm and white;
Her legs and thighs are fashioned to delight.

Her years are in her favor, for she knows
Tricks that a novice never could disclose.
Yes, she is sixty; but, still full of fire,
She'll do, my friend, whatever you desire.

The Living Statue

Here, by the shore, a carven figure shows
    A naked Venus in the morning light.
See how the white and lifeless marble glows,
    And all the waves toss wildly at the sight.

The Young Bather

Bathing herself, a girl with silver feet
Pours water on a skin whiter than milk;
    Her young thighs undulate; the little seat
        Of pleasure shows a few gold hairs of silk.

One small hand half conceals her charm of charms;
    Shyly she crouches there and locks her knees;
Slowly she raises her still glistening arms,
    And archly looks to see if someone sees.

Indignant Protest

"For shame!" cries Cypris as she sees
Her statue by Praxiteles.
"Exposing me to lecherous men!
When did you see me naked! When!"

To a Gnat

Gnat, be my messenger, and fly
To Zenophile; then tell her I
Wait for her, sleepless, and will lie

A prey to wasting misery,
Forever inconsolably,
Till she relent and come to me.

Gnat, should she hearken and give in,
I'll make thee mighty, minikin,
And clothe thee in a lion's skin.

Perfume

I send you perfume fresh as dew
    So that, whenever you may groom
Your body, it will breathe, and you
    Will perfume the perfume.

The Surprise

Her mother watched her closely, yet one day
Alcippa took me to her room to play.
There we made love most quietly, for fear
Some old, suspicious passer-by might hear.

Alas, our ardors grew too wild and rough,
And, at the very climax of our love,
Her mother broke in, crying, "I declare,
This luck is something all of us must share."

The Kiss and the Cup

With maidenly and modest sips
  The festive cup you quaffed.
Oh, that you'd touch me with those lips
  And drink me at one draught!

~∞~

Warning to Cupid

Cupid, beware, there'll come a day
  When, wearied of your stings,
My injured soul will fly away.
  She, too, has wings.

~∞~

The Amorist

Were I a rose, and did you dare
  To pluck me without shame,
You'd place me on your breast, and there
  I'd turn your snow to flame.

~∞~

Consummation

Now put aside the flute; sing no sweet air;
  This is no time for either songs or hymns.
Remove that hindering robe; take down your hair;
  Let naked limbs be locked with naked limbs.

Your thinnest tissued gown is like a wall
  Around some town that must be breached at will.
Now breast to breast, mouth into mouth, till all
  Is plunged into the depths, and we lie still.

~∞~

True Love

My girl is thin, yet that is why
  I'm pleased in every part;
The thinner she, the closer I
  Can press against her heart.

Anacreon

Anacreon, born in the sixth century B.C., was one of the first and certainly the most popular of the Greek poets to unite the triple worship of Wine, Woman, and Song. He lived to be eighty-five, and he died, not because of overindulgence, but, according to Pliny, because of a single grape pit on which he choked.

Most of the translations are adaptations rather than accurate renderings. Nevertheless, the versions by the seventeenth century Abraham Cowley and Thomas Stanley, and those of the nineteenth century Thomas Moore capture the distinct and delicate spirit of the originals in the so-called Anacreontics.

To His Young Mistress

Because, forsooth, you're young and fair,
And fresher than the rose appear,
Gray hairs you treat with scornful eye
And leave me most unmannerly.

Sweetheart, these ashes do contain
Embers that strive to flame again.
And Etna that on top has snow
Feels warmth and constant fire below.

With roses white-haired lilies twine
And in a glowing garland shine;
They, locked in close embraces, lie
And kiss and hug most decently.

TRANSLATED BY ABRAHAM COWLEY

Woman's Arms

Liberal nature did dispense
To all things arms for their defense;
And some, she arms with sinewy force,
And some with swiftness in the course;
Some with hard hoofs or forkèd claws,
And some with horns or tuskèd jaws.
And some with scales and some with wings,
Some with teeth and some with stings.
Wisdom to man she did afford—
Wisdom for shield and wit for sword.

But what for beauteous womankind?
What arms, what armor was she assigned?
Beauty is both, for with the Fair
What arms, what armor can compare?
What gold, what steel, what diamond
More impassible is found?
And what flame, what lightning e'er
Such great and active force did bear?

These are all weapon, and they dart
Like porcupines from every part
Who can, alas, their strength express,
Armed when they themselves undress,
Cap-a-pie with nakedness.

TRANSLATED BY ABRAHAM COWLEY

The Picture

Painter, by unmatch'd desert
Master of the Rhodian art,
Come, my absent mistress take,
As I shall describe her: make
First her hair, as black as bright,
And if colors so much right
Can but do her, let it too
Smell of aromatic dew;
Underneath this shade must thou
Draw her alabaster brow;
Her dark eyebrows so dispose
That they neither part nor close,
But by a divorce so slight
Be disjoin'd, may cheat the sight:
From her kindly killing eye
Make a flash of lightning fly,
Sparkling like Minerva's, yet
Like Cythera's mildly sweet:
Roses in milk swimming seek
For the pattern of her cheek:
In her lip such moving blisses,

As from all may challenge kisses;
Round about her neck (outvying
Parian stone) the Graces flying;
And o'er all her limbs at last
A loose purple mantle cast;
But so ordered that the eye
Some part naked may descry,
An essay by which the rest
That lies hidden, may be guess'd.
  So, to life th' hast come so near,
  All of her, but voice, is here.
TRANSLATED BY THOMAS STANLEY

Heat

Fill, kind misses, fill the bowl
And let the wine refresh my soul.
For now the thirsty heat of day
Has almost drunk my life away;

Whole floods of sweat will not suffice—
It drinks, and still new floods arise:
It drinks till I myself grow dry
And can no longer floods supply.

Now my heat, I pray, relieve,
And now your cooling garlands weave,
Soothing garlands such as may
Invite refreshing winds to play
And chase the tyrant heat away.

But this I do perhaps, you'll guess,
Because I mean to love you less;
Or do't because I'd thus remove
All the flames and heat of love.

Foolish girls, perhaps you know
This to the body good may do.
But love can no abatement find—
Love's the high fever of the mind.

TRANSLATED BY ABRAHAM COWLEY

Design for a Bowl

Sculptor, wouldst thou glad my soul,
Grave for me an ample bowl,
Worthy to shine in hall or bower,
When springtime brings the reveler's hour.
Grave it with themes of chaste design,
Fit for a simple board like mine.
Display not there the barbarous rites
In which religious zeal delights;
Nor any tale of tragic fate
Which History shudders to relate.
No—cull thy fancies from above,
Themes of heaven and themes of love.
Let Bacchus, Jove's ambrosial boy,
Distill the grape in drops of joy,
And while he smiles at every tear,
Let warm-eyed Venus, dancing near,
With spirits of the genial bed,
The dewy herbage deftly tread.
Let Love be there, without his arms,
In timid nakedness of charms;
And all the Graces, linked with Love,
Stray, laughing, through the shadowy grove;
While rosy boys, disporting round,
In circlets trip the velvet ground.
But ah! if there Apollo toys,
I tremble for the rosy boys.

TRANSLATED BY THOMAS MOORE

Lucretius

Little is known of the life of the Roman poet Lucretius (Titus Lucretius Carus) except that he was born toward the beginning of the first century B.C. and lived until his middle forties, when, according to one legend, he died mad as the result of an aphrodisiac administered by his wife. His great work, *De Rerum Natura (On the Nature of Things)* is a long philosophical poem which holds to a materialist interpretation of life—everything is composed of atoms, nothing is created out of nothing—challenges the concept of divine intervention, denounces religious superstition, argues that death is not to be feared since it ends all miseries, and turns myths into moral truths. The preachment is continually uplifted by passages of picturesque and often exquisite poetry.

From *The Nature of Love*

Thus, therefore, he who feels the fiery dart
Of strong desire transfix his amorous heart,
Whether some beauteous boy's alluring face,
Or lovelier maid, with unresisted grace,
From her each part the winged arrow sends,
From whence he first was struck he thither tends;
Restless he roams, impatient to be freed,
And eager to inject the sprightly seed;
For fierce desire does all his mind employ,
And ardent love assures approaching joy.
Such is the nature of that pleasing smart,
Whose burning drops distil upon the heart,
The fever of the soul shot from the fair,
And the cold ague of succeeding care.
If absent, her idea still appears,
And her sweet name is chiming in your ears.
But strive those pleasing phantoms to remove,
And shun th' aërial images of love,
That feed the flame: when one molests thy mind,
Discharge thy loins on all the leaky kind;
For that's a wiser way than to restrain
Within thy swelling nerves that hoard of pain.
For every hour some deadlier symptom shows,
And by delay the gath'ring venom grows,
When kindly applications are not us'd;
The viper, love, must on the wound be bruis'd.
On that one object 't is not safe to stay,
But force the tide of thought some other way;
The squander'd spirits prodigally throw,
And in the common glebe of nature sow.
Nor wants he all the bliss that lovers feign,

Who takes the pleasure, and avoids the pain;
For purer joys in purer health abound,
And less affect the sickly than the sound.

When love its utmost vigor does employ,
Ev'n then 't is but a restless wand'ring joy;
Nor knows the lover in that wild excess,
With hands or eyes, what first he would possess;
But strains at all, and, fast'ning where he strains,
Too closely presses with his frantic pains;
With biting kisses hurts the twining fair,
Which shews his joys imperfect, insincere:

For, stung with inward rage, he flings around,
And strives t' avenge the smart on that which gave the wound.
But love those eager bitings does restrain,
And mingling pleasure mollifies the pain.
For ardent hope still flatters anxious grief,
And sends him to his foe to seek relief:
Which yet the nature of the thing denies;
For love, and love alone of all our joys,
By full possession does but fan the fire;
The more we still enjoy, the more we still desire.
Nature for meat and drink provides a space,
And, when receiv'd, they fill their certain place;
Hence thirst and hunger may be satisfied,
But this repletion is to love denied:
Form, feature, color, whatsoe'er delight
Provokes the lover's endless appetite,
These fill no space, nor can we thence remove
With lips, or hands, or all our instruments of love:
In our deluded grasp we nothing find,
But thin aërial shapes, that fleet before the mind.
As he, who in a dream with drought is curst,
And finds no real drink to quench his thirst,
Runs to imagin'd lakes this heat to steep,
And vainly swills and labors in his sleep;
So love with phantoms cheats our longing eyes,
Which hourly seeing never satisfies:
Our hands pull nothing from the parts they strain,
But wander o'er the lovely limbs in vain.
Nor when the youthful pair more closely join,

When hands in hands they lock, and thighs in thighs they twine,
Just in the raging foam of full desire,
When both press on, both murmur, both expire,
They grip, they squeeze, their humid tongues they dart,
As each would force their way to t'other's heart:
In vain; they only cruise about the coast;
For bodies cannot pierce, nor be in bodies lost,
As sure they strive to be, when both engage
In that tumultuous momentary rage;
So 'tangled in the nets of love they lie,
Till man dissolves in that excess of joy.
Then, when the gather'd bag has burst its way,
And ebbing tides the slacken'd nerves betray,
A pause ensues; and nature nods a while,
Till with recruited rage new spirits boil;
And then the same vain violence returns,
With flames renew'd th' erected furnace burns;
Again they in each other would be lost,
But still by adamantine bars are cross'd.
All ways they try, successless all they prove,
To cure the secret sore of lingering love.

TRANSLATED BY JOHN DRYDEN

Catullus

Considered the greatest lyric poet of ancient Rome, Gaius Valerius Catullus was born about 84 B.C. in Verona, wrote poetry before he was sixteen, and continued to compose until his premature death in 54 B.C. Although there are references to poverty in his verses, he seems to have had ample means; he owned a villa at Tibur, another at Sirmio on beautiful Lake Garda, as well as his own private yacht. He made friends quickly— Cicero was one of them—and enemies with equal ease. The most potent factor in his creative career was his passion for Clodia, the married but promiscuous sister of Clodius, the demagogue. She was the Lesbia of his devoted, distrustful, and tortured love poems, but the disguise deceived no one, including Clodia's various lovers.

Catullus' works—more than 116 pieces—were lost for some three hundred years. After their recovery in fourteenth century Verona, Catullus was not only rediscovered but repeatedly imitated. The Elizabethan lyricists in particular delighted to echo his combination of graceful pleading, desire, and desperation.

My Sweetest Lesbia

My sweetest Lesbia, let us live and love,
And though the sager sort our deeds reprove,
Let us not weigh them. Heaven's great lamps do dive
Into their west, and straight again revive
But, soon as once set is our little light,
Then must we sleep one ever-during night.

If all would lead their lives in love like me,
Then bloody swords and armor should not be;
No drum nor trumpet peaceful sleeps should move,
Unless alarm came from the camp of Love:
But fools do live and waste their little light,
And seek with pain their ever-during night.

When timely death my life and fortune ends,
Let not my hearse be vext with mourning friends,
But let all lovers rich in triumph come
And with sweet pastimes grace my happy tomb:
And, Lesbia, close up thou my little light,
And crown with love my ever-during night.

TRANSLATED BY THOMAS CAMPION

Kiss Me, Sweet [1]

Kiss me, sweet: the wary lover
Can your favors keep, and cover,
When the common courting jay
All your bounties will betray.
Kiss again! no creature comes;
Kiss, and score up wealthy sums

[1] A variation of the following translation.

44

On my lips, thus hardly sundered,
While you breathe. First give a hundred,
Then a thousand, then another
Hundred, then unto the other
Add a thousand, and so more;
Till you equal with the store
All the grass that Romney yields
Or the sands in Chelsea fields,
Or the drops in silver Thames,
Or the stars that gild his streams
In the silent summer-nights,
When youths ply their stolen delights;
That the curious may not know
How to tell 'em as they flow
And the envious when they find
What their number is, be pined.

ADAPTED BY BEN JONSON

To Lesbia

Thy kisses dost thou bid me count,
And tell thee, Lesbia, what amount
My rage for love and thee could tire,
And satisfy and cloy desire?

Many as grains of Libyan sand
Upon Cyrene's spicy land
From prescient Ammon's sultry dome
To sacred Battus' ancient tomb:
Many as stars that silent ken

At night the stolen loves of men.
Yes, when the kisses thou shalt kiss
Have reach'd a number vast as this,
Then may desire at length be stay'd,
And e'en my madness be allay'd:
And when infinity defies
The calculations of the wise;
Nor evil voice's deadly charm
Can work the unknown number harm.

TRANSLATED BY GEORGE LAMB

Dialogue with a Door

PASSERBY

Hail, door, to husband and to father dear!
And may Jove make thee his peculiar care!
Thou who, when Balbus lived, if fame say true,
Wast wont a thousand sorry things to do;
And, when they carried forth the good old man,
For the new bride who didst them o'er again;
Say, how have people this strange notion got,
As if thy former faith thou hadst forgot?

DOOR

So many Caecilius help me, whom I now
Must own my master, as I truly vow—
Be the offences talk'd of great or small;
Still I am free, and ignorant of all:
I boldly dare the worst that can be said;
And yet, what charges to my fault are laid!
No deed so infamous, but straight they cry,
"Fie, wicked door! this is your doing, fie!"

PASSERBY

This downright, bold assertion ne'er will do;
You must speak plainer, and convince us too.

DOOR

I would;—but how, when no one wants to know?

PASSERBY

I want;—collect your facts, and tell them now.

DOOR

First, then, I will deny, for so 'tis thought
That a young virgin to my charge was brought:
Not that her husband, with ungovern'd flame,
Had stolen, in hasty joy, that sacred name;
So vile his manhood, and so cold his blood,
Poor, languid tool! he could not, if he would;
But his own father, 'tis expressly said,
Had stain'd the honors of his nuptial bed;
Whether because, to virtue's image blind,
Thick clouds of lust had darken'd all his mind;

46

Or, conscious of his son's unfruitful seed,
He thought some abler man should do the deed.

PASSERBY

A pious deed, in truth; and nobly done—
A father makes a cuckold of his son!

DOOR

Nor was this all that conscious Brixia knew;
Sweet mother of the country where I grew
In earliest youth! who, from Chinaea's height,
Sees boundless landscapes burst upon the sight;
Brixia! whose sides the yellow Mela laves
With the calm current of its gentle waves:
She also knows what bliss Posthumius proved;
And how, in triumph, gay Cornelius loved;
With both of whom, so wanton was the fair,
She did not blush her choicest gifts to share.
"But how," you'll ask, "could you, a senseless door,
These secrets, and these mysteries explore;
Who never from your master's threshold stirred,
Nor what the people talk'd of ever heard;
Content upon your hinges to remain,
To ope, and shut, and then to ope again."—
Learn, that full oft I've heard the whispering fair,
Who ne'er suspected I had tongue or ear,
To her own slaves her shameful actions tell,
And speak the very names I now reveal.
One more she mention'd, whom I will not speak,
Lest warm displeasure flush his angry cheek:
Thus far I'll tell thee; he's an awkward brute,
Whose spurious birth once caused no small dispute.

TRANSLATED BY JOHN NOTT

Acme and Septimius

Whilst on Septimius' panting breast
(Meaning nothing less than rest)
Acme lean'd her loving head,
Thus the pleas'd Septimius said:

47

"My dearest Acme, if I be
Once alive, and love not thee
With a passion far above
All that e'er was called Love,
In a Lybian desert may
I become some lion's prey,
Let him, Acme, let him tear
My breast, when Acme is not there."

The God of Love who stood to hear him,
(The God of Love was always near him)
Pleas'd and tickl'd with the sound,
Sneez'd aloud, and all around
The little Loves that waited by,
Bow'd and blessed the Augury.

Acme enflam'd with what he said,
Rear'd her gently-bending head,
And her purple mouth with joy
Stretching to the delicious boy.
Twice (twice could scarce suffice)
She kissed his drunken, rolling eyes.

"My little Life, my All" (said she)
"So may we ever servants be
To this best God, and ne'er retain
Our hated liberty again,
So may thy passion last for me,
As I a passion have for thee,
Greater and fiercer much than can
Be conceiv'd by thee a man.
Into my marrow is it gone,
Fixed and settled in the bone,
It reigns not only in my heart,
But runs, like life, through ev'ry part."
She spoke. The God of Love aloud
Sneez'd again, and all the crowd
Of little loves that waited by,
Bow'd and blessed the Augury.

TRANSLATED BY ABRAHAM COWLEY

Catullus Talks to Himself

Catullus, you're a fool. I said,
What's lost is lost, what's dead is dead.
The game is over, that you know;
So let the little strumpet go.

Never was woman held before
With such devotion as we swore.
Never was there a happier lover!
Never such nights! But that's all over.

Stop fretting, stop repining. It's
High time, my boy, to call it quits.
Look at the past without regretting;
Forget the way that she's forgetting.

So farewell to the girl. Good-by,
Good riddance, too, to her, say I.
This is the end; you might have seen it;
But tell her that you're through—and mean it.

Who'll fill her empty hours now?
Who'll praise her arms, her breast, her brow?
Who'll be the ever-welcome one to
Inspire, dream about, and run to?

Who'll give her what her mouth must miss:
Rapturous biting kiss for kiss?
There will be memories, even so.
But let her go, man, let her go.

TRANSLATED BY LOUIS UNTERMEYER

Horace

Unlike Catullus, Horace—Quintus Horatius Flaccus (65–8 B.C.) —never let an unruly passion get the better of him. His odes and epodes are, for the greater part, light-hearted and lightly written verses, playfully satirical, brightly suggestive. Son of a freedman who had been a slave, Horace acquired a patron, Maecenas, and, ensconced on a Sabine estate, took comfortably to a kind of luxurious simplicity. Originally a man-about-town, he became an affable man-about-the-country.

Horace's love poems are casual rather than crucial; they are teasing, sophisticated, ironic, and, even when erotic, humorously restrained. Most of all, they are beautifully made and, for a countryman, singularly urbane.

The first four translations are by Louis Untermeyer; the fifth is by Thomas Charles Baring; the last is by the scapegrace brother of the Brontë sisters, Patrick Branwell Brontë.

The Teasing Lovers

HORACE: Many a time your arms 'round me would cling,
    Before your heart made various excursions;
And I was happier than the happiest king
    Of all the Persians.

LYDIA: As long as I remained your constant flame,
    I was a proud and rather well-sung Lydia,
But now, in spite of all your precious fame,
    I'm glad I'm rid o' ye.

HORACE: Ah well, I've Chloe for my present queen;
    Her voice would thrill the marble bust of Caesar;
And I would exit gladly from the scene
    If it would please her.

LYDIA: And as for me, with every burning breath,
    I think of Calaïs, my handsome lover,
For him not only would I suffer death,
    But die twice over.

HORACE: What if the old love were to come once more
    With smiling face and understanding tacit?
If Chloe went, and I'd unbar the door,
    Would you then pass it?

LYDIA: Though he's a star that's constant, fair and true,
    And you're as light as cork or wild as fever;
With all your faults I'd live and die with you,
    You old deceiver!

51

Barine, The Incorrigible

If only once for every perjured oath,
    Each broken tryst and troth,
One punishment, one scar, one cheek too pale,
    One broken finger-nail
If but one blemish would appear and grieve you,
    I might believe you.

But in your case, with every faithless vow
    You sparkle more somehow.
You go abroad to break, with bright untruth,
    The hearts of all our youth;
You swear still falsely by the gods above you—
    And still they love you!

Yes, Venus gossips with her laughing crew,
    While every Nymph laughs too;
And even Cupid, busy at his art,
    Pointing the fiery dart,
In spite of all his labors pauses nightly,
    And chuckles lightly.

Beguiled by you the lad grows up your slave,
    Freed only by the grave.
And though he leaves you, though the new-wed spouse
    Forsakes your godless house,
He comes back pleading at your doors for mercy—
    Light-hearted Circe!

The Passing of Lydia

No longer now do perfumed swains and merry wanton youths
    Come flocking, loudly knocking at your gate;
No longer do they rob your rest, or mar the sleep that soothes,
    With calling, bawling love-songs until late.

No longer need you bar them out, nor is your window-pane
    Ever shaken, now forsaken here you lie.
Nevermore will lute strings woo you, nor your lover's voice complain,
    " 'Tis a sin, dear; let me in, dear, or I die!"

The little door that used to swing so gaily in and out,
　　Creaks on hinges that show tinges of decay.
For you are old, my Lydia, you are old and rather stout;
　　Not the sort to court or sport with those who play.

Oh now you will bewail the daring insolence of rakes,
　　While you dally in an alley with the crones;
And the Thracian wind goes howling down the avenue and shakes
　　Your old shutters, at it utters mocking moans.

For youth will always call to youth and greet love with a will;
　　And Winter, though you tint her like the Spring,
Beneath the artificial glow she will be Winter still.
　　And who would hold so cold and old a thing?

Too Young for Love

Your heifer's pretty neck is not yet broke
To stand the pressure of a husband's yoke;
　　She's too young yet to bear the weight
　　And duties of the marriage state.
Round the green meadows with the steers to stray
She loves, or in moist osier-beds to play,
　　Or her sun-heated flanks to lave
　　In some cool brook's refreshing wave.
Let not blind passion make you overbold:
Your grasp from yonder unripe grapes withhold,
　　That Autumn soon with purple hue
　　Of varied tint will paint for you.
The wings of Time beat fast, and every year
He takes away from you, he adds to her:
　　With flashing eye and flushing cheek
　　Soon Lalage your love will seek.
Not Chloris then with her developed charms
Will vie, nor Pholoë, who flies your arms,
　　Her shoulders beautiful and bright
　　As moonbeams on the sea at night.
Not Gyges' self will then with her compare;
Though, 'midst a troop of girls, his flowing hair
　　And fair smooth face might well perplex
　　A stranger to discern his sex.

It Always Happens

Grieve not too much, my Albius, since Glycera is no longer
　　As worthy of your constant love and amatory sighs
As in the yesterdays, and since a taller man and younger,
　　Who once embraced her slender waist, seems fairer in her eyes.

Lycoris of the little brow loves Cyrus unrequited;
　　While he in turn will madly burn for rustic Pholoë.
Yet shall Apulian wolves with docile she-goats be united
　　Ere he persuade this wilful maid to smile and turn his way.
Such is the will of Her who rules the destinies of lovers;
　　For Cupid's courts hold cruel sports when wanton Venus reigns.
And underneath her brazen yoke one oftentimes discovers
　　Young couples who, ill-suited to each other, curse their chains.

Thus once the little Myrtalè, a slave-born girl and lowly,
　　As wild and free as is the sea beneath Calabrian skies,
So captured me with pleasing ways I swore to love her solely,
　　While from the glade a worthier maid looked on with longing
　　　　eyes.

Time to Choose a Lover

Why, whenever she can spy me,
Like a fawn will Chloe fly me?
Like a fawn, its mother seeking
O'er the hills, through brambles breaking;
Frightened if the breezes move
But a leaflet in the grove;
Or a branch the zephyr tosses;
Or its path a lizard crosses;
Nothing can its fear dissemble—
Heart and knees together tremble.
Stop, my love. Thou needst not fear me,
For I follow not to tear thee
Like the lion, prowling o'er
Far Letulia's savage shore:
Stop. Thy budding charms discover
'Tis the time to choose a lover.

Ovid

Of all authors of erotic verse Ovid is the most voluminous as well as the most varied. Born in the hills of the Abruzzi forty-three years before the Christian era, Publius Ovidius Naso lived sixty years, during which he wrote passionate lyrics, imaginary love letters, guides to artificial beauty, amatory metamorphoses, and a three-part manual of seduction, *Ars Amatoria (The Art of Love)*, which is considered his masterpiece. Almost equally popular are the shorter poems in *Amores*, written to his mistress, Corinna.

His father, a wealthy aristocrat, hoped his son would be a lawyer and Ovid was prepared for the bar, but he soon abandoned law for literature. He became a state counsellor, married three times, and was well on the way to a high position when he was banished. It has been conjectured that he was sent into exile because of his salacious works, but Roman morals were scarcely strict and, moreover, since the poems were published years before the banishment, it is more likely that he was punished for being involved in political scandals. He died in 17 A.D.

One of the most prolific of Latin poets, Ovid was the laureate of carnal love. He luxuriated not only in the invention of sensual episodes and the rewriting of erotic legends, but in analyzing the processes of love-making. The translations from *Amores* are by the sixteenth century Christopher Marlowe; those from *The Art of Love* are by the eighteenth century John Dryden.

Amores

The Possessive Lover
(BOOK I. ELEGY IV.)

Thy husband to a banquet goes with me,
Pray God it may his latest supper be.
Shall I sit gazing as a bashful guest,
While others touch the damsel I love best?
Wilt lying under him, his bosom clip?
About thy neck shall he at pleasure skip?
Marvel not, though the fair bride did incite
The drunken Centaurs to a sudden fight.
I am no half horse, nor in woods I dwell.
Yet scarce my hands from thee contain I well.
But how thou should'st behave thyself now know,
Nor let the winds away my warnings blow.
Before thy husband come, though I not see
What may be done, yet there before him be,
Lie with him gently, when his limbs be spread.
Upon the bed, but on my foot first tread.
View me, my becks, and speaking countenance;
Take, and return each secret amorous glance,
Words without voice shall on my eyebrows sit,
Lines thou shalt read in wine by my hand writ.
When our lascivious toys come to thy mind,
Thy rosy cheeks be to thy thumb inclined.
If aught of me thou speak'st in inward thought,
Let thy soft finger to thy ear be brought.
When I, my light, do or say aught that please thee,
Turn around thy gold ring, as it were to ease thee.
Strike on the board like them that pray for evil,
When thou dost wish thy husband at the devil.
What wine he fills thee, wisely will him drink,

56

Ask thou the boy, what thou enough dost think.
When thou hast tasted, I will take the cup,
And where thou drink'st, on that part I will sup.
If he gives thee what first himself did taste,
Even in his face his offered goblets cast.
Let not thy neck by his vile arms be prest,
Nor lean thy soft head on his boisterous breast.
Thy bosom's roseate buds let him not finger,
Chiefly on thy lips let not his lips linger.
If thou givest kisses, I shall all disclose,
Say they are mine, and hands on thee impose.
Yet this I'll see, but if thy gown aught cover,
Suspicious fear in all my veins will hover.
Mingle not thighs, nor to his leg join thine,
Nor thy soft foot with his hard foot combine.
I have been wanton, therefore am perplexed,
And with mistrust of the like measure vexed.
I and my wench oft under clothes did lurk,
When pleasure moved us to our sweetest work.
Do not thou so; but throw thy mantle hence,
Lest I should think thee guilty of offence,
Entreat thy husband drink, but do not kiss,
And while he drinks, to add more do not miss;
If he lies down with wine and sleep opprest,
The thing and place shall counsel us the rest.
When to go homeward we rise all along
Have care to walk in middle of the throng,
There will I find thee or be found by thee,
There touch whatever thou canst touch of me.
Ah me! I warn what profits some few hours,
But we must part, when heaven with black night lours,
At night thy husband clips thee: I will weep
And to the doors sight of thyself (will) keep;
Then will he kiss thee, and not only kiss,
But force thee give him my stolen honey bliss.
Constrained against thy will give it the peasant,
Forbear sweet words, and be your sport unpleasant.
To him I pray it no delight may bring,
Or if it do, to thee no joy thence spring.
But, though this night thy fortune be to try it,
To me tomorrow constantly deny it.

In Summer's Heat
(BOOK I. ELEGY V.)

In summer's heat, and mid-time of the day,
To rest my limbs, upon a bed I lay;
One window shut, the other open stood,
Which gave such light as twinkles in a wood,
Like twilight glimpse at setting of the sun,
Or night being past, and yet not day begun;
Such light to shamefaced maidens must be shown
Where they may sport, and seem to be unknown.
Then came Corinna in her long loose gown,
Her white neck hid with tresses hanging down,
Resembling fair Semiramis going to bed,
Or Lais of a thousand wooers sped.
I snatched her gown being thin, the harm was small,
Yet strivèd she to be covered therewithal,
And striving thus as one that would be cast,
Betrayed herself, and yielded at the last.
Stark naked as she stood before mine eyes,
Not one wen in her body could I spy.
What arms and shoulders did I touch and see,
How apt her breasts were to be pressed by me,
How smooth a belly under her waist saw I,
How large a leg, and what a lusty thigh.
To leave the rest, all liked me passing well;
I clinged her naked body, down she fell:
Judge you the rest, being tired she bade me kiss.
Jove send me more such afternoons as this!

Apology for Loose Behavior
(BOOK II. ELEGY IV.)

I mean not to defend the scapes of any,
Or justify my vices being many;
For I confess, if that might merit favor,
Here I display my lewd and loose behavior.
I loathe, yet after that I loathe, I run.
Oh, how the burthen irks, that we should shun.
I cannot rule myself but where love please
And driven like a ship upon rough seas,
No one face likes me best, all faces move,

58

A hundred reasons make me ever love.
If any eye me with a modest look,
I blush, and by that blushful glance am took;
And she that's coy I like, for being no clown,
Methinks she would be nimble when she's down.
Though her sour looks a Sabine's brow resemble,
I think she'll do, but deeply can dissemble.
If she be learned, then for her skill I crave her,
If not, because she's simple I would have her.
Before Callimachus one prefers me far;
Seeing she likes my books, why should we jar?
Another rails at me, and that I write.
Yet would I lie with her, if that I might:
Trips she, it likes me well; plods she, what then?
She would be nimbler lying with a man,
And when one sweetly sings, then straight I long
To quaver on her lips even in her song;
Or if one touch the lute with art and cunning,
Who would not love those hands for their swift **cunning?**
And her I like that with a majesty,
Folds up her arms, and makes low courtesy.
To leave myself, that am in love with all,
Some one of these might make the chastest fall.
If she be tall, she's like an Amazon,
And therefore fills the bed she lies upon:
If short, she lies the rounder, to say troth,
But short and long please me, for I love both.
I think what one undecked would be, being drest;
Is she attired? then show her graces best.
A white wench thralls me, so doth golden yellow;
And nut-brown girls in doing have no fellow.
If her white neck be shadowed with brown hair,
Why so was Leda's, yet was Leda fair.
Amber-tress'd is she? Then on the morn think I:
My love alludes to every history.
A young wench pleaseth, and an old is good,
This for her looks, that for her womanhood:
Nay what is she, that any Roman loves,
But my ambitious ranging mind approves?

The Impotent Lover
(BOOK III. ELEGY VIII.)

Either she was foul, or her attire was bad,
Or she was not the wench I wished to have had.
Idly I lay with her, as if I loved not,
And like a burden grieved the bed that moved not.
Though both of us performed our true intent,
Yet could I not cast anchor where I meant.
She on my neck her ivory arms did throw,
Her arms far whiter than the Scythian snow.
And eagerly she kissed me with her tongue,
And under mine her wanton thigh she flung,
Yes, and she soothed me up, and called me "Sir,"
And used all speech that might provoke and stir.
Yet like as if cold hemlock I had drunk,
It mocked me, hung down the head and sunk.
Like a dull cipher, or rude block I lay,
Or shade, or body was I, who can say?
What will my age do, age I cannot shun,
Seeing in my prime my force is spent and done?
I blush, that being youthful, hot, and lusty,
I prove neither youth nor man, but old and rusty.
Pure rose she, like a nun to sacrifice,
Or one that with her tender brother lies.
Yet boarded I the golden Chie twice,
And Libas, and the white-cheeked Pitho thrice.
Corinna craved it in a summer's night,
And nine sweet bouts had we before daylight.
What, waste my limbs through some Thessalian charms?
May spells and drugs do silly souls such harms?
With virgin wax hath some abased my joints?
And pierced my liver with sharp needle-points?
Charms change corn to grass and make it die:
By charms are running springs and fountains dry.
By charms mast drops from oaks, from vines grapes fall,
And fruit from trees when there's no wind at all.
Why might not then my sinews be enchanted?
And I grow faint as with some spirit haunted?
To this, add shame: shame to perform it quailed me,
And was the second cause why vigor failed me.
My idle thoughts delighted her no more,
Than did the robe or garment which she wore.

Yet might her touch make youthful Pylius fire
And Tithon livelier than his years require.
Even her I had, and she had me in vain,
What might I crave more, if I ask again?
I think the great gods grieved they had bestowed,
This benefit: which lewdly I foreslowed.
I wished to be received in, in I get me.
To kiss, I kiss; to lie with her, she let me.
Why was I blest? why made king to refuse it?
Chuff-like had I not gold and could not use it?
So in a spring thrives he that told so much,
And looks upon the fruits he cannot touch.
Hath any rose so from a fresh young maid,
As she might straight have gone to church and prayed?
Well, I believe, she kissed not as she should,
Nor used the sleight and cunning which she could.
Huge oaks, hard adamants might she have moved,
And with sweet words caused deaf rocks to have loved.
Worthy she was to move both gods and men,
But neither was I man nor lived then.
Can deaf ears take delight when Phaemius sings?
Or Thamyris in curious painted things?
What sweet thought is there but I had the same?
And one gave place still as another came.
Yet, notwithstanding, like one dead it lay,
Drooping more than a rose pulled yesterday.
Now, when he should not yet, he bolts upright,
And craves his task, and seeks to be at fight.
Lie down with shame, and see thou stir no more,
Seeing thou would'st deceive me as before.
Then cozenest me: by thee surprised am I,
And bide sore loss with endless infamy.
Nay more, the wench did not disdain a whit
To take it in her hand, and play with it.
But when she saw it would by no means stand,
But still drooped down, regarding not her hand,
"Why mock'st thou me," she cried, "or being ill,
Why bade thee lie down here against thy will?
Either thou art witched with blood of frogs new dead,
Or jaded cam'st thou from some other's bed."

With that, her loose gown on, from me she cast her,
In skipping out her naked feet much graced her.
And lest her maid should know of this disgrace,
To cover it, spilt water on the place.

Advice to a Fair Wanton
(BOOK III. ELEGY XIV.)

Seeing thou art fair, I bar not thy false playing,
But let not me poor soul know of thy straying.
Nor do I give thee counsel to live chaste,
But that thou would'st dissemble, when 'tis past.
She hath not trod awry, that doth deny it.
Such as confess have lost their good names by it.
What madness is't to tell night-pranks by day?
And hidden secrets openly to bewray?
The strumpet with the stranger will not do,
Before the room be clear, and door put to,
Will you make shipwreck of your honest name,
And let the world be witness of the same?
Be more advised, walk as a puritan,
And I shall think you chaste, do what you can.
Slip still, only deny it when 'tis done,
And, before folk, immodest speeches shun.
The bed is for lascivious toyings meet,
There use all tricks, and tread shame under feet.
When you are up and dressed, be sage and grave,
And in the bed hide all the faults you have.
Be not ashamed to strip you, being there,
And mingle thighs, yours ever mine to bear.
There in your rosy lips my tongue entomb,
Practise a thousand sports when there you come.
Forbear no wanton words you there would speak,
And with your pastime let the bedstead creak
But with your robes put on an honest face,
And blush and seem as you were full of grace.
Deceive all; let me err; and think I'm right,
And like a wittol think thee void of slight.
Why see I lines so oft received and given?
This bed and that by tumbling made uneven?
Like one start up your hair tost and displaced,
And with a wanton's tooth your neck new-rased.

Grant this, that what you do I may not see;
If you weigh not ill speeches, yet weigh me.
My soul fleets when I think what you have done.
And through every vein doth cold blood run.
Then thee whom I must love, I hate in vain,
And would be dead, but dead with thee remain.
I'll not sift much, but hold thee soon excused,
Say but thou wert injuriously accused.
Though while the deed be doing you be took,
And I see when you ope the two-leaved book,
Swear I was blind; deny, if you be wise,
And I will trust your words more than mine eyes.
From him that yields, the palm is quickly got,
Teach but your tongue to say, "I did it not,"
And being justified by two words think
The cause acquits you not, but I that wink.

The Art of Love

(Book I)
In Cupid's school whoe'er would take degree,
Must learn his rudiments, by reading me.
Seamen with sailing arts their vessels move;
Art guides the chariot; art instructs to love.
Of ships and chariots others know the rule;
But I am master in Love's mighty school . . .
You, who in Cupid's rolls inscribe your name,
First seek an object worthy of your flame;
Then strive, with art, your lady's mind to gain;
And last, provide your love may long remain.

On these three precepts all my work shall move:
These are the rules and principles of love.
Before your youth with marriage is oppress'd,
Make choice of one who suits your humor best:
And such a damsel drops not from the sky;
She must be sought for with a curious eye . . .
The face of heav'n with fewer stars is crown'd,
Than beauties in the Roman sphere are found.

Whether thy love is bent on blooming youth,
On dawning sweetness, in unartful truth;
Or courts the juicy joys of riper growth;
Here mayst thou find thy full desires in both.
Or if autumnal beauties please thy sight,
(An age that knows to give and take delight,)
Millions of matrons of the graver sort,
In common prudence, will not balk the sport . . .
But above all, the playhouse is the place;
There's choice of quarry in that narrow chase.
There take thy stand, and sharply looking out,
Soon mayst thou find a mistress in the rout,
For length of time, or for a single bout.
The theaters are berries for the fair:
Like ants on molehills, thither they repair;
Like bees to hives, so numerously they throng,
It may be said, they to that place belong.
Thither they swarm, who have the public voice:
There choose, if plenty not distracts thy choice.
To see and to be seen, in heaps they run;
Some to undo, and some to be undone . . .

Nor shun the chariots, and the courser's race;
The Circus is no inconvenient place.
No need is there of talking on the hand;
Nor nods, nor signs, which lovers understand.
But boldly next the fair your seat provide;
Close as you can to hers, and side by side.
Pleas'd or unpleas'd, no matter; crowding sit,
For so the laws of public shows permit.
Then find occasion to begin discourse;
Enquire whose chariot this, and whose that horse:
To whatever side she is inclin'd,
Suit all your inclinations to her mind;
Like what she likes: from thence your court begin;
And whom she favors, wish that he may win.
But when the statues of the deities,
In chariots roll'd, appear before the prize;
When Venus comes, with deep devotion rise.
If dust be on her lap, or grains of sand,
Brush both away with your officious hand.

64

If none be there, yet brush that nothing thence;
And still to touch her lap make some pretense.
Touch anything of hers; and if her train
Sweep on the ground, let it not sweep in vain;
But gently take it up, and wipe it clean;
And while you wipe it, with observing eyes,
Who knows but you may see her naked thighs!
Observe who sits behind her; and beware,
Lest his incroaching knee should press the fair.
Light service takes light minds; for some can tell
Of favors won by laying cushions well:
By fanning faces some their fortune meet;
And some by laying footstools for their feet.
These overtures of love the Circus gives;
Nor at the swordplay less the lover thrives:
For there the son of Venus fights his prize;
And deepest wounds are oft receiv'd from eyes.
One, while the crowd their acclamations make,
Or while he bets, and puts his ring to stake,
Is struck from far, and feels the flying dart,
And of the spectacle is made a part . . .

Thus far the sportful Muse, with myrtle bound,
Has sung where lovely lasses may be found.
Now let me sing, how she who wounds your mind,
With art, may be to cure your wounds inclin'd.
Young nobles, to my laws attention lend;
And all you vulgar of my school, attend.
First then believe, all women may be won;
Attempt with confidence, the work is done.
The grasshopper shall first forbear to sing
In summer season, or the birds in spring,
Than women can resist your flattering skill:
Ev'n she will yield, who swears she never will.
To secret pleasure both the sexes move;
But women most, who must dissemble love.
'Twere best for us, if they would first declare,
Avow their passion, and submit to prayer.
The cow, by lowing, tells the bull her flame;
The neighing mare invites her stallion to the game.
Man is more temp'rate in his lust than they,
And, more than women, can his passion sway . . .

All women are content that men should woo;
She who complains, and she who will not do.
Rest then secure, whate'er thy luck may prove,
Not to be hated for declaring love.
And yet how canst thou miss, since womankind
Is frail and vain, and still to change inclin'd?
Old husbands and stale gallants they despise,
And more another's than their own they prize.
A larger crop adorns our neighbor's field;
More milk his kine from swelling udders yield.
　　First gain the maid; by her thou shalt be sure
A free access and easy to procure:
Who knows what to her office does belong,
Is in the secret, and can hold her tongue.
Bribe her with gifts, with promises, and pray'rs;
For her good word goes far in love affairs.
The time and fit occasion leave to her,
When she most aptly can thy suit prefer.
The time for maids to fire their lady's blood,
Is, when they find her in a merry mood;
When all things at her wish and pleasure move:
Her heart is open then, and free to love.
Then mirth and wantonness to lust betray,
And smooth the passage to the lover's way.
Troy stood the siege, when filled with anxious care:
One merry mood concluded all the war.
　　If some fair rival vex her jealous mind,
Offer thy service to revenge in kind;
Instruct the damsel, while she combs her hair,
To raise the choler of the injured fair,
And sighing, make her mistress understand
She has the means of vengeance in her hand.
Then, naming thee, thy humble suit prefer,
And swear thou languishest and diest for her.
Then let her lose no time, but push at all,
For women soon are raised and soon they fall.
Give their first fury leisure to relent,
They melt like ice, and suddenly repent.
　　T'enjoy the maid, will that thy suit advance?
'Tis a hard question, and a doubtful chance.
One maid, corrupted, bawds the better for't;

Another for herself will keep the sport.
Thy business may be furthered or delayed,
But by my counsel, let alone the maid;
Even though she should consent to do the feat,
The profit's little and the danger great.
I will not lead thee through a rugged road,
But where the way lies open, safe, and broad.
Yet if thou findst her very much thy friend,
And her good face her diligence commend,
Let the fair mistress have thy first embrace,
And let the maid come after in her place.
  But this I will advise, and mark my words,
For 'tis the best advice my skill affords,
If needs thou with the damsel must begin,
Before the attempt is made, make sure to win,
For then the secret will be better kept,
And she can tell no tales when once she's dipt.
'Tis for the fowler's interest to beware,
The bird entangled should not 'scape the snare.
The fish, once pricked, avoids the bearded hook,
And spoils the sport of all the neighboring brook.
But if the wench be thine, she makes the way,
And for thy sake, her mistress will betray,
Tell all she knows, and all she hears her say . . .

  All things the stations of their seasons keep;
And certain times there are to sow and reap.
Plowmen and sailors for the season stay,
One to plow land, and one to plow the sea:
So should the lover wait the lucky day.
Then stop thy suit, it hurts not thy design;
But think, another hour she may be thine.
When she's in humor, ev'ry day is good.
But than her birthday seldom comes a worse;
When bribes and presents must be sent of course;
And that's a bloody day, that costs thy purse.
Be stanch; yet parsimony will be vain:
The craving sex will still the lover drain.
No skill can shift 'em off, nor art remove;
They will be begging, when they know we love . . .

Invoke the god, and all the mighty powers,
That wine may not defraud thy genial hours.
Then in ambiguous words thy suit prefer,
Which she may know were all address'd to her.
In liquid purple letters write her name,
Which she may read, and reading find thy flame.
Then may your eyes confess your mutual fires;
(For eyes have tongues, and glances tell desires.)
Whene'er she drinks, be first to take the cup;
And, where she laid her lips, the blessing sup.
When she to carving does her hand advance,
Put out thy own, and touch it as by chance.
Thy service ev'n her husband must attend:
(A husband is a most convenient friend.)
Seat the fool cuckold in the highest place,
And with thy garland his dull temples grace.
Whether below, or equal in degree,
Let him be lord of all the company,
And what he says be seconded by thee.
'Tis common to deceive thro' friendship's name;
But, common tho' it be, 'tis still to blame:
Thus factors frequently their trust betray,
And to themselves their masters' gains convey.
Drink to a certain pitch, and then give o'er;
Thy tongue and feet may stumble, drinking more.
Of drunken quarrels in her sight beware;
Pot-valor only serves to fright the fair.
Eurytion justly fell, by wine oppress'd,
For his rude riot at a wedding feast.
Sing, if you have a voice, and shew your parts
In dancing, if endued with dancing arts.
Do anything within your power to please;
Nay, ev'n affect a seeming drunkenness:
Clip every word; and if by chance you speak
Too home, or if too broad a jest you break,
In your excuse the company will join,
And lay the fault upon the force of wine.
True drunkenness is subject to offend;
But when 'tis feign'd, 'tis oft a lover's friend.
Then safely you may praise her beauteous face,
And call him happy, who is in her grace.

Her husband thinks himself the man design'd;
But curse the cuckold in your secret mind.
When all are risen and prepare to go,
Mix with the crowd, and tread upon her toe.

   This is the proper time to make thy court,
For now she's in the vein, and fit for sport.
Lay bashfulness, that rustic virtue, by;
To manly confidence thy thoughts apply.
On Fortune's foretop timely fix thy hold;
Now speak and speed, for Venus loves the bold.
No rules of rhetoric here I need afford;
Only begin, and trust the following word;
It will be witty of its own accord.
Act well the lover; let thy speech abound.
In dying words, that represent thy wound.
Distrust not her belief; she will be mov'd;
All women think they merit to be lov'd.
Sometimes a man begins to love in jest,
And, after, feels the torments he profess'd.
For your own sakes be pitiful, ye fair;
For a feign'd passion may a true prepare.
By flatteries we prevail on womankind,
As hollow banks by streams are undermin'd.
Tell her, her face is fair, her eyes are sweet;
Her taper fingers praise, and little feet.
Such praises ev'n the chaste are pleas'd to hear;
Both maids and matrons hold their beauty dear . . .
Beg her, with tears, thy warm desires to grant;
For tears will pierce a heart of adamant.
If tears will not be squeezed, then rub your eye,
Or noint the lids, and seem at least to cry.
Kiss, if you can: resistance if she make,
And will not give you kisses, let her take.
Fie, fie, you naughty man, are words of course;
She struggles, but to be subdued by force.
Kiss only soft, I charge you, and beware,
With your hard bristles not to brush the fair.
He who has gain'd a kiss, and gains no more,
Deserves to lose the bliss he got before.

If once she kiss, her meaning is express'd;
There wants but little pushing for the rest:
Which if thou dost not gain, by strength or art,
The name of clown then suits with thy desert;
'Tis downright dulness, and a shameful part.
Perhaps, she calls it force; but, if she 'scape,
She will not thank you for th' omitted rape.
The sex is cunning to conceal their fires;
They would be forc'd ev'n to their own desires.
They seem t' accuse you, with a downcast sight,
But in their souls confess you did them right.
Who might be forc'd, and yet untouch'd depart,
Thank with their tongues, but curse you with their heart.

    This is the sex; they will not first begin,
But, when compelled, are pleased to suffer sin.
Is there who thinks that women first should woo,
Lay by thy self-conceit, thou foolish beau.
Begin, and save their modesty the shame;
'Tis well for thee if they receive thy flame.
'Tis decent for a man to speak his mind;
They but expect the occasion to be kind.
Ask, that thou mayst enjoy; she waits for this,
And on thy first advance depends thy bliss. . . .
    But if you find your prayers increase her pride,
Strike sail awhile, and wait another tide.
They fly when we pursue; but make delay,
And when they see you slacken, they will stay.
Sometimes it profits to conceal your end;
Name not yourself her lover, but her friend.
How many skittish girls have thus been caught?
He proved a lover who a friend was thought.
We sin with gust, we love by fraud to gain,
And find a pleasure in our fellows' pain.
From rival foes you may your fair defend,
But, would you ward the blow, beware your friend;
Beware your brother and your next of kin;
But from your bosom friend your care begin.

    Here I had ended, but experience finds
That sundry women are of sundry minds,

With various crotchets filled, and hard to please:
They therefore must be caught by various ways. . . .
So turn thyself, and imitating them,
Try several tricks, and change thy stratagem.
One rule will not for different ages hold:
The jades grow cunning as they grow more old.
Then talk not bawdy to the bashful maid;
Bad words will make her innocence afraid.
Nor to an ignorant girl of learning speak;
She thinks you conjure when you talk in Greek.
And hence 'tis often seen, the simple shun
The learned, and into vile embraces run.
Part of my task is done, and part to do;
But here 'tis time to rest myself and you.

Petronius

We know next to nothing of Petronius except that he is the author of a few poems and *The Satyricon,* a tantalizingly fragmentary masterpiece of ribaldry often called "the first realistic novel." Even his first name is a matter of dispute; Tacitus refers to him as Gaius, Pliny calls him Titus. It is believed that he was also spoken of as Petronius Arbiter, which was evidently a title rather than a part of his name and indicated, if Tacitus is to be trusted, that he was an "Arbiter of Elegance" under Nero. Tacitus has a famous passage about his enjoyment of life, his bad habits, and his enforced suicide. Before his death, says Tacitus, Petronius revenged himself upon Nero by writing out "a list of the Emperor's debaucheries, citing by name each of his sexual partners, male and female, with a catalogue of his sexual experiments."

The liveliest as well as the best translation of *The Satyricon* is by William Arrowsmith. The translations of the following two poems are by the editor.

A Plea for Haste

Why this delay? Why waste the time in kissing?
    What is the very meaning of a kiss?
Think of the best, the ultimate joy we're missing!
    Hasten the moment of our mutual bliss!

Think of the night the little lamplight faltered
    And you lay under me. What love and laughter
We shared that night till morning! Nothing's altered.
    So come to bed; there's time for dawdling after.

A Plea for Postponement [1]

It's all too swift; it's over all too soon—
The quickened pace, the gasps, the final swoon,
The sudden dying down of flame and fire,
The loosened limbs, the loss of all desire.
Let us control it; love is far more than
The itching heat of a stray dog—or man.
Let us put off the moment, let us wait
Before we lose all sense and consummate
What we might well conserve. Let lips and hands
Do all we want to answer our demands.
Let eager mouths and teasing tongues fulfill
Our deepest need until . . . until . . . until . . .

[1] Compare the version ("Against Consummation") by Ben Jonson on page 210

Martial

Marcus Valerius Martial (40–104 A.D.) was born in Spain, came to Rome in his early twenties, and was so disillusioned by what he saw that he became a thoroughly cynical individual. A clever writer, he flattered those in power, adulated them in verse and in person, attracted patrons and attained equestrian rank. Then he turned upon himself and the society of his times.

Martial composed almost twelve hundred poems, many of them epigrams detailing the gaudy grossness of Rome, which he did not excoriate but accepted with a shrug. "Much of his best work," says Chambers's Biographical Dictionary wryly, "unfortunately, is his least pure."

The following translations are by the editor except the last, which is by Thomas Moore.

To His Girl

You're ravishing and, plain to see,
   At any hour you're salable.
Oh, be less beautiful, or be
   A little less available.

A Bad Joke

A fraud, a forger, and informer, too,
   Pander and pimp, the friend of every whore . . .
In spite of this—incredible but true—
   What's the reward of all your schemes? You're poor!

Work and Play

Who is that pretty fellow—
The one that's always hanging around your wife?
The one that's always whispering sweet nothings in her ear,
Who leans against her chair
And casually touches her hair
With jeweled fingers?
"He works for my wife," you answer.
He does, does he? Listen, my friend:
That handsome boy does not do your wife's work.
He does yours.

75

Familiarity Breeds Indifference

Dancing with such salacious gestures
In such transparent vesture
This girl could excite passion
In an ashen corpse or a paralyzed statue.
It's a brave story.
Her master tired of her, sold her as a slave,
And then bought her back as his mistress.

Insufficient Vengeance

You did right, injured husband, to ruin the face
Of the man who shamed you. You cut off
His ears and nose. What a disgrace!
In your place you did right. . . .
But did you cut off enough?

The Incentive

As long as you allowed her complete liberty
And she was free to live her life,
No one went near your wife.
Now that you guard her well it's another matter.
Everyone wants to get at her.

The Too Literal Pupil

Fabulla, sweet virgin, you have learned your lesson too well.
I warned you to hold off impetuous lovers,
To say "No" once, twice, even three times.
But, dear girl for whom I hunger and pine away,
I did not tell you to say "No" forever,
And to me.

Abnegation

I could resign that eye of blue,
   Howe'er its splendor used to thrill me;
And even that cheek of roseate hue
   To lose it, Cloe, would scarcely kill me.

That snowy neck I'd never miss,
   However much I've raved about it;
And sweetly as that lip can kiss,
   I *think* I could exist without it.

In short, so well I've learned to fast,
   That, sooth my love, I know not whether
I might not bring myself at last,
   To do without you altogether.

Juvenal

Perhaps the bitterst satirist that ever lived, Decimus Junius Juvenalis (c. 55-c. 140 A.D.) was, like Ovid, trained to be a lawyer and, like Martial, became an irascible scorner of the social system of his day. His truculence undid him; at eighty he was sent to a remote section of Egypt where he died, says Suetonius "of vexation and disgust."

In a long *Discourse Concerning Satire* prefacing his translations of five of Juvenal's satires, Dryden points to the differences between two favorite Latin poets, Horace and Juvenal:

> *His (Horace's) urbanity is to be commended . . . Juvenal is of a more vigorous and masculine wit; he gives me as much pleasure as I can bear . . . he drives his reader along with him . . . His thoughts are as just as those of Horace, and much more elevated . . . Horace is always on the amble, Juvenal on the gallop. He goes with more impetuosity than Horace, and the swiftness adds a more lively agitation to the spirits.*

Regarding his translation, Dryden implies that he has modernized Juvenal's fiercest satire—the one against women—into a Restoration piece and a vicious commentary on his own age as well as Juvenal's. At the same time Dryden attempts to palliate the sting of Juvenal's scabrous invective. "Let the poet," he wrote with suspicious sarcasm, "bear the blame of his own invention, and let me satisfy the world that I am not of his opinion. Whatever his Roman ladies were, the English are free from his imputations. They will read with wonder and abhorrence the vices of an age which was the most infamous on record." Nevertheless, Dryden ended his preface with this conclusion: "If we take the word of our malicious author: Bad Women are the general standing rule, and Good Women some few exceptions to it."

Against Women

From the Sixth Satire

Yet thou, they say, for marriage dost provide:
Is this an age to buckle with a bride?
They say thy hair the curling art is taught,
The wedding ring perhaps already bought:
A sober man like thee to change his life!
What fury would possess thee with a wife?
Art thou of ev'ry other death bereft,
No knife, no ratsbane, no kind halter left?
(For every noose compar'd to hers is cheap)
Is there no city bridge from whence to leap?
Wouldst thou become her drudge, who dost enjoy
A better sort of bedfellow, thy boy?
He keeps thee not awake with nightly brawls,
Nor with a begg'd reward thy pleasure palls;
Nor with insatiate heavings calls for more,
When all thy spirits were drain'd out before . . .
What revolution can appear so strange,
As such a lecher, such a life to change?
A rank, notorious whoremaster, to choose
To thrust his neck into the marriage noose!
He who so often in a dreadful fright
Had in a coffer scap'd the jealous cuckold's sight,
That he, to wedlock dotingly betray'd,
Should hope in this lewd town to find a maid!
The man's grown mad: to ease his frantic pain,
Run for the surgeon; breathe the middle vein:
But let a heifer with gilt horns be led
To Juno, regent of the marriage bed,
And let him every deity adore,

If his new bride prove not an arrant whore
In head and tail, and every other pore . . .

Think'st thou one man is for one woman meant?
She, sooner, with one eye would be content.
   And yet, 't is nois'd, a maid did once appear
In some small village, tho' fame says not where:
'T is possible; but sure no man she found;
'T was desert all, about her father's ground:
And yet some lustful god might there make bold;
Are Jove and Mars grown impotent and old?
Many a fair nymph has in a cave been spread,
And much good love without a feather bed.
Whither wouldst thou to choose a wife resort,
The Park, the Mall, the Playhouse, or the Court?
Which way soever thy adventures fall,
Secure alike of chastity in all . . .

          . . . You shall hear
What fruits the sacred brows of monarchs bear:
The good old sluggard but began to snore
When from his side up rose the imperial whore;
She who preferr'd the pleasures of the night
To pomps that are but impotent delight,
Strode from the palace, with an eager pace,
To cope with a more masculine embrace;
Muffled she march'd, like Juno in a cloud,
Of all her train but one poor wench allow'd;
One whom in secret service she could trust,
The rival and companion of her lust.
To the known brothel house she takes her way;
And for a nasty room gives double pay;
That room in which the rankest harlot lay.
Prepar'd for fight, expectingly she lies,
With heaving breasts, and with desiring eyes:
Still as one drops, another takes his place,
And baffled still succeeds to like disgrace.
At length, when friendly darkness is expir'd,
And every strumpet from her cell retir'd,
She lags behind, and, ling'ring at the gate,

With a repining sigh submits to fate:
All filth without, and all a fire within,
Tir'd with the toil, unsated with the sin.
Old Caesar's bed the modest matron seeks;
The steam of lamps still hanging on her cheeks
In ropy smut: thus foul, and thus bedight,
She brings him back the product of the night.
 Now should I sing what poisons they provide,
With all their trumpery of charms beside,
And all their arts of death, it would be known
Lust is the smallest sin the sex can own;
Caesinia still, they say, is guiltless found
Of every vice, by her own lord renown'd:
And well she may, she brought ten thousand pound.
She brought him wherewithal to be call'd chaste;
His tongue is tied in golden fetters fast:
He sighs, adores, and courts her every hour;
Who would not do as much for such a dower?
She writes love letters to the youth in grace;
Nay, tips the wink before the cuckold's face;
And might do more; her portion makes it good;
Wealth has the privilege of widowhood.

 These truths with his example you disprove,
Who with his wife is monstrously in love:
But know him better; for I heard him swear,
'Tis not that she's his wife, but that she's fair.
Let her but have three wrinkles in her face,
Let her eyes lessen, and her skin unbrace,
Soon you will hear the saucy steward say:
"Pack up with all your trinkets, and away;
You grow offensive both at bed and board:
Your betters must be had to please my lord."
 Meantime she's absolute upon the throne;
And, knowing time is precious, loses none:
She must have flocks of sheep, with wool more fine
Than silk, and vineyards of the noblest wine;
Whole droves of pages for her train she craves,
And sweeps the prisons for attending slaves.
In short, whatever in her eyes can come,
Or others have abroad, she wants at home.

When winter shuts the seas, and fleecy snows
Make houses white, she to the merchant goes;
Rich crystals of the rock she takes up there,
Huge agate vases, and old China ware:
Then Berenice's ring her finger proves,
More precious made by her incestuous loves,
And infamously dear; a brother's bribe,
Ev'n God's anointed, and of Judah's tribe;
Where barefoot they approach the sacred shrine,
And think it only sin to feed on swine . . .

    Thus the she-tyrant reigns, till, pleas'd with change,
Her wild affections to new empires range:
Another subject-husband she desires;
Divorc'd from him, she to the first retires,
While the last wedding feast is scarcely o'er,
And garlands hang yet green upon the door.
So still the reck'ning rises; and appears,
In total sum, eight husbands in five years.
The title for a tombstone might be fit,
But that it would too commonly be writ.
Her mother living, hope no quiet day;
She sharpens her, instructs her how to flay
Her husband bare, and then divides the prey.
She takes love letters, with a crafty smile,
And in her daughter's answer mends the style.
In vain the husband sets his watchful spies;
She cheats their cunning, or she bribes their eyes.
The doctor's call'd; the daughter, taught the trick,
Pretends to faint; and in full health is sick.
The panting stallion, at the closet door,
Hears the consult, and wishes it were o'er.
Canst thou, in reason, hope, a bawd so known
Should teach her other manners than her own?
Her int'rest is in all th' advice she gives:
'Tis on the daughter's rents the mother lives.
    No cause is tried at the litigious bar,
But women plaintiffs or defendants are;
They form the process, all the briefs they write;
The topics furnish, and the pleas indite;
And teach the toothless lawyer how to bite.

They turn viragoes too; the wrestler's toil
They try, and smear their naked limbs with oil:
Against the post their wicker shields they crush,
Flourish the sword, and at the plastron push.
Of every exercise the mannish crew
Fulfills the parts, and oft excels us to. . . .

Behold the strutting Amazonian whore:
She stands in guard with her right foot before;
Her coats tuck'd up, and all her motions just;
She stamps, and then cries Hah! at every thrust:
But laugh to see her, tir'd with many a bout,
Call for the pot, and like a man piss out.
The ghosts of ancient Romans, should they rise,
Would grin to see their daughters play a prize.
   Besides, what endless brawls by wives are bred!
The curtain lecture makes a mournful bed.
Then, when she has thee sure within the sheets,
Her cry begins, and the whole day repeats.
Conscious of crimes herself, she teases first;
Thy servants are accus'd; thy whore is curst;
She acts the jealous, and at will she cries;
For women's tears are but the sweat of eyes.
Poor cuckold-fool, thou think'st that love sincere,
And suck'st between her lips the falling tear;
But search her cabinet, and thou shalt find
Each tiller there with love epistles lin'd.
Suppose her taken in a close embrace,
This you would think so manifest a case,
No rhetoric could defend, no impudence outface:
And yet even then she cries: "The marriage vow
A mental reservation must allow;
And there's a silent bargain still implied,
The parties should be pleas'd on either side;
And both may for their private needs provide.
Tho' men yourselves, and women us you call,
Yet *homo* is a common name for all."
There's nothing bolder than a woman caught;
Guilt gives 'em courage to maintain their fault.

You ask from whence proceed these monstrous crimes.
Once poor, and therefore chaste, in former times,
Our matrons were: no luxury found room
In low-roof'd houses, and bare walls of loam;
Their hands with labor harden'd while 'twas light,
And frugal sleep supplied the quiet night;
While pinch'd with want, their hunger held 'em straight,
When Hannibal was hov'ring at the gate:
But wanton now, and lolling at our ease,
We suffer all th' invet'rate ills of peace . . .

The secrets of the goddess nam'd the Good,
Are even by boys and barbers understood:
Where the rank matrons, dancing to the pipe,
Jig with their bums, and are for action ripe;
With music rais'd, they spread abroad their hair,
And toss their heads like an enamor'd mare:
Laufella lays her garland by, and proves
The mimic lechery of manly loves.
Rank'd with the lady the cheap sinner lies;
For here not blood, but virtue, gives the prize.
Nothing is feign'd in this venereal strife;
'T is downright lust, and acted to the life.
So full, so fierce, so vigorous, and so strong,
That looking on would make old Nestor young.
Impatient of delay, a general sound,
An universal groan of lust goes round;
For then, and only then, the sex sincere is found.
"Now is the time of action; now begin,"
They cry, "and let the lusty lovers in."
"The whoresons are asleep." "Then bring the slaves,
And watermen, a race of strong-back'd knaves."
I wish, at least, our sacred rites were free
From those pollutions of obscenity:
But 't is well known what singer, how disguis'd,
A lewd audacious action enterpriz'd:
Into the fair, with women mix'd, he went,
Arm'd with a huge two-handed instrument;
A grateful present to those holy choirs,
Where the mouse, guilty of his sex, retires,
And even male pictures modestly are veil'd:

84

Yet no profaneness on that age prevail'd;
No scoffers at religious rites were found;
Tho' now, at every altar they abound.

    I hear your cautious counsel, you would say:
"Keep close your women under lock and key."
But, who shall keep those keepers? Women, nurs'd
In craft, begin with those, and bribe 'em first.
The sex is turn'd all whore; they love the game:
And mistresses and maids are both the same.

The Vigil of Venus

"The Vigil of Venus" is one of the most daintily designed Latin poems. Written in the third century by an unknown poet, it is knit together by a repeating refrain that keeps the lines in continual motion. "Flower-garlanded and myrtle-shrouded, the spring worshippers go dancing through the fields that break before them into a sheet of flowers; among them the boy Love goes with his torch and his arrows." Such was the interpretation of the Scottish classical scholar, J. W. Mackail. The translation is by the seventeenth century Thomas Stanley.

Love he tomorrow, who loved never;
Tomorrow, who hath loved, persever.

The spring appears, in which the earth
Receives a new harmonious birth;
When all things mutual love unites;
When birds perform their nuptial rites;
And fruitful by her watery lover,
Each grove its tresses doth recover.
Love's Queen tomorrow, in the shade,
Which by these verdant trees is made,
Their sprouting tops in wreaths shall bind,
And myrtles into arbors wind;
Tomorrow, raised on a high throne,
Dione shall her laws make known.

Love he tomorrow, who loved never;
Tomorrow, who hath loved, persever.

Then the round ocean's foaming flood
Immingled with celestial blood,
'Mongst the blue purple of the main,

And horses whom two feet sustain,
Rising Dione did beget
With fruitful waters dropping wet.

> *Love he tomorrow, who loved never;*
> *Tomorrow, who hath loved, persever.*

With flowery jewels everywhere
She paints the purple-color'd year;
She, when the rising bud receives
Favonius' breath, thrusts forth the leaves,
The naked roof with these t' adorn;
She the transparent dew o' th' morn,
Which the thick air of night still uses
To leave behind, in rain diffuses;
These tears with orient brightness shine,
Whilst they with trembling weight decline,
Whose every drop, into a small
Clear orb distill'd, sustains its fall.
Pregnant with these the bashful rose
Her purple blushes doth disclose.
The drops of falling dew that are
Shed in calm nights by every star,
She in her humid mantle holds,
And then her virgin leaves unfolds.
I' th' morn, by her command, each maid
With dewy roses is array'd;
Which from Cythera's crimson blood,
From the soft kisses Love bestow'd,
From jewels, from the radiant flame,
And the sun's purple luster, came.
She to her spouse shall married be
Tomorrow; not ashamed that he
Should with a single knot untie
Her fiery garment's purple dye.

> *Love he tomorrow, who loved never;*
> *Tomorrow, who hath loved, persever.*

The goddess bade the nymphs remove
Unto the shady myrtle grove;

The boy goes with the maids, yet none
Will trust, or think Love tame is grown,
If they perceive that anywhere
He arrows doth about him bear.
Go fearless, nymphs, for Love hath laid
Aside his arms, and tame is made.
His weapons by command resign'd,
Naked to go he is enjoin'd,
Lest he hurt any by his craft,
Either with flame, or bow, or shaft.
But yet take heed, young nymphs, beware
You trust him not, for Cupid's fair,
Lest by his beauty you be harm'd;
Love naked is completely arm'd.

> *Love he tomorrow, who loved never;*
> *Tomorrow, who hath loved, persever.*

Fair Venus virgins sends to thee,
Indued with equal modesty:
One only thing we thee desire,
Chaste Delia, for a while retire;
That the wide forest, that the wood,
May be unstain'd with savage blood.
She would with prayers herself attend thee,
But that she knew she could not bend thee;
She would thyself to come have pray'd,
Did these delights beseem a maid.

ANONYMOUS

The Middle Ages and the Renaissance

Wine, Women, and Song

The mythologies and rites of the ancient world gradually dissolved into the flux of violence and ignorance which afflicted the Dark Ages. It is impossible to draw a line which marks an end of medieval turmoil and a beginning of the Renaissance, the time of rebirth and revival of art, literature, and learning. The two periods stretched over approximately a thousand years, starting in the fifth century and covering the greatest contrasts in Christianity and paganism, embracing a tacit acceptance of stern ritual and an outspoken rejection of prescribed morality. "The medieval mind," wrote Reginald Nettel in *Seven Centuries of Popular Song,* "may be compared to medieval architecture—always reaching heavenward . . . but in the buildings there are innumerable little reminders of daily life: contemporary figures, serious, comical, even ribald. To us many of them are possibly obscene; but the medieval minds were at once more pious and more cruel"—and, Nettel may have added, more readily on speaking terms with what many of us still consider unspeakable.

One phenomenon of the twelfth century was the emergence and quickly attained popularity of *Scholares Vagantes,* Wandering Students. They were the *enfants terribles* who enlivened the literature of the twelfth to the fourteenth centuries, a motley antisocial society of jongleurs and strollers, monks who had left their orders, raffish semi-clerics, scholarly vagabonds, singers and satirists who were the displaced bohemians of their times. Their irreverent compositions celebrating the joys of the flesh, the pleasures of guzzling and wooing, as well as the corruption of the clergy, remained unpublished until the nineteenth century when the manuscripts were discovered in a Bavarian monastery.

Two collections endeavor to carry over the spirit of the Latin verses into English, although no translation conveys the full flavor of the originals. The first, *Wine, Women, and Song,* subtitled

91

"Medieval Latin Students' Songs," appeared in 1884 with an introductory essay by John Addington Symonds and prefaced by a motto ascribed to Martin Luther:

> Wer liebt nicht Wein, Weib, und Gesang,
> Der bleibt ein Narr sein Lebenslang.

Which might be translated as:

> The man who shuns wine, woman, and song
> Remains a fool his whole life long.

The second, published in 1949, a set of fresh translations with a running commentary by George F. Whicher, was entitled *The Goliard Poets*. The origin of the word Goliard is obscure. It may have been derived from *gula* or gluttony; it may have come from the Philistine Goliath (Golias in the Vulgate), the sinful giant opposed to the virtuous David. Golias, said Whicher, "eventually became a kind of eponymous hero, typical of the greedy, half-starved reprobates who traveled light with threadbare cloaks and a few staves of Latin verse as their only baggage."

In 1937 a selection of the vagrant songs was put to music by the German composer Carl Orff and performed as a "scenic secular cantata" entitled *Carmina Burana*. It was further popularized by record companies on both continents.

"Invitation to a Mistress" and "Love Laughs at Winter" are translations by George F. Whicher. "The Confessional" is a translation by Louis Untermeyer. All the other translations are by John Addington Symonds.

Love Laughs at Winter

Now wintry blasts have come again
    The toils of love impeding,
From swollen skies come sleet and rain
    Post haste to earthward speeding;
In token of the old campaign
    My cheeks are scarred and bleeding:
Such love is in my breast that I,
When winter is most frigid, fry.

  While goose-flesh makes my skin grow tight,
    The fire within commences;
Sleepless I lie, night after night,
    And daylight racks my senses;
This life, too long continued, might
    Have serious consequences:
Such love is in my breast that I,
When winter is most frigid, fry.

  O Cupid, when the gods divine
    Acknowledge their subdual,
Why pick a worthless heart like mine
    To serve your torch for fuel?
Even cruel cold does not incline
    Stern you to be less cruel:
Such love is in my breast that I,
When winter is most frigid, fry.

  Variety of weather makes
    Our climate so enchanting,
In snow it cools, in sun it bakes,
    No temperature is wanting;

But hot or cold, for ladies' sakes
    My heart is always panting:
Such love is in my breast that I,
When winter is most frigid, fry.

Invitation to a Mistress

Nay, come and visit me, sweet friend,
Heart of my heart, this prayer I send:
Enter, I beg, my little room
So trimly decked — you know for whom.

There stand the chairs, in each a cushion,
And lovely curtains in addition;
About the house are scattered flowers
And scented herbs most sweet in bowers.

There likewise is the table set
Where dainties brought from far are met;
There clear and plenteous wines invite you,
And all things else, dear, to delight you.

And while we dine, sweet sounds shall come
From high-pitched pipe and punctual drum;
Skillful performers, girl and boy,
Will play the songs you most enjoy.

His quill will twang the cither's wire,
Her hand will pluck the sweeter lyre,
While servants from full platters pass
Spiced wine in cups of colored glass.

No joys that banquets can afford
Can match our converse afterward,
For one choice intimacy brings
Delights that cause no surfeitings.

Sweet sister, come — my only goal
And choicer portion of my soul,
Dear beyond all, light of my eyes,
My hope, my joy, my life, my prize.

"I've been alone in darkling woods,
Seeking the deepest solitudes;
I've fled from voices time and again
And kept aloof from sight of men."

No more delay, dearest, permit;
Love is our book — let's open it.
Without you I am scarce alive,
Only by loving can we thrive.

Why not be brave and say that you
Will do soon what you're bound to do?
What sense is there in hesitating?
Come, precious — I'm not good at waiting.

∞

The Confessional

"Father Francisco! Father Francisco!"
    What do you want of Father Francisco?
"Father, a poor old widow's waiting,
    Anxious to confess her sin."
Go, preserve her from temptations
Of the flesh and give me patience
    That the soul may win.

"Father Francisco! Father Francisco!"
    What do you want of Father Francisco?
"Father, a pious matron's waiting,
    Anxious to confess her sin."
Go, protect me from such tattle;
There's no end to women's prattle
    When they once begin.

"Father Francisco! Father Francisco!"
    What do you want of Father Francisco?
"Father, a fair young girl is waiting,
    Anxious to confess her sin."
Heaven praise such holy ardor.
Piously I shall reward her.
    Hurry! Let her in!

95

The Wooing

All the woods are now in flower,
Song-birds sing in field and bower,
Orchards their white blossoms shower:
Lads, make merry in Love's hour!

Sordid grief hath flown away,
Fervid Love is here to-day;
He will tame without delay
Those who love not while they may.

He. "Fairest maiden, list to me;
Do not thus disdainful be;
Scorn and anger disagree
With thy youth, and injure thee.

I am weaker than thou art;
Mighty Love hath pierced my heart;
Scarce can I endure his dart:
Lest I die, heal, heal my smart!"

She. "Why d'you coax me, suitor blind?
What you seek you will not find;
I'm too young for love to bind;
Such vain trifles vex my mind.

Is't your will with me to toy?
I'll not mate with man or boy:
Like the Phoenix, to enjoy
Single life shall be my joy."

He. "Yet Love is tyrannous,
Harsh, fierce, imperious!
He who man's heart can thus
    Shatter, may make to bow
    Maidens as stern as thou!"

She. "Now by your words I'm 'ware
What you wish, what you are;
You know love well, I swear!
    So I'll be loved by you;
    Now I'm on fire too!"

The Lover and the Nightingale

These hours of spring are jolly;
      Maidens, be gay!
Shake off dull melancholy,
      Ye lads, today!
   Oh! all abloom am I!
   It is a maiden love that makes me sigh,
   A new, new love it is wherewith I die!

The nightingale is singing
      So sweet a lay!
Her glad voice heavenward flinging—
      No check, no stay.

Flower of girls love-laden
      Is my sweetheart;
Of roses red the maiden
      For whom I smart.

The promise that she gives me
      Makes my heart bloom;
If she denies, she drives me
      Forth to the gloom.

My maid, to me relenting,
      Is fain to play;
Her pure heart, unconsenting,
      Saith: "Stay, lover, stay!"
Hush, Philomel, thy singing,
      This little rest!
Let the soul's song rise ringing
      Up from the breast!

In desolate Decembers
      Man bides his time:
Spring stirs the slumbering embers;
      Love-juices climb.

Come, mistress, come, my maiden!
      Bring joy to me!

Come, come, thou beauty-laden!
    I die for thee!
O all abloom am I!
It is a maiden love that makes me sigh,
A new, new love it is wherewith I die!

⟨⦵⟩

Wine and Love and Lyre

Sweet in goodly fellowship
    Tastes red wine and rare O!
But to kiss a girl's ripe lip
    Is a gift more fair O!
Yet a gift more sweet, more fine,
    Is the lyre of Maro!
While these three good gifts were mine,
    I'd not change with Pharaoh.

Bacchus wakes within my breast
    Love and love's desire,
Venus comes and stirs the blessed
    Rage of Phœbus' fire;
Deathless honor is our due
    From the laureled sire:
Woe should I turn traitor to
    Wine and love and lyre!

⟨⦵⟩

A Pastoral

There went out in the dawning light
    A little rustic maiden;
Her flock so white, her crook so slight,
    With fleecy new wool laden.

Small is the flock, and there you'll see
    The she-ass and the wether;
This goat's a he, and that's a she,
    The bull-calf and the heifer.

She looked upon the green sward, where
    A student lay at leisure:
"What do you there, young sir, so fair?"
    "Come, play with me, my treasure!"

Invitation to Youth

Take your pleasure, dance and play,
Each with other while ye may:
Youth is nimble, full of grace;
Age is lame, of tardy pace.

We the wars of love should wage,
Who are yet of tender age;
'Neath the tents of Venus dwell
All the joys that youth loves well.

Young men kindle heart's desire;
You may liken them to fire;
Old men frighten love away
With cold frost and dry decay.

Invitation to the Dance

Cast aside dull books and thought;
  Sweet is folly, sweet is play:
Take the pleasure Spring hath brought
  In youth's opening holiday!
Right it is old age should ponder
  On grave matters fraught with care;
Tender youth is free to wander,
  Free to frolic light as air.
      Like a dream our prime is flown,
      Prisoned in a study:
      Sport and folly are youth's own,
      Tender youth and ruddy.

Lo, the Spring of life slips by,
  Frozen Winter comes apace;
Strength is 'minished silently,
  Care writes wrinkles on our face:
Blood dries up and courage fails us,
  Pleasures dwindle, joys decrease,
Till old age at length assails us
  With his troop of illnesses.

Like a dream our prime is flown,
  Prisoned in a study:
Sport and folly are youth's own,
  Tender youth and ruddy.

Live we like the gods above;
  This is wisdom, this is truth:
Chase the joys of tender love
In the leisure of our youth!
Keep the vows we swore together,
  Lads, obey that ordinance;
Seek the fields in sunny weather,
  Where the laughing maidens dance.
      Like a dream our prime is flown,
        Prisoned in a study;
      Sport and folly are youth's own,
        Tender youth and ruddy.

There the lad who lists may see
  Which among the maids is kind:
There young limbs deliciously
  Flashing through the dances wind:
While the girls their arms are raising,
  Moving, winding o'er the lea,
Still I stand and gaze, and gazing
  They have stolen the soul of me!
      Like a dream our prime is flown,
        Prisoned in a study;
      Sport and folly are youth's own,
        Tender youth and ruddy.

Flora's Flower

Rudely blows the winter blast,
Withered leaves are falling fast,
Cold hath hushed the birds at last.
  While the heavens were warm and glowing,
    Nature's offspring loved in May;
  But man's heart no debt is owing
    To such change of month or day
    As the dumb brute-beasts obey.

100

Oh, the joys of this possessing!
How unspeakable the blessing
    That my Flora yields today!

Labor long I did not rue,
Ere I won my wages due,
And the prize I played for drew.
  Flora with her brows of laughter,
    Gazing on me, breathing bliss,
  Draws my yearning spirit after,
    Sucks my soul forth in a kiss:
    Where's the pastime matched with this?
Oh, the joys of this possessing!
How unspeakable the blessing
    Of my Flora's loveliness!

Truly mine is no harsh doom,
While in this secluded room
Venus lights for me the gloom!
  Flora faultless as a blossom
    Bares her smooth limbs for mine eyes;
  Softly shines her virgin bosom,
    And the breasts that gently rise
    Like the hills of Paradise.
Oh, the joys of this possessing!
How unspeakable the blessing
    When my Flora is the prize!

From her tender breasts decline,
In a gradual curving line,
Flanks like swansdown white and fine.
  On her skin the touch discerneth
    Naught of dough; 'tis soft as snow:
  'Neath the waist her belly turneth
    Unto fulness, where below
    In Love's garden lilies blow.
Oh, the joys of this possessing!
How unspeakable the blessing!
    Sweetest sweets from Flora flow!

101

Ah! should Jove but find my fair,
He would fall in love, I swear,
And to his old tricks repair:
  In a cloud of gold descending
    As on Danae's brazen tower,
  Or the sturdy bull's back bending,
    Or would veil his godhood's power
    In a swan's form for one hour.
Oh, the joys of this possessing!
How unspeakable the blessing!
    How divine my Flora's flower!

Phyllis

Think no evil, have no fear,
  If I play with Phyllis;
I am but the guardian dear
  Of her girlhood's lilies,
Lest too soon her bloom should swoon
  Like spring's daffodillies.

All I care for is to play,
  Gaze upon my treasure,
Now and then to touch her hand,
  Kiss in modest measure;
But the fifth act of love's game,
  Dream not of that pleasure!

For to touch the bloom of youth
  Spoils its frail complexion;
Let the young grape gently grow
  Till it reach perfection;
Hope within my heart doth glow
  Of the girl's affection.

Sweet above all sweets that are
  'Tis to play with Phyllis;
For her thoughts are white as snow,
  In her heart no ill is;
And the kisses that she gives
  Sweeter are than lilies.

Love leads after him the gods
    Bound in pliant traces;
Harsh and stubborn hearts he bends,
    Breaks with blows of maces;
Nay, the unicorn is tamed
    By a girl's embraces.

Love leads after him the gods,
    Jupiter with Juno;
To his waxen measure treads
    Masterful Neptune O!
Pluto stern to souls below
    Melts to this one tune O!

Whatsoe'er the rest may do,
    Do not be delaying;
Take the pastime that is due
    While we're yet a-Maying.
I am young and young are you;
    'Tis the time for playing.

Love's Longing

With song I seek my fate to cheer,
As doth the swan when death draws near;
Youth's roses from my cheeks retire,
My heart is worn with fond desire.
    Since care and woe increase and grow, while
        light burns low,
            Poor wretch, I die!
    Heigho! I die, poor wretch I die!
Constrained to love, unloved; such luck have I!

If she could love me whom I love,
I would not then exchange with Jove:
Ah! might I clasp her once, and drain
Her lips as thirsty flowers drink rain!
    With death to meet, his welcome greet, from
        life retreat,

I were full fain!
Heigho! full fain, I were full fain,
Could I such joy, such wealth of pleasure gain!
When I bethought me of her breast,
Those hills of snow my fancy pressed;
Longing to touch them with my hand,
Love's laws I then did understand.
Rose of the south, blooms on her mouth; I felt
love's drouth
That mouth to kiss!
Heigho! to kiss, that mouth to kiss!
Lost in day-dreams and vain desires of bliss.

Anonymous

The Latin songs of the Wandering Students spread through
the streets and inns of Germany and eastern Europe; the songs
of the more serious Provençal jongleurs were, for a long time,
confined to the courts of France. Unlike the rough gaiety of the
Goliard renegades, the lyrics of the Provençal poets were elegant
in style, delicately pastoral, and chivalrous in the traditional ro-
mantic manner.

One of the most beautiful poems of the period is by an anony-
mous Provençal poet. Probably written in the twelfth century, it
has been variously rendered by translators who have sought to
capture its exquisite, heartfelt cry. In one of his early volumes
Ezra Pound presented a version which he called "Alba Innominata"
and which began:

> In a garden where the whitethorn spreads her leaves
> My lady hath her love lain close beside her,
> Till the warder cries the dawn—Ah dawn that grieves!
> Ah God! Ah God! That dawn should come so soon!

About half a century before Pound's forthright translation,
a more rhetorical enlargement was composed by the flamboyant
Algernon Charles Swinburne (see pages 487 to 497). Swinburne
called it "In the Orchard" and acknowledged it as a "Provencal
Burden"

In the Orchard

Leave go my hands, let me catch breath and see;
Let the dewfall drench either side of me;
   Clear apple leaves are soft upon that moon
Seen sidelong like a blossom in the tree.
   Ah God, ah God, that day should be so soon.

The grass is thick and cool; it lets us lie.
Kissed upon either cheek and either eye,
   I turn to thee as some green afternoon
Turns toward the sunset and is loath to die.
   Ah God, ah God, that day should be so soon.

Lie closer, lean your face upon my side,
Feel where the dew fell that has hardly dried,
   Hear how the blood beats that went nigh to swoon;
The pleasure lives there when the sense has died.
   Ah God, ah God, that day should be so soon.

 O my fair lord, I charge you leave me this:
Is it not sweeter than a foolish kiss?
   Nay take it then, my flower, my first in June,
My rose, so like a tender mouth it is.
   Ah God, ah God, that day should be so soon.

Love, till dawn sunder night from day with fire,
Dividing my delight and my desire,
   The crescent life and love the plenilune,
Love me though dusk begin and dark retire.
   Ah God, ah God, that day should be so soon.
Ah, my heart fails, my blood draws back; I know,
When life runs over, life is near to go;

And with the slain of love love's ways are strewn,
And with their blood, if love will have it so.
  Ah God, ah God, that day should be so soon.

Ah, do thy will now; slay me if thou wilt;
There is no building now the walls are built,
  No quarrying now the cornerstone is hewn,
No drinking now the vine's whole blood is spilt.
  Ah God, ah God, that day should be so soon.

Nay, slay me now; nay, for I will be slain;
Pluck thy red pleasure from the teeth of pain,
  Break down thy vine ere yet grape-gatherers prune,
Slay me ere day can slay desire again.
  Ah God, ah God, that day should be so soon.

Yea, with thy sweet lips, thy sweet sword; yea,
Take life and all, for I will die, I say;
  Love, I gave love, is life a better boon?
For sweet night's sake I will not live till day.
  Ah God, ah God, that day should be so soon.

Nay, I will sleep then only; nay, but go.
  Ah sweet, too sweet to me, my sweet, I know
  Love, sleep, and death go to the same sweet tune.
Hold fast my hair, and kiss me through it so.
  Ah God, ah God, that day should be so soon.

O Western Wind

O western wind, when wilt thou blow
  That the small rain down can rain?
Christ, that my love were in my arms
  And I in my bed again!

My Fair Lady

Who shall have my fair lady?
Who shall have my fair lady?
Who but I, who but I, who but I?
Under the leaves so green.

The fairest man
That best love can,
Dandirly, dandirly,
Dandirly, dan,
Under the leaves so green.

Beauty Self

My love in her attire doth show her wit,
  It doth so well become her;
For every season she hath dressings fit,
  For winter, spring, and summer.
No beauty she doth miss
  When all her robes are on;
But Beauty's self she is
  When all her robes are gone.

I Am Dark and Fair to See

I am dark and fair to see,
Young in my virginity,
Rose my color is and white,
Pretty mouth and green my eyes;
And my breast it pricks me so
I may not endure it,
For I meddle me to know
Love, and naught can cure it.

Walter Von Der Vogelweide

The dark days of the Middle Ages were often lightened by bursts of song. In Germany the great twelfth century minnesinger, Walter von der Vogelweide, composed the deathless, tenderly insinuating *Unter den Linden* presented here in a translation by the nineteenth century English poet-dramatist, Thomas Lovell Beddoes. In England the lyric impulse came into power with the packed intensity of the anonymous "O Western Wind," as well as with the delicacy of the four subsequent anonymous poems.

Under the Lime Tree

Under the lime tree on the daisied ground
  Two that I know of made this bed.
There you may see heaped and scattered round
  Grass and blossoms broken and shed
    All in a thicket down in the dale;
Tandaradei—sweetly sang the nightingale.

Ere I set foot in the meadow already
  Some one was waiting for somebody;
There was a meeting—Oh! gracious lady,
  There is no pleasure again for me,
    Thousands of kisses there he took.
Tandaradei—see my lips, how red they look.

Leaf and blossom he had pulled and piled
  For a couch, a green one, soft and high;
And many a one hath gazed and smiled
  Passing the bower and pressed grass by;
    And the roses crushed hath seen,
Tandaradei—where I laid my head between.

In this love passage if any one had been there,
  How sad and shamed should I be;
But what were we adoing alone among the green there
  No soul shall ever know except my love and me,
    And the little nightingale,
Tandaradei—she, I wot, will tell no tale.

Geoffrey Chaucer

Father of English poetry and, added Dryden, "perhaps the prince of it," Geoffrey Chaucer, born in London about 1340, was a typically Renaissance figure. Son of a tavern-keeper, he was, more or less chronologically, a page at court, a soldier, one of the yeomen of the king's chamber, a secret agent, an ambassador to Italy, an appointed comptroller of customs, an elected knight, clerk of the King's Works, and, during his lean later years, a pensioner. At intervals he wrote such masterpieces as *The Parliament of Fowls, Troilus and Cressida,* and *The Canterbury Tales.*

The Canterbury Tales, from which two episodes have been selected, is a mammoth piece of revitalization. Most of the plots were old; Chaucer found them in Ovid, Livy, and in Boccaccio, but he gave them a new and boisterous life. He filled them with raw humor and unbridled freedom of expression, invigorated them with startling details, added outright indecencies to broad innuendoes, and swept the stories on with unflagging gusto. Tolerant of man's foibles, his common frailties and casual adulteries, Chaucer pictured a hurly-burly world in which every person was not only a living individual but also a recognizable and understandable human being.

The Canterbury Tales was a vast undertaking—the plan called for one hundred and twenty tales—and Chaucer did not live to complete his greatest achievement. He died, having established an immortal pageant of humanity, at sixty. He was the first person to be entombed in Westminster Abbey; the place where he was buried became known as the Poet's Corner.

The modern versions of "The Reeve's Tale" and "The Merchant's Tale" are by Frank Ernest Hill.

111

The Reeve's Tale[1]

Not far from Cambridge, close to Trumpington,
Beneath a bridge of stone, there used to run
A brook, and there a mill stood well in view;
And everything I tell you now is true.
Here dwelt a miller many a year and day,
As proud as any peacock, and as gay.
And he could pipe and fish, wrestle and shoot,
Mend nets, and make a well-turned cup to boot,
He wore a long knife belted at his side,
A sword that had a sharp blade and a wide,
And carried in his pouch a handsome dagger.
No man durst touch him, though he boast and swagger.
A Sheffield dirk was hidden in his hose.
His face was round; he had a broad pug nose;
Smooth as an ape's the skull above his face.
He was a bully in the market-place.
No man dared lay a little finger on him
But he would swear to be revenged upon him.
He was indeed a thief of corn and meal.
A sly one, and his habit was to steal;
And scornful Simkin was the name he carried.
A wife of noble kindred he had married:
Her father was the parson of the town!
Many good pans of brass this priest paid down
To win this Simkin to his family!
And she was fostered in a nunnery,
For Simkin would not have a wife, he said,
That was not gently nurtured, and a maid,
To match his standing as a proper yeoman.
As pert as any magpie was this woman.
It was a sight to see them take the road

On holidays. Before her Simkin strode,
His tippet proudly wrapped about his head;
And she came after in a smock of red,
With Simkin clad in stockings of the same.
None dared to call her anything but "dame,"
And there was none that passed them on the way
So bold that he would romp with her or play,
Unless in truth he wished to lose his life
At Simkin's hand by dagger or by knife.
A jealous husband is a dangerous beast—
Or so he wants his wife to think, at least!
And since by birth a little smirched men thought her,
She was as sour of mien as stagnant water,
And haughty in her ways, and full of scorn.
She thought that, since her father was well born,
And she had got a convent education,
A distant air was suited to her station.

    A daughter had these two—a girl a score
Of years in age; and after her, no more,
Except a child a half year old they had,
Still in the cradle, and a proper lad.
This daughter was a stout and full-blown lass
With a pug nose and eyes as gray as glass,
And buttocks broad, and breasts shaped round and high,
And yet her hair was fair, I will not lie.

    The parson of the town, since she was fair,
Had it in mind that she should be his heir
Unto his house and goods and everything.
He was severe about her marrying.
He meant to place her in some family
Of worthy blood and lofty ancestry;
For holy church's goods must be expended
On those from holy church's blood descended;
His holy blood—he would do honor to it,
Though he devoured holy church to do it!

    This miller took great toll, ye need not doubt,
On wheat and malt from all the land about,
And from a certain college most of all,
At Cambridge, which was known there as King's Hall,
That brought their wheat and barley to his mill.
It happened once, the manciple lay ill,

And with his malady was kept a-bed,
And he was sure to die of it, men said.
Therefore this miller stole of corn and meal
A hundred times what he had dared to steal
Before; for then he took his toll discreetly,
But now the fellow was a thief completely,
Which made the warden fume and scold and swear,
Yet the bold miller did not give a tare;
But boasted loud, and swore it was not true.
 Among the Cambridge students there were two
In dwelling at the Hall of which I tell.
Headstrong they were, and quick and bold as well.
And all for lustihood and jollity
They begged the warden long and eagerly
For his permission to be gone until
They saw their grain ground at the miller's mill.
Each offered sturdily to lay his neck
The miller should not steal a half a peck
Whether by trickery or force, and so
At length the warden gave them leave to go.
One was named John, and Alan was the other;
Born in the same town both—a place called Strother—
Far to the north—I cannot tell you where.
 This Alan for the journey doth prepare,
And brought a horse to put their sack upon,
And off they go, this Alan and this John,
Each with a sword and buckler by his side.
John knew the way; they did not need a guide;
And at the mill at length the sack he lay'th.
Alan spoke first: "Hail, Simon, by my faith!
How fares thy daughter fair, and thy good wife?"
 Said Simkin: "Welcome, Alan, by my life!
And John the same! How now, what do ye here?"
 "Simon," said John, "By God, need has no peer.
Who hath no servant, as the clerks have said,
Unless a fool, must serve himself instead.
Our manciple, I fear, will soon be dead,
The poor man's jaws are waggling in his head;
So I am come, and Alan, with our sack,
To have our grain ground, and to bear it back.
I pray you, put it quickly through the mill."

"Now by my faith," this Simkin said, "I will.
What will ye while I have the thing in hand?"
  "By God, right by the hopper will I stand,"
Said John, "and see the grain go down the maw;
For by my father's kin, I never saw
The way a hopper waggles to and fro."
  Alan replied: "What, John, and wilt thou so?
Then I will stand beneath it, by my crown,
And I will watch the meal come falling down
Into the trough; so shall I have my fun.
For, John, in faith, when all is said and done,
I am as poor a miller as are ye."
  The miller smiled at this simplicity.
"All this is but a trick of theirs," he thought.
"They think they cannot be deceived or caught;
But I shall pull the wool across their eyes
However shrewdly they philosophize.
The more involved the stratagems they make,
The more shall be the stealing when I take!
Instead of flour they shall be served with bran!
'The greatest clerk is not the wisest man,'
As the wolf heard the proverb from the mare.
I count this art of theirs not worth a tare!"
  Then when he saw his opportunity,
He slipped out through the doorway stealthily,
And looked about him when he stood outside,
And found the student's horse, which they had tied
Behind the mill, beneath an arbor there.
Then he approached it with a friendly air,
And straightway stripped the bridle from its head.
And when the horse found he was loose, he fled
Off toward the fen, where wild mares ran at play;
"We-hee!" Through thick and thin he streaked away.
  The miller then came back. No word he spoke,
But did his work, or sometimes cracked a joke,
Until the grain was well and fairly ground.
And when the meal at length was sacked and bound,
This John found that his horse had run away;
And "Help!" he shouted, and "Alackaday!
Our horse is gone! Alan, come out!" he cried,
"By God's bones, man, step lively! Come outside!

Alas! Our warden's palfrey hath been lost!"
All thought of meal and grain this Alan tossed
Into the wind, and all economy.
"What! Which way is he gone?" demanded he.
    The wife came leaping in among them then.
"Alas!" she said. "Your horse makes for the fen
With the wild mares, as fast as he can go!
Bad luck upon the hand that tied him so,
That should have bound him better with the rein!"
    "Alas!" cried John. "Now, Alan, for Christ's pain,
Off goes my sword; lay thine beside it here.
God knows I be as nimble as a deer;
He shall not get away from both of us.
Alan, thou wast a fool to tie him thus.
Why didst na' put the nag into the stable?"
    These students ran as fast as they were able
Off to the fen, this Alan and this John,
And when the miller saw that they were gone
He took a half a bushel of their flour
And bade his wife go knead it up that hour
Into a cake. "These students were a feared!
A miller still can trim a student's beard
For all his art! Now let them go their way!
Look where they run! Yea, let the children play;
They will not get him quickly, by my crown!"
    These simple students scurried up and down
With "Whoa there, whoa!" "Hold hard!" "Look to the rear!"
"Go whistle to him while I keep him here!"
But, to be brief, until the edge of night
They could not, though they strove with all their might,
Capture their horse, he ran away so fast.
Till in a ditch they cornered him at last.
    Like cattle in the rain, wet through and through,
And wearied out, they plodded back, the two.
"Alas!" cried John, "the day that I was born!
Now we are brought to mockery and scorn!
Our grain is stolen; each will be called a fool
Both by the warden and our friends at school,
And by the miller most. Alackaday!"
    Thus John came back, complaining all the way,
With Bayard's rope in hand, through brush and mire.

He found the miller sitting by the fire,
For it was night. Return they did not dare,
And begged him he would give them lodging there,
For love of God, and they would pay their penny.
    The miller answered: "Yea, if there be any,
Such as it is, that will I share with you.
My house is small; but ye are schooled, ye two,
And by your arguments can make a place
A mile in breadth from twenty feet of space!
Let us see now if this will hold us all,
Or talk it larger, if it be too small!"
    "Now by St. Cuthbert, Simon, shrewdly spoke!"
This John replied. "Always thou hast thy joke!
They say a man must choose between two things:
Take what he finds, or do with what he brings.
But specially I pray thee, landlord dear,
Get us some meat and drink, and make good cheer,
And we will pay in full upon demand.
No one can lure a hawk with empty hand;
Lo!—here our silver ready to be spent."
    This miller to the town his daughter sent
For ale and bread, and roasted them a goose,
And tied their horse so it should not get loose—
And in his own room laid them out a bed
With sheets and blankets well and fairly spread,
Not more than ten or twelve feet from his own.
His daughter had one for herself alone,
In the same chamber, in its proper place.
Better it might not be—the little space
Within the house had made it necessary.
They sat and supped and talked and made them merry
And drank strong ale, and so the evening sped.
At midnight, or about, they went to bed.
    Well was this miller varnished in the head:
So pale with drink his face was drained of red.
He hiccoughs, and his voice comes through his nose
As if he had a cold. To bed he goes,
And by his side the good wife goes her way.
She was as light and saucy as a jay,
So well her merry whistle had been wet.
At the bed's foot the baby's crib they set,

117

To rock it, and to give the child the dug.
And when the ale was emptied from the jug
The daughter followed with no more ado;
And then to bed went John and Alan too.
No need of drugs to send them off to sleep;
This miller of the ale had drunk so deep
He snorted like a horse, nor had a mind
For any noises from his tail behind.
His wife sang with him—such a lusty singing
Two furlongs off ye might have heard it ringing;
The wench snored loudly, too, *pour compagnie.*
    Alan the student heard this melody,
And nudging John he whispered: "Sleepest thou?
Heardst ever such a song as this ere now?
Lo! what an evening liturgy they make!
May wild fire all their cursèd bodies take!
Who ever heard so weird a chant ascending?
Yea, they deserve the flower of all bad ending!
All this long night I shall not get my rest.
No matter—all shall happen for the best.
For John, as I have hope to thrive," he said,
"I shall go lay that wench in yonder bed.
The law allows some easement unto us:
For, John, there is a law that puts it thus:
That if a man in one point shall be grieved,
Then in another he shall be relieved!
Our grain is stolen—there is no saying nay,
Ill luck hath dogged us all this livelong day.
Now since for this I get no compensation,
I mean to salve my loss with consolation.
By God's soul, this shall be the way, I swear!"
    This John replied, "Nay, Alan, have a care.
This miller is a dangerous man," he said,
"And if ye wake him as he lies in bed,
He might do both of us an injury."
    Alan replied: "I count him not a fly,"
And rose, and to the wench's bed he crept.
The girl lay on her back and soundly slept.
Before she knew what Alan was about
It was too late for her to cry or shout,
And, to be brief, the two were soon as one.

Now, Alan, play! for I will speak of John.
    John lay in silence while a man might go
A furlong, and he moaned for very woe.
"Alas! This is a wicked jest," cried he.
"Plainly it makes a clumsy ape of me.
My comrade gets some pay for all his harms;
He holds the miller's daughter in his arms;
He hath adventured, and his quest hath sped,
And I lie like a sack of bran in bed.
And when this prank of ours is told at school,
I shall be held a milk-sop and a fool!
I will arise and risk it, by my faith!
'No pluck, no luck,' is what the proverb saith."
And up he rose, and with a noiseless tread
Stole to the cradle, and bore it to his bed,
And at the foot he set it on the flooring.
    Soon after this the wife left off her snoring,
Rose and relieved herself, and came again,
But by her bed she missed the cradle then,
And in the darkness groped about and sought.
"Alas! I almost went amiss," she thought,
"I would have climbed into the students' bed!
Eh, *ben'cite!* That would be bad!" she said.
And groped, and found the cradle, and went past
With hand outstretched, and reached the bed at last.
And had no thought but everything was good
Because the baby's cradle by it stood,
And in the dark she knew not where she went.
So she crept in, relieved and well content,
And there lay still, and would have gone to sleep.
But soon this John the student with a leap
Was on this wife, at work with all his might;
So merry she had not been for many a night;
He pricketh hard and deep, as he were mad.
And thus a jolly life these students had
Until at length the third cock started crowing.
    Alan, with dawn a little weary growing,
For all night he had labored hard and well:
"Sweetheart, dear Malin, I must say farewell.
Day comes; I cannot stay beyond this kiss;
But always, as my soul may win to bliss,

I am thy student, where I go or ride."
"So then, dear love, farewell," the wench replied.
"But one thing, while thou lie beside me still—
When thou art going homeward by the mill—
Right at the entry door—look thou behind;
A loaf of half a bushel wilt thou find,
Kneaded and baked it was from thine own meal
Which yesterday I helped my father steal.
Now, sweetheart, may God save thee well, and keep."
And with that word almost began to weep.

Alan arose. "Before the night shall end,
I will go creep in bed beside my friend,"
And touched the cradle as he groped along.
"By God," he muttered, "I am going wrong;
My head is dizzy from my work this night
And hath confused me, so I go not right,
For by the cradle I can surely tell;
Here lies the miller and his wife as well."
By twenty devils, forth he goes his way,
And found the bed in which the miller lay,
And crawled in softly where his comrade slept,
As he supposed, and to the miller crept,
And caught him by the neck, and softly spake,
Saying: "Thou, John, thou swine's head! What! Awake!
And hear, for Christ's soul, of this noble sport;
For by St. James, although this night was short,
Thrice have I laid the miller's daughter flat
Upon her back, and had her, and all that
While like a coward thou hast lain in bed."

"Yea, hast thou, lecherous rogue?" the miller said.
"Ha! thou false student, traitor false!" cried he.
"Thou shalt be dead, yea, by God's dignity!
Who dare disgrace," he cried in fearful rage,
"My daughter, come of such a lineage?"
And caught this Alan by the Adam's apple,
And choked him as the two began to grapple,
And smote him with his fist full on the nose.
Down on his breast the warm blood spurting flows,
And on the floor; his nose and mouth were broke.
They wallow like two pigs tied in a poke,
And up they go, then down again are thrown,

Until the miller on a paving stone
Stumbled, and fell down backward on his wife,
That lay there dead to all this crazy strife,
For she began a little sleep to take
By John, that all night long had been awake,
And started from her slumber when he fell.
"Help, cross of Bromholm!" she began to yell.
"*In manus tuas!* Lord, I call on thee!
Simon, awake! The fiend hath fallen on me;
My heart is cracked! Help! I am all but dead!
One on my belly, one upon my head!
Help, Simon! for these lying students fight!"
　　This John jumped up as quickly as he might,
And back and forth along the wall he flew
To find a staff, and she had jumped up too,
And knew the room much better than he knew it,
And where a staff was, and went quickly to it,
And saw a little shimmering of light,
For through a hole the moon was shining bright,
And by the light in struggle saw the two,
But did not know for certain who was who,
But saw a glimmer there of something white,
And with this white thing dancing in her sight,
She thought, because she could not see it clearer,
It was a student's night-cap, and drew nearer,
And would have hit this Alan, but instead
She struck the bald spot on the miller's head,
And down he went, and cried out: "Help, I die!"
These students beat him well and let him lie,
And dressed themselves, and got their horse and meal,
And on their homeward journey off they steal.
And at the mill they got the loaf of bread—
Of half a bushel—and away they sped.
　　Thus was the haughty miller roundly beat,
And got no pay for grinding all their wheat,
And paid for supper ere the game was through
For Alan and John, that thrashed him soundly, too.
His wife and daughter are both of them disgraced;
So fares a miller that is double-faced
And false: the proverb tells the honest truth:
"Let him not look for good that evil do'th;"
He that deceives, himself deceived shall be.

The Merchant's Tale

(Shorter version)

Once on a time a knight of high degree,
Though born in Pavia, dwelt in Lombardy,
And there he lived a rich and prosperous life.
For sixty years this knight had had no wife,
But ever fed his bodily delight
On women, where he had an appetite,
As foolish laymen do. But when at last
With course of time his sixtieth year was passed,
In dotage, or in fear for his salvation
I know not which, a great determination
Fell on this knight to be a wedded man,
And day and night he labors all he can
To find where he might marry fittingly,
Praying our Lord to grant him clemency
That he for once might know the blissful life
Shared always by a husband and his wife,
Living beneath the bond God gave to man
And women when their common life began.
"No other life is worth a bean, for sure,
For wedlock is so easy and so pure,
That here on earth it is a paradise!"
Thus said this knight, who thought himself so wise . . .

Now careful thoughts of how he ought to marry
Mingled within the soul of January[1]
Day after day, with visions high and rare.
Many fair forms, and many a face as fair
Went passing through his heart, night after night
As one who takes a mirror burnished bright,
And sets it in the general market place,
Shall there behold full many a figure pace
Within his mirror—so in the same way
The thoughts of January began to play
Among the maidens that were dwelling by him.
He could not tell which best would satisfy him.
For if one had a loveliness of face
Another stood so well in people's grace
For sober ways and kindness, that these gave her

[1] January was the name given by Chaucer to the old knight.

122

The greatest voice to have the people's favor.
Though rich, some had a name not of the best.
But in the end, through earnestness and jest,
He found one maiden that he set apart,
And let the others vanish from his heart,
And chose her, on his own authority,
For love is always blind, and cannot see.
At night, as in his bed he lay reclining,
He saw in heart and mind fair visions shining
Of her fresh beauty and her youth so tender,
Her little waist, her arms so long and slender,
And thought her wise and staid as he had seen her,
Of gentle ways and womanly demeanor.
And once his fancy by this maid was caught,
His choice could not have been improved, he thought . . .
Now when they saw at last that it must be,
By contract they arranged it skilfully,
With prudence, that this maid, whose name was May,
Should with the shortest possible delay
Be bound in wedlock to this January.
I think it were too long for you to tarry
If I should tell what bonds and bills they planned,
By which she was enfeoffed with all his land,
Or tell of all this maiden's rich array
Against the wedding. Finally the day
Arrived, and to the church this couple went
There to receive the holy sacrament.
His stole about his neck, the priest appeared.
Like Sarah and Rebecca be revered,
He told her, as a wise wife and a true;
And prayed, as it is usual to do,
And asked God's grace, and with the cross he signed them,
And went through holy rites enough to bind them.
    Thus they are married ceremoniously,
And at the feast are seated, he and she,
And other worthies on the dais there;
And joy was in the palace everywhere;
And music; and fair victual stood revealed,
The daintiest all Italy could yield.
And there were instruments to play upon,
So fine that Orpheus or Amphion
Never made melody so fine and proud . . .

May sat there with so ravishing an air
It was as if she cast a faery spell.
Queen Esther never let her eyes so dwell
Upon Ahasuerus, with a glance
So meek. I cannot paint her radiance
In full for you, but thus much I can say:
That she was bright as morning is in May,
And full of all sweet beauty and delight.

Each time he fed his eyes upon this sight
Old January sat ravished in a trance.
And in his heart the threat began to dance
That he would clasp her soon with such an ardor
That Paris never strained Queen Helen harder
Against his breast. And yet his mood was tender
To think how with the night he must offend her.
"Alas!" he thought, "O tender thing and pure,
I would to God that ye could well endure
All of my love! So it is sharp and strong
I fear ye cannot well sustain it long!
Yet God forbid I work with all my power . . .
I would that it were night this very hour,
And that the night forever more would stay.
I wish these people all were gone away!"
And finally, as well as he can plan,
Saving his honor, he does the best he can
To speed them from the feast in shortest season.

The time came when to rise was only reason,
And then to dance and drink the people fall,
And spices strew about by room and hall,
And full of joy and bliss was every man—
All but a squire, a youth called Damian,
Who carved before the knight on many a day.
He was so ravished with his lady May
Pain all but drove his reason from its seat;
Almost he swooned and fainted on his feet,
So sorely Venus hurt him with her brand
As she went dancing by him, torch in hand;
And to his bed in haste he stole away.
Now for the time no more of him I say,
But leave him there to weep and to complain
Till lovely May has pity on his pain.

O perilous fire that in the bedstraw lurks!
O household foe, eager for evil works!
O traitor-servant, truthful still of mien,
O adder in the bosom, false, unseen,
God from acquaintance with you shield us all!
O January, drunk with the festival
Of marriage, see now how thy Damian,
Thine own squire, that was born thy very man,
Is scheming in his heart to bring thee woe.
God grant thou may'st espy thine household foe,
For in this world no worse a plague can try thee
Than such a foe forever dwelling by thee.

The sun had traversed his diurnal arc;
His body could no longer hold the dark
From the horizon, in that latitude.
Night came, and spread his mantle dark and rude,
The hemisphere about to overcloud.
And so departed all this lusty crowd
From January, with thanks on every side.
Home to their houses merrily they ride,
Each busy there with that which pleased him best,
And when their time had come, they went to rest.
Soon after that this eager January
Must go to bed, no longer would he tarry;
But first drank claret to increase his spirit,
And spiced vernage as strong as he could bear it
And many a fortifying syrup fine,
Such as the cursèd monk Sir Constantine
Describes well in his book, *De Coitu;*
He took them all, omitting none he knew,
And to his close friends whispered urgently,
"For love of God, as soon as it may be,
In courteous fashion get them to retire!"
And soon they managed after his desire;
Men drank, then forth to draw the curtain sped;
Still as a stone, the bride was brought to bed.
Then came the priest, the bed was duly blessed,
Forth from the room departed every guest,
And January with May in rapture lies,
Clasping his fresh young mate, his paradise.

125

He lulled and kissed her, and her cheek was speared
With bristles of his thick and prickly beard,
Sharp as the skin of dogfish, or a briar,
For he was newly shorn. Hot with desire
He rubbed her tender face, and said to her:
"Alas! Now must I be a trespasser
On you, my wife, and I may much offend
Before the time shall come when I descend.
Yet none the less, consider this," said he;
"There is no workman, whosoever he be,
That works in haste, whose work will bear inspection;
And this needs leisure to attain perfection.
It matters not how long we lie at play;
We two are joined in wedlock from this day,
And blessèd be the yoke that we are in,
For nothing that we do can be a sin.
A man can do no sin with his own wife;
He cannot hurt himself with his own knife,
For by the law we have full leave to play."
And so he labored till the break of day,
Then in fine clarey dipped a sop of bread,
And ate, and then he sat erect in bed,
And fell to singing in a loud, clear strain,
And kissed his wife, and played with her again.
Coltish he was, riding his passion high,
And full of chatter as a speckled pie.
And while he sang the slack skin at his throat
Shook, and he chanted with a croaking note.
God knows what thoughts this fair May had to hide
While in his shirt he sat there by her side,
With night-cap, and his neck all loose and lean;
She did not think his capers worth a bean!
"The day is come," he said, "and I will take
My rest; for now I cannot stay awake;"
And so lay down, and slept till it was prime.
Then somewhat later, when he thought it time,
This January arose; but fresh young May
Kept to her chamber unto the fourth day,
As wives still do by custom, for the best.
For every labor must be crowned with rest,
Or he that labors cannot long endure;

That is, no living creature can, for sure,
Be it a fish, or bird, or beast, or man.
　　　Now will I speak of woeful Damian,
That languishes for love, as ye shall hear;
And I address him as will now appear.
I say: "O hapless Damian, alas!
Answer to what I ask thee in this pass!
How shalt thou tell thy lovely lady May
The woe thou hast? For she will answer, 'Nay;'
And also, if thou speak, she will betray thee;
All I can say is, May God help and stay thee."
　　　This fevered Damian in Venus' fire
So burns, he all but dies of his desire.
And so he puts his life on the assay;
He could not suffer longer in this way.
In secrecy a pen-case did he borrow,
And in a letter wrote out all his sorrow,
Giving it form of a complaint or lay
Unto his fresh and lovely lady May,
And put it in a silken purse, and strung it
Over his shirt; against his heart he hung it.
　　　The moon, that at the noontide of that day
When January had wedded fresh young May,
In Taurus hung, had into Cancer passed—
So long had May kept to her chamber fast,
As do these noble ladies, one and all.
A bride must never eat within the hall
Until four days go by, or three at least;
Then let her go, indeed, and join the feast.
From noon to noon the fourth day now was sped,
And so, the high mass being duly said,
This January sits in his hall, and May,
As fresh as any shining summer's day.
And now it happened that this worthy man
Called to his memory this Damian.
"St. Mary!" he exclaimed, "how can it be
That Damian is not here to wait on me?
What is the cause? Is he still sick?" he cried.
His squires, that stood in waiting at his side,
Excused him; for his sickness, as they said,
Hindered his duty; were he not a-bed

127

No other cause, indeed, could make him tarry.
"That grieves me greatly," said this January;
"For by my faith, a gentle squire is he;
If he should die, it were calamity;
He is as wise, as subtle, and discreet
In his degree as any ye may meet,
Ready to serve, and ever manly, too,
And like to prosper ere his days are through.
But after meat I shall not long delay
To visit him myself, and so shall May,
To give him all the comfort that I can."
And for that word they blessed him, every man,
That had in noble kindness this desire
To go and bring such comfort to his squire
That lay there sick. It was a noble deed.
"Dame," said this January, "take good heed
That after meat, ye and your women all,
Returning to your chamber from this hall,
Go all of you to see this Damian;
And cheer him up; he is a gentle man;
And tell him I will visit him as well
When I have rested but a little spell.
And do it quickly; I will wait for you
To come and sleep by me when ye are through."
And with that word he raised his voice to call
A squire, one that was marshal of his hall,
And told him certain things he wished to say.
Then with her women fresh and lovely May
Went straight to Damian's chamber after that,
And close beside his bed this lady sat,
And gave him all she could of happy cheer.
This Damian, when he saw his time appear,
In secret slipped the purse, in which reposed
The rhyme in which his passion was disclosed,
Into the hand of May, and did no more,
Save that he sighed then wondrous deep and sore,
And in a whisper said, "Mercy, I pray thee!
And for the love of God, do not betray me,
For I am dead if this should come to light!"
She slipped it in her bosom out of sight,
And went her way; ye get no more from me.

128

Back to this January repaireth she,
Who sat upon his bed and waited for her.
He took her, and with kisses overbore her,
And then lay down, and soon he slept, indeed.
And she pretended she must go of need
Where all folks must, as ye are well aware.
When she had read the note she carried there,
She tore it into little bits at last,
And in the privy all the pieces cast.

    Who ponders now but fresh and lovely May?
Down by this aged January she lay,
Who slept until awakened by his cough.
He prayed her then to take her garments off.
For he would have, he said, some pleasure of her,
And clothes were an encumbrance to a lover;
And like the thing or not, she must obey.
Some nice folk might be angry should I say
How he performed, and so I dare not tell,
Or whether she thought it paradise or hell;
But at their work the afternoon they passed
Till evensong, when they must rise at last.

    Now were it chance or destiny began it,
Or nature, by the working of some planet
Or constellations shaping such a state
Within the skies, that it was fortunate
To slip a billet of Venus on that day
(For all things have their times, as scholars say)
To any woman, with hope to win her love,
I cannot say; but the great God above
Who knows that cause and act can never cease—
Let Him decide, for I will hold my peace.
But this is true, that what occurred that day
Made such impression on this fresh young May,
Rousing her pity for sick Damian,
That in her heart, let her do what she can,
The wish to heal this lover haunts her still.
She thought: "Let this dispease whomever it will—
Here I assure him, all my promise giving,
To love him best of any creature living,
Although his shirt were all that he possessed."
Ah, swift is pity in a noble breast!

Here ye may see the generosity
Of women, when they ponder carefully.
Some tyrant (and indeed, there's many a one!)
That has a heart as hard as any stone,
Might have preferred to be his murderer
Than grant the grace he begged so hard of her,
Would have rejoiced in cruel, unyielding pride,
And cared not though she were a homicide!
    This gentle May, with pity sorely smitten,
A letter with her own fair hand hath written,
In which she fully granted him her grace;
Only the day was lacking, and the place,
Where pain and passion both should be appeased;
For all should be, she wrote him, as he pleased.
    And when she saw her chance, upon a day,
To visit Damian goes lovely May,
And slipped beneath his pillow, soft and still.
Her letter. Let him read it if he will!
She took his hand, and hard she wrung and pressed it,
So secretly, that there was none that guessed it,
And bade him soon be whole, and forth she went
To January, when after her he sent.
    And Damian arises on the morrow;
All vanished are his sickness and his sorrow.
He preens and pranks himself, and combs his hair,
And does his lady's liking well and fair,
And unto January he is as docile
As any dog is to the bowman's whistle;
And speaks to all in such a pleasant way
(If one can use it, tact will always pay)
None has a word to say of him but good;
And fully in his lady's grace he stood.
Now let him do the things he has to do
While I proceed to tell my tale to you.
      Some writers say he wins the fullest measure
Of happiness who gets the greatest pleasure;
And so this January, with all his might,
And honorably, as well befits a knight,
Had planned his life to live in happiness.
His house was wrought, his furnishings and dress,
As nobly for his station as a king's.

And there he fashioned, among other things,
A garden, that was walled about with stone;
Nowhere was any fairer garden known.
For past all doubt, I must indeed suppose,
That he who wrote the Romance of the Rose
Could not describe the beauty of it well;
Nor would Priapus have the tongue to tell,
Though God of gardens and their flowering,
The beauty of the place, or of the spring
Beneath a laurel that was always green.
There many a time had Pluto and his queen
Prosperina, and all their company
Of fairies, it was said, with melody
Danced by the spring in sport, and made them merry.
    This noble knight, this aged January,
Loved so to walk and play within the wall
That he would trust the key to none at all
Except himself; for he would constantly
Bear for a gate a little silver key
With which he would unlock it when it pleased him.
And there in summer, when the longing seized him,
To pay his wife the debt that was her due,
With May his wife, and none beside the two,
He went, and things that were not done a-bed
There in the garden were performed and sped.
Thus in this way, for many a day full merry,
Lived lovely May and this old January.
But worldly joy, alas! endureth never
Neither for him, nor any man whatever.

    O chance, O Fortune, false and fickle one!
Dyed in deception, like the scorpion!
What words of flattery lie upon thy lip
While strikes thy tail, death poised upon the tip!
O brittle joy! O venom sweet and strange!
O monster, that canst paint a subtle change
Upon thy gifts, that seem so all-enduring
That high and low are victims of thy luring!
Why, having been his friend, as he believed,
Hast thou poor January thus deceived?
And now of both his eyes hast thou bereft him,
Until he cries that death alone is left him.

Alas! this generous, noble January,
So prosperous, so lusty, and so merry!
All sudden goes blind—his eyesight fails!
How piteously he sighs and weeps and wails,
While fire of jealousy so rages through him,
With fear of folly that his wife might do him,
Searing his heart, that he were nothing loath
If someone with a sword had slain them both.
For while he lived and after he was buried
He wished her neither to be loved nor married,
But all in black to keep a widow's state,
Lone as the turtle that has lost its mate.
But in the end, after a month or two,
A little less at length his sorrow grew;
For when he knew that nothing else could be,
He took in patience his adversity;
Save that from this he never could recover:
That he continued to be jealous of her;
Which jealousy was so inordinate
That neither in his room, nor when he ate,
Nor in another place, if she went out,
Would he permit his wife to go about
Unless her hand in his he safely kept.
And lovely May for this cause often wept,
For now so sweetly she had come to cherish
Her Damian, that she thought that she must perish
Or have him at her will, to love and take.
She waited for her very heart to break.

    And on his part this lover Damian
Is sunk in sorrow more than any man
That ever was, for neither night nor day
Could he address a word to lovely May
Or speak his purpose with a lover's spirit,
But January would be sure to hear it,
That always had a hand upon her fast.
And yet by writing to and fro at last
He knew her meaning, and by secret signs;
And she too knew the end of his designs.

    O January, what profit or avail,
Though thou couldst see as far as ships can sail?

As well be blind and bear such treachery,
As be deceived, alack! when thou canst see.
Lo, what could Argus do, the hundred-eyed?
It made no difference how he peered or pried,
He was deceived—and others, too, God knows,
Not half so wise as often they suppose.
But skipping this is pleasure, so no more.

    This lovely May, of whom I spoke before,
Has pressed in wax the key which January
Had for the little gate, and used to carry,
And with it to his garden often went.
And Damian, that knew her full intent,
In secret had another like it made.
Now there is nothing more to be conveyed,
Except that if ye wait, there shall appear
A marvel through this key, which ye shall hear.

    O noble Ovid, God knowest thou sayst truly
There is no trick a lover will not duly
Unravel, long and hard though it may be.
Of Pyramus and Thisbe men may see
How, though so strictly guarded, after all
They spoke together, whisperering through a wall;
Who could detect a ruse so strange and sly?

    But to my tale. Before eight days went by—
Before July—urged by his fair wife May,
This January was so possessed one day
To play about within his garden fair—
They two alone, with no attendants there—
That on a morning to this May he cries:
"Rise up, my wife, my noble lady, rise;
Sweet dove, the turtle in the sun is singing;
Winter is gone, and all his cold and stinging
Rains are no more; O dove-eyed sweetheart mine.
Come forth; thy breasts are lovelier than wine!
Walled is the garden safely, all about.
Come forth, my fair white spouse; ah, never a doubt
But thou hast pierced my very heart, O wife!
I've known no blemish in thee all my life.
Come, then, and let us go and take our pleasure;

133

I chose thee for my comfort, wife, and treasure!"
    Such lewd old words he spoke, this doting man;
And she has made a sign to Damian
That he should go before them with his key.
This Damian for the gate made instantly
And went inside, but took great pains to bear him
That none about should either see or hear him;
And crouched beneath a bush there, all alone.
    This January, as blind as any stone,
Holding May's hand, with no one else around,
Seeks the fresh beauty of the garden ground,
And claps the gate behind him suddenly.
"Now none is here," he said, "but thee and me,
Thee, wife, whom best of all the world I love.
For, by the Lord that sits in heaven above,
Far rather would I die upon a knife
Than to offend thee, dear and faithful wife!
For God's sake, give a little thought to this:
The way I chose thee—not for avarice,
But only for the love I had for thee.
And even if I am old and cannot see,
Be true to me, and I will tell thee why.
Three things for certain shall ye win thereby;
First, love of Christ; and for yourself great dower
Of honor; and my holdings, town and tower;
I give them to you—draw then as ye please
The deeds; tomorrow we shall finish these
Before the sun sets, as I hope for bliss!
And first, in covenant, I ask a kiss.
And though I may be jealous, yet be kind;
Ye are so deeply graven in my mind
That, when your beauty in my thought appears,
And I remember my unfitting years,
I cannot, though it were the death of me,
Bear any parting of our company
For very love; lo, this is past all doubt.
Now kiss me, wife, and let us roam about."
    This fair May, having heard these words he cried
All mild and kind to January replied,
But first, before she spoke, began to weep.
"I have," she said to him, "a soul to keep

134

As well as ye, and have mine honor, too,
And tender flower of wifehood, fresh and new,
Set in your hands, my lord, as justly due you
With the priest's words that bound my body to you.
Then by your leave, my lord I love so dear,
Thus will I speak in answer to you here:
I pray God there shall never dawn the day
I shall not die, as foul as woman may,
If I shall do my kin so great a shame
And so besmirch the honor of my name
As to be false; and if I do that sin,
Strip me, and get a sack to put me in,
And in the nearest river let me die.
A gentlewoman and no wench am I!
Why do ye speak like this? But falseness taints
You men—ye greet us still with fresh complaints!
Ye have no other pretext, I should guess,
But talk about reproof and faithlessness."
    And with that word she saw where Damian
Sat beneath the bush, and she began
To cough and then made signals urgently
That Damian at once should climb a tree
Laden with fruit, and up this lover went,
For of a truth he knew well what she meant,
And all the meaning that her signs might carry
Better than did her husband, January.
For in a letter she had made it clear
How he should go about this matter here.
And thus I leave him sitting in the tree
While January and May roam merrily.
    Bright was the day and blue the firmament,
And Phœbus down his streams of gold hath sent
And with his bright warmth gladdened every flower.
He was, I think, in Gemini at that hour,
But close to Cancer and his declination,
Which brings to Jupiter his exaltation.
And so it fell, on that bright morning-tide,
That in the garden, at the farther side,
Pluto, that is the king of Fairyland,
With many a fairy lady in his band
All following his wife, Queen Proserpine,

Each after each, as straight as any line—
While she was gathering flowers in the mead,
Ye may in Claudian the story read
How off he bore her in his chariot grim—
This king of Fairyland now seated him
Upon a bench of turves all fresh and green,
And in this manner soon addressed his queen:
     "My wife," he said, "no one can say this Nay:
Experience keeps proving every day
The treason that ye women do to men.
Of your untruth and fickleness, again,
Ten hundred thousand stories could be told.
O Solomon, so shrewd, so rich in gold,
So full of worldly glory, and so wise,
Thy words are worthy ones to keep and prize
For all who value wit and reason well.
The good that lies in men now hear him tell:
'Among a thousand men I found but one;
Among all living women I found none.'
     "Thus says the king that knows your wickedness;
And Jesus, son of Sirach, as I guess,
Can seldom speak of you with reverence.
A wild fire and corrupting pestilence
This very evening on your bodies light!
Do ye not see this honorable knight
That his own man will shame here in his fold
Because, alas! he is both blind and old?
Lo, there he sits, the lecher, in the tree!
Now I will promise, of my majesty,
To this old blind and honorable knight
That he shall once more wholly have his sight
When his wife wrongs him. So then shall he see
And know the sum of all her harlotry
To the reproach of her and others, too."
     His queen replied: "Is this what ye will do?
I swear now by my mother's father's soul
That she shall have an answer, good and whole,
And women ever after, for her sake;
Though found in guilt, they shall have wit to make
A bold defense that always will excuse them
And bear down any men that shall accuse them.

136

None shall be slain for want of good replies.
For though a man shall see with both his eyes
Yet shall we women boldly face it out,
So subtly scold, so weep and swear and shout,
That men shall be as ignorant as geese.
What do I care for your authorities?"
   "Dame," Pluto said, "be angry now no more.
I give it up. And yet, because I swore
That I would let him have his sight again,
My word must stand. That much is clear and plain.
I am a king; it fits me not to lie."
     Said she: "The queen of Fairyland am I,
And she shall have her answer, too—I swear.
But let us talk no more of this affair;
I would no longer play your adversary."

    Now let us turn again to January,
That in the garden, with his lovely May,
Goes singing merrier than a popinjay,
"I love you best, none will I love but you!"
Thus many a garden path he wandered through,
Until at length he reached the very tree
Where Damian sat above him merrily
High up, among green leaves and many a pear.
   This lovely May, that looked so bright and fair,
Began to sigh, and said: "Alas! my side!
Whatever happens, this is sure," she cried,
"Sir, I must taste these pears that I can see
Or I shall die, such longing comes to me
To eat these pears, so small and sweet and green.
Now help me, for the love of heaven's queen!
I tell you that a woman in my plight
May long for fruit with such an appetite
That she may die if she must go without."
   "Alas!" said he, "had I a boy about
That might climb up! Alas! Alas!" cried he,
"That I am blind!" "No matter, sir," said she.
"But for God's sake, I beg of you, draw near,
And put your arms about the pear tree here
(For well I know ye are suspicious of me);
Then I could climb up by these limbs above me,

If I could set my foot upon your back."

"Truly," he answered, "there ye shall not lack;
Would I could help you with my own heart's blood!"
Then he stooped down, and on his back she stood,
And pulled herself up quickly by a bough.
Ladies, I pray you, be not angry now;
I cannot gloss it—I am a rough man.
All in a flash this lover Damian
Pulled up the smock, and he was in ere long.

At once when Pluto saw this monstrous wrong,
He gave his sight to January once more,
And made him see as well as ever before.
And when he found himself restored to sight,
No man was ever filled with such delight;
But always thinking of his wife, he raised
His eyes aloft, and in the tree he gazed,
And saw how Damian, that was hard at play,
So held his wife as I could never say
If with a courteous tongue I tell my tale.
At once he raised a mighty roar and wail
As does a mother that fears her child will die.
"Alas! Help! Harrow!" he began to cry,
"O bold, bad woman, what is this ye do?"

But she replied: "Sir, what is wrong with you?
Have patience; and let reason rule your mind!
I have restored your eyes, that both were blind!
For by my soul's rest, let me tell no lies:
Thus was I taught—if I would heal your eyes,
There was no better way to make you see
Than struggling with a man within a tree;
God knows, I did a good, sire, and no sin!"

"Struggle!" he cried. "I saw it going in!
God gave you both a shameful death to die!
He laid thee—yea, I saw it with mine eye,
Let them go hang me if it be not true!"

"Why then, my medicine is bad for you,"
She said, "for certainly, if ye could see
Then ye would speak no words like these to me;
Your sight is but a glimmer, not yet good."

"I see," cried he, "as well as ever I could,
Thanks be to God, with both mine eyes, I know;

And by my truth, I thought he had thee so."
    "Ye are confused, good sire, confused," said she.
"This is my thanks for having made you see.
Alas!" she cried, "that I was ever so kind."
    "Now, Dame," he answered, "put it out of mind.
Come down, my love; if I have spoken amiss
I am sorry for it, as God may give me bliss.
But by my father's soul, it seemed to me
That Damian was lying there with thee,
And that thy smock upon his breast was lying."
    "Yea, sire, think as ye please," she said, replying.
"But, sire, a man when first awakening
Out of his sleep, may not behold a thing
All of a sudden in any perfect way
Until he grow accustomed to the day.
And so a man that hath been blind for long,
He sees not suddenly so well and strong
The first time that he hath his sight anew,
As one that has it for a day or two.
Until ye grow accustomed to your sight
Ye may not see full many a thing aright.
Beware, I pray you; for by heaven's King,
Full many a man thinks that he sees a thing
That in reality is otherwise.
His judgment then will err, as did his eyes."
And with that word she leapt down from the tree.
    This January—who now is glad but he?
He kissed her, and embraced her with sweet sighs,
And stroked her softly in between her thighs,
And led her to his palace happily.

And now, good men, I pray you merry be.

The Boy and the Mantle

The story of "The Boy and the Mantle" was a favorite of troubadours and minnesingers; it was variously interpreted in the European courts of the thirteenth century, one version being the French fabliau, *Cort Mantel*. As an Arthurian ballad, "The Boy and the Mantle" was a cherished piece of minstrelsy.

The Boy and the Mantle

On the third day of May
    To Carlisle did come
A kind, courteous child
    That knew much of wisdom.

A kirtle and a mantle
    This child had upon,
With brooches and rings
    Full richly bedone.

"God speed thee, King Arthur,
    Sitting at thy meat.
And the goodly Queen Guenevere,
    I cannot her forget.

"I tell you, lords in this hall,
    I bid you all to heed,
Except you be full sure
    Is for you to dread."

He plucked out his pouch
    And longer would not dwell,
He pulled forth a pretty mantle
    Between two nut shells.

"Have this here, King Arthur,
    Have this here from me.
Give it to thy comely queen
    Shaped as you see.

141

"It shall never become that wife
    That hath once done amiss."
Then every knight in the king's court
    Began to care for his.

Forth came dame Guenevere,
    To the mantle she hied;
The lady was inconstant,
    Yet she was not afraid.

When she had put on the mantle
    She stood as she had been made;
From the top to the toe
    As if shears had it shred.

At times it was red,
    At times it was green,
At times it was blue;
    Ill did it her beseem.

Another time it was black,
    And bore the worst hue.
"By my troth," quoth King Arthur,
    "I think thou art not true."

She threw down the mantle
    So bright that it bled,
Fast with a red face
    To her chamber she fled.

She cursed the weaver,
    The cloth he had wrought,
And bade a vengeance on his crown
    That hither had it brought.

"I had rather be in a wood
    Under a green tree
Than in King Arthur's court
    Shamed for to be."

Kay called forth his lady
    And bade her come near;

Said, "Madam, if thou be guilty
    I pray thee stay there."

Forth came his lady
    Shortly and anon,
Boldly to the mantle
    The lady is gone.

When she had ta'en the mantle
    And cast it her about,
Then she was bare
    Before all the rout.

Then every knight
    That was in the king's court,
Talked, laughed, and shouted
    Full oft at the sport.

She threw down the mantle
    So bright that it bled,
Fast with a red face
    To her chamber she fled.

Forth came an old knight
    Pattering o'er a creed,
He proffered this little boy
    Twenty marks for his deed,

And all the time of Christmas
    Willingly to feed,
If this bright mantle might
    Do his wife some need.

When she had ta'en the mantle
    Of cloth that was made,
She had no more left on her
    Than a tassel and a thread.
Then every knight in the king's court
    Bade evil might she speed.

She threw down the mantle
　　So bright that it bled,
Fast with a red face
　　To her chamber she fled.

Craddock called forth his lady
　　And bade her come to.
Said, "Win this mantle, lady,
　　Without more ado.

"Win this mantle, lady,
　　And it shall be thine,
If thou never did amiss
　　Since thou wast mine."

Forth came Craddock's lady
　　Shortly and anon
Boldly to the mantle,
　　Then she put it on.

When she had ta'en the mantle
　　And cast it her about,
Up at her great toe
　　It began to rise and draw out.
She said, "Bow down, mantle,
　　And shame me not for nought.

"Once I did amiss,
　　I tell you certainly,
When I kissed Craddock's mouth
　　Under a green tree,
When I kissed Craddock's mouth
　　Before he married me."

When she had shriven
　　And her sin she had told,
The mantle stood about her
　　Right as she would,

Seemly of color,
    Glittering like gold.
Then every knight in Arthur's court
    Did her behold.

Then spake dame Guenevere
    To Arthur her king,
"She hath ta'en yonder mantle
    Not with right but with wrong.

"See you not yonder woman
    That maketh herself so clean—
I have seen ta'en out of her bed
    Of men fifteen,

"Priests, clerks, and wedded men
    Noble and mean.
Yet she taketh the mantle
    And maketh herself clean!"

Then spoke the little boy
    That kept the mantle in hold;
Said, "King, chasten thy wife;
    With her words she is too bold.

"She is a bitch and a witch
    And a whore bold.
King, in thine own hall
    Thou art a cuckold."

The little boy stood
    Looking out of the door,
And as he was looking
    He saw a wild boar.

He saw a wild boar
    Would have worried a man;
He pulled forth a wood knife,
    And thither he ran.

He brought in the boar's head,
    Wondrous to behold;

145

He said there was never a cuckold's knife
    Carve it that could.

Some rubbed their knives
    Upon a whetstone;
Some threw them under the table
    And said they had none.

King Arthur and the child
    Stood looking on them;
All their knives' edges
    Turned back again.

Craddock had a little knife
    Of iron and of steel,
He carved up the boar's head
    Wondrous well,
So that every knight in the king's court
    Could have a morsel.

The little boy had a horn
    Of red gold that rang;
He said that no cuckold
    Could drink of his horn,
But he would shed his drink
    Either behind or beforne.

Some shed on their shoulder,
    And some on their knee.
He that could not hit his mouth
    Shed it in his e'e;
So that he that was a cuckold
    Everyone might see.

Craddock won the horn
    And the boar's head;
His lady won the mantle
    Unto her meed.
Every such a loving lady
    God help her with speed.

François Villon

"Villon, our sad bad glad mad brother's name!" This is the repeated last line of each stanza in Swinburne's ballade apostrophizing the lawless vagabond poet. He was born in 1431 of a well-established family; his name, before he changed it, was François de Montcorbier, and he entered the University of Paris at fifteen, receiving his M.A. three years later. A precocious student, he fell into bad company and accidentally killed a priest in a brawl. Forced to flee the city, he joined a notorious gang, returned to Paris, took part in a robbery, was sentenced to be hanged but, somehow, escaped the death penalty. He was barely thirty when, as the result of further criminalities, he was banished from Paris. With his banishment he disappears from history; where he went, how he lived, and when he died is unknown.

During his first thirty years Villon wrote ballads and testaments which, like Chaucer's tales, rouse the reader because of their unaffected vitality. He wrote to entertain his companions: purse-snatchers, prostitutes, thieves and cut-throats; and his poems were as raw, ironic, bitter, and realistic as the life he led with them. Nevertheless, the poetry attained a wide popularity. Within eighty years after his death thirty-four editions of his works had been published, and their author became the subject of legends, plays, and novels.

The first three of the following translations are by John Payne; the fourth and fifth (the last usually expurgated) are by Algernon Charles Swinburne.

147

Ballade of Villon and Fat Margot

Because I love and serve a whore *sans glose,*
  Think not therefore a knave or fool am I.
She hath in her such goods as no man knows.
  For love of her, target and dirk I ply:
  When clients come, I hend a pot there nigh
And get me gone for wine, without word said:
Before them water, fruit, bread, cheese, I spread.
  If they pay well, I bid them "Well God aid!
Come here again, when you by lust are led,
  In this the brothel where we ply our trade."

But surely before long an ill wind blows
  When, coinless, Margot comes by me to lie.
I hate the sight of her, catch up her hose,
  Her gown, her surcoat and her girdle tie,
  Swearing to pawn them, meat and drink to buy.
She grips me by the throat and cuffs my head,
Cries "Antichrist!" and swears by Jesus dead,
  It shall not be; till I, to quell the jade,
A potsherd seize and score her nose with red,
  In this the brothel where we ply our trade.

Then she, peace made, to show we're no more foes,
  A hugeous crack of wind at me lets fly
And laughing sets her fist against my nose,
  Bids me "Go to" and claps me on the thigh;
  Then, drunk, like logs we sleep till, by and by,
Awaking, when her womb is hungered,
To spare the child beneath her girdle stead,
  She mounts on me, flat as a pancake laid.
With wantoning she wears me to the thread,
  In this the brothel where we ply our trade.

Hail, rain, freeze, ready baked I hold my bread:
Well worth a lecher with a wanton wed!
Which is the worse? They differ not a shred.
 Ill cat to ill rat; each for each was made.
We flee from honor; it from us hath fled:
Lewdness we love, that stands as well in stead,
 In this the brothel where we ply our trade.

Ballade of Ladies' Love

Whoso in love would bear the bell,
 Needs must he prank him gallantly,
Swagger and ruffle it, hold and snell,
 And when to his lady's sight comes he,
 Don cloth of gold and embroidery;
For ladies liken a goodly show.
 This should serve well; but, by Marie,
Not all can nick it that will, heigho!

Once on a season in love I fell
 With a lady gracious and sweet to see,
Who spoke me fair, that she liked me well
 And gladly would harken to my plea,
 But first I must give to her for fee
Fifty gold crowns, not less nor mo'.
 Fifty gold crowns?—O' right good gree!
Not all can nick it that will, heigho!

To bed I went with the damsèl
 And there four times right merrily
I did to her what I may not tell
 In less than an hour and a half, perdie.
 Then with a failing voice she said,
"Once more, I prithee! my heart is woe."
 Once more, quotha, sweetheart? Ah me,
Not all can nick it that will, heigho!

Great God of love, I crave of thee,
  If ever again I lay her low,
Ne'er let my lance untempered be,
Not all can nick it that will, heigho!

Ballade of the Fair Helm-Maker

To the Light o' Loves

Now think on't, Nell the glover fair,
  That once my scholar used to be,
And you, Blanche Slippermaker there,
  Your case in mine I'd have you see:
  Look all to right and left take ye;
Forbear no man; for trulls that bin
  Old have nor course nor currency,
No more than money that's called in.

You, sausage-huckstress debonair,
  That dance and trip it brisk and free,
And Guillemette Upholstress there,
  Look you transgress not Love's decree:
  Soon must you shut up shop, perdie;
Soon old you'll grow, faded and thin,
  Worth, like some old priest's visnomy,
No more than money that's called in.

Jenny the hatter, have a care
  Lest some false lover hamper thee;
And Kitty Spurmaker, beware,
  Deny no man that proffers fee.
  For girls that are not bright of blee[1]
Man's scorn and not their service win;
  Foul age gets neither love nor gree,[2]
No more than money that's called in.

[1] Bright of blee: clever. [2] Gree: good will.

Wenches, give ear and list (quoth she)
  Wherefore I weep and make this din:
'Tis that there is no help for me—
  No more than money that's called in.

Ballade of the Women of Paris

Albeit the Venice girls get praise
  For their sweet speech and tender air,
And though the old women have wise ways
  Of chaffering for amorous ware,
  Yet at my peril dare I swear,
Search Rome, where God's grace mainly tarries,
  Florence and Savoy, everywhere,
There's no good girl's lip out of Paris.

The Naples women, as folk prattle,
  Are sweetly spoken and subtle enough;
German girls are good at tattle,
  And Prussians make their boast thereof;
  Take Egypt for the next remove,
Or that waste land the Tartar harries,
  Spain or Greece, for the matter of love,
There's no good girl's lip out of Paris.

Breton and Swiss know nought of the matter,
  Gascony girls or girls of Toulouse;
Two fishwomen with a half-hour's chatter
  Would shut them up by three and twos;
  Calais, Lorraine, and all their crews,
(Names enow the mad song marries,)
  England and Picardy, search them and choose,
There's no good girl's lip out of Paris.

Prince, give praise to our French ladies
  For the sweet sound their speaking carries;
'Twixt Rome and Cadiz many a maid is,
  But no good girl's lip out of Paris.

Complaint of the Fair Armoress

Meseemeth I heard cry and groan
   The sweet who was the armorer's maid.
For her young years she made sore moan,
   And right upon this wise she said:
   "Ah, fierce old age with foul bald head,
To spoil fair things thou art ever fain.
   Who holds me? Who? Would I were dead!
Would God I were well dead and slain!

"Lo, thou hast broken the sweet yoke
   That my high beauty held above
All priests and clerks and merchantfolk;
   There was not one but for my love
   Would give me gold and gold enough,
Though sorrow his very heart had riven,
   To win from me such wage thereof
As now no thief would take if given.

"I was right chary of the same,
   God wot it was my great folly,
For love of one sly knave of them,
   Good store of that same sweet had he;
   For all my subtle wiles, perdie,
God wot I loved him well enow;
   Right evilly he handled me,
But he loved well my gold, I trow.

"Though I gat bruises green and black,
   I loved him never the less a jot;
Though he bound burdens on my back,
   If he said 'Kiss me, and heed it not,'
   Right little pain I felt, God wot,
When that foul thief's mouth, found so sweet,
   Kissed me— Much good thereof I got!
I keep the sin and the shame of it.

"And he died thirty years agone.
   I am old now, no sweet thing to see;
By God, though, when I think thereon,

And of that glad good time, woe's me,
  And stare upon my changed bodie,
Stark naked, that had been so sweet,
  Lean, wizened, like a small dry tree,
I am nigh mad with the pain of it.

"Where is my forehead's faultless white,
  The lifted eyebrows, soft gold hair,
Eyes wide apart and keen of sight,
  With subtle skill in the amorous air;
  The straight nose, great nor small, but fair,
The small carved ears of shapeliest growth,
  Chin dimpling, color good to wear,
And sweet red splendid kissing mouth.

"The shapely slender shoulders small,
  Long arms, hands wrought in glorious wise,
Round little breasts, the hips withal
  High, full of flesh, not scant in size,
  Fit for all amorous masteries;
Wide flanks, and the fresh sweet flower
  Of youth, between the perfect thighs,
That hides within its pretty bower.

"A wrinkled forehead, hair gone gray,
  Fallen eyebrows, eyes gone blind and red,
Their laughs and looks all fled away,
  Yea, all that smote men's hearts are fled;
  The bowed nose, fallen from goodlihead;
Foul flapping ears like water flags;
  Peaked chin, and cheeks all waste and dead,
And lips that are two skinny rags.

"Thus endeth all the beauty of us.
  The arms made short, the hands made lean,
The shoulders bowed and ruinous,
  The breasts, alack! all fallen in;
  The flanks too, like the breasts, grown thin;
The flower of love no longer sweet;
  For the lank thighs, no thighs but skin
That are speckled with spots like sausage meat.

153

"So we make moan for the old sweet days,
  Poor old light women, two or three
Squatting above the straw fire's blaze,
  The bosom crushed against the knee,
  Like fagots on a heap we be,
Round fires soon lit, soon quenched and done;
  And we were once so sweet—even we!
Thus fareth many and many an one!"

Elizabethan Voices and Echoes

The Elizabethans luxuriated in music and verse. Every other person was a poet; rhyme was not an odd method of communication but a natural way of expressing oneself. Thomas Deloney was a ballad-writer as well as a silk weaver; even a shoemaker, said he, could "sound the trumpet or play upon the flute and bear his part in a three-man's song." The Elizabethan lyrics are especially rich in their reflection of the pomp and circumstance of the age. Some of the liveliest pieces in *Pills to Purge Melancholy*, a series of anthologies which began appearing in the seventeenth century, were circulated long before their authorship was acknowledged, and maintained their popularity long after their publication.

So much poetry was produced, published, quoted, and imitated that much of it fell into a pattern. "Heart" was inevitably rhymed with "dart"; "fire" was followed by "expire," "moon" by "swoon," and "eyes" (or "prize") by "dies." In 1578 Barnabe Riche ridiculed the stereotypes employed by writers of love poems. "Her hairs are wires of gold, her cheeks are made of lilies and roses, her brows are arches, her eyes sapphires, her looks lightning, her mouth coral, her teeth pearls, her paps alabaster, her body straight, her belly soft, and from thence downward to her knees is all sugar candy." Shakespeare mocked the artificial prettifications and the whole catalogue of clichés when he wrote the sonnet beginning "My mistress' eyes are nothing like the sun. . . ."

It was an age of songbooks, anthologies, miscellanies. The last quarter of the sixteenth century saw countless collections bearing such fancy titles as *The Paradise of Dainty Devices, A Gorgeous Gallery of Gallant Inventions, The Forest of Fancy, A Handful of Pleasant Delights, The Phoenix Nest, The Passionate Pilgrim,* and (an anthology of anthologies) *England's Helicon.* Many of the contributors to these compilations are known, but the authorship of some of the finest lyrics cannot be determined. The following is a selection of the anonymous poems.

Kisses Make Men Loath to Go

My Love bound me with a kiss.
  That I should no longer stay;
When I felt so sweet a bliss
  I had less power to part away:
Alas! that women do not know
Kisses make men loath to go.

Yes, she knows it but too well,
  For I heard when Venus' dove
In her ear did softly tell
  That kisses were the seals of love:
O muse not then though it be so,
Kisses make men loath to go.

Wherefore did she thus inflame
  My desires, heat my blood,
Instantly to quench the same
  And starve whom she had given food?
Ay, ay, the common sense can show,
Kisses make men loath to go.

Had she bid me go at first
  It would ne'er have grieved my heart.
Hope delayed had been the worst;
  But ah to kiss and then to part!
How deep it struck, speak, gods! you know
Kisses make men loath to go.

Give Me a Kiss

Give me a kiss from those sweet lips of thine
And make it double by enjoining mine,
Another yet, nay yet and yet another,
And let the first kiss be the second's brother.
Give me a thousand kisses and yet more;
And then repeat those that have gone before;
Let us begin while daylight springs in heaven,
And kiss till night descends into the even,
And when that modest secretary, night,
Discolors all but thy heaven beaming bright,
We will begin revels of hidden love
In that sweet orb where silent pleasures move.
In high new strains, unspeakable delight,
We'll vent the dull hours of the silent night:
Were the bright day no more to visit us,
Oh, then for ever would I hold thee thus,
Naked, enchained, empty of idle fear,
As the first lovers in the garden were.
I'll die betwixt thy breasts that are so white,
For, to die there, would do a man delight.
Embrace me still, for time runs on before,
And being dead we shall embrace no more.
Let us kiss faster than the hours do fly,
Long live each kiss and never know to die.
Yet, if that fade and fly away too fast,
Impress another and renew the last;
Let us vie kisses, till our eyelids cover,
And if I sleep, count me an idle lover;
Admit I sleep, I'll still pursue the theme,
And eagerly I'll kiss thee in a dream.
Oh, give me way: grant love to me thy friend!
Did hundred thousand suitors all contend
For thy virginity, there's none shall woo
With heart so firm as mine; none better do
Than I with your sweet sweetness; if you doubt,
Pierce with your eyes my heart, or pluck it out.

157

O Jealous Night

O Night, O jealous Night, repugnant to my measures!
    O Night so long desired, yet cross to my content!
There's none but only thou that can perform my pleasures,
    Yet none but only thou that hindereth my intent.

Thy beams, thy spiteful beams, thy lamps that burn too brightly,
    Discover all my trains, and naked lay my drifts,
That night by night I hope, yet fail my purpose nightly,
    Thy envious, glaring beam defeateth so my shifts.

Sweet Night, withhold thy beams, withhold them till tomorrow,
    Whose joy in lack so long a hell of torment breeds!
Sweet Night, sweet gentle Night, do not prolong my sorrow:
    Desire is guide to me, and love no lodestar needs.

Let sailors gaze on stars and moon so freshly shining;
    Let them that miss the way be guided by the light;
I know my lady's bower, there needs no more divining:
    Affection sees in dark, and Love hath eyes by night.

Dame Cynthia, couch awhile! hold in thy horns for shining,
    And glad not lowering Night with thy too glorious rays;
But be she dim and dark, tempestuous and repining,
    That in her spite my sport may work thy endless praise!

And when my will is wrought, then, Cynthia, shine, good lady,
    All other nights and days in honour of that night,
That happy heavenly night, that night so dark and shady,
    Wherein my Love had eyes that lighted my delight!

The Amorous Silvy

On a time the amorous Silvy
Said to her shepherd, "Sweet, how do you?
Kiss me this once, and then God be wi' you,
               My sweetest dear!
Kiss me this once and then God be wi' you,
For now the morning draweth near."

With that, her fairest bosom showing,
Opening her lips, rich perfumes blowing,
She said, "Now kiss me and be going,
                              My sweetest dear!
Kiss me this once and then be going,
For now the morning draweth near."

With that the shepherd waked from sleeping,
And, spying where the day was peeping,
He said, "Now take my soul in keeping,
                              My sweetest dear!
Kiss me, and take my soul in keeping,
Since I must go, now day is near."

Poor Is the Life That Misses

Poor is the life that misses
    The lover's greatest treasure,
Innumerable kisses,
    Which end in endless pleasure.
    Oh, then, if this be so,
    Shall I a virgin die? Fie no!

The Gordian Knot

The Gordian knot, which Alexander great
    Did whilom cut with his all-conquering sword,
Was nothing like thy busk-point,[1] pretty peat,[2]
    Nor could so fair an augury afford;
Which if I chance to cut or else untie,
Thy little world I'll conquer presently.

[1] Busk-point: corset-laces. [2] Peat: pet.

A Pretty Thing

Fair would I have a pretty thing
  To give unto my lady:
I name no thing, nor I mean no thing,
  But as pretty a thing as may be.

Twenty journeys would I make,
  And twenty ways would hie me,
To make adventure for her sake
  To set some matter by me.
      But I would fain have a pretty thing, &c.

Some do long for pretty knacks,
  And some for strange devices:
God send me that my lady lacks,
  I care not what the price is.
      Thus fain would I have a pretty thing, &c.

Some go here and some go there
  Where gazes be not geason;[1]
And I go gaping everywhere,
  But still come out of season.
      Yet fain would I have a pretty thing, &c.

I walk the town and tread the street,
  In every corner seeking:
The pretty thing I cannot meet
  That's for my lady's liking.
      Fain would I have a pretty thing, &c.

The mercers pull me going by;
  The silk-wives say, "What lack ye?"
"The thing you have not," then say I,
  "Ye foolish fools, go pack ye!"
      But fain would I have a pretty thing, &c.

It is not all the silk in Cheape,
  Nor all the golden treasure,
Nor twenty bushels on a heap,
  Can do my lady pleasure.
      But fain would I have a pretty thing, &c.

¹ Geason: uncommon.

160

The gravers of the golden shows
  With jewels do beset me;
The shemsters in the shops, that sews,
  They do nothing but let me.
      But fain would I have a pretty thing, &c.

But were it in the wit of man
  By any means to make it,
I could for money buy it then,
  And say, "Fair lady, take it!"
      Thus fain would I have a pretty thing, &c.

O lady, what a luck is this—
  That my good willing misseth
To find what pretty thing it is
  That my good lady wisheth!
      Thus fain would I have had this pretty thing
        To give unto my lady:
      I said no harm, nor I meant no harm,
        But as pretty a thing as may be.

❧

Court and Country Love

You courtiers scorn us country clowns,
  We country clowns do scorn the court;
We can be as merry upon the downs
  As you are at midnight with all your sport.

You hawk, you hunt, you lie upon pallets,
  You eat, and drink, the Lord knows how;
We sit upon hillocks, and pick up our sallets,[1]
  And sup up our sillabubs[2] under a cow.

Your masques are made of knights and lords,
  And ladies that are fresh and gay;
We dance with such music as bagpipes affords,
  And trick up our lasses as well as we may.

Your suits are made of silk and satin,
  And ours are made of good sheep's gray;

---

[1] Sallets: salads   [2] Sillabubs: desserts made of sweetened milk.

161

You mix your discourses with pieces of Latin,
    We speak our old English as well as we may.

Your rooms are hung with cloth of Arras,
    Our meadows are decked as fresh as may be,
And from this pastime you never shall bar us,
    Since Joan in the dark is as good as my lady.

Ralegh and Others

Shakespeare's immediate predecessors included such notable poets as Sir Thomas Wyatt, Nicholas Breton, Edmund Spenser, Sir Walter Ralegh, Sir Philip Sidney, and Thomas Lodge—Queen Elizabeth herself wrote poetry.

Of these, the most spectacular was Walter Ralegh—usually spelled Raleigh. Born in 1552, he became a soldier, ship designer, navigator, explorer, government administrator, member of Parliament, promoter of colonies, captain of the Queen's Guard, and one of her chief favorites. A truly Renaissance man, continually in action, Ralegh was also a poet, pamphleteer, and historian, author of a huge *History of the World*. His reckless pride was his undoing; he had tremendous charm, great intelligence, and no political judgment. In 1618 he was charged with conspiring against the ruler, found guilty and executed. His finesse if not his flamboyance persists in his poetry.

A Description of Love

Now what is Love, I pray thee, tell?
  It is that fountain and that well
  Where pleasure and repentance dwell;
  It is, perhaps, the saucing bell
  That tolls all into heaven or hell;
  And this is Love, as I hear tell.

Yet what is Love, I prithee, say?
  It is a work on holiday,
  It is December matched with May,
  When lusty bloods in fresh array
  Hear ten months after of the play;
  And this is Love, as I hear say.

Yet what is Love, good shepherd, sayn?
  It is a sunshine mixed with rain,
  It is a toothache or like pain,
  It is a game where none hath gain;
  The lass saith no, yet would full fain;
  And this is Love, as I hear sayn.

Yet, shepherd, what is Love, I pray?
  It is a yes, it is a nay,
  A pretty kind of sporting fray,
  It is a thing will soon away.
  Then, nymphs, take vantage while ye may;
  And this is Love, as I hear say.

Yet what is Love, good shepherd, show?
A thing that creeps, it cannot go,

A prize that passeth to and fro,
A thing for one, a thing for moe,
And he that proves shall find it so;
And shepherd, this is Love, I trow.

SIR WALTER RALEGH (1552–1618)

Come to Me Soon

As at noon Dulcina rested
   In her sweet and shady bower,
Came a shepherd and requested
   In her lap to sleep an hour;
      But from her look
      A wound he took
So deep that, for a further boon,
      The nymph he prays;
      Whereto she says,
"Forego me now; come to me soon."

In vain did she conjúre him
   To leave her presence so,
Having a thousand tongues t'allure him,
   And but one to bid him go.
      Where lips invite
      And eyes delight
And cheeks as fresh as rose in June
      Persuade to stay,
      What use to say,
"Forego me now; come to me soon."

Words whose hopes might have enjoined
   Him to let Dulcina sleep,
Could a man's love be confined
   Or a maid her promise keep;
      But he her waist

165

Still holds as fast
As she was constant to her tune.
And still she spake,
"For Cupid's sake,
Forego me now; come to me soon."

He demands what time or pleasure
Can there be more soon than now?
She says night gives love the leisure
That the day does not allow.
The sun's kind sight
Forgives delight,
Quoth he, more easily than the moon;
When Venus plays,
Be bold. She says
"Forego me now; come to me soon."

How at last agreed these lovers?
He was fair and she was young.
Tongue may tell what eye discovers;
Joys unseen are never sung.
Did she consent
Or he relent?
Accepts he night or grants she noon?
Left he a maid?
Or not? She said,
"Forego me now; come to me soon."

SIR WALTER RALEGH (1552–1618)

Importune Me No More

When I was fair and young, and favor gracëd me,
Of many was I sought, their mistress for to be:
But I did scorn them all, and answered them therefore,
"Go, go, go, seek some otherwhere!
Importune me no more!"

166

How many weeping eyes I made to pine with woe,
How many sighing hearts, I have no skill to show:
Yet I the prouder grew, and answered them therefore,
   "Go, go, go, seek some otherwhere!
         Importune me no more!"

Then spake fair Venus' son, that proud victorious boy,
And said, "Fine Dame, since that you be so coy,
I will so pluck your plumes that you shall say no more,
   " 'Go, go go, seek some otherwhere!
         Importune me no more!' "

When he had. spake these words, such change grew in my breast
That neither night nor day since that, I could take any rest.
Then, lo! I did repent that I had said before,
   "Go, go, go, seek some otherwhere!
         Importune me no more!"

QUEEN ELIZABETH (1553–1603)

The Lover Forsaken

They flee from me that sometime did me seek,
   With naked foot stalking within my chamber:
Once have I seen them gentle, tame, and meek,
   That now are wild, and do not once remember
   That sometime they have put themselves in danger
To take bread at my hand; and now they range,
Busily seeking in continual change.

Thanked be fortune, it hath been otherwise
   Twenty times better; but once especiàl—
In thin array, after a pleasant guise,
   When her loose gown did from her shoulders fall,
   And she me caught in her arms long and small,
And therewithal so sweetly did me kiss,
And softly said, "Dear heart, how like you this?"

It was no dream; for I lay broad awaking:
  But all is turn'd now, through my gentleness,
Into a bitter fashion of forsaking;
  And I have leave to go of her goodness;
  And she also to use new-fangleness.
But since that I unkindly so am servèd,
"How like you this?"—what hath she now deservèd?

SIR THOMAS WYATT (1503–1542)

Phillida and Coridon

In the merry month of May,
In a morn by break of day,
Forth I walked by the wood-side
When as May was in his pride:
There I spièd all alone
Phillida and Coridon.
Much ado there was, God wot!
He would love and she would not.
She said, Never man was true;
He said, None was false to you.
He said, He had loved her long;
She said, Love should have no wrong.
Coridon would kiss her then;
She said, Maids must kiss no men
Till they did for good and all.
Then she made the shepherd call
All the heavens to witness truth
Never loved a truer youth.
Thus with many a pretty oath,
Yea and nay, and faith and troth,
Such as silly shepherds use
When they will not Love abuse,
Love, which had been long deluded,
Was with kisses sweet concluded.
And Phillida, with garlands gay,
Was made the Lady of the May.

NICHOLAS BRETON (c.1545–c.1626)

A Dialogue Between the Lovelorn Sir Hugh and Certain Ladies of Venice

The Ladies: Welcome to Venice, gentle courteous Knight;
      Cast off care and entertain content.
  If any here be gracious in thy sight,
      Do but request and she shall soon consent.
  Love's wings are swift, then be thou not so slow.
Sir Hugh: O that fair Winifred would once say so.

The Ladies: Within my lap lay down thy comely head,
      And let me stroke those golden locks of thine;
  Look on the tears that for thy sake I shed,
      And be thou lord of anything that's mine.
  One gentle look upon thy love bestow—
Sir Hugh: O that fair Winifred would once say so.

The Ladies: Embrace with joy thy lady in thine arms,
      And with all pleasures pass to thy delight;
  If thou dost think the light will work our harms
      Then come to bed and welcome all the night;
  There thou shalt find what lovers ought to know.
Sir Hugh: O that fair Winifred would once say so.

The Ladies: Give me those pearls as pledges of thy love,
      And with those pearls the favor of thy heart;
  Do not from me thy sugared breath remove
      Which double comfort gives to every part.
  Nay, stay, Sir Knight, from hence thou shalt not go.
Sir Hugh: O that fair Winifred would once say so.

THOMAS DELONEY (c. 1550–1600)

Anthony Munday

Anthony Munday (1553–1633) was a poet and a playwright who also managed to combine a career as actor and stationer. Pamphlets and pageants were his stock in trade and, when he was not otherwise occupied, he spied on the activities of English Catholics in Europe. Nothing of his work has survived except a lyric or two.

Beauty Sat Bathing

Beauty sat bathing by a spring
  Where fairest shades did hide her;
The winds blew calm, the birds did sing,
  The cool streams ran beside her.
My wanton thoughts enticed mine eye
  To see what was forbidden:
But better memory said, fie!
  So vain desire was chidden.

Into a slumber then I fell,
  When fond imagination
Seemèd to see, but could not tell
  Her feature or her fashion.
But even as babes in dreams do smile,
  And sometime fall a-weeping,
So I awaked, as wise this while
  As when I fell a-sleeping.

Sir Philip Sidney

Like Walter Ralegh, Sir Philip Sidney (1554–1586) was a perfect pattern of the Elizabethan man. He was a soldier, poet, statesman, and a favorite of the Queen. He fell in love with Lord Essex's daughter, and addressed an interrelated series of more than one hundred sonnets, *Astrophel to Stella,* to her. Whether or not she returned his passion is unknown—she married someone else—but the poems started a vogue for elaborate sonnet sequences.

Sidney attempted to join Drake on one of his expeditions—he was fascinated by colonization in America—but the Queen forbade the venture. Instead he was sent to the Netherlands and there, defending the natives against the invading Spaniards, he died. He was not yet thirty-two when, fatally wounded in battle, and about to put a cup of water to his lips, he passed the drink to another wounded soldier. "Thy need is greater than mine," he said.

Only Joy! Now Here You Are

Only Joy! now here you are,
Fit to hear and ease my care,
Let my whispering voice obtain
Sweet reward for sharpest pain:
Take me to thee, and thee to me.
No, no, no, no, my Dear, let be.

Night hath closed all in her cloak,
Twinkling stars love-thoughts provoke,
Danger hence good care doth keep,
Jealousy itself doth sleep:
Take me to thee, and thee to me.
No. no, no, no, my Dear, let be.

Better place no wit can find,
Cupid's knot to loose or bind;
These sweet flowers on fine bed too,
Us in their best language woo:
Take me to thee, and thee to me.
No, no, no, no, my Dear, let be.

This small light the moon bestows
Serves thy beams but to disclose;
So to raise my hap more high,
Fear not else, none can us spy;
Take me to thee, and thee to me.
No, no, no, no, my Dear, let be.

That you heard was but a mouse,
Dumb sleep holdeth all the house:

Yet asleep, methinks they say,
"Young folks, take time while you may":
Take me to thee, and thee to me.
No, no, no, no, my Dear, let be.

Niggard Time threats, if we miss
This large offer of our bliss,
Long stay, ere he grant the same:
Sweet, then, while each thing doth frame,
Take me to thee, and thee to me.
No, no, no, no, my Dear, let be.

Your fair mother is a-bed,
Candles out and curtains spread;
She thinks you do letters write;
Write, but first let me indite:
"Take me to thee, and thee to me."
No, no, no, no, my Dear, let be.

Sweet, alas, why strive you thus?
Concord better fitteth us;
Leave to Mars the force of hands,
Your power in your beauty stands:
Take me to thee, and thee to me.
No, no, no, no, my Dear, let be.

Woe to me! and do you swear
Me to hate, but I forbear?[1]
Cursèd be my destines[2] all,
That brought me so high to fall!
Soon with my death I will please thee.
No, no, no, no, my Dear, let be.

[1] But I forbear: unless I restrain myself. [2] Destines: destinies.

173

George Peele

It was always the custom to flatter noblemen, monarchs, or possible patrons with poems of adulation, and the work of George Peele (c. 1558–1598) was no exception. His *Arraignment of Paris* is a long pastoral full of ingenious tributes to Queen Elizabeth. It was properly rewarded, but it did not keep the poet from a dissolute life. Peele died in poverty and distress.

∽༄∾

What Thing is Love?

What thing is love? for, well I wot, love is a thing.
It is a prick, it is a sting,
It is a pretty pretty thing;
It is a fire, it is a coal,
Whose flame creeps in at every hole;
And as my wit doth best devise,
Love's dwelling is in ladies' eyes:
From whence do glance love's piercing darts
That make such holes into our hearts;
And all the world herein accord
Love is a great and mighty lord,
And when he list to mount so high,
With Venus he in heaven doth lie,
And evermore hath been a god
Since Mars and she played even and odd.

Thomas Lodge

Son of a Lord Mayor of London, intended to be a lawyer, Thomas Lodge (c. 1558–1625) abandoned law for literature, took part in sea expeditions, and rollicked his way through life. At forty he became a Roman Catholic, studied medicine, and qualified as a physician. Among other activities, he wrote *A History of the Plague*, translations from the Latin, biographies, poems, and plays. One of his comedies, *Rosalynde*, is not only the basis of Shakespeare's *As You Like It* but also supplies many of the incidents.

Coridon's Song

A blithe and bonny country lass,
    Heigh-ho, the bonny lass,
Sat sighing on the tender grass
    And, weeping, asked, would none come woo her.
A limber lad, a lithe young swain,
    Heigh-ho, the lithe young swain,
That in his love was wanton fain,
    With smiling looks came straight unto her.

When as the wanton wench espied,
    Heigh-ho, when she espied,
The means to make herself a bride,
    She simpered like a bonny bell,
The swain that saw her looking kind,
    Heigh-ho, the looking kind,
His arms about her body twined,
    With, "Fair lass, how fare ye, well?"

The country kit said, "Well, forsooth,
    Heigh-ho, well, forsooth,
But that I have a longing tooth,
    A longing tooth that makes me cry."
"Alas," said he, "what makes thy grief?
    Heigh-ho, what makes thy grief?"
"A wound," quoth she, "without relief;

    I fear a maiden I shall die."
"If that be all," the shepherd said,
    "Heigh-ho," the shepherd said,
"I'll make thee wive it, gentle maid,
    "And so I'll cure thy malady."
Whereon they kissed with many an oath,
    Heigh-ho, with many an oath,
And 'fore god Pan did plight their troth,
    Then to the church they both did hie.

Rosaline

Like to the clear in highest sphere
Where all imperial glory shines,
Of selfsame color is her hair
Whether unfolded, or in twines:
    Heigh-ho, fair Rosaline!
Her eyes are sapphires set in snow
Resembling heaven by every wink;
The Gods do fear whenas they glow,
And I do tremble when I think,
    Heigh-ho, would she were mine!

Her cheeks are like the blushing cloud
That beautifies Aurora's face,
Or like the silver crimson shroud
That Phœbus' smiling looks doth grace:
    Heigh-ho, fair Rosaline!
Her lips are like two budded roses
Whom ranks of lilies neighbor nigh,
Within which bounds she balm encloses
Apt to entice a deity:
    Heigh-ho, would she were mine!

Her neck is like a stately tower
Where Love himself imprisoned lies,
To watch for glances every hour
From her divine and sacred eyes:
    Heigh-ho, fair Rosaline!
Her paps are centers of delight,
Her breasts are orbs of heavenly frame,
Where Nature molds the dew of light
To feed perfection with the same:
    Heigh-ho, would she were mine!

With orient pearl, with ruby red,
With marble white, with sapphire blue
Her body every way is fed,
Yet soft in touch and sweet in view:
    Heigh-ho, fair Rosaline!
Nature herself her shape admires;
The Gods are wounded in her sight;
And Love forsakes his heavenly fires
And at her eyes his brand doth light:
    Heigh-ho, would she were mine!

Then muse not, Nymphs, though I bemoan
The absence of fair Rosaline,
Since for a fair there's fairer none,
Nor for her virtues so divine:
    Heigh-ho, fair Rosaline!
Heigh-ho, my heart! would God that she were mine!

Rosalind's Madrigal

Love in my bosom like a bee
    Doth suck his sweet:
Now with his wings he plays with me,
    Now with his feet.
Within mine eyes he makes his nest,
His bed amidst my tender breast;
My kisses are his daily feast,
And yet he robs me of my rest:
    Ah! wanton, will ye?

And if I sleep, then percheth he
        With pretty flight,
And makes his pillow of my knee
        The livelong night.
Strike I my lute, he tunes the string;
He music plays if so I sing;
He lends me every lovely thing,
Yet cruel he my heart doth sting:
        Whist, wanton, still ye!

Else I with roses every day
        Will whip you hence,
And bind you, when you long to play,
        For your offence.
I'll shut mine eyes to keep you in;
I'll make you fast it for your sin;
I'll count your power not worth a pin.
—Alas! what hereby shall I win
        If he gainsay me?

What if I beat the wanton boy
        With many a rod?
He will repay me with annoy,
        Because a god.
Then sit thou safely on my knee;
Then let thy bower my bosom be;
Lurk in mine eyes, I like of thee;
O Cupid, so thou pity me,
        Spare not, but play thee!

Michael Drayton

Michael Drayton (1563–1631) spent years writing *Poly-Olbion,*
an epic survey which was to give "a chorographical description of
all the tracts, rivers, mountains, forests, and other parts of Great
Britain." Its thousands of monotonous twelve-syllable couplets are,
except for a few picturesque passages, unreadable. So are most of
the historical narratives, legends, pastorals, "heroical epistles," and
plays which Drayton composed. Today he is remembered for his
shorter works: the stripped sonnets in the sequence entitled "Idea,"
the bravura "Battle of Agincourt," and a few whimsical antiques
like the following fancy.

179

Dowsabel

Far in the country of Arden,
There won'd a knight, hight[1] Cassemen,
   As bold as Isenbras:
Fell was he, and eager bent,
In battle and in tournament,
   As was the good Sir Topas.

He had, as antique stories tell,
A daughter cleped[2] Dowsabel,
   A maiden fair and free:
And for she was her father's heir,
Full well she was y-cond the leir[3]
   Of mickle courtesy.

The silk well could she twist and twine,
And make the fine march-pine,[4]
   And with the needle work:
And she could help the priest to say
His matins on a holy-day,
   And sing a psalm in kirk.

She wore a frock of frolick green,
Might well beseem a maiden queen,
   Which seemly was to see;
A hood to that so neat and fine,
In colour like the columbine,
   Y-wrought full featously.[5]

Her features all as fresh above,
As is the grass that grows by Dove;
   And like as lass of Kent.

---

[1] Hight: called. [2] Cleped: named. [3] Y-cond the leir: learned in the lore. [4] March-pine: marzipan, a sweetmeat made of almonds. [5] Featously: neatly.

Her skin as soft as Lemster wool,
As white as snow on Peakish Hull,
  Or swan that swims in Trent.

This maiden in a morn betime
Went forth, when May was in her prime,
  To get sweet cetewall,[6]
The honey-suckle, the harlock,[7]
The lily and the lady-smock,
  To deck her summer hall.

Thus, as she wand'red here and there,
Y-picking of the bloomed brere,[8]
  She chanced to espy
A shepherd sitting on a bank;
Like chanteclere he crowed crank,[9]
  And piped full merrily.

He lear'd[10] his sheep as he him list,
When he would whistle in his fist,
  To feed about him round;
Whilst he full many a carol sung,
Until the fields and meadows rung,
  And all the woods did sound.

In favor this same shepherd's swain
Was like the bedlam[11] Tamburlane,
  Which held proud kings in awe:
But meek he was as lamb mought be;
And innocent of ill as he
  Whom his lewd brother slaw.

The shepherd wore a sheep-gray cloak,
Which was of the finest loke,
  That could he cut with shear:
His mittens were of bauzens[12] skin,
His cockers were of cordiwin,[13]
  His hood of menivere.[14]

His awl and lingell[15] in a thong,
His tar-box on his broad belt hong,

6 Cetewall: valerian. 7 Harlock: cornflower. 8 Brer: briar. 9 Crank: merrily. 10 Lear'd: taught.
11 Bedlam: mad. 12 Bauzens: badgers. 13 Cockers . . . cordiwin: gaiters . . . leather. 14 Menivere: fur. 15 Lingell: thread.

His breech of Coyntrie blue:
Full crisp and curlèd were his locks,
His brows as white as Albion rocks:
  So like a lover true,

And piping still he spent the day,
So merry as the popinjay;
  Which likèd Dowsabel:
That would she ought, or would she nought,
This lad would never from her thought;
  She in love-longing fell.

At length she tuckèd up her frock,
White as a lily was her smock,
  She drew the shepherd nigh;
But then the shepherd piped a good,
That all his sheep forsook their food,
  To hear his melody.

"Thy sheep," quoth she, "cannot be lean,
That have a jolly shepherd's swain,
  The which can pipe so well."
"Yea but," saith he, "their shepherd may,
If piping thus he pine away
  In love of Dowsabel."

"Of love, fond boy, take thou no keep,"
Quoth she, "Look thou unto thy sheep,
  Lest they should hap to stray."
Quoth he, "So had I done full well,
Had I not seen fair Dowsabel
  Come forth to gather may."

With that she gan to veil her head,
Her cheeks were like the roses red,
  But not a word she said:
With that the shepherd gan to frown,
He threw his pretty pipes adown,
  And on the ground him laid.

Saith she, "I may not stay till night,
And leave my summer-hall undight,

And all for long of thee."
"My coat," saith he, "nor yet my fold
Shall neither sheep nor shepherd hold,
    Except thou favor me."

Saith she, "Yet liever were I dead,
Than I should lose my maiden-head,
    And all for love of men."
Saith he, "Yet are you too unkind,
If in your heart you cannot find
    To love us now and then.

"And I to thee will be as kind,
As Colin was to Rosalind,
    Of courtesy the flower."
"Then will I be as true," quoth she,
"As ever maiden yet might be
    Unto her paramour."

With that she bent her snow-white knee,
Down by the shepherd kneelèd she,
    And him she sweetly kissed:
With that the shepherd whooped for joy,
Quoth he, "There's never shepherd's boy
    That ever was so blest."

Christopher Marlowe

Christopher Marlowe (1564–1593), the poet-dramatist whom fellow-poets called "the muses' darling" and who threatened to rival Shakespeare, did not live beyond his twenty-ninth year. He was stabbed to death in a tavern brawl, not as formerly thought, because of a romantic struggle over a girl, but because of a sordid quarrel over the payment of a bill. Shakespeare quoted from him and acknowledged his indebtedness—Marlowe's *The Jew of Malta* is the forerunner of *The Merchant of Venice*. The young genius wrote four flamboyant plays in the short space of six years and gave blank verse such a resonance that it seemed a new language. His "The Passionate Shepherd to His Love" was continually imitated by the Elizabethan lyricist, and "Hero and Leander" (which contains the much-quoted "Who ever loved, that loved not at first sight?") was a favorite erotic poem of the period.

Marlowe luxuriated in his own rhetoric and even expanded it in the translations from Ovid on pages 55-63.

184

The Passionate Shepherd to His Love

Come live with me and be my Love,
And we will all the pleasures prove
That hills and valleys, dale and field,
And all the craggy mountains yield.

There will we sit upon the rocks
And see the shepherds feed their flocks,
By shallow rivers, to whose falls
Melodious birds sing madrigals.

There will I make thee beds of roses
And a thousand fragrant posies,
A cap of flowers, and a kirtle
Embroidered all with leaves of myrtle.

A gown made of the finest wool,
Which from our pretty lambs we pull,
Fair linèd slippers for the cold,
With buckles of the purest gold.

A belt of straw and ivy buds
With coral clasps and amber studs:
And if these pleasures may thee move,
Come live with me and be my Love.

Thy silver dishes for thy meat
As precious as the gods do eat,
Shall on an ivory table be
Prepared each day for thee and me.

The shepherd swains shall dance and sing
For thy delight each May-morning:
If these delights thy mind may move,
Then live with me and be my Love.

From *Hero and Leander*

She stay'd not for her robes, but straight arose.
And, drunk with gladness, to the door she goes;
Where seeing a naked man, she screech'd for fear,
(Such sights as this to tender maids are rare.)
And ran into the dark herself to hide
(Rich jewels in the dark are soonest spied).
Unto her was he led, or rather drawn
By those white limbs which sparkled through the
          lawn.
The nearer that he came, the more she fled,
And, seeking refuge, slipt into her bed;
Whereon Leander sitting, thus began,
Through numbing cold, all feeble, faint, and wan.
"If not for love, yet, love, for pity-sake,
Me in thy bed and maiden bosom take;
At least vouchsafe these arms some little room,
Who, hoping to embrace thee, cheerly swoom:
This head was beat with many a churlish billow,
And therefore let it rest upon thy pillow."
Herewith affrighted, Hero shrunk away,
And in her lukewarm place Leander lay;
Whose lively heat, like fire from heaven fet,
Would animate gross clay, and higher set
The drooping thoughts of base-declining souls,
Than dreary-Mars-carousing nectar bowls.
His hands he cast upon her like a snare:
She, overcome with shame and sallow fear,
Like chaste Diana when Actæon spied her,
Being suddenly betray'd, div'd down to hide
          her;
And, as her silver body downward went,
With both her hands she made the bed a tent,
And in her own mind thought herself secure,
O'ercast with dim and darksome coverture.
And now she lets him whisper in her ear,
Flatter, entreat, promise, protest, and swear:
Yet ever, as he greedily assay'd
To touch those dainties, she the harpy play'd,
And every limb did, as a soldier stout,

Defend the fort, and keep the foeman out;
For though the rising ivory mount he scal'd,
Which is with azure circling lines empal'd,
Much like a globe, (a globe may I term this,
By which Love sails to regions full of bliss,)
Yet there with Sisyphus he toil'd in vain,
Till gentle parley did the truce obtain.
Even as a bird, which in our hands we wring,
Forth plungeth, and oft flutters with her wing,
She trembling strove: this strife of hers, like that
Which made the world, another world begat
Of unknown joy. Treason was in her thought,
And cunningly to yield herself she sought.
Seeming not won, yet won she was at length:
In such wars women use but half their strength.
Leander now, like Theban Hercules,
Enter'd the orchard of th' Hesperides;
Whose fruit none rightly can describe, but he
That pulls or shakes it from the golden tree.
Wherein Leander, on her quivering breast,
Breathless spoke something, and sigh'd out the
            rest;
Which so prevail'd, as he, with small ado,
Enclos'd her in his arms, and kiss'd her too:
And every kiss to her was as a charm,
And to Leander as a fresh alarm:
So that the truce was broke, and she, alas,
Poor silly maiden, at his mercy was.
Love is not full of pity, as men say,
But deaf and cruel where he means to prey.

And now she wish'd this night were never done,
And sigh'd to think upon th' approaching sun;
For much it griev'd her that the bright day-light
Should know the pleasure of this blessed night,
And them, like Mars and Erycine, display
Both in each other's arms chain'd as they lay.
Again, she knew not how to frame her look,
Or speak to him, who in a moment took
That which so long, so charily she kept;
And fain by stealth away she would have crept,

And to some corner secretly have gone,
Leaving Leander in the bed alone.
But as her naked feet were whipping out,
He on the sudden cling'd her so about,
That, mermaid-like, unto the floor she slid;
One half appear'd, the other half was hid.
Thus near the bed she blushing stood upright,
And from her countenance behold ye might
A kind of twilight break, which through the air,
As from an orient cloud, glimps'd here and there;
And round about the chamber this false morn
Brought forth the day before the day was born.
So Hero's ruddy cheek Hero betray'd,
And her all naked to his sight display'd.

William Shakespeare

Holding the mirror up to nature, William Shakespeare (1564–1616) was himself a mirror of mankind. He concealed nothing. He revealed man's highest dreams and his lowest thoughts; he matched nobility and ecstasy with clowning vulgarity. Even his tragedies intermingle the tremendous with the trifling. The exquisite *Romeo and Juliet* opens with jokes about maidenheads and later, Juliet's Nurse cackles lewdly when she recalls her charge's innocent *double entendre*. *King Lear* has a mad scene which is full of images of copulation. When Hamlet's Ophelia loses her reason she also loses her modesty and sings bawdy ditties disclosing unfulfilled sexual desire. Even the songs scattered through the plays intermingle lyric charm with light ribaldry, while *Venus and Adonis* is a rich tapestry of erotic imagery. No love scene has ever surpassed the passages in which the radiant Queen of Love attempts to seduce the beautiful and reluctant mortal.

189

From *Venus and Adonis*

O, what a war of looks was then between them!
Her eyes petitioners to his eyes suing;
His eyes saw her eyes as they had not seen them;
Her eyes woo'd still, his eyes disdain'd the wooing:
  And all this dumb play had his acts made plain
  With tears, which chorus-like her eyes did rain.

Full gently now she takes him by the hand,
A lily prison'd in a gaol of snow,
Or ivory in an alabaster band;
So white a friend engirts so white a foe:
  This beauteous combat, wilful and unwilling,
  Show'd like two silver doves that sit a-billing.

Once more the engine of her thoughts began:
"O fairest mover on this mortal round,
Would thou wert as I am, and I a man,
My heart all whole as thine, thy heart my wound;
  For one sweet look thy help I would assure thee,
  Though nothing but my body's bane would cure thee!"

"Give me my hand," saith he, "why dost thou feel it?"
"Give me my heart," saith she, "and thou shalt have it;
O, give it me, lest thy hard heart do steel it,
And being steel'd, soft sighs can never grave it:
  Then love's deep groans I never shall regard,
  Because Adonis' heart hath made mine hard.

. . . .

190

"Who sees his true-love in her naked bed,
Teaching the sheets a whiter hue than white,
But, when his glutton eye so full hath fed,
His other agents aim at like delight?
   Who is so faint, that dare not be so bold
   To touch the fire, the weather being cold?"

      . . . .

"I know not love," quoth he, "nor will not know it,
Unless it be a boar, and then I chase it;
'Tis much to borrow, and I will not owe it;
My love to love is love but to disgrace it;
   For I have heard it is a life and death,
   That laughs and weeps, and all but with a breath.

      . . . .

"You hurt my hand with wringing; let us part,
And leave this idle theme, this bootless chat:
Remove your siege from my unyielding heart;
To love's alarms it will not ope the gate:
   Dismiss your vows, your feignèd tears, your flattery;
   For where a heart is hard they make no battery."

"What canst thou talk?" quoth she, "hast thou a tongue?
O, would thou hadst not, or I had no hearing!
Thy mermaid's voice hath done me double wrong;
I had my load before, now press'd with bearing:
   Melodious discord, heavenly tune harsh-sounding,
   Ear's deep-sweet music, and heart's deep-sore wounding.

"Had I no eyes but ears, my ears would love
That inward beauty and invisible;
Or were I deaf, thy outward parts would move
Each part in me that were but sensible:
   Though neither eyes nor ears, to hear nor see,
   Yet should I be in love by touching thee."

      . . . .

And at his look she flatly falleth down,
For looks kill love and love by looks reviveth;
A smile recures the wounding of a frown;

191

But blessed bankrupt, that by love so thriveth!
　The silly boy, believing she is dead,
　　Claps her pale cheek, till clapping makes it red;

And all amazed brake off his late intent,
For sharply he did think to reprehend her,
Which cunning love did wittily prevent:
Fair fall the wit that can so well defend her!
　For on the grass she lies as she were slain,
　　Till his breath breatheth life in her again.

He wrings her nose; he strikes her on the cheeks;
He bends her fingers; holds her pulses hard;
He chafes her lips; a thousand ways he seeks
To mend the hurt that his unkindness marr'd.
　He kisses her; and she, by her good will,
　　Will never rise, so he will kiss her still.

The night of sorrow now is turn'd to day:
Her two blue windows faintly she up-heaveth,
Like the fair sun, when in his fresh array
He cheers the morn, and all the earth relieveth:
　And as the bright sun glorifies the sky,
　　So is her face illumined with her eye.

　　　　　　　． ． ． ．

"Oh, where am I?" quoth she, "in earth or heaven,
Or in the ocean drench'd, or in the fire?
What hour is this? or morn or weary even?
Do I delight to die, or life desire?
　But now I lived, and life was death's annoy;
　　But now I died, and death was lively joy.

"O, thou didst kill me: kill me once again:
Thy eyes' shrewd tutor, that hard heart of thine,
Hath taught them scornful tricks and such disdain,
That they have murder'd this poor heart of mine;
　And these mine eyes, true leaders to their queen,
　　But for thy piteous lips no more had seen.

　　　　　　　． ． ． ．

"A thousand kisses buys my heart from me;
And pay them at thy leisure, one by one.

What is ten hundred touches unto thee?
Are they not quickly told and quickly gone?
   Say, for non-payment that the debt should double,
   Is twenty hundred kisses such a trouble?"

"Fair queen," quoth he, "if any love you owe me,
Measure my strangeness with my unripe years:
Before I know myself, seek not to know me;
No fisher but the ungrown fry forbears:
   The mellow plum doth fall, the green sticks fast,
   Or being early pluck'd is sour to taste.

"Now let me say 'Good night,' and so say you;
If you will say so, you shall have a kiss."
"Good night," quoth she; and, ere he says "Adieu,"
The honey fee of parting tender'd is:
   Her arms do lend his neck a sweet embrace;
   Incorporate then they seem; face grows to face.

Till, breathless, he disjoin'd, and backward drew
The heavenly moisture, that sweet coral mouth,
Whose precious taste her thirsty lips well knew,
Whereon they surfeit, yet complain on drouth:
   He with her plenty press'd, she faint with dearth,
   Their lips together glued, fall to the earth.

Now quick desire hath caught the yielding prey,
And glutton-like she feeds, yet never filleth;
Her lips are conquerors, his lips obey,
Paying what ransom the insulter willeth;
   Whose vulture thought doth pitch the price so high,
   That she will draw his lips' rich treasure dry:

And having felt the sweetness of the spoil,
With blindfold fury she begins to forage;
Her face doth reek and smoke, her blood doth boil,
And careless lust stirs up a desperate courage,
   Planting oblivion, beating reason back,
   Forgetting shame's pure blush and honor's wrack.

Hot, faint, and weary, with her hard embracing,
Like a wild bird being tamed with too much handling,

Or as the fleet-foot roe that's tired with chasing,
Or like the froward infant still'd with dandling,
He now obeys, and now no more resisteth,
While she takes all she can, not all she listeth.

. . . .

For pity now she can no more detain him;
The poor fool prays her that he may depart:
She is resolved no longer to restrain him;
Bids him farewell, and look well to her heart,
The which, by Cupid's bow she doth protest,
He carries thence incagèd in his breast.

"Sweet boy," she says, "this night I'll waste in sorrow,
For my sick heart commands mine eyes to watch.
Tell me, Love's master, shall we meet tomorrow?
Say, shall we? shall we? wilt thou make the match?"
He tells her, no; tomorrow he intends
To hunt the boar with certain of his friends.

"The boar!" quoth she; whereat a sudden pale,
Like lawn being spread upon the blushing rose,
Usurps her cheek; she trembles at his tale,
And on his neck her yoking arms she throws:
She sinketh down, still hanging by his neck,
He on her belly falls, she on her back.

Now is she in the very lists of love,
Her champion mounted for the hot encounter:
All is imaginary she doth prove,
He will not manage her, although he mount her;
That worse than Tantalus' is her annoy,
To clip Elysium and to lack her joy.

Even as poor birds, deceived with painted grapes,
Do surfeit by the eye and pine the maw,
Even so she languisheth in her mishaps,
As those poor birds that helpless berries saw.
The warm effects which she in him finds missing
She seeks to kindle with continual kissing.

But all in vain; good queen, it will not be:
She hath assay'd as much as may be proved;
Her pleading hath deserved a greater fee;
She's Love, she loves, and yet she is not loved.
   "Fie, fie," he says, "you crush me; let me go;
   You have no reason to withhold me so."

"Thou hadst been gone," quoth she, "sweet boy, ere this,
But that thou told'st me thou wouldst hunt the boar.
O, be advised! thou know'st not what it is
With javelin's point a churlish swine to gore,
   Whose tushes never sheathed he whetteth still,
   Like to a mortal butcher bent to kill.

        .   .   .   .

"Lie quietly, and hear a little more;
Nay, do not struggle, for thou shalt not rise:
To make thee hate the hunting of the boar,
Unlike myself thou hear'st me moralize,
   Applying this to that, and so to so;
   For love can comment upon every woe.

"Where did I leave?" "No matter where," quoth he,
"Leave me, and then the story aptly ends:
The night is spent." "Why, what of that?" quoth she.
"I am," quoth he, "expected of my friends;
   And now 'tis dark, and going I shall fall."
   "In night," quoth she, "desire sees best of all."

Ophelia's Song

Tomorrow is Saint Valentine's day
   All in the morning betime,
And I a maid at your window,
   To be your Valentine.

Then up he rose, and donn'd his clothes,
   And dupp'd the chamber-door;
Let in the maid, that out a maid
   Never departed more.

By Gis and by Saint Charity,
  Alack, and fie for shame!
Young men will do 't, if they come to 't;
  By cock, they are to blame.

Quoth she, before you tumbled me,
  You promised me to wed.
So would I ha' done, by yonder sun,
  An thou hadst not come to my bed.

When Daffodils Begin to Peer

When daffodils begin to peer,
  With heigh! the doxy over the dale,
Why, then comes in the sweet o' the year;
  For the red blood reigns in the winter's pale.

The white sheet bleaching on the hedge,
  With heigh! the sweet birds, oh, how they sing!
Doth set my pugging tooth on edge;
  For a quart of ale is a dish for a king.

The lark, that tirra-lirra chaunts,
  With heigh! with heigh! the thrush and the jay,
Are summer songs for me and my aunts
  While we lie tumbling in the hay.

It Was a Lover and His Lass

It was a lover and his lass,
  With a hey, and a ho, and a hey nonino,
That oe'r the green corn field did pass
  In the spring time, the only pretty ring time,
When birds do sing, hey ding a ding, ding;
Sweet lovers love the spring.

Between the acres of the rye,
  With a hey, and a ho, and a hey nonino,
These pretty country folks would lie,

In the spring time, the only pretty ring time,
When birds do sing, hey ding a ding, ding;
Sweet lovers love the spring.

This carol they began that hour,
  With a hey, and a ho, and a hey nonino,
How that a life was but a flower
  In the spring time, the only pretty ring time,
When birds do sing, hey ding a ding, ding;
Sweet lovers love the spring.

And therefore take the present time.
  With a hey, and a ho, and a hey nonino,
For love is crownèd with the prime
  In the spring time, the only pretty ring time,
When birds do sing, hey ding a ding, ding;
Sweet lovers love the spring.

Crabbèd Age and Youth

Crabbèd Age and Youth
Cannot live together:
Youth is full of pleasance,
Age is full of care;
Youth like summer morn,
Age like winter weather;
Youth like summer brave,
Age like winter bare.
Youth is full of sport,
Age's breath is short;
Youth is nimble, Age is lame;
Youth is hot and bold,
Age is weak and cold;
Youth is wild, and Age is tame.
Age, I do abhor thee;
Youth, I do adore thee;
O, my Love, my Love is young!
Age, I do defy thee:
O, sweet shepherd, hie thee!
For methinks thou stay'st too long.

Thomas Campion

Even in a time of marvels, Thomas Campion (1567–1620) was a marvelously gifted man. He was an eminent doctor, a pure poet, and a popular composer; some of the most cherished Elizabethan songs were his lyrics which he had set to music. Campion was also something of a paradox; he wrote a critical protest against "the vulgar and artificial custom of rhyming," yet he was one of the most accomplished rhymesters of his day. His four *Books of Airs* show the influence of Catullus, who delighted him and whom he translated (see page 43). Besides his *Observations in the Art of English Poesy*, Campion published a guide to musical composition, *A New Way of Making Four Parts in Counterpoint*. These works, as well as his delicate and almost transparent lyrics, were lost for three hundred years until they were unearthed in the nineteenth century.

The Place of Cupid's Fire

Beauty, since you so much desire
To know the place of Cupid's fire,
About you somewhere doth it rest,
Yet never harbour'd in your breast,
Nor gout-like in your heel or toe—
What fool would seek Love's flame so low?
But a little higher, but a little higher,
There, there, O there lies Cupid's fire.

Think not, when Cupid most you scorn.
Men judge that you of ice were born;
For though you cast love at your heel,
His fury yet sometimes you feel:
And whereabouts if you would know,
I tell you still not in your toe:
But a little higher, but a little higher,
There, there, O there lies Cupid's fire.

When We Court and Kiss

I care not for these ladies,
That must be wooed and prayed:
Give me kind Amarillis,
The wanton country maid.
Nature art disdaineth,
Her beauty is her own.
  Her when we court and kiss,
  She cries, "Forsooth, let go!"
  But when we come where comfort is,
  She never will say "No!"

If I love Amarillis,
She gives me fruit and flowers:
But if we love these ladies,
We must give golden showers.
Give them gold, that sell love,
Give me the nut-brown lass,
  Who, when we court and kiss,
  She cries, "Forsooth, let go!"
  But when we come where comfort is,
  She never will say "No!"

These ladies must have pillows,
And beds by strangers wrought;
Give me a bower of willows,
Of moss and leaves unbought,
And fresh Amarillis,
With milk and honey fed;
  Who when we court and kiss,
  She cries, "Forsooth, let go!"
  But when we come where comfort is,
  She never will say "No!"

What Harvest Half So Sweet Is

What harvest half so sweet is
As still to reap the kisses
  Grown ripe in sowing?
And straight to be receiver
Of that which thou art giver,
  Rich in bestowing?
Kiss then, my Harvest Queen,
  Full garners heaping!
Kisses, ripest when th' are green,
  Want only reaping.

The dove alone expresses
Her fervency in kisses,
  Of all most loving:
A creature as offenseless

200

As those things that are senseless
  And void of moving.
Let us so love and kiss,
  Though all envy us:
That which kind, and harmless is,
  None can deny us.

Bar Not the Door

Sweet, exclude me not, nor be divided
  From him that ere long must bed thee:
All thy maiden doubts law hath decided;
  Sure we are, and I must wed thee.
Presume then yet a little more:
Here's the way, bar not the door.

Tenants, to fulfil their landlord's pleasure,
  Pay their rent before the quarter:
'Tis my case, if you it rightly measure;
  Put me not then off with laughter.
Consider then a little more:
Here's the way to all my store.

Why were doors in love's despight devised?
  Are not laws enough restraining?
Women are most apt to be surprised
  Sleeping, or sleep wisely feigning.
Then grace me yet a little more:
Here's the way, bar not the door.

It Fell on a Summer's Day

It fell on a summer's day,
While sweet Bessy sleeping lay,
In her bower, on her bed,
Light with curtains shadowed,
Jamy came: she him spies,
Opening half her heavy eyes.

201

Jamy stole in through the door,
She lay slumb'ring as before;
Softly to her he drew near,
She heard him, yet would not hear:
Bessy vowed not to speak,
He resolved that dump to break.

First a soft kiss he doth take,
She lay still and would not wake;
Then his hands learned to woo,
She dreamt not what he would do,
But still slept, while he smiled
To see love by sleep beguiled.

Jamy then began to play,
Bessy as one buried lay,
Gladly still through this sleight
Deceived in her own receit;
And since this trance begoon,
She sleeps every afternoon.

Your Fair Looks Inflame My Desire

Your fair looks inflame my desire:
   Quench it again with love!
Stay, O strive not still to retire:
   Do not inhuman prove!
If love may persuade,
   Love's pleasures, dear, deny not.
Here is a silent grovy shade;
   O tarry then, and fly not!

Have I seized my heavenly delight
   In this unhaunted grove?
Time shall now her fury requite
   With the revenge of love.
Then come, sweetest, come,
   My lips with kisses gracing!
Here let us harbor all alone,
   Die, die in sweet embracing!

Will you now so timely depart,
  And not return again?
Your sight lends such life to my heart
  That to depart is pain.
Fear yields no delay,
  Secureness helpeth pleasure:
Then, till the time gives safer stay,
  O farewell, my life's treasure!

Be Wise, and Fly Not [1]

Your fair looks urge my desire:
  Calm it, sweet, with love!
Stay; O why will you retire?
  Can you churlish prove?
If love may persuade,
  Love's pleasures, dear, deny not:
Here is a grove secured with shade:
  O then be wise, and fly not.

Hark, the birds delighted sing,
  Yet our pleasure sleeps:
Wealth to none can profit bring,
  Which the miser keeps.
O come, while we may,
  Let's chain love with embraces;
We have not all times time to stay,
  Nor safety in all places.

What ill find you now in this,
  Or who can complain?
There is nothing done amiss
  That breeds no man pain.
'Tis now flow'ry May;
  But even in cold December,
When all these leaves are blown away,
  This place shall I remember.

[1] A variation on the preceding poem.

Fain Would I Wed a Fair Young Man

Fain would I wed a fair young man that day
    and night could please me,
When my mind or body grieved that had the
    power to ease me.
Maids are full of longing thoughts that breed
    a bloodless sickness,
And that, oft I hear men say, is only cured
    by quickness.
Oft I have been wooed and prayed, but never
    could be moved;
Many for a day or so I have most dearly loved,
But this foolish mind of mine straight loathes
    the thing resolved;
If to love be sin in me that sin is soon absolved.
Sure I think I shall at last fly to some holy order;
When I once am settled there then can I fly no
    farther.
Yet I would not die a maid, because I had a
    mother:
As I was by one brought forth I would bring
    forth another.

A Maid's Complaint

My love hath vowed he will forsake me,
    And I am already sped;
Far other promise he did make me
    When he had my maidenhead.
If such danger be in playing
    And sport must to earnest turn,
I will go no more a-maying.

Had I foreseen what is ensued,
    And what now with pain I prove,
Unhappy then I had eschewed

204

This unkind event of love:
Maids foreknow their own undoing,
　But fear naught till all is done,
When a man alone is wooing.

Dissembling wretch, to gain thy pleasure,
　What didst thou not vow and swear?
So didst thou rob me of the treasure
　Which so long I held so dear.
Now thou provest to me a stranger:
　Such is the vile guise of men
When a woman is in danger.

Turn Back, You Wanton Flyer

Turn back, you wanton flyer,
And answer my desire,
With mutual greeting:
Yet bend a little nearer,
True beauty still shines clearer,
In closer meeting.
Hearts, with hearts delighted,
Should strive to be united;
Either other's arms with arms enchaining:
Hearts with a thought,
Rosy lips with a kiss still entertaining.

What harvest half so sweet is
As still to reap the kisses
Grown ripe in sowing?
And straight to be receiver
Of that, which thou art giver,
Rich in bestowing?
There's no strict observing
Of times' or seasons' swerving;
There is ever one fresh spring abiding.
Then what we sow with our lips,
Let us reap, love's gains dividing!

In the Dark What the Day Doth Forbid

Hark, all you ladies that do sleep!
  The fairy-queen Proserpina
Bids you awake and pity them that weep:
    You may do in the dark
    What the day doth forbid;
  Fear not the dogs that bark,
    Night will have all hid.

But if you let your lovers moan,
  The fairy-queen Proserpina
Will send abroad her fairies every one,
    That shall pinch black and blue
      Your white hands and fair arms
    That did not kindly rue
      Your paramours' harms.

In myrtle arbors on the downs
  The fairy-queen Proserpina,
This night by moonshine leading merry rounds,
    Holds a watch with sweet love,
      Down the dale, up the hill;
    No plaints or groans may move
      Their holy vigil.

All you that will hold watch with love,
  The fairy-queen Proserpina
Will make you fairer than Dione's dove;
    Roses red, lilies white,
      And the clear damask hue,
    Shall on your cheeks alight:
      Love will adorn you.

All you that love or loved before,
  The fairy-queen Proserpina
Bids you increase that loving humor more:
    They that have not fed
      On delight amorous,
    She vows that they shall lead
      Apes in Avernus.[1]

---

[1] Avernus: Hades. It was once believed that, after death, spinsters would be compelled to lead apes through the underworld.

Ben Jonson

Beginning as a bricklayer working with his stepfather, Ben Jonson (1572–1637) became a soldier, an actor, and a swaggering hot-headed roisterer before he became a playwright turning out a succession of comedies, tragedies, satires, ballets, allegories, and productions for which there is no convenient category. At twenty-six he quarreled with and killed a fellow actor, was condemned to be hanged, became a Catholic in prison, escaped the gallows through "benefit of clergy," recanted, and rejoined the Church of England. A friend and idolator of Shakespeare, an inspirer of younger poets, Jonson died in his sixty-fourth year and was buried in Westminster Abbey. His tombstone is inscribed with this tribute: "O Rare Ben Jonson."

Love

So Love, emergent out of chaos, brought
        The world to light!
And gently moving on the waters, wrought
        All form to sight!
        Love's appetite
        Did beauty first excite!
        And left imprinted in the air
    Those signatures of good and fair,
Which since have flow'd, flow'd forth upon the sense
To wonder first, and then to excellence,
By virtue of divine intelligence!

The Kiss

O that joy so soon should waste!
    Or so sweet a bliss
    As a kiss
Might not forever last!

So sugared, so melting, so soft, so delicious!
    The dew that lies on roses
    When the morn itself discloses
Is not so precious.

O rather that I would it smother
Were I to taste such another;
    It should be my wishing
    That I might die kissing!

For Love's Sake

For Love's sake, kiss me once again!
I long, and should not beg in vain.
Here's none to spy, or see;
Why do you doubt, or stay?
I'll taste as lightly as the bee,
That doth but touch his flower, and flies away.

Once more, and faith, I will be gone—
Can he that loves ask less than one?
Nay, you may err in this,

And all your bounty wrong:
This could be called but half a kiss;
What we're but once to do, we should do long.

I will but mend the last, and tell
Where, how, it would have relished well;
Join lip to lip, and try:
Each suck the other's breath,
And whilst our tongues perplexèd lie,
Let who will think us dead, or wish our death!

So White, So Soft, So Sweet

Have you seen but a bright lily grow
   Before rude hands have touch'd it?
Have you marked but the fall of the snow
   Before the soil hath smutch'd it?
Have you felt the wool of beaver,
   Or swan's down ever?
Or have smelt o' the bud o' the brier,
   Or the nard in the fire?
Or have tasted the bag of the bee?
O so white, O so soft, O so sweet is she!

To Celia

Come, my Celia, let us prove,
While we may, the sports of love;
Time will not be ours for ever;
He at length our good will sever;
Spend not then his gifts in vain.
Suns that set may rise again;
But if once we lose this light,
'Tis with us perpetual night.
Why should we defer our joys?
Fame and rumor are but toys.
Cannot we delude the eyes

Of a few poor household spies;
Or his easier ears beguile,
So removed by our wile?
'Tis no sin love's fruit to steal,
But the sweet theft to reveal:
To be taken, to be seen,
These have crimes accounted been.

~o&~

Against Consummation [1]

Doing a filthy pleasure is, and short,
And done, we straight repent us of the sport.
Let us not then rush blindly on unto it
Like lustful beasts that only know to do it;
For lust will languish and its heat decay.
But thus, thus, keeping endless holiday,
Let us together closely lie and kiss,
There is no labor nor no shame in this;
This hath pleased, doth please, and long will please; never
Can this decay, but is beginning ever.

[1] A variation on Petronius' "A Plea for Postponement," page 73.

Heywood and Others

Thomas Heywood (1574–1641), John Marston (1576–1634), John Fletcher (1579–1625), Francis Beaumont (1584–1616), and Philip Massinger (1583–1640) were Shakespeare's fellow dramatists. Like their most famous contemporary, they interlarded their plays with songs, a few of which follow.

She That Denies Me

She that denies me I would have;
    Who craves me I despise:
Venus hath power to rule mine heart,
    But not to please mine eyes.

Temptations offered I still scorn;
    Denied, I cling them still;
I'll neither glut mine appetite,
    Nor seek to starve my will.

Diana, double-clothed, offends;
    So Venus, naked quite:
The last begets a surfeit, and
    The other no delight.

That crafty girl shall please me best,
    That no, for yea, can say;
And every wanton willing kiss
    Can season with a nay.

THOMAS HEYWOOD

211

Delicious Beauty

Delicious beauty that doth lie
Wrapped in a skin of ivory,
Lie still, lie still upon thy back
And, Fancy, let no sweet dreams lack
To tickle her, to tickle her with pleasing thoughts.

But if thy eyes are open full,
Then deign to view an honest gull
That stands, that stands expecting still
When that thy casement open will;
And bless his eyes, and bless his eyes with one kind glance.

JOHN MARSTON

Love's Emblems

Now the lusty spring is seen;
  Golden yellow, gaudy blue,
Daintily invite the view:
Everywhere on every green
Roses blushing as they blow,
  And enticing men to pull,
Lilies whiter than the snow,
  Woodbines of sweet honey full:
    All love's emblems, and all cry,
    "Ladies, if not plucked, we die."

Yet the lusty spring hath stayed;
Blushing red and purest white
  Daintily to love invite
Every woman, every maid:
Cherries kissing as they grow,
  And inviting men to taste,
Apples even ripe below,
  Winding gently to the waist:
    All love's emblems, and all cry,
    "Ladies, if not plucked, we die."

JOHN FLETCHER

The Power of Love

Hear, ye ladies that despise
  What the mighty Love has done;
Fear examples and be wise:
  Fair Callisto was a nun;
Leda, sailing on the stream
  To deceive the hopes of man,
Love accounting but a dream,
  Doted on a silver swan;
    Danaë, in a brazen tower,
    Where no love was, loved a shower.

Hear, ye ladies that are coy,
  What the mighty Love can do;
Fear the fierceness of the boy:
  The chaste Moon he makes to woo;
Vesta, kindling holy fires,
  Circled round about with spies,
Never dreaming loose desires,
  Doting at the altar dies;
    Ilion, in a short hour, higher
    He can build, and once more fire.

JOHN FLETCHER

From *The Maid's Tragedy*

To Bed, To Bed
To bed, to bed; come, Hymen, lead the bride,
And lay her by her husband's side;
  Bring in the virgins every one,
  That grieve to lie alone:
That they may kiss while they may say, a maid;
Tomorrow, 'twill be other, kiss'd, and said.
  Hesperus be long a-shining.
  Whilst those lovers are a-twining.

Hold Back Thy Hours

Hold back thy hours, dark Night, till we have done;
  The day will come too soon;
Young maids will curse thee if thou steal'st away,
And leav'st their losses open to the day:
    Stay, stay, and hide
    The blushes of the bride.

Stay, gentle Night, and with thy darkness cover
  The kisses of her lover.
Stay, and confound her tears, and her shrill cryings,
Her weak denials, vows, and often dyings;
    Stay, and hide all:
    But help not, though she call.

FRANCIS BEAUMONT and JOHN FLETCHER

A Song of Pleasure

The blushing rose and purple flower,
  Let grow too long, are soonest blasted.
Dainty fruits, though sweet, will sour
  And rot in ripeness, left untasted.
    Yet here is one more sweet than these:
    The more you taste, the more she'll please.

Beauty, though enclosed with ice,
  Is a shadow chaste as rare;
Then how much those sweets entice
  That have issue full as fair!
    Earth cannot yield from all her powers
    One equal, for Dame Venus' bowers.

PHILLIP MASSINGER

George Wither

George Wither (1588–1616) was not a playwright but a lyricist. His "I Loved a Lass" seems to parallel "Greensleeves" (page 398) in its author's complaint about a mistress whom he loved desperately and supplied liberally—" 'Twas I that paid for all things;/'Twas others drank the wine"—and who, after taking his love and presents, ruthlessly deserted him.

I Loved a Lass

I loved a lass, a fair one,
 As fair as e'er was seen;
She was indeed a rare one,
 Another Sheba Queen:
But, fool as then I was,
 I thought she loved me too:
But now, alas! sh'as left me,
 Falero, lero, loo!

Her hair like gold did glister,
 Each eye was like a star,
She did surpass her sister,
 Which passed all others far;
She would me honey call,
 She'd—oh, she'd kiss me too!
But now, alas! sh'as left me,
 Falero, lero, loo!
But now, alas! sh'as left me,
 Falero, lero, loo!

215

In summer time to Medley
    My Love and I would go:
The boatmen there stood ready
    My Love and I to row;
For cream there would we call,
    For cakes and for prunes too:
But now, alas! sh'as left me,
    Falero, lero, loo!

Many a merry meeting
    My Love and I have had;
She was my only sweeting,
    She made my heart full glad;
The tears stood in her eyes
    Like to the morning dew:
But now, alas! sh'as left me,
    Falero, lero, loo!

And as abroad we walkèd,
    As lovers' fashion is,
Oft as we sweetly talkèd
    The sun would steal a kiss;
The wind upon her lips
    Likewise most sweetly blew:
But now, alas! sh'as left me,
    Falero, lero, loo!

Her cheeks were like the cherry,
    Her skin as white as snow;
When she was blithe and merry
    She angel-like did show;
Her waist exceeding small,
    The fives did fit her shoe;
But now, alas! sh'as left me,
    Falero, lero, loo!

In summer time or winter
    She had her heart's desire;
I still did scorn to stint her
    From sugar, sack, or fire:
The world went round about,

No cares we ever knew:
But now, alas! sh'as left me,
    Falero, lero, loo!

As we walked home together,
    At midnight, through the town,
To keep away the weather
    O'er her I'd cast my gown;
No cold my Love should feel,
    Whate'er the heavens could do:
But now, alas! sh'as left me,
    Falero, lero, loo!

Like doves we would be billing,
    And clip and kiss so fast,
Yet she would be unwilling
    That I should kiss the last:
They're Judas kisses now,
    Since that they proved untrue:
For now, alas! sh'as left me,
    Falero, lero, loo!

To maidens' vows and swearing
    Henceforth no credit give;
You may give them the hearing,
    But never them believe;
They are as false as fair,
    Unconstant, frail, untrue:
For mine, alas! has left me,
    Falero, lero, loo!

'Twas I that paid for all things;
    'Twas others drank the wine;
I cannot now recall things,
    Live but a fool to pine;
'Twas I that beat the bush,
    The bird to others flew:
For she alas! hath left me,
    Falero, lero, loo!

If ever that Dame Nature,
    For this false lover's sake,

Another pleasing creature
　　Like unto her would make,
Let her remember this—
　　To make the other true:
For this, alas! hath left me,
　　Falero, lero, loo!

No riches now can raise me,
　　No want make me despair,
No misery amaze me,
　　Nor yet for want I care;
I have lost a world itself:
　　My earthly heaven, adieu!
Since she, alas! hath left me,
　　Falero, lero, loo!

The Kiss

Now gentle sleep hath closèd up those eyes
Which, waking, kept my boldest thoughts in awe;
And free access unto that sweet lip lies,
From whence I long the rosy breath to draw.
Methinks no wrong it were, if I should steal
From those two melting rubies one poor kiss;
None sees the theft that would the theft reveal,
Nor rob I her of aught that she can miss.
Nay, should I twenty kisses take away,
There would be little sign I would do so.
Why then should I this robbery delay?
O, she may wake, and therewith angry grow!
Well, if she do, I'll back restore that one,
And twenty hundred thousand more for loan.

Robert Herrick

A quiet little country vicar, Robert Herrick (1591–1674) wrote some of the naughtiest of English poems. Son of a London goldsmith, apprenticed to his uncle, a jeweler, he prepared for the ministry and at thirty-eight was presented with a living at Dean Prior in Devon. At a time when the country was ravaged by civil war, Herrick amused himself with hundreds of "cleanly wanton" lyrics. The paradoxical phrase is exact, for though Herrick's models were the Latin poets, he resembles the temperate Horace rather than the impassioned Catullus; his love poems to Julia, Electra, Anthea, Corinna, Perenna, and other "mistresses" are more polite than pagan. He never married and died in his eighty-fourth year.

Forgotten for about two hundred years, Herrick's works were rediscovered during the nineteenth century; his "delight in disorder," his naïve indelicacies, and his simple erotic imagery charmed all readers. Too facile to be enjoyed *in toto*—he wrote more than 1400 poems—Herrick will remain the laureate of precise and polished trivialities; his playful verse is assured of perennial life.

The Vision

I dreamed we both were in bed
Of roses almost smotherèd:
The warmth and sweetness and me there
Made lovingly familiar,
But that I heard thy sweet breath say,
"Faults done by night will blush by day."
I kissed thee, panting, and I call
Night to the record, that was all
But ah! if empty dreams so please,
Love, give me more such nights as these.

❧

Show Me Thy Feet

Show me thy feet, show me thy legs, thy thighs,
Show me those fleshy principalities;
Show me that hill where smiling love doth sit,
Having a living fountain under it;
Show me thy waist; then let me there withal,
By the ascension of thy lawn, see all.

❧

When I Thy Parts Run O'er

When I thy parts run o'er, I can't espy
In any part the least indecency,
But every line and limb diffusèd thence,
A fair and unfamiliar excellence:
So that the more I look, the more I prove
There's still more cause why I the more should love.

The Vine

I dreamed this mortal part of mine
Was metamorphosed to a vine,
Which, crawling one and every way,
Enthralled my dainty Lucia.
Methought, her long small legs and thighs
I with my tendrils did surprise;
Her belly, buttocks, and her waist
By my soft nervelets were embraced:
About her head I writhing hung,
And with rich clusters hid among
The leaves, her temples I behung:
So that my Lucia seemed to me
Young Bacchus ravished by his tree.
My curls about her neck did crawl,
And arms and hands they did enthrall,
So that she could not freely stir,
All parts there made one prisoner.
But when I crept with leaves to hide
Those parts which maids keep unespied,
Such fleeting pleasures there I took
That with the fancy I awoke;
And found, ah me! this flesh of mine
More like a stock than like a vine.

What Kind of Mistress He Would Have

Be the mistress of my choice
Clean in manners, clear in voice;
Be she witty, more than wise;
Pure enough, though not precise:
Be she showing in her dress,
Like a civil wilderness;
That the curious may detect
Order in a sweet neglect;
Be she rolling in her eye,
Tempting all the passers-by;
And each ringlet of her hair
An enchantment, or a snare

221

For to catch the lookers on,
But herself held fast by none.
Let her Lucrece all day be,
Thaïs in the night to me.
Be she such, as neither will
Famish me, nor overfill.

To His Mistresses

Help me! help me! now I call
To my pretty witchcrafts all:
Old I am, and cannot do
That I was accustomed to.
Bring your magics, spells, and charms,
To enflesh my thighs and arms.
Is there no way to beget
In my limbs their former heat?
Æson had, as poets fain,
Baths that made him young again:
Find that medicine, if you can,
For your dry, decrepit man;
Who would fain his strength renew,
Were it but to pleasure you.

Upon the Nipples of Julia's Breast

Have ye beheld (with much delight)
A red rose peeping through a white?
Or else a cherry (double graced)
Within a lily's centre placed?
Or ever marked the pretty beam,
A strawberry shows half drowned in cream?
Or seen rich rubies blushing through
A pure smooth pearl, and orient too?
So like to this, nay all the rest,
Is each neat niplet of her breast.

222

Upon Julia's Petticoat

Thy azure robe I did behold,
As airy as the leaves of gold;
Which erring here, and wandering there,
Pleased with transgression everywhere.
Sometimes 't would pant, and sigh, and heave,
As if to stir it scarce and leave:
But having got it, thereupon,
'T would make a brave expansión;
And pounced with stars, it showed to me
Like a celestial canopy.
Sometimes 't would blaze, and then abate,
Like to a flame grown moderate:
Sometimes away 't would wildly fling,
Then to thy thighs so closely cling,
That some conceit did melt me down,
As lovers fall into a swoon;
And all confused, I there did lie
Drowned in delights, but could not die.
That leading cloud I followed still,
Hoping t' have seen of it my fill;
But ah! I could not: should it move
To life eternal, I could love.

The Night-Piece

Her eyes the glowworm lend thee;
The shooting stars attend thee;
    And the elves also,
    Whose little eyes glow
Like the sparks of fire, befriend thee.

No will-o'-th'- wisp mislight thee,
Nor snake or slow worm bite thee;
    But on, on thy way,
    Not making a stay,
Since ghost there's none to affright thee.

223

Let not the dark thee cumber;
What though the moon does slumber?
    The stars of the night
    Will lend thee their light
Like tapers clear, without number.

Then, Julia, let me woo thee,
Thus, thus, to come unto me;
    And when I shall meet
    Thy silvery feet,
My soul I'll pour into thee.

I'll Come to Thee

I'll come to thee in all those shapes
As Jove did when he made his rapes;
Only, I'll not appear to thee
As he did once to Semele.
Thunder and lightning I'll lay by,
To talk with thee familiarly:
Which done, then quickly we'll undress
To one and th' others nakedness;
And ravished, plunge into the bed,
Bodies and souls commingléd,
And kissing, so as none may hear,
We'll weary all the fables there.

More White Than Whitest Lilies

More white than whitest lilies far,
Or snow, or whitest swans you are:
More white than are the whitest creams,
Or moonlight tinseling the streams:
More white than pearls, or Juno's thigh,
Or Pelop's arm of ivory.
True, I confess, such whites as these
May me delight, not fully please,
Till, like Ixion's cloud, you be
White, warm, and soft to lie with me.

What Shame Forbids to Speak

Ah, my Anthea! Must my heart still break?
Love makes me write what shame forbids to speak.
Give me a kiss, and to that kiss a score;
Then to that twenty, add an hundred more;
A thousand to that hundred; so kiss on,
To make that thousand up a million;
Treble that million, and when that is done,
Let's kiss afresh, as when we first begun.
But yet, though love likes well such scenes at these,
There is an act that will more fully please:
Kissing and glancing, soothing, all make way
But to the acting of this private play:
Name it I would; but being blushing red,
The rest I'll speak, when we meet both in bed.

On Himself

Young I was who now am old,
But I am not yet grown cold.
I can play and I can twine
'Bout a virgin like a vine;
In her lap too I can lie
Melting, and in fancy die,
And return to life if she
Claps my cheek or kisses me.
Thus, and thus it now appears
That our love outlasts our years.

Chop-Cherry

Thou gav'st me leave to kiss,
Thou gav'st me leave to woo,
Thou mad'st me think by this
And that, thou lov'dst me too.

But I shall ne'er forget
How for to make me merry
Thou mad'st me chop, but yet
Another snapped the cherry.

225

Upon Julia's Fall

Julia was careless, and withal
She rather took than got a fall.
The wanton ambler chanced to see
Part of her legs' sincerity;
And, ravished thus, it came to pass
The nag (like to the prophet's ass)
Began to speak, and would have been
A-telling what rare sights he'd seen,
And had told all, but did refrain
Because his tongue was tied again.

Sitting Alone

Sitting alone, as one forsook,
Close by a silver-shedding brook,
With hands held up to love, I wept,
And after sorrows spent, I slept:
Then in a vision I did see
A glorious form appear to me:
A virgin's face she had; her dress
Was like a sprightly Spartaness.
A silver bow, with green silk strung,
Down from her comely shoulders hung;
And as she stood, the wanton air
Dandled the ringlets of her hair.
Her legs were such Diana shows,
When tucked up she a hunting goes,
With buskins shortened to descry
The happy dawning of her thigh:
Which when I saw, I made access
To kiss that tempting nakedness;
But she forbade me, with a wand
Of myrtle she had in her hand,
And chiding me, said, "Hence, remove.
Herrick, thou art too coarse to love."

226

The Second Vision

Methought I saw (as I did dream in bed)
A crawling vine about Anacreon's head:
Flushed was his face; his hairs with oil did shine;
And as he spake, his mouth ran o'er with wine.
Tippled he was; and tippling lisped withal;
And lisping reeled, and reeling like to fall.
A young enchantress close by him did stand
Tapping his plump thighs with a myrtle wand:
She smiled; he kissed; and kissing, culled her, too;
And being cup-shot, more he could not do.
For which (methought) in pretty anger she
Snatched off his crown, and gave the wreath to me:
Since when (methinks) my brains about do swim,
And I am wild and wanton like to him.

Fresh Cheese and Cream

Would ye have fresh cheese and cream?
Julia's breast can give you them.
And if more, each nipple cries
To your cream here's strawberries.

Love Perfumes All Parts

If I kiss Anthea's breast,
There I smell the Phoenix' nest:
If her lip, the most sincere
Attar of incense, I smell there.
Hands, and thighs, and legs, are all
Richly aromatical.
Goddess Isis can't transfer
Musks and ambers more from her,
Nor can Juno sweeter be,
When she lies with Jove, than she.

227

To Virgins

Hear ye virgins, and I'll teach
What the times of old did preach.
Rosamond was in a bower
Kept, as Danae in a tower:
But yet love, who subtle is,
Crept to that, and came to this.
Be ye locked up like to these,
Or the rich Hesperides;
Or those babies in your eyes,
In their crystal nunneries:
Notwithstanding love will win,
Or else force, a passage in;
And as coy be, as you can,
Gifts will get ye, or the man.

Thomas Carew

By birth an aristocrat, Thomas Carew (1595–1639) was one of the friends and followers of Ben Jonson. He wrote plays, arranged masques, and prepared various "entertainments" for the court until he died at forty-four. It is said that on his deathbed he repented of a life "spent with less severity than it ought to have been."

There was some reason for repentance. Carew was one of the most licentious as well as one of the most mocking of poets. Nevertheless, his "A Rapture" is a minor classic and, with the somewhat less lascivious "Second Rapture" and other lyrics, will be preserved as long as there is freedom to reprint them.

Give Me More Love

Give me more love or more disdain;
    The torrid or the frozen zone
Bring equal ease unto my pain;
    The temperate affords me none.
Either extreme, of love or hate,
Is sweeter than a calm estate.

Give me a storm; if it be love,
    Like Danae in that golden shower,
I swim in pleasure; if it prove
    Disdain, that torrent will devour
My vulture-hopes; and he's possess'd
Of Heaven that's but from Hell releas'd.
Then crown my joys or cure my pain;
Give me more love or more disdain.

I Will Enjoy Thee Now

(From *A Rapture*)

I will enjoy thee now, my Celia, come,
And fly with me to Love's Elysium.
The giant, Honor, that keeps cowards out
Is but a masquer, and the servile rout
Of baser subjects only bend in vain
To the vast idol; whilst the nobler train
Of valiant lovers daily sail between
The huge Colossus' legs, and pass unseen
Unto the blissful shore. Be bold and wise,
And we shall enter; the grim Swiss denies
Only to tame fools a passage, that not know
He is but form and only frights in show
The duller eyes that look from far; draw near
And thou shalt scorn what we were wont to fear . . .

Come, then, and mounted on the wings of Love
We'll cut the flitting air and soar above
The monster's[1] head, and in the noblest seats
Of those blest shades quench and renew our heats.
There shall the queens of love and innocence,
Beauty and Nature, banish all offense
From our close ivy-twines; there I'll behold
Thy baréd snow and thy unbraided gold;
There my enfranchised hand on every side
Shall o'er thy naked polish'd ivory slide.
No curtain there, though of transparent lawn,
Shall be before thy virgin-treasure drawn;
But the rich mine, to the enquiring eye
Exposed, shall ready for mintage lie,
And we will coin young Cupids. There a bed
Of roses and fresh myrtles shall be spread,
Under the cooler shades of cypress groves;
Our pillows of the down of Venus' doves,
Whereon our panting limbs we'll gently lay,
In the faint respites of our active play;
That so our slumbers may in dreams have leisure

[1] The "monster" is Honor.

To tell the nimble fancy our past pleasure,
And so our souls, that cannot be embraced,
Shall the embraces of our bodies taste.
Meanwhile the bubbling stream shall court the shore,
Th' enamor'd chirping wood-choir shall adore
In varied tunes the deity of love;
The gentle blasts of western winds shall move
The trembling leaves, and through their close boughs breathe
Still music, whilst we rest ourselves beneath
Their dancing shade; till a soft murmur, sent
From souls entranced in amorous languishment,
Rouse us, and shoot into our veins fresh fire,
Till we in their sweet ecstasy expire.
Then, as the empty bee that lately bore
Into the common treasure all her store,
Flies 'bout the painted field with nimble wing,
Deflow'ring the fresh virgins of the spring,
So will I rifle all the sweets that dwell
In my delicious paradise, and swell
My bag with honey, drawn forth by the power
Of fervent kisses from each spicy flower.
I'll seize the rosebuds in their perfumed bed,
The violet knots, like curious mazes spread
O'er all the garden, taste the ripen'd cherry,
The warm firm apple, tipp'd with coral berry;
Then will I visit with a wand'ring kiss
The vales of lilies and the bower of bliss;
And where the beauteous region doth divide
Into two milky ways, my lips shall slide
Down those smooth alleys, wearing as they go
A track for lovers on the printed snow;
Thence climbing o'er the swelling Apennine,
Retire into thy grove of eglantine,
Where I will all those ravish'd sweets distill
Through Love's alembic, and with chemic skill
From the mix'd mass of one sovereign balm derive,
Then bring that great elixir to thy hive.

Now in more subtle wreaths I will entwine
My sinewy thighs, my legs and arms with thine;
Thou like a sea of milk shalt lie display'd

Whilst I the smooth calm ocean invade
With such a tempest, as when Jove of old
Fell down on Danaë in a storm of gold;
Yet my tall pine shall in the Cyprian strait
Ride safe at anchor and unlade her freight:
My rudder with thy bold hand, like a tried
And skilful pilot, thou shalt steer, and guide
My bark into love's channel, where it shall
Dance, as the bounding waves do rise or fall.
Then shall thy circling arms embrace and clip
My willing body, and thy balmy lip
Bathe me in juice of kisses, whose perfume
Like a religious incense shall consume,
And send up holy vapors to those powers
That bless our loves and crown our sportful hours,
That with such halcyon calmness fix our souls
In steadfast peace, as no affright controls.
There no rude sounds shake us with sudden starts;
No jealous ears, when we unrip our hearts,
Such our discourse is; no observing spies
This blush, that glance traduce; no envious eyes
Watch our close meetings; nor are we betray'd
To rivals by the bribèd chambermaid.
No wedlock bonds unwreathe our twisted loves,
We seek no midnight arbor, no dark groves
To hide our kisses; there the hated name
Of husband, wife, lust, modest, chaste, or shame,
Are vain and empty words, whose very sound
Was never heard in the Elysian ground.
All things are lawful there, that may delight
Nature or unrestrainèd appetite.
Like and enjoy, to will and act is one:
We only sin when Love's rites are not done.

The Roman Lucrece reads there the divine
Lectures of love's great master, Aretine,
And knows as well as Lais how to move
Her pliant body in the act of love;
To quench the burning ravisher she hurls
Her limbs into a thousand winding curls,
And studies artful postures, such as be

Carved on the bark of every neighboring tree
By learned hands, that so adorned the rind
Of those fair plants which, as they lay entwined,
Have fanned their glowing fires. The Grecian dame,
That in her endless web toiled for a name
As fruitless as her work, doth there display
Herself before the youth of Ithaca,
And amorous sports of gamesome nights prefer
Before dull dreams of the lost traveler.
Daphne hath broke her bark, and that swift foot
Which th' angry gods had fastened with a root
To the fixed earth, doth now unfettered run
To meet th' embraces of the youthful Sun.
She hangs upon him like his Delphic lyre;
Her kisses blow the old and breathe new fire . . .

Come then, my Celia, we'll no more forbear
To taste our joys, struck with a panic fear,
But will depose from his imperious sway
This proud usurper and walk free as they.

The Second Rapture

No, worldling, no, 'tis not thy gold,
Which thou dost use but to behold,
Nor fortune, honor, nor long life,
Children, or friends, nor a good wife,
That makes thee happy: these things be
But shadows of felicity.
Give me a wench about thirteen,
Already voted to the queen
Of lust and lovers; whose soft hair
Fanned with the breath of gentle air,
O'erspreads her shoulders like a tent,
And is her veil and ornament;
Whose tender touch will make the blood
Wild in the agèd and the good;
Whose kisses, fasten'd to the mouth
Of three-score years and longer slouth,
Renew the age; and whose bright eye

Obscures those lesser lights of sky;
Whose snowy breasts (if we may call
That snow, that never melts at all,)
Make Jove invent a new disguise,
In spite of Juno's jealousies;
Whose every part doth re-invite
The old decayèd appetite;
And in whose sweet embraces I
May melt my self to lust, and die.
This is true bliss, and I confess
There is no other happiness.

A Song

In her fair cheeks two pits do lie,
To bury those slain by her eye;
So, spite of death, this comforts me,
That fairly buried I shall be,
My grave with rose and lily spread;
O 'tis a life to be so dead!
    Come then, and kill me with thy eye,
    For, if thou let me live, I die.

When I behold those lips again,
Reviving what those eyes have slain,
With kisses sweet, whose balsam pure
Love's wounds, as soon as made, can cure,
Methinks 'tis sickness to be sound,
And there's no health to such a wound.
    Come then, and kll me with thy eye,
    For, if thou let me live, I die.

When in her chaste breast I behold
Those downy mounts of snow, ne'er cold;
And those blest hearts her beauty kills,
Revived by climbing those fair hills,
Methinks there's life in such a death,
And so t'expire inspires new breath.
    Come then, and kill me with thy eye,
    For, if thou let me live, I die.

Nymph, since no death is deadly, where
Such choice of antidotes are near,
And your keen eyes but kill in vain
Those that are sound, as soon as slain;
That I, no longer dead, survive,
Your way's to bury me alive
In Cupid's cave, where happy I
May dying live, and living die.
    Come then, and kill me with thy eye,
    For, if thou let me live, I die.

Fear Not, Dear Love

Fear not, dear love, that I'll reveal
Those hours of pleasure we two steal;
No eyes shall see, nor yet the sun
Descry, what thou and I have done;
No ear shall hear our love, but we
Silent as the night will be;
The god of love himself (whose dart
Did first wound mine, and then thy heart)
Shall never know, that we can tell,
What sweets in stol'n embraces dwell.
This only means may find it out:
If, when I die, physicians doubt
What caus'd my death, and there to view
Of all their judgments which was true,
Rip up this heart, O then, I fear,
The world will see thy picture there.

Boldness in Love

Mark how the bashful morn in vain
    Courts the amorous marigold
With sighing blasts and weeping rain,
    Yet she refuses to unfold;

But when the planet of the day
Approacheth with his powerful ray,
Then she spreads, then she receives
His warmer beams into her virgin leaves.

So shalt thou thrive in love, fond boy:
   If thy tears and sighs discover
Thy grief, thou never shalt enjoy
   The just reward of a bold lover;
But when with moving accents thou
Shalt constant faith and service vow,
Thy Celia shall receive those charms
With open ears, and with unfolded arms.

Love's Courtship

Kiss, lovely Celia, and be kind;
Let my desires freedom find,
     Sit thee down,
And we will make the gods confess
Mortals enjoy some happiness.

Mars would disdain his mistress' charms
If he beheld thee in my arms,
     And descend,
Thee his mortal queen to make,
Or live as mortal for thy sake.

Venus must lose her title now,
And leave to brag of Cupid's bow;
     Silly Queen!
She hath but one, but I can spy
Ten thousand Cupids in thy eye.

Nor may the sun behold our bliss,
For sure thy eyes do dazzle his;
     If thou fear
That he'll betray thee with his light,
Let me eclipse thee from his sight!

And while I shade thee from his eye
Oh! let me hear thee gently cry,
      Celia yields!
Maids often lose their maidenhead
Ere they set foot in nuptial bed.

Francis Davison

Son of a Privy Councillor and Queen Elizabeth's Secretary of State, Francis Davison (c.1575–1619) was one of the best anthologists of his day. His *Poetical Rhapsody* includes some of his original poems, and it is believed that "Cupid's Pastime" is his own composition.

Cupid's Pastime

It chanced of late a shepherd swain,
   That went to seek his straying sheep,
Within a thicket on a plain
   Espied a dainty nymph asleep.

Her golden hair o'erspread her face;
   Her careless arms abroad were cast;
Her quiver had her pillow's place;
   Her breast lay bare to every blast.

The shepherd stood and gazed his fill;
   Nought durst he do; nought durst he say;
Whilst chance, or else perhaps his will,
   Did guide the god of love that way.

The crafty boy that sees her sleep,
  Whom if she waked he durst not see;
Behind her closely seeks to creep,
  Before her nap should ended be.

Then come, he steals her shafts away,
  And puts his own into their place;
Nor dares he any longer stay,
  But, ere she wakes, hies thence apace.

Scarce was he gone, but she awakes,
  And spies the shepherd standing by:
Her bended bow in haste she takes,
  And at the simple swain lets fly.
Forth flew the shaft, and pierced his heart,
  That to the ground he fell with pain:
Yet up again forthwith he start,
  And to the nymph he ran amain.

Amazed to see so strange a sight,
  She shot, and shot, but all in vain:
The more his wounds, the more his might,
  Love yielded strength amidst his pain.

Her angry eyes were great with tears,
  She blames her hand, she blames her skill;
The bluntness of her shaft she fears,
  And try them on herself she will.

Take heed, sweet nymph, try not thy shaft,
  Each little touch will pierce thy heart:
Alas! thou knows't not Cupid's craft;
  Revenge is joy; the end is smart.

Yet try she will, and pierce some bare;
  Her hands were glov'd, but next to hand
Was that fair breast, that breast so rare,
  That made the shepherd senseless stand.

That breast she pierced; and through that breast
   Love found an entry to her heart:
At feeling of this new-come guest,
   Lord! how this gentle nymph did start!

She runs not now; she shoots no more;
   Away she throws both shaft and bow:
She seeks for what she shunned before,
   She thinks the shepherd's haste too slow.

Though mountains meet not, lovers may:
What other lovers do, did they.
The god of love sat on a tree,
And laughed that pleasant sight to see.

Suckling and Others

Sir John Suckling (1609–1642), Richard Lovelace (1618–1657), Edmund Waller (1606–1687), and William Habington (1605–1654) were Cavalier poets who loved sportive, graceful, and sometimes lightly metaphysical verse. The first two, like Carew, became court poets.

Suckling was the most reckless as well as the most spendthrift— he insisted that the actors of his elaborate plays wear costumes to match and furnished them with real lace and decorations of pure silver and gold. His "A Ballad upon a Wedding" is a rustic contrast to most of his cynical verse; it is casual, colloquial, a bit boisterous, and spiced with a faint trace of bawdiness.

A Ballad upon a Wedding

I tell thee, Dick, where I have been,
Where I the rarest things have seen,
  Oh, things without compare!
Such sights again can not be found
In any place on English ground,
  Be it at wake or fair.

At Charing Cross, hard by the way
Where we, thou know'st, do sell our hay,
  There is a house with stairs;
And there did I see coming down
Such folk as are not in our town,
  Forty at least, in pairs.

241

Amongst the rest, one pestilent fine
(His beard no bigger though than thine,)
   Walked on before the rest:
Our landlord looks like nothing to him;
The King (God bless him!) 'twould undo him
   Should he go still so dressed.

At course-a-park,[1] without all doubt,
He should have first been taken out
   By all the maids i' the town,
Though lusty Roger there had been,
Or little George upon the Green,
   Or Vincent of the Crown.

But wot you what? the youth was going
To make an end of all his wooing;
   The parson for him stayed:
Yet by his leave, for all his haste,
He did not so much wish all past,
   Perchance, as did the maid.

The maid—and thereby hangs a tale,
For such a maid no Whitson-ale [2]
   Could ever yet produce:
No grape that's kindly ripe could be
So round, so plump, so soft as she,
   Nor half so full of juice.

Her finger was so small, the ring
Would not stay on which he did bring,
   It was too wide a peck;
And to say truth (for out it must)
It looked like the great collar, just,
   About our young colt's neck.

Her feet beneath her petticoat
Like little mice stole in and out,
   As if they feared the light;
But, Dick! she dances such a way,
No sun upon an Easter day
   Is half so fine a sight.

Course-a-park: a country game. ² Whitson-ale: festivities at Whitsuntide.

242

He would have kissed her once or twice,
But she would not, she was so nice,
  She would not do 't in sight;
And then she looked as who should say
I will do what I list today,
  And you shall do 't at night.

Her cheeks so rare a white was on,
No daisy makes comparison,
  (Who sees them is undone,)
For streaks of red were mingled there
Such as are on a Katherine pear,
  The side that's next the sun.

Her lips were red, and one was thin
Compared to that was next her chin—
  Some bee had stung it newly:
But, Dick, her eyes so guard her face,
I durst no more upon them gaze
  Than on the sun in Jùly.

Her mouth so small, when she does speak,
Thou'dst swear her teeth her words did break,
  That they might passage get;
But she so handled still the matter,
They came as good as ours, or better,
  And are not spent a whit.

If wishing should be any sin
The parson himself had guilty bin,
  She looked that day so purely;
And did the youth so oft the feat
At night, as some did in conceit,
  It would have spoiled him, surely.

Passion o' me! how I run on!
There's that that would be thought upon,
  I trow, besides the bride:
The business of the kitchen's great,
For it is fit that men should eat;
  Nor was it there denied.

Just in the nick the cook knocked thrice,
And all the waiters in a trice
   His summons did obey;
Each serving-man with dish in hand
Marched boldly up, like our trained band,
   Presented, and away.

When all the meat was on the table
What man of knife, or teeth, was able
   To stay to be intreated?
And this the very reason was
Before the parson could say grace
   The company was seated.

Now hats fly off, and youths carouse;
Healths first go round, and then the house,
   The bride's came thick and thick;
And when 'twas named another's health,
Perhaps he made it hers by stealth:
   (And who could help it? Dick!)

O' the sudden up they rise and dance;
Then sit again, and sigh, and glance;
   Then dance again and kiss:
Thus several ways the time did pass,
Whilst every woman wished her place,
   And every man wished his.

By this time all were stol'n aside
To counsel and undress the bride,
   But that he must not know:
But yet 'twas thought he guessed her mind,
And did not mean to stay behind
   Above an hour or so.

When in he came, Dick, there she lay
Like new-fall'n snow melting away,
   ('Twas time, I trow, to part,)
Kisses were now the only stay,
Which soon she gave, as who would say
   Good boy with all my heart.

But just as heavens would have to cross it
In came the bridesmaids with the posset:
   The bridegroom ate in spite;
For had he left the women to 't,
It would have cost two hours to do 't,
   Which were too much that night.

At length the candle's out, and now
All that they had not done they do.
   What that is, who can tell?
But I believe it was no more
Than thou and I have done before
   With Bridget and with Nell.

SIR JOHN SUCKLING

❦

The Rejected Offer

It is not four years ago
   I offered forty crowns
To lie with her a night or so.
   She answered me with frowns.

Not two years since, she, meeting me,
   Did whisper in my ear
That she would at my service be,
   If I contented were.

I told her I was cold as snow
   And had no great desire,
But should be well content to go
   To twenty, but no higher.

Some three months since or thereabout,
   She that so coy had been,
Bethought herself and found me out,
   And was content to sin.

245

I smiled at that, and told her I
  Did think it somewhat late,
And that I'd not repentance buy
  At more than half the rate.

This present morning early she
  Forsooth came to my bed,
And gratis there she offered me
  Her high-prized maidenhead.

I told her that I thought it then
  Far dearer than I did,
When I at first the forty crowns
  For one night's lodging bid.

SIR JOHN SUCKLING

To Amarantha
That She Should Dishevel Her Hair

Amarantha sweet and fair,
Braid no more that shining hair!
As my curious hand or eye
Hovering round thee, let it fly!

Let it fly as unconfined
As its calm ravisher, the wind,
Who hath left his darling, th' East,
To wanton o'er that spicy nest.

Every tress must be confest,
But neatly tangled at the best;
Like a clue of golden thread
Excellently ravellèd.

Do not then wind up that light
In ribbands, and o'ercloud in night
Like the sun in's early ray;
But shake your head, and scatter day!

RICHARD LOVELACE

246

A Plea for Promiscuity

Phyllis, why should we delay
Pleasures shorter than the day?
Could we (which we never can!)
Stretch our lives beyond their span,
Beauty like a shadow flies,
And our youth before us dies.
Or, would youth and beauty stay,
Love hath wings, and will away.
Love hath swifter wings than Time:
Change in love to Heaven does climb.
Gods, that never change their state,
Vary oft their love and hate.

Phyllis, to this truth we owe
All the love betwixt us two:
Let not you and I inquire
What has been our past desire;
On what shepherd you have smiled,
Or what nymphs I have beguiled.
Leave it to the planets, too,
What we shall hereafter do.
For the joys we now may prove.
Take advice of present love.

EDMUND WALLER

On a Girdle

That which her slender waist confined,
Shall now my joyful temples bind;
No monarch but would give his crown,
His arms might do what this has done.

It was my heaven's extremest sphere,
The pale which held that lovely deer,
My joy, my grief, my hope, my love,
Did all within this circle move!

A narrow compass! and yet there
Dwelt all that's good, and all that's fair!
Give me but what this ribband bound,
Take all the rest the sun goes round!

EDMUND WALLER

~◦◦~

To Roses in the Bosom of Castara

Ye blushing virgins happy are
  In the chaste nunnery of her breasts—
For he'd profane so chaste a fair,
  Whoe'er should call them Cupid's breasts—

Transplanted thus how bright ye grow!
  How rich a perfume do ye yield!
In some close garden cowslips so
  Are sweeter than in the open field.

In those white cloisters live secure
  From the rude blasts of wanton breath!
Each hour more innocent and pure,
  Till you shall wither into death.

Then that which living gave you room
  Your glorious sepulcher shall be.
There wants no marble for a tomb
  Whose breast hath marble been to me.

WILLIAM HABINGTON

248

A World of Wit

The period between the middle of the seventeenth and the end of the eighteenth centuries was characterized variously as the Restoration, the Age of Enlightenment, the Age of Reason, and the Decline of Elegance. It was a time in which cleverness and subtlety were dominant; it was a world of wit, of nimble raillery and cruel satire, of sensibility and metaphysical sensualism.

The poetry of the period ranged from the tortured ingenuities of John Donne through the superb artifice of John Dryden and the frank lubricity of John Wilmot, Earl of Rochester, to the thrusting epigrams of Alexander Pope. The ancient battle between the sexes took on a new militancy. Every courtship was a campaign; lovers "laid siege" to their ladies, made gallant "conquests," and overcame planned resistance. The amatory warfare allowed for countless physical variations, painful as well as joyful, in which no detail was spared. No poet of the period—or, for that matter, any other age—combined sensitivity and sensuality, delight and despair, more brilliantly than John Donne.

John Donne

Midway between the Elizabethan singers and the later meta-physicians, John Donne (1573–1631) brought the writing of erotic poems to a height of eloquence and a nobility never before achieved. His life was a long struggle between flesh and spirit, success and defeat, rebellion and religion. Son of a wealthy ironmonger and a mother related to Sir Thomas More, Donne prepared for the law, was a soldier for two years, became secretary to Sir Thomas Egerton, fell in love with Lady Egerton's young niece, Anne, and eloped with her. This act almost ruined his career; he summed up the situation to his mother in a punning sentence: "John Donne—Anne Donne—Undone."

At forty-two, Donne forsook the Catholic faith of his father and took orders in the Anglican Church; James I promptly appointed him his chaplain. Six years later he became Dean of St. Paul's. A passionate preacher, famous for his "Devotions"—one beginning "No man is an Iland" took on new meaning in the twentieth century—he died, survived by six of his twelve children, at fifty-eight.

Most of Donne's daring love poems, the half-sensual, half-cynical songs, and the extraordinarily lively "elegies" were written during his twenties, although none saw publication until he was near forty. In these sensitivity attains a pitch of high seriousness, and what might have been merely suggestive becomes a series of mounting tensions, sometimes agonizing and never less than force-fully dramatic.

To His Mistress Going to Bed

Come, madam, come, all rest my powers defy,
Until I labor, I in labor lie.
The foe ofttimes having the foe in sight,
Is tired with standing though he never fight.
Off with that girdle, like heaven's zone glittering,
But a far fairer world encompassing.
Unpin that spangled breastplate which you wear
That th' eyes of busy fools may be stopped there.
Unlace yourself, for that harmonious chime
Tells me from you that now it is bedtime.
Off with that happy busk, which I envie,
That still can be, and still can stand so nigh.
Your gown going off such beauteous state reveals
As when from flowery meads th'hills shadow steals.
Off with that wiry coronet and show
The hairy diadem which on you doth grow;
Now off with those shoes, and then safely tread
In this love's hallowed temple, this soft bed.
In such white robes, heaven's angels used to be
Received by men. Thou, angel, bring'st with thee
A heaven like Mahomet's paradise; and though
Ill spirits walk in white, we easily know,
By this these angels from an evil sprite:
Those set our hairs, but these our flesh upright.

License my roving hands, and let them go,
Before, behind, between, above, below.
O my America! my New-found-land,
My kingdom, safeliest when with one man manned,
My mine of precious stones, my empery,

How blest am I in this discovering thee!
To enter in these bonds is to be free;
Then where my hand is set my seal shall be.

   Full nakedness! All joys are due to thee,
As souls unbodied, bodies unclothed must be
To taste whole joys. Gems which you women use
Are like Atlanta's ball cast in men's views
That when a fool's eye lightest on a gem
His earthly soul may covet that, not them.
Like pictures or like book's gay covering made
For laymen are all women thus arrayed;
Themselves are mystic books, which only we
(Whom their imputed grace will dignify)
Must see revealed. Then since that I may know,
As liberally as to a midwife show
Thyself: cast all, yea, this white linen hence;
There is no penance due to innocence.

   To teach thee, I am naked first. Why, then,
What need'st thou have more covering than a man?

⌒ ･9℮ ⌒

The Good-Morrow

I wonder, by my troth, what thou and I
Did till we loved? Were we not weaned till then?
But sucked on country pleasures childishly?
Or snorted we in the Seven Sleepers' den?
'T was so; but this, all pleasures fancies be;
If ever any beauty I did see,
Which I desired, and got, 't was but a dream of thee.

And now good-morrow to our waking souls,
Which watch not one another out of fear;
For love all love of other sights controls,
And makes one little room an everywhere.
Let sea-discoverers to new worlds have shown;
Let us possess one world; each hath one, and is one.

My face in thine eye, thine in mine appears,
And true plain hearts do in the faces rest;

252

Where can we find two better hemispheres
Without sharp north, without declining west?
Whatever dies, was not mixed equally;
If our two loves be one, or thou and I
Love so alike that none can slacken, none can die.

The Sun Rising

Busy old fool, unruly Sun,
    Why dost thou thus
Through windows and through curtains call on us?
Must to thy motions lovers' seasons run?
        Saucy pedantic wretch, go chide
        Late schoolboys and sour prentices;
    Go tell court-huntsmen that the king will ride,
    Call country ants to harvest offices;
Love, all alike, no season knows nor clime,
Nor hours, days, months, which are the rags of time.

        Thy beams so reverend and strong
        Why shouldst thou think?
I could eclipse and cloud them with a wink,
But that I would not lose her sight so long.
        If her eyes have not blinded thine,
        Look, and tomorrow late tell me,
    Whether both th' Indias of spice and mine
    Be where thou left'st them, or lie here with me.
Ask for those kings whom thou saw'st yesterday,
And thou shalt hear, "All here in one bed lay."

        She's all states, and all princes I;
        Nothing else is;
Princes do but play us; compared to this,
All honor's mimic, all wealth alchemy.
        Thou, Sun, art half as happy as we,
        In that the world's contracted thus;
    Thine age asks ease, and since thy duties be
    To warm the world, that's done in warming us.
Shine here to us, and thou art everywhere;
This bed thy center is, these walls thy sphere.

The Indifferent

I can love both fair and brown;
Her whom abundance melts, and her whom want betrays,
Her who loves loneness best, and her who masks and plays,
Her whom the country formed, and whom the town,
Her who believes, and her who tries,
Her who still weeps with spongy eyes,
And her who is dry cork, and never cries;
I can love her, and her, and you and you,
I can love any, so she be not true.

Will no other vice content you?
Will it not serve your turn to do as did your mothers?
Or have you all old vices spent, and now would find out others?
Or doth a fear that men are true torment you?
Oh, we are not, be not you so.
Let me, and do you, twenty know.
Rob me, but bind me not, and let me go.
Must I who came to travail through you
Grow your fixed subject because you are true?

Venus heard me sigh this song,
And by Love's sweetest part, variety, she swore
She heard not this till now; and that it should be so no more.
She went, examined, and returned ere long
And said, "Alas, some two or three
Poor heretics in love there be,
Which think to 'stablish dangerous constancy.
But I have told them, 'Since you will be true,
You shall be true to them who are false to you.' "

The Canonization

For God's sake hold your tongue, and let me love;
  Or chide my palsy, or my gout;
  My five grey hairs, or ruined fortune flout;
With wealth your state, your mind with arts improve;
    Take you a course, get you a place,
    Observe his Honor, or his Grace;

Or the King's real, or his stampèd face
  Contemplate; what you will, approve,
  So you will let me love.

Alas! alas! who's injured by my love?
  What merchant's ships have my sighs drowned?
  Who says my tears have overflowed his ground?
When did my colds a forward spring remove?
    When did the heats which my veins fill
    Add one more to the plaguy bill? [1]
Soldiers find wars, and lawyers find out still
  Litigious men, which quarrels move,
  Though she and I do love.

Call us what you will, we are made such by love;
  Call her one, me another fly,
  We are tapers too, and at our own cost die,
And we in us find the eagle and the dove.
    The phoenix riddle hath more wit
    By us; we two being one, are it;
So, to one neutral thing both sexes fit,
  We die and rise the same, and prove
  Mysterious by this love.

We can die by it, if not live by love,
  And if unfit for tombs and hearse
  Our legends be, it will be fit for verse;
And if no piece of chronicle we prove,
    We 'll build in sonnets pretty rooms;
    As well a well-wrought urn becomes
The greatest ashes, as half-acre tombs,
  And by these hymns all shall approve
  Us canonized for love;

And thus invoke us, "You, whom reverend love
  Made one another's hermitage;
  You, to whom love was peace, that now is rage;
Who did the whole world's soul contract, and drove
    Into the glasses of your eyes,

[1] Plaguy bill: A weekly bill of mortality sent during the time of the plague.

255

o made such mirrors, and such spies,
   they did all to you epitomize—
untries, towns, courts beg from above
   pattern of your love."

The Ecstasy

Where like a pillow on a bed,
   A pregnant bank swelled up to rest
The violet's reclining head,
   Sat we two, one another's best.

Our hands were firmly cementéd
   With a fast balm which thence did spring,
Our eye-beams twisted, and did thread
   Our eyes upon one double string;

So t' intergraft our hands as yet
   Was all the means to make us one,
And pictures in our eyes to get
   Was all our propagatión.

As 'twixt two equal armies, Fate
   Suspends uncertain victory,
Our souls (which to advance their state,
   Were gone out) hung 'twixt her and me.

And whilst our souls negotiate there,
   We like sepulchral statues lay;
All day the same our postures were
   And we said nothing all the day.

If any, so by love refined,
   That the soul's language understood
And by good love were grown all mind,
   Within convenient distance stood,

He (though he knew not which soul spake,
   Because both meant, both spake the same)
256

Might thence a new concoction take,
   And part far purer than he came.

This ecstasy doth unperplex
   (We said) and tell us what we love,
We see by this, it was not sex,
   We see, we saw not what did move:

But as all several souls contain
   Mixture of things they know not what,
Love these mixed souls doth mix again,
   And makes both one, each this and that.

A single violet transplant,
   The strength, the color, and the size,
(All which before was poor, and scant),
   Redoubles still, and multiplies.

When love, with one another so
   Inter-inanimates two souls,
That abler soul, whence doth flow,
   Defects of loneliness controls.

We then who are this new soul know
   Of what we are composed and made,
For th' Atomies of which we grow
   Are souls whom no change can invade.

But O alas, so long, so far
   Our bodies why do we forbear?
They are ours though they are not we. We are
   The intelligences, they are spheres.

We owe them thanks because they thus
   Did us to us at first convey,
Yielded their forces, sense, to us,
   Nor are dross to us but allay.

On man heaven's influence works not so,
   But that it first imprints the air
So soul into the soul may flow
   Though it to body first repair.

As our blood labors to beget
    Spirits as like souls as it can
Because such fingers need to knit
    That subtle knot which makes us man:

So must pure lovers' souls descend
    T' affections and to faculties
Which sense may reach and apprehend,
    Else a great Prince in prison lies.

To our bodies turn we then that so
    Weak men on love revealed may look;
Love's mysteries in souls do grow
    But yet the body is his book;

And if some lover, such as we
    Have heard this dialogue of one,
Let him still mark us, he shall see
    Small change, when we're to bodies gone.

Johannes Secundus

Celebrated as the author of the alluring *Basia,* a favorite sequence of the seventeenth century, Johannes Secundus was not, as the name might indicate, a classic Latin poet. His real name was Jan Everts and he was born at the Hague in Holland in 1611. He studied law at Bourges, became secretary to the archbishop of Toledo, moved to Utrecht where he joined the staff of another church dignitary, and then became part of the entourage of Charles V. It was a brief career; he died in 1636, barely twenty-five years old.

Whatever his position or place, Everts remained a poet. As Johannes Secundus he wrote exceptionally neat and sometimes naughty verse. Although he served various masters more or less perfunctorily, it was to *Basia* (or *Kisses*) that he gave more than—the pun is inevitable—lip service.

The first two translations are by the eighteenth-century John Nott; the third is by George Ogle.

Neaera's Kisses

(From *Basia*)

While tenderly around me cast
Your arms, Neaera, hold me fast;
And hanging o'er, to view confest,
Your neck, and gently-heaving breast;
Down on my shoulders soft decline
Your beauties more than half divine;
With wand'ring looks that o'er me rove,
And fire the melting soul with love:

While you, Neaera, fondly join
Your little pouting lips with mine;
And frolic bite your am'rous swain
Complaining soft if bit again;
And sweetly-murm'ring pour along
The trembling accents of your tongue,
Your tongue, now here now there that strays,
Now here now there delighted plays;
That now my humid kisses sips,
Now wanton darts between my lips;
And on my bosom raptured lie,
Venting the gently-whisper'd sigh;
A sigh that kindles warm desires,
And kindly fans life's drooping fires;
Soft as the zephyr's breezy wing,
And balmy as the breath of spring:

While you, sweet nymph! with am'rous play,
In kisses suck my breath away;
My breath with wasting warmth replete,
Parch'd by my breast's contagious heat;
Till, breathing soft, you pour again
Returning life through every vein;
Thus soothe to rest my passion's rage,
Love's burning fever thus assuage:
Sweet nymph! whose breath can best allay
Those fires that on my bosom prey,

Breath welcome as the cooling gale,
That blows when scorching heats prevail:

Then, more than blest, I fondly swear,
"No power can with Love's power compare!
None in the starry court of Jove
Is greater than the god of Love!
If any can yet greater be,
Yes, my Neaera! yes, 'tis thee!"

The Insatiate

(From *Basia*)

Bright as Venus' golden star,
Fair as Dian's silver car,
Nymph, with every charm replete,
Give me hundred kisses sweet;
Then as many kisses more
O'er my lips profusely pour,
As th' insatiate bard could want,
Or his bounteous Lesbia grant;
As the vagrant Loves that stray
On thy lips' nectareous way;
As the dimpling Graces spread
On thy cheeks' carnation'd bed;
As the deaths thy lovers die;
As the conquests of thine eye,
Or the cares, and fond delights,
Which its changeful beam incites;
As the hopes and fears we prove,
Or th' impassion'd sighs, in love;
As the shafts by Cupid sped,
Shafts by which my heart has bled;
As the countless stores that still
All his golden quiver fill.
Whisper'd plaints, and wanton wiles;
Speeches soft, and soothing smiles;
Teeth-imprinted, tell-tale blisses,

Intermix with all thy kisses.
So, when Zephyr's breezy wing
Wafts the balmy breath of spring,
Turtles thus their loves repeat,
Fondly billing, murm'ring sweet,
While their trembling pinions tell
What delights their bosoms swell.

Kiss me, press me, till you feel
All your raptured senses reel;
Till your eyes, half-closed and dim,
In a dizzy transport swim,
And you murmur faintly, "Grasp me,
Swooning, in your arms oh, clasp me."
In my fond sustaining arms
I will hold your drooping charms;
While the long, life-teeming kiss
Shall recall your soul to bliss;
And, as thus the vital store
From my humid lips I pour,
Till exhausted with the play,
All my spirit wastes away;
Sudden, in my turn, I'll cry,
"Oh! support me, for I die."
To your fost'ring breast you'll hold me,
In your warm embrace enfold me;
While your breath, in nectar'd gales,
O'er my sinking soul prevails;
While your kisses sweet impart
Life and rapture to my heart.
    Thus, when youth is in its prime,
Let's enjoy the golden time;
For, when smiling youth is past,
Age these tender joys shall blast:
Sickness, which our bloom impairs;
Slow-consuming, painful cares;
Death, with dire remorseless rage;
All attend the steps of age.

The Wedding Night

(From the Epithalamium of Johannes Secundus)

Thrice happy maid; supremely blest,
Of every wish in one possest;
To thee, on wings of love and truth,
Comes, all-devote, the raptured youth.
Thy bending neck with eager hold,
Thy waist, impatient to enfold.
While, for that hair of easy flow,
While, for that breast of virgin snow,
While, for that lip of rosy dye,
While, for that sweetly-speaking eye,
With silent passion he expires,
And burns with still consuming fires;
Now Phoebus, slow to quit the skies,
Now loit'ring Phoebe, slow to rise
Persists, alternate, to upbraid.
Thrice happy youth! thrice happy maid!

See where the maid, all-panting, lies,
(Ah, never more a maid to rise!)
And longs, yet trembles at thy tread;
Her cheeks suffused with decent red;
Expressing half her inward flame!
Half springing from ingenuous shame!
Tears from her eyes, perhaps, may steal,
Her joys the better to conceal;
Then sighs, with grief unreal fraught,
Then follow plaints of wrongs unthought.
But cease not thou with idle fears,
For all her plaints, or sighs, or tears.
Kiss'd be the tears from off her eyes;
With tender murmurs stopp'd her sighs;
With soothings soft her plaints allay'd.
Thrice happy youth! thrice happy maid!

The maid, in decent order placed,
With every bridal honor graced,
Through all her limbs begin to spread
The glowings of the genial bed;

263

And languid sleep dispose to take,
Did not the youth, more watchful, wake,
And the mild queen of fierce desire,
With warmth not disproportion'd, fire:
Taught hence, nor purpled kings to prize?
Nor scepter'd Jove that rules the skies.
Soon for soft combats he prepares,
And gentle toils of amorous wars.
Declared, but with no dreaded arms;
Kisses! which, wanton as he strays,
He darts a thousand wanton ways,
At mouth or neck, at eyes or cheeks.
Him humbly, she full oft bespeaks,
Entreats, "a helpless maid to spare!"
And begs, with trembling voice, "Forbear!"
Full oft his rudeness loudly blames,
His boundless insolence proclaims.
His lips, with lips averse, withstands,
With hands, restrains his roving hands,
Resistance sweet; delicious fight!
O night! O doubly-happy night!

Contention obstinate succeeds.
The tender Loves contention feeds;
By that redoubled ardor burns;
By that redoubled strength returns.
Now o'er her neck take nimble flight;
Her breast as spotless ivory white;
Her waist of gradual rising charms;
Soft-molded legs; smooth-polish'd arms:
Search all the tracts, in curious sport,
Conductive to the Cyprian court.
Through all the dark recesses go,
And all the shady coverts know.
To this, unnumber'd kisses join,
Unnumber'd as the stars that shine,
Commingling rays of blended light.
O night! O doubly-happy night!

Then spare no blandishments of love;
Sounds, that with soft'ning flattery move;

Sighs, that with soothing murmur please,
The injured virgin to appease;
Such, as when Zephyr fans the grove,
Or coos the am'rous billing dove;
Or sings the swan with tuneful breath,
Conscious of near approaching death;
Till, pierced by Cupid's powerful dart,
As by degrees relents her heart,
The virgin, less and less severe,
Quits, by degrees, her stubborn fear;
Now on your arms her neck reclines;
Now with her arms your neck entwines;
As Love's resistless flames incite.
O night! O doubly-happy night!

Sweet kisses shall reward your pains,
Kisses which no rude rapine stains;
From lips on swelling lips that dwell;
From lips on dwelling lips that swell;
That play return with equal play;
That bliss with equal bliss repay;
That vital stores, from either heart,
Imbibing, soul for soul impart;
Till now the maid, adventurous grown,
Attempts new frolics of her own;
Now suffers, strangers to the way,
Her far more daring hands to stray.
Now sports far more salacious seeks,
Now words far more licentious speaks;
Words that past sufferings well requite.
O night! O doubly-happy night!

To arms! to arms! now Cupid sounds.
Now is the time for grateful wounds,
Here Venus waves the nimble spear—
Venus is warlike goddess here.
Here not thy sister, Mars, presides,
Thy mistress in these conflicts prides;
While close engage the struggling foes,
And, restless, breast to breast oppose;
While, eager, this disputes the field,

And that alike disdains to yield;
Till, lo! in breathless transports tost,
Till in resistless raptures lost,
Their limbs with liquid dews distil;
Their hearts with pleasing horrors thrill;
And faint away in wild delight.
O night! O doubly-happy night!

John Cleveland

One of the lesser Cavalier poets, John Cleveland (1613–1658), son of a poor country clergyman, opposed Cromwell, lost his fellowship at St. John's, and joined the king's army. When the garrison at Newark surrendered, he was arrested, but was pardoned by Cromwell who admired the man's courage. A semi-fictional account of his career is Rose Macaulay's novel, *They Were Defeated*.

Whenas the Nightingale

Whenas the nightingale chanted her vespers,
And the wild forester couched on the ground,
Venus invited me in the evening whispers
Unto a fragrant field with roses crowned;
    Where she before had sent
    My wishes' complement,
    Unto my heart's content
Played with me on the green;
    Never Mark Anthony
    Dallied more wantonly
    With the fair Egyptian Queen.

First on her cherry cheeks I mine eyes feasted,
Thence fear of surfeiting made me retire;
Next on her warmer lips, which when I tasted
My duller spirits made active as fire;
    Then we began to dart,
    Each at another's heart,
    Arrows that knew no smart;
Sweet lips and smiles between.

Never Mark Anthony
Dallied more wantonly
With the fair Egyptian Queen.

Wanting a glass to plait her amber tresses,
Which like a bracelet rich bedecked mine arm,
Gaudier than Juno wears whenas she graces
Jove with embraces more stately than warm;
    Then did she peep in mine
    Eyes' humor crystalline,
    I in her eyes was seen,
  As if we one had been.
    Never Mark Anthony
    Dallied more wantonly
    With the fair Egyptian Queen.

Mystical grammar of amorous glances;
Feeling of pulses, the physic of love,
Rhetorical courtings and musical dances,
Numbering of kisses arithmetic prove
    Eyes like astronomy,
    Straight-limbed geometry:
    In her heart's ingeny
  Our wits are sharp and keen.
    Never Mark Anthony
    Dallied more wantonly
    With the fair Egyptian Queen.

Andrew Marvell

One of the most independent poets of the pre-Restoration period, son of the Master of Hull Grammar School, Andrew Marvell (1621-1658) acquired a wide cultural background during many years of travel on the Continent. Tutor to Cromwell's ward, he became Milton's assistant as Latin secretary to Cromwell. When the Stuarts regained the throne, he was tolerant of Charles II but continued to praise Cromwell and refused to accept favors from the king. He attacked the corrupt court and maintained that the only solution was a republic.

Although an able satirist, Marvell excelled in charming delicacies about nature, love, and the passing of time. These concerns are beautifully combined in his most famous poem, "To His Coy Mistress," a witty treatment of a familiar formula: the persuasive lover and the hesitant lady.

To His Coy Mistress

Had we but world enough and time,
This coyness, lady, were no crime.
We would sit down and think which way
To walk and pass our long love's day.
Thou by the Indian Ganges' side
Should'st rubies find: I by the tide
Of Humber would complain. I would
Love you ten years before the Flood,
And you should, if you please, refuse
Till the conversion of the Jews.

My vegetable love should grow
Vaster than empires, and more slow.
An hundred years should go to praise
Thine eyes, and on thy forehead gaze:
Two hundred to adore each breast:
But thirty thousand to the rest;
An age at least to every part,
And the last age should show your heart.
For, lady, you deserve this state,
Nor would I love at lower rate.

    But at my back I always hear
Time's wingèd chariot hurrying near:
And yonder all before us lie
Deserts of vast eternity.
Thy beauty shall no more be found;
Nor, in thy marble vault, shall sound
My echoing song: then worms shall try
That long-preserved virginity,
And your quaint honor turn to dust,
And into ashes all my lust.
The grave's a fine and private place,
But none, I think, do there embrace.

    Now, therefore, while the youthful hue
Sits on thy skin like morning dew,
And while thy willing soul transpires
At every pore with instant fires,
Now let us sport us while we may:
And now, like amorous birds of prey,
Rather at once our Time devour,
Than languish in his slow-chapt power.
Let us roll all our strength and all
Our sweetness up into one ball,
And tear our pleasures with rough strife
Through the iron gates of life.
Thus, though we cannot make our Sun
Stand still, yet we will make him run.

Jean De La Fontaine

A serious scholar who was also one of the most frivolous of versifiers, Jean De La Fontaine (1621–1695) was born at Chateau-Thierry in Champagne, where he assisted his father, a forest ranger. At twenty-four he published a translation of Terence; at twenty-six he married a girl of fifteen who brought him a large dowry and, according to one biographer, drove him to despair. He left her, went to Paris, found several patronesses, including two "high born ladies who kept him from experiencing the pangs of love and hunger." One of them, Mme de la Sablière, maintained him in her household for twenty years.

La Fontaine's *Fables*, based on Aesop's, are his best-known work, but the *Tales and Novels* are equally adroit pieces of rhyming. The plots were taken from various story-tellers, including Margaret of Navarre, but chiefly from Boccaccio, although some are founded on contemporary scandals. Accused of impropriety, La Fontaine recalled Cicero's rejoinder that "propriety consists in saying what is appropriate to the time, the place, and the person."

To Promise is One Thing,

To Perform is Another

John courts Perrette, but all in vain;
  Love's sweetest oaths and tears and sighs
All potent spells her heart to gain
  The ardent lover vainly tries;
Fruitless his arts to make her waver,
She will not grant the smallest favor.
  A ruse our youth resolved to try
  The cruel fair to mollify:
  Holding his fingers ten outspread
  To Perrette's gaze, and with no dread:
  "So often," said he, "can I prove,
  "My sweet Perrette, how warm my love."
  When lover's last avowals fail
To melt the maiden's coy suspicions,
  A lover's sign will oft prevail
To win the way to soft concessions.

  Half won she takes the tempting bait,
Smiles on him, draws her lover nearer,
  With heart no longer obdurate
She teaches him no more to fear her—
  A pinch,—a kiss,—a kindling eye,—
  Her melting glances,—nothing said.—
  John ceases not his suit to ply
  Till his first finger's debt is paid.
  A second, third and fourth he gains,
  Takes breath, and e'en a fifth maintains.
  But who could long such contest wage?
  Not I, although of fitting age,
  Nor John himself, for here he stopped,
  And further effort sudden dropped.
  Perrette, whose appetite increased

Just as her lover's vigor ceased,
In her fond reckoning defeated,
Considered she was greatly cheated—
    If duty, well discharged, such blame
    Deserve; for many a highborn dame
    Would be content with such deceit.
    But Perrette, as already told,
    Out of her count, began to scold
    And call poor John an arrant cheat
For promising and not performing.
John calmly listened to her storming,
    And well content with work well done,
    Thinking his laurels fairly won,
    Coolly replied, on taking leave:
    "No cause I see to fume and grieve,
    Or for such trifle to dispute;
    To promise and to execute
    Are not the same, be it confessed,
    Suffice it to have done one's best.
    With time I'll yet discharge what's due;
    Meanwhile, my sweet Perrette, adieu!"

A Fair Exchange

As William walking with his wife was seen,
A man of rank admired her lovely mien.
"Who gave you such a charming fair?" he cried.
"May I presume to kiss your beauteous bride?"
"With all my heart," replied the humble swain.
"You're welcome, sir. I beg you'll not refrain.
She's at your service. Take the boon I pray;
You will not get such offers every day."

The gentleman proceeded as desired.
To get a kiss alone he had aspired;
Howe'er, so fervently he pressed her lip
That Petronella blushed at every sip.

A week had scarcely run when, to his arms,
The noble took a wife with seraph charms;

And William was allowed to take a kiss
That filled his soul with soft, ecstatic bliss.
"I wish," cried he, "and truly I am grieved,
That when the gentleman a kiss received
From her I love, he'd gone to greater height
And with my Petronella spent the night."

The Superfluous Saddle

A famous painter, jealous of his wife,
Whose charms he valued more than fame or life,
When going on a journey used his art
To paint an Ass upon a certain part,
(Umbilical, 'tis said) and like a seal:
Impressive token, nothing thence to steal.

A brother painter, favored by the dame,
Now took advantage and declared his flame.
The Ass effaced, though God knows how 'twas done,
Another soon howe'er he had begun,
And finished well, upon the very spot—
In painting, few more skill had ever got.
But, with misguided zeal, it came to pass
He put a saddle on the Ass.

The husband, when returned, desired to look
At what he drew, when leave he lately took.
"Yes, see my dear," the wily wife replied.
"The Ass is witness, faithful I abide."
"Zounds!" said the painter, when he got a sight,
"What!—you'd persuade me ev'ry thing is right?
I wish the witness you display so well,
And him who saddled it, were both in Hell!"

The Gascon Punished

A Gascon, being heard one day to swear
That he'd possessed a certain lovely fair,
Was played a wily trick and nicely served;

'Twas clear from truth he shamefully had swerved.
The dame indeed the Gascon only jeered,
Denied herself to him when he appeared;
For when she met the man who sought to shine
And called her "angel, beauteous and divine,"
She fled and hastened to a female friend.
Where she could laugh and at her ease unbend.

Near Phillis (our fair fugitive) there dwelled
One Eurilas, his nearest neighbor held;
His wife was Cloris—'twas with *her* our dove
Took shelter from the Gascon's forward love,
Whose name was Dorilas—and Damon young
(The Gascon's friend) on whom gay Cloris hung.

Sweet Phillis, by her manner, you might see,
From sly amours and dark intrigues was free;
The value to possess her no one knew,
Though all admired the lovely belle at view.
Just twenty years she counted at the time,
And now a widow was, though in her prime,
(Her spouse, an aged dotard, worth a plum—
Of those whose loss to mourn no tears e'er come.)

Our seraph fair, such loveliness possessed,
In num'rous ways a Gascon could have blessed;
Above, below, appeared angelic charms;
'Twas Paradise, 'twas Heav'n, within her arms!

The Gascon was—a *Gascon*—would you more?
Who knows a Gascon knows at least a score.
I need not say what solemn vows he made;
Alike with Normans Gascons are portrayed;
Their oaths, indeed, won't pass for Gospel truth;
But we believe that Dorilas (the youth)
Loved Phillis to his soul, our lady fair,
Yet he would fain be thought *successful* there.

One day, said Phillis, with unusual glee
(Pretending with the Gascon to be free)
"Do me a favor—nothing very great—

Assist to dupe one jealous of his mate.
You'll find it very easy to be done,
And doubtless 'twill produce a deal of fun.
'Tis my request (the plot you'll say is deep),
That you this night with Cloris' husband sleep.
Some disagreement with her gay gallant
Requires that she at least a night should grant
To settle diff'rences. Now I desire
That you'll to bed with Eurilas retire.
There's not a doubt he'll think his Cloris near;
He never touches her, so nothing fear.
For whether jealousy or other pains,
He constantly from intercourse abstains,
Snores through the night and, if a cap he sees,
Believes his wife in bed and feels at ease.
We'll properly equip you as a belle,
And I will certainly reward you well."

To gain but Phillis' smiles, the Gascon said
He'd with the very devil go to bed.

The night arrived, our man the chamber traced;
The lights extinguished; Eurilas, too, placed.
The Gascon 'gan to tremble in a trice,
And soon with terror grew as cold as ice;
Durst neither spit nor cough; still less encroach;
And seemed to shrink, lest t'other should approach;
Crept near the edge; would scarcely room afford,
And could have passed the scabbard of a sword.

Oft in the night his bed-fellow turned round;
At length a finger on his nose he found,
Which Dorilas exceedingly distressed;
But more inquietude was in his breast,
For fear the husband amorous should grow,
From which incalculable ills might flow.

Our Gascon ev'ry minute knew alarm;
'Twas now a leg stretched out, and then an arm;
He even thought he felt the husband's beard;
But presently arrived what more he feared.

A bell, conveniently, was near the bed,
Which Eurilas to ring was often led;
At this the Gascon swooned, so great his fear,
And swore for ever he'd renounce his dear.
But no one coming, Eurilas once more
Resumed his place, and 'gan again to snore.

At length, before the sun his head had reared,
The door was opened, and a torch appeare1.
Misfortune then he fancied full in sight;
More pleased he'd been to rise without a light,
And clearly thought 'twas over with him now;
The flame approached—the drops ran o'er his brow;
With terror he for pardon humbly prayed.
"You have it," cried a fair. "Be not dismayed."
'Twas Phillis spoke, who Eurilas's place
Had filled, throughout the night, with wily grace,
And now to Damon and his Cloris flew,
With ridicule the Gascon to pursue;
Recounted all the terrors and affright,
Which Dorilas had felt throughout the night.
To mortify still more the silly swain,
And fill his soul with every poignant pain,
She gave a glimpse of beauties to his view,
And from his presence instantly withdrew.

The Ear-Maker and the Mould-Mender

When William went from home (a trader styled),
Six months his better half he left with child,
A simple, comely, modest, youthful dame,
Whose name was Alice; from Champaign she came.
Her neighbor Andrew visits now would pay;
With what intention, needless 'tis to say.
A master who but rarely spread his net,
But, first or last, with full success he met;
And cunning was the bird that 'scaped his snare,
Without surrendering a feather there.

Quite raw was Alice; for his purpose fit;
Not overburdened with a store of wit;

277

Of this indeed she could not be accused,
And Cupid's wiles by her were never used.
Poor lady, all with her was honest part,
And naught she knew of stratagem or art.

Her husband then away, and she alone,
This neighbor came, and in a whining tone,
To her observed, when compliments were o'er—
"I'm all astonishment, and you deplore,
To find that neighbor William's gone from hence,
And left your child's completing in suspense,
Which now you bear within, and much I fear,
That when 'tis born you'll find it wants an ear.
Your looks sufficiently the fact proclaim,
For many instances I've known the same."
"Good heav'ns!" replied the lady in a fright;
"What say you, pray?—the infant won't be right?
Shall I be mother to a one-eared child?
And know you no relief that's certain styled?"
"Oh yes, there is," rejoined the crafty knave,
"From such mishap I can the baby save;
Yet solemnly I vow, for none but you
I'd undertake the toilsome job to do.
The ills of others, if I may be plain,
Except your husband's, never give me pain;
But him I'd serve for ever, while I've breath;
To do him good I'd e'en encounter death.
Now let us see, without more talk or fears,
If I know how to forge the bantling ears."
"Remember," cried the wife, "to make them like."
"Leave that to me," said he, "I'll justly strike."
Then he prepared for work—the dame gave way;
Not difficult she proved—well pleased she lay.
Philosophy was never less required,
And Andrew's process much the fair admired,
Who, to his work extreme attention paid;
'Twas now a tendon; then a fold he made,
Or cartilage, of which he formed enough,
And all without complaining of the stuff.
"Tomorrow we will polish it," said he:
"Then in perfection soon the whole will be;

And from repeating this so oft, you'll get
As perfect issue as was ever met."
"I'm much obliged to you," the wife replied,
"A friend is good in whom we may confide."

Next day, when tardy Time had marked the hour,
That Andrew hoped again to use his pow'r,
He was not plunged in sleep, but briskly flew,
His purpose with the charmer to pursue.
Said he, "All other things aside I've laid,
This ear to finish, and to lend you aid."
"And I," the dame replied, "was on the eve,
To send and beg you not the job to leave;
Above stairs let us go": away they ran,
And quickly recommenced as they began.
The work so oft was smoothed that Alice showed
Some scruples lest the ear he had bestowed
Should do too much, and to the wily wight,
She said, "So little you the labor slight,
'Twere well if ears no more than two appear."
"Of that," rejoined the other, "never fear;
I've guarded thoroughly against defects,
Mistakes like that shall ne'er your senses vex."

The ear howe'er was still in hand the same,
When from his journey home the husband came.
Saluted Alice, who with anxious look,
Exclaimed, "Your work how finely you forsook,
And, but for neighbor Andrew's kindness here,
Our child would incomplete have been—an ear.
I could not let a thing remain like this,
And Andrew would not be to friends remiss,
But, worthy man, he left his thriving trade,
And for the babe a proper ear has made."

The husband, not conceiving how his wife,
Could be so weak and ignorant of life,
The circumstances made her fully tell,
Repeat them o'er and on each action dwell.
Enraged at length, a pistol by the bed
He seized and swore at once he'd shoot her dead.

279

The belle with tears replied, howe'er she'd swerved,
Such cruel treatment never she deserved.
Her innocence, and simple, gentle way,
At length appeared his frantic rage to lay.
"What injury," continued she, "is done?
The strictest scrutiny I would not shun;
Your goods and money, ev'ry thing is right;
And Andrew told me, nothing he would slight;
That you would find much more than you could want;
And this I hope to me you'll freely grant.
If falsehood I advance, my life I'll lose;
Your equity, I trust, will me excuse."

A little cooled, then William thus replied,
"We'll say no more; you have been drawn aside;
What passed you fancied acting for the best,
And I'll consent to put the thing at rest;
To nothing good such altercations tend;
I've but a word: to that attention lend;
Contrive tomorrow that I here entrap
This fellow who has caused your sad mishap;
You'll utter not a word of what I've said.
Be secret, or at once I'll strike you dead.
Adroitly you must act. For instance, say
I'm on a second journey gone away;
A message or a letter to him send,
Soliciting that he'll on *you* attend,
That something you have got to let him know—
To come, no doubt, the rascal won't be slow;
Amuse him then with converse most absurd,
But of the EAR remember—not a word;
That's finished now, and nothing can require;
You'll carefully perform what I desire."
Poor innocent! the point she nicely hit;
Fear oft gives simpletons a sort of wit.

The arch gallant arrived. The husband came:
Ascended to the room where sat his dame.
Much noise he made, his coming to announce.
The lover, terrified, began to bounce;
Now here, now there, no shelter could he meet;

Between the bed and wall he put his feet,
And lay concealed, while William loudly knocked;
Fair Alice readily the door unlocked,
And, pointing with her hand, informed the spouse,
Where he might easily his rival rouse.

The husband ev'ry way was armed so well,
He four such men as Andrew could repel;
In quest of succor howsoe'er he went:
To kill him surely William never meant,
But only take an ear, or what the Turks,
Those savage beasts, cut off from Nature's works,
Which doubtless must be infinitely worse:
Infernal practice and continual curse.
'Twas this he whispered should be Andrew's doom,
When with his easy wife he left the room;
She nothing durst reply. The door he shut,
And our gallant 'gan presently to strut
Around and round, believing all was right,
And William unacquainted with his plight.

The latter having well the project weighed,
Now changed his plan, and other schemes surveyed;
Proposed within himself revenge to take,
With less parade: less noise it then would make,
And better fruit the action would produce
Than if he were apparently profuse.
Said he to Alice, "Go and seek his wife;
To her relate the whole that caused our strife;
Minutely all from first to last detail;
And then the better on her to prevail,
To hasten here, you'll hint that you have fears,
That Andrew risks the loss of—more than ears,
For I have punishment severe in view,
Which greatly she must wish I should not do;
But if an ear-maker, like this, is caught,
The worst of chastisement is always sought;
Such horrid things as scarcely can be said:
They make the hair to stand upon the head;
That he's upon the point of suff'ring straight,
And only for her presence things await;

That though she cannot all proceedings stay
Perhaps she may some portion take away.
Go. Bring her instantly. Haste quickly. Run.
And if she comes, I'll pardon what's been done."

With joy to Andrew's house fair Alice went;
The wife to follow her appeared content;
Quite out of breath, alone she ran up stairs,
And, not perceiving him who shared her cares,
Believed he was imprisoned in a room;
And while with fear she trembled for his doom,
The master (having laid aside his arms)
Now came to compliment the lady's charms;
He gave the belle a chair, who looked most nice.
Said he, "Ingratitude's the worst of vice;
To me your husband has been wondrous kind;
So many services has done I find,
That, ere you leave this house, I'd wish to make
A like return, and this you will partake.
When I was absent from my loving dear,
Obligingly he made her babe an ear.
The compliment of course I must admire;
Retaliation is what I desire,
And I've a thought—your children all have got
The nose a little short, which is a blot;
A fault within the mould no doubt's the cause,
Which I can mend, and any other flaws.
The business now let's execute I pray,"
On which the dame he took without delay,
And placed her near where Andrew hid his head,
Then 'gan to operate as he was led.

The lady patiently his process bore,
And blessed her stars that Andrew's risk was o'er:
That she had thus the dire return received,
And saved the man for whom her bosom grieved.
So much emotion William seemed to feel,
No grace he gave, but all performed with zeal;
Retaliated ev'ry way so well,
He measure gave for measure—ell for ell.

How true the adage, that revenge is sweet!
The plan he followed clearly was discrete;
For since he wished his honor to repair—
Of any better way I'm not aware.

The whole without a murmur Andrew viewed,
And thanked kind Heav'n that nothing worse ensued;
One ear most readily he would have lost,
Could he be certain *that* would pay the cost.
He thought 'twould lucky be, could he get out,
For all considered, better 'twere no doubt,
Howe'er ridiculous the thing appears,
To have a pair of horns than lose his ears.

The Cudgelled But Contented Cuckold

Some time ago from Rome, in smart array,
A younger brother homeward bent his way,
Not much improved, as frequently the case
With those who travel to that famous place.
Upon the road oft finding, where he stayed,
Delightful wines and handsome belle or maid.
With careless ease he loitered up and down . . .
One day there passed him in a country town,
Attended by a page, a lady fair,
Whose charming form and all-engaging air,
At once his bosom fired with fond desire;
And nearer still, her beauties to admire.
He most gallantly saw her safely home—
Attentions charm the sex where'er we roam.

Our thoughtless rambler pleasures always sought:
From Rome this spark had num'rous pardons brought;
But—as to virtues (this too oft we find),
He'd left them—with his holiness behind!

The lady was, by ev'ry one, confessed,
Of beauty, youth, and elegance possessed;
She wanted naught to form her bliss below,
But one whose love would ever fondly flow.

Indeed so fickle proved this giddy youth,
That nothing long would please his heart or tooth;
Howe'er he earnestly inquired her name,
And ev'ry other circumstance the same.
She's lady, they replied, to great 'squire Good,
Who's almost bald from age 'tis understood;
But as he's rich, and high in rank appears,
Why that's a recompense, you know, for years.

These facts our young gallant no sooner gained,
But ardent hopes at once he entertained;
To wily plots his mind he quickly bent,
And to a neighb'ring town his servants sent;
Then, at the house where dwelled our noble 'squire,
His humble services proposed for hire.

Pretending ev'ry sort of work he knew,
He soon a fav'rite with old Square-toes grew,
Who (first advising with his charming mate),
Chief falc'ner made him o'er his fine estate.

The new domestic much the lady pleased;
He watched, and eagerly the moment seized
His ardent passion boldly to declare,
In which he showed a novice had no share.

'Twas managed well, for nothing but the chase
Could Square-toes tempt to quit her fond embrace,
And then our falc'ner must his steps attend:
The very time he wished at home to spend.
The lady similar emotions showed;
For opportunity their bosoms glowed.
And who will feel in argument so bold,
When this I say, the contrary to hold?
At length with pity Cupid saw the case,
And kindly lent his aid to their embrace.

One night the lady said, with eager eyes,
My dear, among our servants, which d'ye prize,
For moral conduct most and upright heart?
To this her spouse replied, the faithful part

Is with the falc'ner found, I must decide:
To *him* my life I'd readily confide.

Then you are wrong, said she, most truly so,
For he's a good-for-nothing wretch I know;
You'll scarcely credit, but t'other day,
He had the barefaced impudence to say,
He loved me much, and then his passion pressed:
I'd nearly fallen, I was so distressed.
To tear his eyes out, I designed at first,
And e'en to choke this wretch, of knaves the worst;
By prudence solely was I then restrained,
For fear the world should think his point was gained.

The better then to prove his dark intent,
I feigned an inclination to consent,
And in the garden, promised as tonight,
I'd near the pear-tree meet this roguish wight.
Said I, my husband never moves from hence;
No jealous fancy, but to show the sense
He entertains of my pure, virtuous life,
And fond affection for a loving wife.
Thus circumstanced, your wishes see are vain,
Unless when he's asleep a march I gain,
And softly stealing from his torpid side,
With trembling steps I to my lover glide.
So things remain, my dear, an odd affair.
On this Square-toes 'gan to curse and swear;
But *his* fond rib most earnestly besought,
His rage to stifle, as she clearly thought,
He might in person, if he'd take the pain,
Secure the rascal and redress obtain.
You know, said she, the tree is near the door,
Upon the left and bears of fruit great store;
But if I may my sentiments express,
In cap and petticoats you'd best to dress;
His insolence is great, and you'll be right,
To give your strokes with double force tonight;
Well work his back; flat lay him on the ground;
A rascal honorable ladies round,
No doubt he many times has served the same;
'Tis such impostors characters defame.

To rouse his wrath the story quite sufficed;
The spouse resolved to do as she advised.
Howe'er to dupe him was an easy lot;
The hour arrived, his dress he soon had got,
Away he ran with anxious fond delight.
In hopes the wily spark to trap that night.
But no one there our easy fool could see,
And while he waited near the fav'rite tree,
Half dead with cold, the falc'ner slyly stole,
To her who had so well contrived the whole;
Time, place, and disposition, all combined.
The loving pair to mutual joys resigned.
When our expert gallant had with the dame
An hour or more indulged his ardent flame,
Though forced at length to quit the loving lass
'Twas not without the favourite parting glass.
He then the garden sought, where long the 'squire,
Upon the knave had wished to vent his ire.

No sooner he the silly husband spied,
But feigning 'twas the wily wife he eyed,
At once he cried, "Ah, vilest of the sex!
Are these thy tricks, so good a man to vex?
Oh shame upon thee! thus to treat his love,
As pure as snow, descending from above.
I could not think thou hadst so base a heart,
But clear it is, thou need'st a friendly part,
And that I'll act: I asked this rendezvous
With full intent to see if thou wert true;
And, God be praised, without a loose design,
To plunge in luxuries pronounced divine.
Protect me Heav'n! poor sinner that I'm here!
To guard thy honor I will persevere.
My worthy master could I thus disgrace?
Thou wanton baggage with unblushing face,
Thee on the spot I'll instantly chastise,
And then thy husband of the fact advise."

The fierce harangue o'er Squares-toes pleasure spread,
Who, muttering 'tween his teeth, with fervor said:
"O gracious Lord! to thee my thanks are due—

286

To have a wife so chaste—a man so true!
But presently he felt upon his back
The falc'ner's cudgel vigorously thwack,
Who soundly basted him as on he ran,
To gain the house, with terror, pale and wan.

    The 'squire had wished his trusty man, no doubt,
Had not, at cudgelling, been quite so stout;
But since he showed himself so true a friend,
And with his actions could such prudence blend,
The master fully pardoned what he knew,
And quickly to his wife in bed he flew,
When he related every thing that passed:
Were we, cried he, a hundred years to last,
My lovely dear, we ne'er on earth could find
A man so faithful, and so well inclined.
I'd have him take within our town a wife,
And you and I'll regard him during life.
In that, replied the lady, we agree,
And heartily thereto I pledged will be.

Charles Cotton

Charles Cotton (1630–1687) could do almost anything; his versatility prevented him from doing any one thing greatly. He translated Montaigne, burlesqued the Latin poets, showed himself to be a good gardener in *The Planter's Manual*, reveled as a tipster in *The Compleat Gamester*, and was enough of an expert to furnish a supplement to Izaak Walton's *The Compleat Angler*—his initials and Walton's were intertwined above Walton's door. Cotton's poetic talent was limited but distinct; his lyrics are clean-cut, candid, and spiced with unaffected wit.

Alice

Alice is tall and upright as a pine,
White as blanched almonds or the falling snow,
Sweet as are damask roses when they blow,
And doubtless fruitful as the swelling vine.

Ripe to be cut and ready to be pressed,
Her full-cheeked beauties very well appear;
And a year's fruit she loses every year,
Wanting a man to improve her to the best.

Full fain she would be husbanded; and yet,
Alas, she cannot a fit laborer get
To cultivate her to his own content.

Fain would she (God wot) about her task,
And yet (forsooth) she is too proud to ask,
And (which is worse) too modest to consent.

Margaret

Margaret of humbler stature by the head
Is (as it oft falls out with yellow hair)
Than her fair sister, yet so much more fair
As her pure white is better mixed with red.

This, hotter than the other ten to one,
Longs to be put unto her mother's trade,
And loud proclaims she lives too long a maid,
Wishing for one to untie her virgin zone.

She finds virginity a kind of ware
That's very, very troublesome to bear,
And being gone she thinks will ne'er be missed:

And yet withal the girl has so much grace,
To call for help I know she wants the face,
Though, asked, I know not how she would resist.

John Dryden

A proud poet laureate and a greedy opportunist, John Dryden (1631–1700) was called "the glory and the shame of our literature." He despised the taste of his day and catered to it; he aimed to write tragedies in the grand manner, but when the public demanded frivolous plays, Dryden, who disliked comedies, supplied them. He turned out a new play almost every year for nineteen years. There was nothing he could not do. Before he died at seventy he had written in every possible vein: odes, tracts, essays, librettos for Purcell's music, modernizations of Chaucer, adaptations of Shakespeare, translations from Latin poets, especially Lucretius, Ovid, and Juvenal (see pages 39, 55, and 78), heroic stanzas, religious poems, an attempt to enliven *Paradise Lost* by adding rhymes, and two of the greatest satires of all time.

As a person Dryden was both shy and aloof; as a wit his conversation was taciturn rather than tart. "My humor is saturnine," he said. "I am none of those who endeavor to break jests in company or make repartees." Nevertheless, his poems are full of brisk playfulness, and the lyrics interspersed throughout his plays run from the piquant to the provocatively libidinous. They were so popular that many were incorporated in the songbooks of the period and were sung long after the dramas were forgotten.

After the Pangs

(From *An Evening's Love*)

After the pangs of a desperate lover
When a day and night I have sighed all in vain,
Ah, what a pleasure it is to discover
In her eyes pity who causes my pain.

When with unkindness our love at a stand is
And both have punish'd our selves with the pain,
Ah, what a pleasure the touch of her hand is!
Ah, what a pleasure to touch it again!

When the denial comes fainter and fainter
And her eyes give what her tongue does deny,
Ah, what a trembling I feel when I venture,
Ah, what a trembling does usher my joy!

When, with a sigh, she accords me the blessing,
And her eyes twinkle 'twixt pleasure and pain,
Ah, what a joy 'tis beyond all expressing!
Ah, what a joy to hear, "Shall we again?"

Whilst Alexis Lay Prest

(From *Marriage à la Mode*)

Whilst Alexis lay prest
In her arms he loved best
With his hands round her neck
And his head on her breast
He found the fierce pleasure too hasty to stay,
And his soul in the tempest just flying away.

When Celia saw this,
With a sigh and a kiss,
She cried, "Oh, my dear, I am robbed of my bliss!
'Tis unkind to your love, and unfaithfully done,
To leave me behind you, and die all alone."

The youth, though in haste
And breathing his last
In pity died slowly, while she died more fast;
Till at length she cried, "Now, my dear, now let us go:
Now die, my Alexis, and I will die too!"

Thus entranced they did lie,
Till Alexis did try
To recover new breath that again he might die.
Then often they died; but the more they did so,
The nymph died more quick, and the shepherd more slow.

Beneath a Myrtle Shade

(From *The Conquest of Granada*)

Beneath a myrtle shade,
Which love for none but happy lovers made,
I slept; and straight my love before me brought
Phyllis, the object of my waking thought;
Undressed she came my flames to meet,
While Love strowed flowers beneath her feet;
Flowers which, so pressed by her, became more sweet.

From the bright vision's head
A careless veil of lawn was loosely spread;
From her white temples fell her shaded hair,
Like cloudy sunshine, not too brown nor fair;
Her hands, her lips, did love inspire;
Her every grace my heart did fire:
But most her eyes, which languished with desire.

"Ah, charming fair," said I,
"How long can you my bliss and yours deny?
By nature and by love this lonely shade
Was for revenge of suff'ring lovers made.
Silence and shades with love agree:

Both shelter you and favor me;
You cannot blush, because I cannot see."

  "No, let me die," she said,
"Rather than lose the spotless name of maid!"
Faintly, methought, she spoke; for all the while
She bid me not believe her, with a smile.
"Then die," said I: she still denied:
"And is it thus, thus, thus," she cried,
"You use a harmless maid?"—and so she died!

  I waked, and straight I knew
I loved so well, it made my dream prove true:
Fancy, the kinder mistress of the two,
Fancy had done what Phyllis would not do!
Ah, cruel nymph, cease your disdain;
While I can dream, you scorn in vain—
Asleep or waking, you must ease my pain.

Sylvia, the Fair

(From *Sylvae*)

Sylvia the fair, in the bloom of fifteen
Felt an innocent warmth as she lay on the green:
She had heard of a pleasure, and something she guessed
By the towzing and tumbing and touching her breast:
She saw the men eager, but was at a loss,
What they meant by their sighing and kissing so close;
    By their praying and whining
    And clasping and twining
    And panting and wishing
    And sighing and kissing
    And sighing and kissing so close.

Ah! she cry'd, ah! for a languishing maid
In a country of Christians to die without aid.
Not a Whig, or a Tory, or Trimmer at least,
Or a Protestant parson or Catholic priest
To instruct a young virgin that is at a loss
What they meant by their sighing and kissing so close;

By their praying and whining
And clasping and twining
And panting and wishing
And sighing and kissing
And sighing and kissing so close.

Cupid in shape of a swain did appear,
He saw the sad wound, and in pity drew near,
Then show'd her his arrow, and bid her not fear,
For the pain was no more than a maiden may bear;
When the balm was infus'd she was not at a loss
What they meant by their sighing and kissing so close;
By their praying and whining
And clasping and twining
And panting and wishing
And sighing and kissing
And sighing and kissing so close.

Sung by a Young Girl

Young I am, and yet unskill'd
How to make a lover yield:
How to keep or how to gain,
When to love and when to feign.

Take me, take me, some of you,
While I yet am young and true;
Ere I can my soul disguise;
Heave my breasts and roll my eyes.

Stay not till I learn the way,
How to lie and to betray:
He that has me first is blest,
For I may deceive the rest.

Could I find a blooming youth,
Full of love and full of truth,
Brisk, and of a jaunty mien
I should long to be fifteen.

Hourly I Die

(From *Amphitryon*)

Fair Iris I love and hourly I die,
But not for a slip nor a languishing eye:
She's fickle and false and there we agree;
For I am as false and as fickle as she:
We neither believe what either can say;
And neither believing we neither betray.

'Tis civil to swear, and say things of course;
We mean not the taking for better or worse;
When present, we love, when absent, agree;
I think not of Iris, nor Iris of me:
The legend of love no couple can find
So easy to part, or so equally joined.

Kiss Me, Dear

Chloe found Amyntas lying
   All in tears upon the plain,
Sighing to himself and crying,
   Wretched I to love in vain!
Kiss me, dear, before my dying;
   Kiss me once and ease my pain.

Sighing to himself and crying,
   Wretched I to love in vain!
Ever scorning and denying
   To reward your faithful swain.
Kiss me, dear, before my dying;
   Kiss me once and ease my pain!

Ever scorning and denying
   To reward your faithful swain.
Chloe, laughing at his crying,
   Told him that he lov'd in vain:
Kiss me, dear, before my dying;
   Kiss me once and ease my pain!

Chloe, laughing at his crying,
   Told him that he lov'd in vain;
But repenting and complying,
   When he kiss'd she kiss'd again:
Kiss'd him up before his dying;
   Kiss'd him up and eas'd his pain.

Sir George Etherege

In common with other poets of his day, Sir George Etherege (c. 1635–1692) was a dramatist who put his dissolute life into his plays. Inspired by Molière, he devoted himself to the comedy of wit and intrigue; in turn he influenced Goldsmith and Sheridan and was a forerunner of the comedy of manners. A diplomat in the service of two kings, he drank, flirted, and finessed his way from Turkey to Holland and Germany and died in Paris.

To Little or No Purpose

To little or no purpose I spent many days
In ranging the Park, the Exchange, and the Plays;
For ne'er in my rambles till now did I prove
So lucky to meet with the man I could love.
   Oh! how I am pleased when I think on this man,
   That I find I must love, let me do what I can!

How long I shall love him I can no more tell
Than, had I a fever, when I should be well.
My passion shall kill me before I will show it,
And yet I would give all the world he did know it;
   But oh, how I sigh when I think should he woo me,
   I cannot deny what I know would undo me!

Charles Sackville

Sixth Earl of Dorset, Charles Sackville (1638–1706) was in the first Parliament of King Charles II. Like many of his colleagues, he was a scapegrace fellow; he became, says Chambers' *Biographical Dictionary,* "an especial favorite of the king, notorious for his boisterous and indecorous frolics." Although he wrote several satires, he survives by virtue—if that is the right word—of a few lyrics.

May the Ambitious Ever Find

May the ambitious ever find
  Reward in crowds and noise,
Whilst gentle love does fill my mind
  With silent real joys.

May fools and knaves grow rich and great
  And the world think 'em wise,
Whilst I lie dying at her feet
  And all the world despise.

Let conquering kings new trophies raise
  And melt in court delights:
Her eyes shall give me brighter days,
  Her arms much softer nights.

The Fire of Love

The fire of love in youthful blood,
Like what is kindled in brushwood,
    But for a moment burns;
Yet in that moment makes a mighty noise;
It crackles, and to vapor turns,
    And soon itself destroys.

But when crept into agèd veins
It slowly burns and then long remains
    And with a silent heat,
Like fire in logs, it glows and warms them long;
And though the flame be not so great,
    Yet is the heat as strong.

Aphra Behn

Aphra Behn (1640–1689) was a multiple woman formed by multiple contradictions. She was the daughter of a barber and a housemaid, her early life was (says one commentator) "obscure and probably improper," yet she married a wealthy merchant, queened it in society, and at nineteen was known as "the Incomparable." A wit skilled in intrigue, she was the first woman to support herself by her pen. At forty she was the author of fifteen plays, countless poems, a popular pseudo-autobiographical novel, and many tales. As if this were not enough for one woman, she was also a spy. Her charm was so great that, when Charles II sent her to Antwerp at the outbreak of the Dutch war, she had no trouble getting secret information from the enemy.

Jealousy brought about her downfall; toward the end of her life she fell out of favor into poverty and a debtor's prison. However, in spite of scandal, she was buried in Westminster Abbey.

That Beauty I Ador'd Before

That beauty I ador'd before
  I now as much despise:
'Tis money only makes the whore:
  She that for love with her crony lies,
Is chaste: But that's the whore that kisses for prize.

Let Jove with gold his Danaë woo
  It shall be no rule for me:
Nay, 't may be I may do so too
  When I'm as old as he.
Till then I'll never hire the thing that's free.

If coin must your affection imp
   Pray get some other friend:
My pocket ne'er shall be my pimp
   I never that intend,
Yet can be noble too, if I see they mend.

Since loving was a liberal art
   How canst thou trade for gain?
'Tis pleasure is on your part,
   'Tis we men take the pain:
And being so, must Women have the gain?

No, no, I'll never farm your bed
   Nor your smock-tenant be:
I hate to rent your white and red,
   You shall not let your love to me:
I court a Mistress, not a Landlady.

A pox take him that first set up
   The exercise of flesh and skin:
And since it will no better be
   Let's both to kiss begin;
To kiss freely: if not, you may go spin.

When Damon First Began to Love

When Damon first began to love
He languisht in a soft desire
And knew not how the gods do move
To lessen or increase his fire,
For Celia in her charming eyes
Were all love's sweets, and all his cruelties.

But as beneath a shade he lay
Weaving of flowers for Celia's hair
She chanced to lead her flock that way
And saw the amorous shepherd there.
She gazed around upon the place
And saw the grove (resembling night)
To all the joys of love invite,

301

Whilst guilty smiles and blushes drest her face
At this the bashful youth all transport grew
And with kind force he taught the virgin how
To yield what all his sighs could never do.

O What Pleasure 'Tis to Find

O what pleasure 'tis to find
   A coy heart melt by slow degrees
When to yielding 'tis inclined,
   Yet her fear a ruin sees;
When her tears do kindly flow
And her sighs do come and go!

O how charming 'tis to meet
   Soft resistance from the fair,
When her pride and wishes meet
   And by turns increase her care;
O how charming 'tis to know
She would yield but can't tell how!

O how pretty is her scorn
   When, confused 'twixt love and shame,
Still refusing, tho' she burn,
   The soft pressures of my flame!
Her pride in her denial lies
And mine is in my victories.

The Willing Mistress

Amyntas led me to a grove
   Where all the trees did shade us;
The sun itself, though it had strove,
   It could not have betray'd us:
The place secur'd from human eyes,
   No other fear allows,
But when the winds that gently rise
   Do kiss the yielding boughs.

302

Down there we sat upon the moss
And did begin to play
A thousand amorous tricks to pass
The heat of all the day.
A many kisses he did give:
And I return'd the same
Which made me willing to receive
That which I dare not name.

His charming eyes no aid requir'd
To tell their softening tale;
On her that was already fir'd
'Twas easy to prevail.
He did but kiss and clasp me round
Whilst those his thoughts expressed:
And lay'd me gently on the ground;
Ah! who can guess the rest?

Beneath a Cool Shade

Beneath a cool shade, where some here have been,
Convenient for lovers, most pleasant and green,
Alexis and Chloris lay pressing soft flowers,
She close in his arms with her head on his breast,
And fainting with pleasure; you guess at the rest:
She blushed and she sighed with a joy beyond measure,
All ravished with billing and dying with pleasure.

But while thus in transports extended they lay,
A handsome young shepherd was passing that way.
She saw him and cried, "Oh, Alexis, betrayed!
Oh what have you done? You have ruined a maid!"
But the shepherd, being modest, discreetly past by,
And left them again at their leisure to die.
And often they languished with joy beyond measure,
All ravished with billing and dying with pleasure.

Thomas Shadwell

The man who succeeded Dryden as poet laureate, Thomas Shadwell (c. 1642–1692), is famous only because of Dryden's scorn. Shadwell was foolish enough to attack Dryden, whereupon the latter made him the butt of ridicule in his savage "MacFlecknoe" and "Absalom and Achitophel." Of Shadwell's works, which run to five large volumes, little remains; his name persists chiefly because of Dryden's lines supposedly spoken by a deceased minor poet:

> Shadwell alone my perfect image bears,
> Mature in dullness from his tender years;
> Shadwell alone of all my sons is he
> Who stands confirmed in full stupidity.
> The rest to some faint meaning make pretense,
> But Shadwell never deviates into sense.

Love and Wine

The delights of the bottle and charms of old wine
To the power and the pleasure of love must resign;
Though the night in the joy of good drinking be passed,
The debauches but till the next morning will last.
But love's great debauch is more lasting and strong
For that often lasts a man all his life long.

Love and wine are the bonds that fasten us all;
The world but for these to confusion would fall.
Were it not for the pleasures of love and good wine
Mankind for each trifle their loves would resign;
They'd not value life nor could live without thinking,
Nor would kings rule the world but for love and good drinking.

John Wilmot, Earl of Rochester

The court of Charles II was largely composed of profligates, perverts, rogues and rakehells. John Wilmot, Earl of Rochester (1647–1680) was one of the ringleaders, a boon companion of the king, whom he both patronized and satirized. Sometimes he went too far and was expelled from the court, but his "exile" was spent on his own luxurious estate, and he was soon back to accompany the king on another licentious escapade. A serious as well as a scurrilous poet, Rochester died at thirty-three.

Several of his poems seem written by a satyr rather than a satirist. Impotence at the crucial moment was a problem that bothered Rochester considerably. He wrote at least three variations on the theme. It is interesting to compare "The Disappointment" with "The Imperfect Enjoyment." The first is phrased in the approved pastoral manner, prettily artificial in its pseudo-formality. The second is colloquial in language, candid in style, and reaches its climax—or anti-climax—in a brutal tirade against the member which betrayed his manhood.

Most of Rochester's works were published posthumously, but many remained in manuscript. It was not until 1926, more than two and a half centuries after their composition, that a large collection was printed in England and forbidden entry to the United States. The salacious "Ramble in St. James Park" and a play, *Sodom* (adequately described by its subtitle, "The Quintessence of Debauchery"), are still on the prohibited list.

The Disappointment

One day the amorous Lysander,
  By an impatient passion swayed,
  Surprised fair Cloris, that loved maid,
Who could defend herself no longer;
All things did with his love conspire.
  The gilded planet of the day,
In his gay chariot, drawn by fire,
  Was now descending to the sea,
And left no light to guide the world,
But what from Cloris' brighter eyes was hurled.

In a lone thicket made for love,
  Silent as yielding maid's consent,
  She, with a charming languishment
Permits his force, yet gently strove.
Her hands his bosom softly meet,
  But not to put him back designed,
  Rather to draw him on inclined,
Whilst he lay trembling at her feet.
Resistance 'tis too late to show;
She wants the power to say, "Ah! What d'you do!"

Her bright eyes sweet and yet severe,
  Where love and shame confus'dly strive,
  Fresh vigor to Lysander give;
And, whisp'ring softly in his ear,
She cried, "Cease, cease your vain desire,
  Or I'll call out 'What would you do?'
  My dearer honor even to you,
I cannot, must not, give. Retire,
Or take that life whose chiefest part
I gave you with the conquest of my heart."

But he, as much unused to fear,
  As he was capable of love,
  The blessèd minutes to improve,
Kisses her lips, her neck, her hair!
Each touch her new desires alarms!
  His burning, trembling hand he pressed
  Upon her melting, snowy breast,
While she lay panting in his arms!
All her unguarded beauties lie,
The spoils and trophies of the enemy.

And now without respect or fear,
  He seeks the object of his vows.
  His love no modesty allows.
By swift degrees, advancing where
His daring hand that altar seized,
  Where gods of love do sacrifice.
  That awful throne! That Paradise!
Where rage is tamed and anger pleased.
That living fountain from whose trills
The melted soul in liquid drops distills!

Her balmy lips encountering his,
  Their bodies as their souls they joined,
  Where both in transports unconfined,
Extend themselves upon the moss.
Cloris half dead and breathless lay,
  Her eyes appeared like humid light,
  Such as divides the day and night,
Or falling stars whose fires decay;
And now no sign of life she shows,
But what, in short-breathed sighs, returns and goes.

He saw how at her length she lay;
  He saw her rising bosom bare;
  Her loose thin robes, through which appear
A shape designed for love and play.
Abandoned by her pride and shame,
  She does her softest sweets dispense,
  Off'ring her virgin innocence
A victim to love's sacred flame.

Whilst the o'er-ravished shepherd lies,
Unable to perform the sacrifice.

Ready to taste a thousand joys,
   The too-transported, hapless swain
   Found the vast pleasure turned to rain.
Pleasure! which too much love destroys!
The willing garment by he laid
   And heaven all opened to his view.
   Mad to possess himself he threw
On the defenseless, lovely maid!
But oh! what envious gods conspire
To snatch his power, yet leave him the desire!

Nature's support, without whose aid,
   She can no human being give,
   Itself now wants the art to live.
Faintness its slackened nerves invade.
In vain th' enragèd youth assayed
   To call his fleeting vigor back;
   No motion 'twill from motion take;
Excessive love is love betrayed.
In vain he toils, in vain commands.
Th' insensible fell weeping in his hands.

Cloris returning from the trance,
   Which love and soft desire had bred,
   Her timorous hand she gently laid,
Or guided by design or chance,
Upon that fabulous priapus,
   That potent god (as poets feign),
But never did young shepherdess,
   Gath'ring of fern upon the plain,
More nimbly draw her fingers back,
Finding beneath the verdant leaves a snake.

Then Cloris her fair hand withdrew,
   Finding that god of her desires
   Disarmed of all his powerful fires,
And cold as flowers bathed in morning dew.
Who can the nymph's confusion guess?

The blood forsook the kinder place
And strewed with blushes all her face,
Which doth disdain and shame express;
And from Lysander's arms she fled,
Leaving him fainting on the gloomy bed.

Like lightning through the grove she hies,
    Or Daphne from the Delphic god.
    No print upon the grassy road
She leaves t'instruct pursuing eyes.
The wind that wantoned in her hair
    And with her ruffled garments played,
    Discovered in the flying maid
All that the gods e'er made of fair.
So Venus when her love was slain,
With fear and haste flew o'er the fatal plain.

The nymph's resentment none but I
    Can well imagine and condole.
    But none can guess Lysander's soul
But those who swayed his destiny.
His silent griefs swell up in storms,
    And not one god his fury spares;
    He cursed his birth, his fate, his stars,
But more the shepherdess's charms,·
Whose soft bewitching influence
Had damn'd him to the depths of impotence.

The Imperfect Enjoyment

Naked she lay, clasped in my longing arms,
I filled with love, and she all over charms,
Both equally inspired with eager fire,
Melting through kindness, flaming in desire.
With arms, lips, legs close clinging to embrace,
She clips me to her breast, and sucks me to her face.
The nimble tongue (love's lesser lightning) played
Within my mouth, and to my thoughts conveyed
Swift orders that I should prepare to throw

309

The all-dissolving thunderbolt below.
My fluttering soul, sprung with the pointed kiss,
Hangs hovering o'er her balmy limbs of bliss.
But whilst her busy hand would guide that part
Which should convey my soul up to her heart,
In liquid raptness I dissolve all o'er,
Melting in love, such joys ne'er felt before.
A touch from any part of her had done't,
Her hand, her foot, her very looks had charms upon't.
Smiling, she chides in a soft murmuring noise,
And sighs to feel the too-too hasty joys;
When with a thousand kisses, wand'ring o'er
My panting breast—and is there then no more?
She cries: All this to love and raptures due,
Must we not pay a debt to pleasure too?

But I the most forlorn, lost man alive
To show my wish'd obedience vainly strive.
I sigh, alas, and kiss, but cannot drive.
Eager desires confound my first intent,
Succeeding shame does more success prevent,
And rage at last confirms me impotent.
Even her fair hands which might bid heat return
To frozen age, and make cold hermits burn,
Applied to my dead cinder warms no more
Than fire to ashes could past flames restore.
Trembling, confused, despairing, limber, dry,
A wishing, weak, unmoving lump I lie.
This dart of love, whose piercing point oft tried
With virgin blood, a hundred maids has dyed,
Which nature still directed with such art
That it, through every port, reached every heart.
Stiffly resolved, turned careless I invade,
Where it essayed, nor ought its fury stayed,
Where e'er it pierced, entrance it found or made,
Now languid lies, in this unhappy hour,
Shrunk up and sapless, like a withered flower.

Thou treacherous, base, deserter of my flame,
False to my passion, fatal to my fame,
By what mistaken magic dost thou prove

So true to lewdness, so untrue to love?
What oyster, cinder, beggar, common whore,
Didst thou e'er fail in all they life before?
When vice, disease, and scandal led the way
With what officious haste didst thou obey?
Like a rude-roaring Hector in the streets
That scuffles, cuffs, and ruffles all he meets;
But if his King or country claim his aid
The rascal villain shrinks and hides his head;
E'en so is thy brutal valour displayed,
Breaks every stews, does each small crack invade,
But if great love the onset does command,
Base recreant to thy Prince, thou dost not stand.
Worst part of me and henceforth hated most,
Through all the town the common rubbing-post,
On whom each wretch relieves her lustful want,
As hogs on goats do rub themselves and grunt,
May'st thou to ravenous shankers be a prey,
Or in consuming weepings waste away;
May stranguries and stone thy days attend.
May'st thou not piss who did'st so much offend
When all my joys did on false thee depend.
And may ten thousand abler men agree
To do the wrong'd Corinna right for thee.

Upon Leaving His Mistress

'Tis not that I am weary grown
Of being yours, and yours alone;
But with what face can I incline
To damn you to be only mine—
You, whom some kinder power did fashion,
By merit, and by inclination,
The joy at least of a whole nation?

Let meaner spirits of your sex
With humble aims their thoughts perplex,
And boast if by their arts they can
Contrive to make one happy man;
While, moved by an impartial sense,

Favors, like Nature, you dispense
With universal influence.

See, the kind seed-receiving earth
To every grain affords a birth:
On her no showers unwelcome fall;
Her willing womb retains them all.
And shall my Celia be confined?
No, live up to thy mighty mind,
And be the mistress of mankind!

The Platonic Lady

I could love thee till I die
Wouldst thou love me modestly,
And ne'er press, whilst I do live
For more than willingly I would give;
Which should sufficient be to prove
I understand the art of love.

I hate the thing that's called enjoyment;
Besides it is a dull employment;
It cuts off all that's life and fire
From that which may be termed desire,
Just like the bee, whose sting is gone,
Converts the owner to a drone.

I love a youth [if] he'd give me leave
His body in my arms to wreathe,
To press him gently and to kiss,
To sigh, and look with eyes that wish
For what, if I could once obtain,
I would neglect with flat disdain.

I'd give him liberty to toy
And play with me and count it joy;
Our freedom should be full, complete,
And nothing wanting but the feat.
Let's practice then, and we shall prove
These are the only sweets of love.

The Fall

How blessed was the created state
    Of man and woman ere they fell,
Compared to our unhappy fate;
    We need not fear another hell.

Naked, beneath cool shades, they lay;
    Enjoyment waited on desire;
Each member did their wills obey,
    Nor could a wish set pleasure higher.

But we, poor slaves to hope and fear,
    Are never of our joys secure;
They lessen still as they draw near,
    And none but dull delights endure.

Then, Chloris, while I duty pay,
    The nobler tribute of my heart,
Be not you so severe to say
    You love me for a frailer part.

A Song

As Chloris full of harmless thoughts
    Beneath a willow lay,
Kind love a youthful shepherd brought
    To pass the time away.

She blushed to be encountered so,
    And chid the amorous swain;
But as she strove to rise and go
    He pulled her down again.

A sudden passion seized her heart
    In spite of her disdain;
She found a pulse in every part
    And love in every vein.

Ah, Youth (said she), what charms are these
    That conquer and surprise?

Ah, let me[1]—for unless you please,
 I have no power to rise.

She fainting spoke and trembling lay,
 For fear he should comply;
Her lovely eyes her heart betray
 And give her tongue the lie.

Thus she whom princes had denied,
 With all their pomp and train,
Was, in the lucky moment, tried,
 And yielded to a swain.

A Description of Maidenhead

Have you not in a chimney seen
A sullen faggot, wet and green,
How coyly it receives the heat,
And at both ends does fume and sweat?

So fares it with the harmless maid
When first upon her back she's laid.
But the kind, experienced dame
Cracks, and rejoices in the same.

Et Cetera

In a dark, silent, shady grove,
Fit for the delights of love,
As on Corinna's breast I panting lay,
My right hand playing with *Et Cetera*,

A thousand words and amorous kisses
Prepared us both for more substantial blisses;
And thus the hasty moments slipped away,
Lost in the transports of *Et Cetera*.

[1] Let me: leave me.

She blushed to see her innocence betrayed
And the small opposition she had made;
Yet hugged me close and, with a sigh, did say,
Once more, my dear, once more, *Et Cetera.*

But, oh! the power to please this nymph was past;
Too violent a flame can never last.
So we remitted to another day
The prosecution of *Et Cetera.*

∽◦◦◦◦◦◦◦◦∽

A Pastoral Courtship

Behold these woods, and mark, my sweet,
How all these boughs together meet.
The cedar his fair arms displays
And mixes branches with the bays.
The lofty pine deigns to descend;
The sturdy oaks do gently bend;
One with another subtly weaves
Into one loom their various leaves . . .

Being set, let's sport a while, my fair.
I will tie love-knots in thy hair.
See, Zephyrus through the leaves doth stray
And has free liberty to play
And braid thy locks. And shall I find
Less favor than a fancy wind . . .

Come, let me touch those breasts that swell
Like two fair mountains, and may well
Be styled the Alps, but that I fear
The snow has much less whiteness there . . .
Fie, fie, this belly, Beauty's mint,
Blushes to see no coin stamped in't.
Employ it then, for though it be
Our wealth, it is your royalty;
And Beauty will have current grace
That bears the image of your face.
How to the touch the ivory thighs
Veil gently, and again do rise,

315

As pliable to the impressión
As Virgin's Wax or Barian Stone
Dissolved to softness; plump and full,
More white and soft than Cotsall wool.
These on two marble pillars raised
Make me in doubt which should be praised:
They or their columns most. But when
I view those feet that I have seen
So nimbly trip it o'er the lawns,
That all the satyrs and the fawns
Have stood amazed, when they would pass
Over the leas, and not a grass
Would feel the weight, nor rush, nor bent,
Drooping betray which way you went.

O then I feel my hot desires
Burn more and flame with double fires.
Come, let those thighs, those legs, those feet
With mine in thousand windings meet,
And woven in more subtle twines
Than woodbine, ivy, or the vines.
Now let us kiss, would you be gone?
Manners at least allows me one.
Blush you at this? Pretty one, stay,
And I will take that kiss away.
Thus with a second, and that, too,
A third wipes off. So will we go
To numbers that the stars outrun,
And all the atoms in the sun . . .

Are kisses all? They but forerun
Another duty to be done.
What would you of that minstrel say
That tunes his pipes and will not play?
Say what are blossoms in their prime
That ripen not in harvest time?
Or what are buds that ne'er disclose
The longed-for sweetness of the rose?
So kisses to a lover's guest
Are invitations, not the feast.

From *A Panegyric on Nelly*[1]

Of a great heroine I mean to tell
And by what just degrees her titles swell
To Mrs. Nelly, grown from Cinder Nell.

Much did she suffer, first on bulk and stage
From the blackguards and bullies of the age.
Much more her growing virtue did sustain
While dear Charles Hart and Buckhurst sued in vain;
In vain they sued. Cursed be the envious tongue
That her undoubted chastity would wrong.
For should we fame believe, we then might say
That thousands lay with her as well as they.
But, fame, thou liest; for her prophetic mind
Foresaw her greatness. Fate had well designed
And her ambition chose to be, before
A virtuous countess, an imperial whore.

Ev'n in her native dirt her soul was high
And did at crowns and shining monarchs fly.
Ev'n while the cinders raked, her swelling breast
With thoughts of glorious whoredom was possessed.
Still did she dream (nor could her birth withstand)
Of dangling scepters in her dirty hand.

But first the basket her fair arm did suit,
Laden with pippins and Hesperian fruit.
This first step raised, to th'wond'ring pit she sold
The lovely fruit smiling with streaks of gold.
Fate now for her did its whole force engage,
And from the pit she mounted to the stage.
There, in full luster did her glories shine
And, long eclipsed, spread forth their light divine;
There Hart's and Rowley's soul she did ensnare
And made a king the rival to a player.
The king o'ercomes, and to the royal bed

---

[1] Eleanor (Nell) Gwyn. Reared in poverty, she sold oranges in the pit of Drury Lane Theatre, went on the stage, and attracted attention as a comedienne in "breeches parts." Her first protector was Lord Buckhurst; later she became the favorite mistress of Charles II.

The dunghill offspring is in triumph led.
Nor let the envious her first rags object
To her that's now in tawdry gayness decked.
Her merit does from this much greater show,
Mounting so high that took her rise so low.

Less famed that Nelly was, whose cuckold's rage
In ten years' wars did half the world engage;
She's now the darling strumpet of the crowd;
Forgets her state and talks to them aloud;
Lays by her greatness and descends to prate
With those 'bove whom she's raised by wondrous fate . . .

From Oxford prison many did she free;
There died her father, and there gloried she
In giving others life and liberty.
Nor was her mother's funeral less her care;
No cost, no velvet did the daughter spare;
Fine gilded 'scutcheons did the hearse enrich
To celebrate this martyr of the ditch;
Burnt brandy did in flaming brimmers flow,
Drunk at her funeral, while her well-pleased shade
Rejoiced ev'n in the sober fields below
At all the drunkenness her death had made . . .

Thus we in short have all the virtues seen
Of the incomparable Madam Gwyn.
No wonder others are not with her shown;
She who no equal has, must be alone.

John Sheffield, Duke of Buckinghamshire

When John Sheffield (1648–1721) was ten years old, he suc-
ceeded his father as third earl of Musgrave. Subsequently he served
in both the army and the navy, became Lord Chamberlain to James
II and a cabinet-councilor under William III. Queen Anne made
him Duke of Buckingham—William II had already made him Mar-
quis of Normandy—and he was Lord Steward until, at Anne's death,
he fell from power.

Sheffield's brilliant career as politician and leader obscured his
role as poet, but, friend of Dryden and Pope, he wrote metrical
essays on satire and poetry, produced two tragedies, and amused
himself with light and sometimes licentious verse. The following
is one of his nimblest pieces.

The Happy Night

Since now my Silvia is as kind as fair,
Let wit and joy succeed my dull despair,
O what a night of pleasure was the last!
A full reward for all my troubles past;
And on my head if future mischiefs fall,
This happy night shall make amends for all.
Nay, tho' my Silvia's love should turn to hate,
I'll think of this, and die contented with my fate,
Twelve was the lucky minute when we met,
And on her bed we close together set;
Tho' listening spies might be perhaps too near,
Love filled our hearts; there was no room for fear.
Now, whilst I strive her melting heart to move;
With all the powerful eloquence of love;
In her fair face I saw the color rise,
And an unusual softness in her eyes;
Gently they look, I with joy adore,
That only charm they never had before,
The wounds they made, her tongue was used to heal,
But now these gentle enemies reveal
A secret, which that friend would still conceal.
My eyes transported too with amorous rage,
Seem fierce with expectation to engage;
But fast she holds my hands, and close her thighs,
And what she longs to do, with frowns denies.
A strange effect on foolish women wrought,
Bred in disguise, and by custom taught:
Custom, that prudence sometimes overrules,
But serves instead of reason to the fools!
Custom, which all the world to slavery brings,
The dull excuse for doing silly things.

She, by this method of her foolish sex,
Is forced awhile me and herself to vex:
But now, when thus we had been struggling long,
Her limbs grow weak, and her desires grow strong;
How can she hold to let the hero in?
He storms without, and love betrays within.
Her hands at last, to hide her blushes, leave
The fort unguarded, willing to receive
My fierce assault made with a lover's haste,
Like lightning piercing and as quickly past.
Thus does fond nature with her children play;
Just shows us joy, then snatches it away.
'Tis not the excess of pleasure makes it short,
The pain of love's as raging as the sport;
And yet, alas! that lasts: we sigh all night
With grief; but scarce one moment with delight.
Some little pain may check her kind desire,
But not enough to make her once retire.
Maids wounds for pleasure bear, as men for praise;
Here honor heals, there love the smart allays,
The world, if just, would harmful courage blame,
And this more innocent reward with fame.
Now she her well contented thoughts employs
On her past fears, and on her future joys:
Whose harbinger did roughly all remove,
To make fit room for great, luxurious love.
Fond of the welcome guest, her arms embrace
My body, and her hands another place:
Which with one touch so pleased and proud doth grow,
It swells beyond the grasp that made it so:
Confinement seems, in any straiter walls,
Than those of love, where it contented falls.
Tho' twice o'erthrown, he more enflamed does rise,
And will, to the last drop, fight out the prize.
She like some Amazon in story proves,
That overcomes the hero whom she loves.
In the close strife she takes so much delight,
She then can think of nothing but the fight:
With joy she lays him panting at her feet,
But with more joy does his recovery meet.
Her trembling hands first gently raise his head:

She almost dies for fear that he is dead:
Then binds his wounds up with her busy hand,
And with that balm enables him to stand,
'Til by her eyes she conquers him once more,
And wounds him deeper than she did before.
Tho' fallen from the top of Pleasure's Hill,
With longing eyes we look up thither still;
Still thither our unwearyed wishes tend,
'Til we that height of happiness ascend
By gentle steps: the ascent itself exceeds
All joys but that alone to which it leads:
First then, so long and lovingly we kiss,
As if, like doves, we knew no dearer bliss.
Still in one mouth our tongues together play,
While grouping hands are pleased no less than they.
Thus clinged together, now a while we rest,
Breathing our souls into each other's breast;
Then give a general kiss of all our parts,
While this way we make exchange of hearts.
Here, would my praise, as well as pleasure, dwell:
Enjoyment's self I scarcely like so well:
The little kiss comes short of rage and strength
So largely recompensed with endless length.
This is a joy would last, if we could stay:
But love's too eager to admit delay,
And hurries us along to smooth a way.
Now, wanton with delight, we nimble move
Our pliant limbs, in all the slopes of love;
Our motions not like those of gamesome fools,
Whose active bodies show their heavy souls:
But sports of love, in which a willing mind
Make us as able, as our hearts are kind:
At length, all languishing, and out of breath,
Panting, as in the agonies of death,
We lie entranced, 'til one provoking kiss
Transports our ravished souls to Paradise,
O Heaven of Love; thou moment of delight!
Wronged by my words, my fancy does thee right.
Methinks I lie all melting in her charms,
And fast locked up within her legs and arms;
Bent on our minds, and all our thoughts on fire,

Just laboring in the pangs of fierce desire.
At once, like misers, wallowing in their store,
In full possession; yet desiring more.
Thus with repeated pleasures, while we waste
Our happy hours that like short minutes past,
To such a sum of bliss our joys amount,
The numbers now become too great to count.
Silent, as night, are all sincerest joys,
Like deepest waters running with least noise.
But now, at last, for want of further force,
From deeds alas; we fall into discourse;
A Fall, which each of us in rain bemoans;
A greater Fall than that of kings from thrones.
The tide of pleasure flowing now no more,
We lie like fish left gasping on the shore;
And now, as after fighting, wounds appear,
Which we in heat did neither feel, nor fear:
She, for her sake, entreats me to give o'er,
And yet for mine would gladly suffer more.
Her words are coy, while all her motions woo
And, when she asks me, if it please me too,
I rage to show how well, but 'twill not do.
Thus would hot love run itself out of breath,
And wanting rest, find it too soon in death;
Did not wise nature with gentle force,
Restrain its rage, and stop its headlong course:
Indulgently severe, she well does spare
This child of hers, that most deserves her care.

Peter Anthony Motteux

Known chiefly as a translator of Rabelais and Cervantes—his *Don Quixote* was the favorite version for generations—Peter Anthony Motteux was born in France in 1660, left Rouen for London in his mid-twenties, and established himself there as a journalist. Although most of his verse-making was mediocre, he was the author of "Man is for Woman Made," which is still sung, is considered a folk song, and is usually credited to "Anonymous."

Man is for Woman Made

Man is for woman made,
And the woman made for man;
As the spur is for the jade,
As the scabbard for the blade,
As for digging is the spade,
As for liquor is the can,
So man is for the woman made
And the woman made for man.

As the sceptre's to be swayed,
As for night's the serenade,
As for pudding is the pan
And to cool us is the fan,
So man is for the woman made
And the woman made for man.

Be she widow, wife, or maid,
Be she wanton, be she staid,
Be she well or ill arrayed,
Whore, or bawd, or harridan,
Yet man is for the woman made
And the woman made for man.

Strephon

Strephon the brisk and gay,
  Young Strephon's Nature's wonder,
Whose eyes let forth bright flames of day,
Whose every look does souls betray,
  Or splits an heart asunder.

Strephon has every grace
  And wears 'em still about him;
The nymph whose greedy eye does trace
The swarming beauties of his face
  Yields heaven's no heaven without him.

Who views his mien or air
  The lovely youth confounds her;
He is so charming and so fair,
The heedless virgin, unaware,
  Plays with the dart that wounds her.

JOHN SMYTH (1662–1717)

Matthew Prior

A Tory diplomat who was imprisoned for making a dubious treaty, Matthew Prior (1664–1721) fancied himself as a satiric and serious poet. He is, however, forgotten as the author of lengthy soliloquies and remembered as the adept fashioner of neat and even endearing trifles.

The Lover's Anger

As Cloe came into the room t'other day,
I peevish began: "Where so long could you stay?
In your life-time you never regarded your hour:
You promised at two; and (pray look, child) 'tis four.
A lady's watch needs neither figures nor wheels:
'Tis enough, that 'tis loaded with baubles and seals.
A temper so heedless no mortal can bear—"
Thus far I went on with a resolute air.
"Lord bless me," said she, "Let a body but speak:
Here's an ugly hard rosebud fall'n into my neck:
It has hurt me, and vexed me to such a degree—
See here! for you never believe me; pray see,
On the left side my breast what a mark it has made!"
So saying, her bosom she careless displayed.
That seat of delight I with wonder surveyed,
And forgot every word I designed to have said.

Sir John Vanbrugh

An architect who designed Haymarket Theatre, the colossal Blenheim Palace, and his own Palladian Castle Howard, John Vanbrugh (1664–1726) was also, and originally, a dramatist. He wrote as he talked; his fellow playwright, Colley Cibber, said that Vanbrugh's dialogues were "common conversations committed to paper." It was reported that his highly successful *The Relapse* was conceived and written in less than six weeks. Unlike the bitter ironies of Wycherley, to whom he was compared, Vanbrugh delighted in farce. "In the Sprightly Month of May" is from his comedy, *Aesop*.

In the Sprightly Month of May

(From *Aesop*)

In the sprightly month of May,
When males and females sport and play,
And kiss and toy away the day;
An eager sparrow and his mate
Chirping on a tree were sate,
Full of love—and full of prate.
They talk'd of nothing but their fires,
Of raging heats and strong desires,
Of eternal constancy:
How true and faithful they would be,
Of this and that, and endless joys,
And a thousand more such toys:
The only thing they apprehended,
Was that their lives would be so short,
They could not finish half their sport
Before their days were ended.
But as from bough to bough they rove,
    They chanced at last
    In furious haste,
On a twig with birdlime spread,
(Want of a more downy bed)
To act a scene of love.
Fatal it proved to both their fires.
For though at length they broke away,
And balk'd the schoolboy of his prey,
Which made him weep the livelong day,
The bridegroom in the hasty strife,
Was stuck so fast to his dear wife,
That though he used his utmost art,
He quickly found it was in vain,
To put himself to further pain,

They never more must part.
A gloomy shade o'creast his brow;
He found himself—I know not how:
He look'd—as husbands often do
Where'er he moved he felt her still,
She kiss'd him oft against his will:
Abroad, at home, at bed and board,
With favors she o'erwhelmed her lord.
Oft he turned his head away,
And seldom had a word to say.
Which absolutely spoiled her play,
For she was better stored.
Howe'er at length her stock was spent.
(For female fires sometimes may be
Subject to mortality;)
So back to back they sit and sullenly repent.
But the mute scene was quickly ended,
The lady, for her share, pretended
The want of love lay at his door;
For her part she had still in store
Enough for him and twenty more,
Which could not be contended.
He answer'd her in homely words.
(For sparrows are but ill-bred birds,)
That he already had enjoy'd.
So much, that truly he was cloy'd.
Which so provoked her spleen,
That after some good hearty prayers,
A jostle, and some spiteful tears,
They fell together by the ears,
And ne'er were fond again.

Jonathan Swift

Jonathan Swift (1667–1745) was the victim of his own savagery; his furious indignations finally drove him mad. He wanted a world of justice, truth, and love, and saw about him nothing but injustice, hypocrisy, and hate. He longed for beauty, but a beauty so idealized that it bore no resemblance to anything human; a beautiful woman reminded him that she was nothing but flesh, that flesh decays, and that the body is a corrupting mass of ordure. He could not accustom himself to the naturalness of bodily functions but was preoccupied with men's (and particularly woman's) normal "dirty" habits, with their animality, their digestions and excretions. "He hated them, certainly," says Edgar Johnson in *A Treasury of Satire*, "and he bathed in the squelchy imagination of them, stained clouts, smeared chemises, grimy towels, defiled and fascinated at the same time."

The author of *Gulliver's Travels* was a poet as well as a satirist. His vehement disgusts are even more apparent in his verse than in his prose. "A Beautiful Young Nymph Going to Bed," with its sneering subtitle ("Written for the Honor of the Fair Sex") is Swift at his ugliest and most scarifying. A contrast to most of the pages in this collection, it is one of the most violently anti-erotic poems ever written.

A Beautiful Young Nymph Going to Bed

Written for the Honor of the Fair Sex

Corinna, pride of Drury-Lane,
For whom no shepherd sighs in vain;
Never did Covent-Garden boast
So bright a batter'd strolling toast!
No drunken rake to pick her up,
No cellar where on tick to sup;
Returning at the midnight hour,
Four stories climbing to her bower;
Then, seated on a three-legg'd chair,
Takes off her artificial hair;
Now picking out a crystal eye,
She wipes it clean, and lays it by.
Her eyebrows from a mouse's hide
Stuck on with art on either side,
Pulls off with care, and first displays 'em,
Then in a play-book smoothly lays 'em.
Now dext'rously her plumpers draws,
That serve to fill her hollow jaws,
Untwists a wire, and from her gums
A set of teeth completely comes;
Pulls out the rags contrived to prop
Her flabby dugs, and down they drop.
Proceeding on, the lovely goddess
Unlaces next her steel-ribb'd bodice,
Which, by the operator's skill,
Press down the lumps, the hollows fill.
Up goes her hand, and off she slips
The bolsters that supply her hips;
With gentlest touch she next explores
Her chancres, issues, running sores;

331

Effects of many a sad disaster,
And then to each applies a plaster:
But must, before she goes to bed,
Rub off the daubs of white and red,
And smooth the furrows in her front
With greasy paper stuck upon't.
She takes a bolus ere she sleeps;
And then between two blankets creeps.
With pains of love tormented lies;
Or, if she chance to close her eyes,
Of Bridewell and the Compter dreams,
And feels the lash, and faintly screams;
Or, by a faithless bully drawn,
At some hedge-tavern lies in pawn;
Or to Jamaica seems transported
Alone, and by no planter courted;
Or, near Fleet-ditch's oozy brinks,
Surrounded with a hundred stinks,
Belated, seems on watch to lie,
And snap some cully passing by;
Or, struck with fear, her fancy runs
On watchmen, constables, and duns,
From whom she meets with frequent rubs;
But never from religious clubs;
Whose favor she is sure to find,
Because she pays them all in kind.

   Corinna wakes. A dreadful sight!
Behold the ruins of the night!
A wicked rat her plaster stole,
Half eat, and dragg'd it to his hole.
The crystal eye, alas! was miss'd;
And puss had on her plumpers piss'd,
A pigeon pick'd her issue-pease:
And Shock her tresses fill'd with fleas.

   The nymph, though in this mangled plight,
Must ev'ry morn her limbs unite.
But how shall I describe her arts
To re-collect the scatter'd parts?
Or show the anguish, toil, and pain,
Of gathering up herself again?
The bashful Muse will never bear

332

In such a scene to interfere.
Corinna, in the morning dizen'd,
Who sees, will spew; who smells, be poison'd.

A Wicked Treasonable Libel

While the king and his ministers keep such a pother,
And all about changing one whore for another,
Think I to myself, what need all this strife,
His majesty first had a whore of a wife,
And surely the difference mounts to no more
Than, now he has gotten a wife of a whore.
Now give me your judgment a very nice case on;
Each queen has a son, say which is the base one?
Say which of the two is the right Prince of Wales,
To succeed, when, (God bless him,) his majesty fails;
Perhaps it may puzzle our loyal divines
To unite these two Protestant parallel lines,
From a left-handed wife, and one turn'd out of doors,
Two reputed king's sons, both true sons of whores;
No law can determine it, which is first oars.
But, alas! poor old England, how wilt thou be master'd;
For, take which you please, it must needs be a bastard.

William Congreve

The Mourning Bride by William Congreve (1670–1729) contains two quotations which have become so generally accepted as to be proverbs: "Hell hath no fury like a woman scorned" and "Music hath charms to soothe the savage breast." Besides *The Mourning Bride*, his one tragedy, Congreve wrote vivacious comedies which have never lost their popularity: *The Way of the World, Love for Love*, and *The Double Dealer*. He satirized the callous immorality of his day in the last of these, and imitated the classic poets as well in his own vein as contributor to Dryden's collection of Latin translations. A cataract almost blinded him during his thirties, but he was able to live comfortably, thanks to a series of sinecure positions, until he was close to sixty. After a fatal accident, he was buried in Westminster Abbey.

A Nymph and a Swain

A nymph and a swain to Apollo once prayed,
The swain had been jilted, the nymph been betrayed:
Their intent was to try if his oracle knew
E'er a nymph that was chaste, or a swain that was true.

Apollo was mute, and had like t' have been posed,
But sagely at length he this secret disclosed:
"He alone won't betray in whom none will confide;
And the nymph may be chaste that has never been tried."

The Better Bargain

Tell me no more I am deceived,
  That Chloe's false and common;
By Heaven! I all along believed
  She was a very woman;
As such I liked, as such caressed,
She was constant—when possessed;
  She could do more for no man.

But oh! her thoughts on others ran,
  And that you think a hard thing?
Perhaps she fancied you the man?
  Why, what care I one farthing?
You think she's false, I'm sure she's kind,
I'll take her body, you her mind:
  Who has the better bargain?

Pious Selinda

Pious Selinda goes to prayers
  If I but ask the favor;
And yet the tender fool's in tears
  When she believes I'll leave her.

Would I were free from this restraint,
  Or else had hopes to win her;
Would she could make of me a saint,
  Or I of her a sinner!

Richard Brinsley Sheridan

Before he was twenty-four Richard Brinsley Sheridan (1751–1816) had written *The Rivals,* a comedy that has maintained its place in the theatre for almost two centuries. Within the next two years, he produced a farce; a cleaned-up version of Vanbrugh's *The Relapse;* a comic opera, *The Duenna;* and his masterpiece, *The School for Scandal.* The last-named merited its title, for Sheridan had trouble getting it staged; a license was procured only because of the friendship of the Lord Chamberlain. *The Critic,* a critical burlesque, was written at twenty-eight.

Sheridan's success as a playwright helped him achieve prominence as a politician. He entered Parliament in his thirtieth year and achieved an immediate reputation as a brilliant orator. He opposed the Revolutionary War in America, upheld the right of non-intervention as against those who denounced the French Revolution, and became a member of the Privy Council. He lived extravagantly, gambled wildly, and was hounded by creditors; only the fact that he was a Member of Parliament saved him from being arrested for debt at sixty. He died in utter poverty and would have been gratified by the sumptuous funeral that was accorded his body when it was buried in Westminster Abbey.

The Geranium

In the close covert of a grove,
By nature formed for scenes of love,
Said Susan in a lucky hour,
"Observe yon sweet geranium flower;
How straight upon its stalk it stands,
And tempts our violating hands:
Whilst the soft bud as yet unspread,
Hangs down its pale declining head:
Yet, soon as it is ripe to blow,
The stems shall rise, the head shall glow."

"Nature," said I, "my lovely Sue,
To all her followers lends a clue;
Her simple laws themselves explain,
As links of one continued chain;
For her the mysteries of creation,
Are but the work of generation:
Yon blushing, strong, triumphant flower,
Is in the crisis of its power:
But short, alas! its vigorous reign,
He sheds his seed, and drops again;
The bud that hangs in pale decay,
Feels not, as yet, the plastic ray;
Tomorrow's sun shall bid him rise,
Then, too, he sheds his seed and dies:
But words, my love, are vain and weak,
For proof, let bright example speak.
Then straight before the wondering maid,
The tree of life I gently laid.
"Observe, sweet Sue, his drooping head,
How pale, how languid, and how dead;
Yet, let the sun of thy bright eyes,

337

Shine but a moment, it shall rise;
Let but the dew of thy soft hand
Refresh the stem, it straight shall stand:
Already, see, it swells, it grows,
Its head is redder than the rose,
Its shrivelled fruit, of dusky hue,
Now glows, a present fit for Sue:
The balm of life each artery fills,
And in o'erflowering drops distils."
"Oh me," cried Susan, "what is this?
What strange tumultuous throbs of bliss!
Sure, never mortal, till this hour,
Felt such emotion at a flower:
Oh, serpent! cunning to deceive,
Sure, 'tis this tree that tempted Eve;
The crimson apples hang so fair,
Alas! what woman could forbear?"
"Well, hast thou guessed, my love," I cried,
"It is the tree by which she died;
The tree which could content her,
All nature, Susan, seeks the center.
Yet, let us still, poor Eve forgive,
It's the tree by which we live;
For lovely woman still it grows,
And in the center only blows.
But chief for thee, it spreads its charms,
For paradise is in thy arms."

I ceased, for nature kindly here
Began to whisper in her ear:
And lovely Sue lay softly panting,
While the geranium tree was planting.
'Til in the heat of amorous strife,
She burst the mellow tree of life.
"Oh, heaven!" cried Susan, with a sigh,
"The hour we taste—we surely die;
Strange raptures seize my fainting frame,
And all my body glows with flame;
Yet let me snatch one parting kiss
To tell my love I die with bliss:
That pleased, thy Susan yields her breath;
Oh, who would live if this be death!"

Williams and Others

The next eight poems are by various minor poets of the eighteenth century. The best known among them is Charles Hanbury Williams (1708–1750), whose imitations of Martial and other Latin bards were often quoted although his *Works* did not achieve publication until the nineteenth century. The other poets are occasionally encountered in collections of the period.

Come, Chloe, and Give Me Sweet Kisses

Come, Chloe, and give me sweet kisses,
    For sweeter sure never girl gave;
But why in the midst of my blisses,
    Do you ask me how many I'd have?
I'm not to be stinted in pleasure,
    Then, prithee, my charmer, be kind,
For whilst I love thee above measure,
    To numbers I'll ne'er be confined.

Count the bees that on Hybla are playing,
    Count the flowers that enamel its fields,
Count the flocks that on Tempe are straying,
    Or the grain that rich Sicily yields,
Go number the stars in the heaven,
    Count how many sands on the shore,
When so many kisses you've given,
    I still shall be craving for more.

To a heart full of love, let me hold thee,
    To a heart that, dear Chloe, is thine;
In my arms I'll for ever enfold thee,
    And twist round thy limbs like a vine.
What joy can be greater than this is?
    My life on thy lips shall be spent!
But the wretch that can number his kisses,
    With few will be ever content.

CHARLES HANBURY WILLIAMS

Sweet, Let Me Go

Sweet, let me go, sweet, let me go!
What do you mean to vex me so?
Cease your pleading force!
Do you thing thus to extort remorse?
Now, now! no more! alas, you overbear me,
And I would cry—but some would hear, I fear me.

WILLIAM CORKINE

Song

    When thy beauty appears
    In its graces and airs
All bright as an angel new dropp'd from the sky,
At distance I gaze and am awed by my fears:
    So strangely you dazzle my eye!

    But when without art
    Your kind thoughts you impart,
When your love runs in blushes through every vein;
When it darts from your eyes, when it pants in your heart,
    Then I know you're a woman again.

    There's a passion and pride
    In our sex (she replied),
And thus, might I gratify both, I would do:
Still an angel appear to each lover beside,
    But still be a woman to you.

THOMAS PARNELL

Fair, and Soft, and Gay, and Young

Fair, and soft, and gay, and young,
All charm! She played, she danced, she sung!
There was no way to 'scape the dart,
No care could guard the lover's heart.
"Ah! why," cried I, and dropped a tear
(Adoring, yet despairing e'er
To have her to myself alone),
"Was so much sweetness made for one?"

But growing bolder, in her ear
I in soft numbers told my care:
She heard, and raised me from her feet,
And seemed to glow with equal heat.
Like heaven's, too mighty to express,
My joys could but be known by guess.
"Ah, fool!" said I, "what have I done,
To wish her made for more than one?"

But long she had not been in view,
Before her eyes their beams withdrew:
Ere I had reckoned half her charms,
She sank into another's arms.
But she, that once could faithless be,
Will favor him no more than me:
He, too, will find he is undone,
And that she was not made for one.

ROBERT GOULD

❧

The Unfortunate Reminder

As Dolly and her favorite swain
Were interrupted by the rain,
From tedding out the fragrant hay;
Beneath a sheltering cock they lay:
When thus the lovely, longing jade,
Unto the drowsy shepherd said,
"Nay, prithee Lobby, why so sleepy?
Indeed, upon my word I'll nip ye.
How pretty might we sit and chat,

341

Tell o'er old stories, and all that.
But you—O Lord, the careless beast!
As if folks lie down to take rest."

Lob, half asleep, made no replies,
Or answered with a grunt her sighs.
While she to be revenged, arose,
And played a tickler on his nose.
(But come, the virgin to disgrace,
We'll say, 'twas in another place.)

Be that as 'twill, she waked the swain,
And tickled him with words again.
"Come sweeting, Lobby, come my dear,
I'm sure that nobody is near;
Indeed we may, pray be'n't afraid,
Poor I am, but an harmless maid.
For since you're so disposed to rest,
Pray take a nap upon my breast.
You see time, leisure, place, and all
For such enjoyment seem to call.
And you remember people say,
When the sun shines, then make your hay."

"Augh! augh!" quoth Lob, waked with surprise,
To see the sun flame in his eyes.
"Heigh Ho! Come Doll, for as you say.
The sun shines, we must make our hay.
So reach me here my rake and prong,
'Twas well you waked—we've slept too long."

WILLIAM PATTISON

The Penitent Nun

Dame Jane a sprightly nun and gay,
And formed of very yielding clay,
Had long with resolution strove
To guard against the shafts of love.
Fond Cupid smiling, spies the fair,
And soon he baffles all her care;

In vain she tries her pain to smother,
The nymph too frail becomes a mother.

But once these little follies o'er,
She firmly vows she'll sin no more;
No more to vice will fall a prey,
But spend in prayer each fleeting day.
Close in her cell immured she lies,
Nor from the cross removes her eyes;
While sisters crowding at the gate,
Spend all their time in worldly prate.
The abbess, overjoyed to find
This happy change in Jenny's mind,
The rest, with air composed, addressing,
"Daughters, if you expect a blessing,
From pious Jane, example take,
The world and all its joys forsake."
"We will," they all replied as one,
"But first let's do as Jane has done."

JOHN LOCKMAN

Maria

One day, by appointment, Maria I met,
That day of delight I remember it yet;
As the meadow we cross'd to avoid the town's crowd,
The sun seem'd eclips'd, by a black spreading cloud:
Escaping the shower, to barn we fast fled,
There safe heard the pattering rain overhead.

Some moments I suffer'd my fair to take breath,
Then, sighing, she cry'd, "Lord I'm frighted to death;
"Suppose nay, now by any one I should be seen?
"Nay, nay, now—nay, pray now—dear—what do you
      mean?
"Had I thought you wou'd be half so rude—fie! for
      shame!
"I wish I'd been wet to the skin ere I came.

"You will have a kiss, then!—why, take one or two!
"I beg you won't tease me!—Lord! what wou'd you do?

343

"You'll tear all one's things—I ne'er saw such a man!
"I will hold your hands too!—Aye, do if you can:
"Is this your love for me? Is this all you care?
"I'll never come near you again—now, I swear!"

As she push'd me away, love explain'd by her eyes,
Resistance was only to heighten the prize;
Her face chang'd alternate, from scarlet to snow,
Her neck rose and fell fast, her language was low:
Such beauty! but more of that scene was not shown—
For Decency here bid her curtain drop down.

The storm being over, all sunshine the air,
When instant rose up, the yet love-looking fair,
Crying, hark! there's one listens—do look out, dear,
I must be bewitch'd, I am sure, to come here,
My things how they are rumpled!—Lord, let me be gone;
What have you been doing? and what have I done?

Into this fatal place, I most solemnly vow,
I innocent enter'd—but am I so now?
I'm ruin'd—I never myself can forgive—
I'll leap in the brook—for I'm sure I can't live!—
If I do, my whole life will be wasted in grief,
Unless here tomorrow you'll give me relief.

G. A. STEVENS

Anonymous

Some of the lightest as well as the liveliest stanzas of the period are unsigned. It is suspected that Rochester, Sackville, and possibly Dryden may have had a hand in them, but this is conjecture. Thomas D'Urfey, part author and part compiler of a much-ransacked collection, *Pills to Purge Melancholy*, is usually credited with the first of the following poems. Charming many of them are, and this section concludes with a representative assortment of anonymous favorites.

Kissing's No Sin

Some say that kissing's a sin;
    But I think it's nane ava,[1]
For kissing has wonn'd in this warld
    Since ever that there was twa.

O, if it wasna lawfu'
    Lawyers wadna allow it;
If it wasna holy,
    Ministers wadna do it.

If it wasna modest,
    Maidens wadna tak' it;
If it wasna plenty,
    Puir folk wadna get it.

[1] Nane ava: none at all.

Chloe

Chloe's a nymph in flowery groves,
    A nereid in the streams;
Saint-like she in the temple moves,
    A woman in my dreams.

Love steals artillery from her eyes,
    The Graces point her charms;
Orpheus is rivalled in her voice,
    And Venus in her arms.

Never so happily in one
    Did heaven and earth combine:
And yet 'tis flesh and blood alone
    That makes her so divine.

The Willow

Under the willow shades they were
    Free from the eye-sight of the sun,
For no intruding beam could there
    Peep through to spy what things were done:
        Thus sheltered they unseen did lie,
        Surfeiting on each other's eye;
Defended by the willow shades alone,
The sun's heat they defied and cool'd their own.

Whilst they did embrace unspied,
    The conscious willow seem'd to smile,
That them with privacy supplied,
    Holding the door, as 'twere, the while;

346

And when their dalliances were o'er,
The willows, to oblige them more,
Bowing, did seem to say, as they withdrew,
"We can supply you with a cradle too."

I Dreamed My Love

I dreamed my love lay in her bed:
    It was my chance to take her:
Her legs and arms abroad were spread;
    She slept; I durst not wake her.
O pity it were, that one so fair
    Should crown her love with willow;
The tresses of her golden hair
    Did kiss her lovely pillow.

Methought her belly was a hill
    Much like a mount of pleasure,
Under whose height there grows a well;
    The depth no man can measure.
About the pleasant mountain's top
    There grows a lovely thicket,
Wherein two beagles trampled,
    And raised a lively pricket.[1]

They hunted there with pleasant noise
    About the pleasant mountain,
Till he by heat was forced to fly,
    And skip into the fountain.
The beagles followed to the brink,
    And there at him they barked;
He plunged about, but would not shrink;
    His coming forth they waited.

Then forth he came, as one half lame,
    Were weary, faint, and tired;
And laid him down betwixt her legs,
    As help he had required.
The beagles being refresht again,
    My love from sleep bereavèd;
She dreamed she had me in her arms,
    And she was not deceivèd.

[1] A punning reference to a young male deer with upright, unbranched antlers.

The Reluctant Lady

Nay, pish; nay, phew! nay, faith and will you? fie!
A gentleman and use me thus! I'll cry!
Nay, God's body, what means this? Nay, fie for shame,
Nay, faith, away! Nay, fie, you are to blame.
Hark! somebody comes! hands off, I pray!
I'll pinch, I'll scratch, I'll spurn, I'll run away.
Nay, faith, you strive in vain, you shall not speed.
You mar my ruff, you hurt my back, I bleed.
Look how the door stands open! Someone sees!
Your buttons scratch, in faith you hurt my knees.
What will men say? Lord, what a coil is here!
You make me sweat, i' faith, here's goodly gear.
Nay, faith, let me entreat you, if you list;
You mar my clothes, you tear my smock, but, had I wist
So much before, I would have shut you out.
Is it a proper thing you go about?
I did not think you would have used me this,
But now I see I took my aim amiss.
A little thing would make me not be friends:
You've used me well! I hope you'll make amends.
Hold still, I'll wipe your face, you sweat amain:
You have got a goodly thing with all your pain.
Alas! how hot am I! what will you drink?
If you go sweating down what will men think?
Remember, sir, how you have used me now;
Doubtless ere long I will be meet with you.
If any man but you had used me so,
Would I have put it up? in faith, sir, no.
Nay, go not yet; stay here and sup with me,
And then at cards we better shall agree.

The Cautious Struggle

Be quiet, sir! Begone, I say!
Lord bless us, how you romp and tear!
There!
I swear!
Now you have laid my bosom bare!

348

I do not like such boisterous play,
So take that saucy hand away. . . .
Why! Now you're ruder than before!
Nay, I'll be hanged if I comply—
    Fie!
    I'll cry!
Oh, I can't bear it—I shall die!
I vow I'll never see you more!
But—are you sure you shut the door?

A Lamentable Case

Ye famed physicians of this place,
Hear Strephon's and poor Chloe's case,
    Nor think that I am joking;
When she would, he cannot comply,
When he would drink, she's not a-dry.
    And is not this provoking?

At night when Strephon comes to rest,
Chloe received him on her breast,
    With fondly folding arms:
Down, down he hangs his drooping head,
Falls fast asleep, and lies as dead,
    Neglecting all her charms.

Reviving when the morn returns,
With rising flames young Strephon burns,
    And then would fain be doing:
But Chloe, now asleep or sick,
Has no great relish for the trick,
    And sadly balks his wooing.

O cruel and disastrous case,
When in the critical embrace
    That only one is burning!
Dear doctors, set this matter right;
Give Strephon spirits in the night,
    Or Chloe in the morning.

Two Puritans

It was a puritanical lad
    His name it was Matthias,
And he would go to Amsterdam
    To speak with Ananias.
He had not gone but half a mile
    When he met a holy sister;
He laid his Bible under her breech,
    And merrily he kissed her.

"Alas! What would the wicked say,"
    Quoth she, "if they had seen it!
My buttocks lie too low; I wish
    Apocrypha were in it!"
"Peace, sweetheart, for ere we part—
    I speak in pure devotion—
By yea and nay I'll not away
    Till thou feel my spirit's motion."

They huffed and puffed with many heaves,
    Till that they both were tired.
"Alas!" quoth she, "you'll spoil the leaves;
    My petticoat's all mired!
If we professors should be known
    To all the congregation
Either at Leyden or Amsterdam,
    It would disgrace our nation."

"But since it is that part we must,
    Though I am much unwilling,
Brother, let's have another thrust,
    And take thee this fine shilling
To bear thy charges when thou goest
    As passage o'er the ocean."
Then down she laid and, so tis said,
    She quenched his spirit's motion.

The Shepherd and the Milkmaid

I'll tell you a tale of my love and I,
  How often we did a-milking go;
And when I looked merrily then she would cry
  And still in her fits she would use me so.
At last I plainly did tell her my mind,
  And then she began to love me.
I asked her the cause of her being unkind,
  And she said it was only to prove me.

Then did I give her a kiss or two;
  She returned them with interest still;
I thought I had now no more to do
  But that at last I might have my will.
Yet she, being taught by her thoughtful Dad,
  Began to be cautious and wary,
And told me if I my will had had
  The Devil a bit would I marry.

So married we were, and when it was o'er,
  I told her plain in the Parsonage Hall,
That if she had giv'n me my will before,
  The Devil a bit I'd have married at all.
She smiled, and presently told me her mind:
  She had vowed she'd never do more so
Because she was cozen'd, for being too kind,
  By three or four men before so.

She Lay All Naked

She lay all naked in her bed,
  And I myself lay by;
No veil but curtains about her spread,
  No covering but I.
Her head upon her shoulders seeks
  To hang in careless wise,
And full of blushes were her cheeks,
  And of wishes were her eyes.

Her blood still fresh into her face,
    As on a message came,
To say that in another place
    It meant another game;
Her cherry lip moist, plump, and fair,
    Millions of kisses crown,
Which ripe and uncropt dangled there
    And weighed the branches down.

Her breasts, that well'd so plump and high,
    Bred pleasant pain in me,
For all the world I do defy
    The like felicity;
Her thighs and belly, soft and fair,
    To me were only shown:
To see such meat, and not to eat,
    Would anger any stone.

Her knees lay upward gently bent,
    And all lay hollow under,
As if on easy terms, they meant
    To fall unforc'd asunder;
Just so the Cyprian Queen[1] did lie,
    Expecting in her bower;
When too long stay had kept the boy[2]
    Beyond his promis'd hour.

"Dull clown," quoth she, "why dost delay
    Such proffered bliss to take?
Canst thou find out no other way
    Similitudes to make?"
Mad with delight I thundering
    Threw both my arms about her,
But pox upon 't 'twas but a dream.
    And so I lay without her.

[1] Cyprian Queen: Venus. [2] The boy: Adonis.

Joan to Her Lady

Lady, sweet, now do not frown,
Nor in anger call me clown,
For your servant Joan may prove,
Like your self, as deep in love;
And as absolute a bit,
Man's sweet liquorish tooth to fit.
The smock alone the difference makes,
'Cause yours is spun of finer flax.

What avails the name of Madam?
Came not all from Father Adam?
Where does one exceed the other?
Was not Eve our common Mother?
Then what odds 'twixt you and Joan?
Truly in my judgment, none.

Ladies are but blood and bone,
Skin and sinews, so is Joan.
Joan's a piece for a man to bore,
With his wimble, yours no more.
Then what odds 'twixt you and Joan?
Truly in my judgment, none.

It is not your flaunting tires [1]
Are the cause of men's desires;
They're other darts which lusts pursue,
Those Joan has as well as you.
Then what odds 'twixt you and Joan?
Truly in my judgment, none.

What care we for glorious lights,
Women are used in the nights;
And in night in women-kind,
Kings and clowns like sport do find.
Then what odds 'twixt you and Joan?
Truly in my judgment, none.

Where there's two in bed together,
There's no a pin to chuse 'twixt either;

[1] Tires: attire, clothes.

Both have eyes, and both have lips;
Both have thighs and both have hips.
Then what odds 'twixt you and Joan?
Truly in my judgment, none.

When your hand puts out the candle,
And you at last begin to handle,
Then you go about to do
What you should be done unto.
Then what odds 'twixt you and Joan?
Truly in my judgment, none.

Who can but in conscience say,
Fie, fie, for shame away, away,
Putting finger in the eye,
Till you have a fresh supply.
Then what odds 'twixt you and Joan?
Truly in my judgment, none.

Young Strephon and Phillis

Young Strephon and Phillis,
    They sat on a hill;
But the shepherd was wanton,
    And would not sit still:
His head on her bosom,
    And arms round her waist;
He hugged her, and kissed her,
    And clasped her so fast:
    Till playing and jumbling,
    At last they fell tumbling;
And down they got 'em,
But oh! they fell soft on the grass at the bottom.

As the shepherdess tumbled,
    The rude wind got in,
And blew up her clothes,
    And her smock to her chin:
The shepherd he saw
    The bright Venus, he swore,

For he knew her own dove,
By the feathers she wore:
Till furious love sallying,
At last he fell dallying,
And won, down he got him,
But oh! oh! how sweet, and how soft at the bottom.

The shepherdess blushing,
To think what she'd done;
Away from the shepherd,
She fain would have run;
Which Strephon perceiving,
The wand'rer did seize;
And cried do be angry,
Fair Nymph if you please:
'Tis too late to be cruel,
Thy frowns my dear jewel,
Now no more stings have got 'em,
For oh! Thou'rt all kind, and all soft at the bottom.

As On Serena's Panting Breast

As on Serena's panting breast
The happy Strephon lay,
With love and beauty doubly blest
He passed the hours away.
Fierce rapture of transporting love
And pleasure struck him dumb;
He envied not the powers above
Nor all the joys to come.
As zealous bees far off do rove
To bring their treasure home,
So Strephon ranged the field of love
To make his honey-comb.
Her ruby lips he sucked and pressed
From whence all sweets derive;
Then, buzzing 'round her snowy breast,
He crept into the hive.

355

My Mistress Makes Music

My mistress is in music passing skillful,
And plays and sings her part at the first sight,
But in her play she is exceeding willful,
And will not play but for her own delight,
Nor touch one string, nor play one pleasing strain,
Unless you take her in a pleasing vein.

Also she hath a sweet delicious touch
Upon the instrument whereon she plays,
And thinks that she doth never do too much,
Her pleasures are dispers'd so many ways;
She hath such judgment both in time and mood,
That for to play with her 'twill do you good.

And then you win her heart: but here's the spite,
You cannot get her for to play alone,
But play with her, and she will play all night,
And next day too, or else 'tis ten to one,
And run division with you in such sort,
Run ne'er so swift she'll make you come too short.

Still so she sent for me one day to play,
Which I did take for such exceeding grace,
But she so tired me ere I went away,
I wished I had been in another place.
She knew to play much better than I could,
And still she kept me time for heart and blood.

I love my mistress, and I love to play,
So she will let me play with intermission:
But when she ties me to it all the day,
I hate and loathe her greedy disposition;
Let her keep time, as nature doth require,
And I will play as much as she'll desire.

Ballads and Folk Songs

Anonymous

The range of ballads sung or spoken covers a seemingly endless stretch of time and the widest possible area of places and subjects. Most ballads were not only sung by itinerant balladmongers but also hawked about the streets on song sheets and broadsides; they were crude in style and coarse in matter. Seductions and adulteries vied with murders as favorite subjects; the lines were salted with casual vulgarities and spiced with double meanings which everyone understood. There was much about tools of various trades and professions, many references to instruments, pipes, flutes, fiddles, yardsticks, hammers, kettles, candles, keys to fit locks, and such transparent sexual symbols as plucking flowers, catching birds, finding bowers of bliss, mowing (a common figure for copulation) and dying (a favorite and fitting description of the final ecstasy).

Not that all ballads are ribald. Many of them are lightly frolicsome and even innocent; many are familiar folk tales and racy narratives set to rhyme. But a great many, compounded with earthy humor, are audacious and downright bawdy. Examples of every sort may be found in the priceless *Reliques of Ancient Poetry* by Thomas Percy, Lord Bishop of Dromore; *English and Scottish Popular Ballads* collected by the pioneering Francis James Child; and the more recent anthology of British ballad poetry, *The Common Muse*, edited by Vivian de Sola Pinto and Allan Edwin Rodway. Whatever their contents, the best ballads are vigorous, usually enlivened with high spirits, and never without a sense of vital humanity.

Their variations are endless. More than one hundred versions of a single folk song, "Barbara Allen," are in the archives of the Library of Congress, and in one state, Vermont, Helen Harkness Flanders assembled nine thousand ballads sung in New England.

Where do the ballads come from? It used to be thought that they were the result of communal creation, that groups of people either originated or formed the story-songs. But a song or story must begin with an individual creator. It is inevitably the work of a single author, often unknown, reshaped by oral repetitions and variations until, by the process of evolution, it becomes a folk song.

The following examples are by a variety of unknown authors who have relished the spontaneity of the folk song and the freedom accorded the traditional ballad.

Our Goodman

Home came our goodman,
    Home came he,
And there he saw a saddle-horse,
    Where never a horse should be.

"What's this now, goodwife?
    What's this I see?
How came this horse here
    Without the leave of me?"

"Shame on your silly face,
    For surely you can see
'Tis nothing but a brood-sow
    My mother sent to me."

"I've traveled far," our goodman said,
    "I've traveled wide," said he.
"But a saddle on a sow's back
    Never did I see."

Home came our goodman,
    Home came he,
And there he saw a pair of boots
    Where never boots should be.

"What's this now, goodwife?
    What's this I see?
How came these boots here
    Without the leave of me?"

"Shame on your silly face,
    For surely you can see
They're but a pair of pewter jugs
    My mother sent to me."

"I've traveled far," our goodman said,
    "I've traveled wide," said he.
"But silver spurs on pewter jugs
    Never did I see."

Home came our goodman,
    Home came he,
And there he saw a sword
    Where never a sword should be.

"What's this now, goodwife?
    What's this I see?
How came this sword here
    Without the leave of me?"

"Shame on your silly face,
    For surely you can see
It's nothing but a porridge stick
    My mother sent to me."

"I've traveled far," our goodman said,
    "I've traveled wide," said he.
"But a two-edged, cutting porridge stick
    Never did I see."

Home came our goodman,
    Home came he,
And there he saw a great-coat
    Where never a coat should be.

"What's this now, goodwife?
    What's this I see?
How came this coat here
    Without the leave of me?"

"Shame on your silly face,
    For surely you can see

It's but a pair of blankets
  My mother sent to me."

"I've traveled far," our goodman said,
  "I've traveled wide," said he.
"But buttons upon blankets
  Never did I see."

Inside went our goodman,
  To the inner room went he,
And in the bed he spied a man
  Where never a man should be.

"What's this now, goodwife?
  What's this I see?
How came this man here
  Without the leave of me?"

"Shame on your silly face,
  For surely you can see
It's only a new milking-maid
  My mother sent to me."

"I've traveled far," our goodman said,
  "I've traveled wide," said he.
"But a maiden with a long beard
  Never did I see."

The Friar and the Fair Maid

O hearken and hear the while I will tell
Of a friar that loved a maiden too well.

The friar he came to this maiden's bed
And there he asked for her maidenhead.

"O I would grant you your heart's desire
But I am afraid of hell's burning fire."

363

"Of hell's burning fire you need have no doubt,
For though you were in, I would whistle you out."

"O if I should grant you this very thing
Some money first to me you must bring."

He brought her the money and then, so they tell,
She spread a white cloth in front of the well.

"My master is coming," she suddenly cried.
"O," said the friar, "then where shall I hide?"

"O you will be safe behind yonder screen
For then by my master you will not be seen."

Hastily behind the screen he went
And fell in the well by accident.

"O help," he cried with a piteous moan,
"O help! Help me out, or else I will drown."

"You said you would whistle me out of hell;
Now whistle yourself right out of the well."

She helped him out and bade him be gone;
Then the friar asked for his money again.

"As for your money, it's a very small matter,
And you should pay more for fouling our water."

Now all who have heard must commend this fair maid
For the nimble trick on the friar she played.

The Riddle

Down in a garden sits my dearest Love,
Her skin more white than is the Down of Swan,
More tender-hearted than the Turtle Dove,
And far more kind than is the Pelican;

I courted her, she blushing, rose and said,
Why was I born to live and die a Maid?

If that be all your grief, my Sweet, said I,
I soon shall ease you of your care and pain,
Yielding a mean to cure your misery,
That you no more shall cause have to complain,
Then be content, Sweeting, to her, I said,
Be ruled by me, thou shalt not die a Maid.

A Medicine for thy grief I can procure,
Then wail no more (my Sweet) in discontent,
My love to thee for ever shall endure,
I'll give no cause whereby thou shouldst repent,
The Match we make: for I will constant prove
To thee, my Sweeting, and my dearest Love.

Then sigh no more, but wipe thy watery eyes,
Be not perplexed, my Honey, at the heart,
Thy beauty doth my Heart and thoughts surprise
Then yield me love, to end my burning smart.
Shrink not from me, my bonny Love, I said,
For I have vowed thou shalt not die a Maid.

Pity it were, so fair a one as you,
Adorned with Nature's chiefest Ornaments,
Should languish thus in pain, I tell you true,
Yielding in love, all danger still prevents.
Then seem not coy, nor Love be not afraid,
But yield to me, thou shalt not die a Maid.

Yield me some comfort, Sweeting, I entreat,
For I am now tormented at the heart,
My affection's pure, my love to thee is great,
Which makes me thus my thoughts to thee impart:
I love thee dear, and shall do evermore,
O pity me, for love I now implore.

For her I plucked a pretty Marigold,
Whose leaves shut up even with the Evening Sun,
Saying, Sweetheart, look now and do behold
A pretty Riddle in it to be shown:

This Leaf shut in, even like a Cloistered Nun,
Yet will it open, when it feels the Sun.

What mean you by this Riddle, Sir, she said,
I pray expound it. Then he thus began:
Women were made for Men, and Men for Maids
With that she changed her color, and looked wan,
Since you this Riddle to me so well have told
Be you my Sun, I'll be your Marigold.

~∘∘~

The Swimming Lady [1]

The four and twentieth Day of May,
    Of all Times of the Year,
A Virgin-Lady bright in and gay,
    Did privately appear
Close by a River-side, which she
    Did single out the rather,
'Cause she was sure, she was secure,
    And had an Intent to bath her.

With glittering Glance, her jealous Eyes,
    Did slyly look about,
To see if any lurking Spies,
    Were hid to find her out;
And being well resolv'd that none
    Could view her Nakedness;
She puts her Robes off, one by one
    And doth her self undress.

A purple Mantle (fringed with Gold)
    Her Ivory Hands unpin,
It would have made a Coward bold,
    Or tempted a Saint to sin;
She turns about to look again,
    I hope, says she, I am safe,
And then a Rosy Petticoat,

[1] When these verses appeared in a collection of ballads in 1723 they were preceded by a caption which read: "A true relation of a coy lady betray'd by her lover as she was stark naked and swimming in a river near Oxford."

She presently put off.
The Snow-White Smock which she had on
    Transparently so decked her,
It looked like Cambrick-Lawn, upon
    An Alabaster Picture,
Thro' which your Eye might faintly spy
    Her Belly and her Back;
Her Limbs were strait, and all was white
    But that which should be black.

The Part which she's ashamed to see
    Without a bashful Blush,
Appeared like curious Tiffany
    Displayed upon a Bush:
But that Posterior extreme Limb
    She cannot look upon,
Did like a twisted Cherry seem
    Before the white was gone.

As when a Masquing Scene is drawn,
    And new Lights do appear,
When she put off her Smock of Lawn,
    Just such a Sight was there:
The bright Reflection of her Eyes,
    In every Limb was strowed,
As when the radiant Sun doth rise,
    And gild each neighboring Cloud,

Into a fluent Stream she leapt,
    Which look'd like liquid Glass;
The Fishes from all Quarters crept,
    To see what Angel 'twas;
She did so like a Vision look,
    Or Fancy in a Dream,
'Twas thought the Sun the Sky forsook,
    And dropt into the Stream,

Each Fish did wish himself a Man,
    About her all were drawn,
And at the Sight of her began
    To spread abroad their Spawn:

She turned to swim upon her Back,
    And so display'd her Banner,
If Jove had then in Heaven been
    He would have dropt upon her.

Thus was the River's Diamond Head,
    With Pearl and Sapphire crowned:
Her legs did shove, her Arms did move,
    Her Body did rebound;
She that did quaff the Juice of Joy,
    (Fair Venus Queen of Love)
With Mars did never in more ways,
    Of melting Motion move.

A Lad that long her Love had been,
    And could obtain no Grace,
For all her prying, lay unseen;
    Hid in a secret Place;
Who having been repulsed when he
    Did often come to woo her,
Pull'd off his Clothes, and furiously
    Did run and leap in to her.

She shrieks, she strives, and down she dives,
    He brings her up again,
He got her o'er, upon the Shore,
    And then, and then, and then!
As Adam did old Eve enjoy,
    You may guess what I mean;
Because she all uncovered lay,
    He covered her again.

With wat'ry Eyes, she pants, and cries
    I'm utterly undone,
If you'll not be wedded unto me,
    Ere the next Morning Sun;
He answered her, I'll never stir
    Out of thy Sight 'till then;
We'll both clasp Hands, in Wedlock Bands,
    Marry, and to't again.

The Foolish Miller

Come all who desire to hear of a jest;
Come listen and learn from one of the best.
'Tis the tale of a miller that lived very near;
The like of his story you never did hear.

A handsome young country lass came to his mill;
To have her corn ground with right earnest will.
The miller beheld her with joy and delight
And asked her to stay with him all of the night.

He told her, "My dear, you must wait until morn
When Lawrence, my man, can start grinding your corn.
But meanwhile, if you will but hearken to me,
At home in my parlor your lodging shall be.
You have set me on fire because of your charms
And therefore this night you must sleep in my arms.
'Tis no use to argue or answer me no;
I swear on my life that it needs must be so."

The maid when she heard this, all blushing did stand;
But the masterful miller took her by the hand
And, leading her home to Gillian, his wife,
Said, "Honey, my darling, the joy of my life,
Be kind to this girl, for her father I know,
And let her sleep here in the parlor below.
Young Lawrence, my servant, and I will both stay
All night in the mill till the dawning of day."

The wife at his bidding agreed to his will,
And straightway the miller did hie to the mill;
He almost was ready to leap from his skin
To think of the bed that he meant to lie in.

Now when he was gone, the girl told his intent
To Gillian, and they a new scheme did invent.
The maid and the wife they changed beds for that night;
So that when the miller prepared for delight
Straightway to the parlor bed he did repair,

And instead of the maiden, his Gillian was there,
Which he did imagine was just the young lass.
And, after some hours in pleasure went past,
He returned to the mill, but a thought drove him wild
For fear he had got the young maiden with child.

Then to Lawrence, his servant, the miller did say,
"I have left a young maiden both bonny and gay;
Her eyes are like diamonds, her cheeks sweet and fair,
They may with the rose and the lily compare;
Her lips they are warm and their color is red.
This lass is at home in the parlor bed;
So if you go there you may freely enjoy
With her every pleasure, for she is not coy."

His master's kind offer he did not refuse;
He rose brisk and airy and pleased with the news.
He said, "To yourself much beholden I am,
In return for this favor I'll give you my ram."
With this lusty Lawrence gets up and goes;
He strips off his coat, his shoes and his hose,
And went into bed with Gillian, the dame.
Yet Lawrence for this was not worthy of blame.

He little imagined the dame was in bed,
And therefore his heart was the freer from dread;
The moments in pastime and pleasure they spent,
While each of them dallied and tasted content.
Now after young Lawrence the dame had embraced
He rose and returned to the mill in all haste;
He then told the miller of all the delight
Which he had enjoyed with the damsel that night.

Next morning the maid to the mill did repair;
The miller and Lawrence, his servant, were there.
The miller then whispered this word in her ear,
"How like you to lie with a miller, my dear?"
At this the young maiden, laughing outright,
Said, "I changed beds with your Gillian last night.
If you enjoyed any, it was your sweet wife,
For I never lay with a man in my life."

At this he began to rave, stamp and swear,
He beat on the table and tore at his hair;
A madman distracted, about he did run
And oftentimes crying, "Ah! What have I done;
Was ever a miller so badly betrayed!
By Lawrence, my man, I a cuckold am made!"
The maiden she laughed and was pleased in her mind,
And said he was very well served in his kind.

The London Prentice

A Worthy London Prentice,
    Came to his Love by Night;
The Candles were lighted,
    The Moon did shine so bright:
He knocked at the Door,
    To ease him of his Pain;
She rose and let him in, Love,
    And went to Bed again.

He went into the Chamber,
    Where his true Love did lie;
She quickly gave consent,
    For to have his Company:
She quickly gave consent,
    The Neighbors peeping out;
So take away your Hand,
    Love, let's blow the Candle out.

I would not for a Crown, Love,
    My Mistress should it know;
I'll in my Smock step down, Love,
    And I'll out the Candle blow;
The Streets they are so nigh,
    And the People walk about;
Some may peep in and spy, Love,
    Let's blow the Candle out.

My Master and my Mistress,
    Upon the Bed do lie;
Enjoying one another,

Why should not you and I;
My Master kiss'd my Mistress,
    Without any fear or doubt;
And we'll kiss one another,
    Let's blow the Candle out.

I prithee speak more softly,
    Of what we have to do;
Least that our noise of Talking,
    Should make our Pleasure rue:
For kissing one another,
    Will make no evil rout;
Then let us now be silent,
    And blow the Candle out.

But yet he must be doing,
    He could no longer stay;
She strove to blow the Candle out,
    And push'd his Hand away:
The young Man was so hasty,
    To lay his Arms about;
But she cried I pray, Love,
    Let's blow the Candle out.

As this young Couple sported,
    The Maiden she did blow;
But how the Candle went out,
    Alas I do not know!
  Said she I fear not now, Sir,
    My Master nor my Dame;
And what this Couple did, Sir,
    Alas I dare not Name.

An Amorous Dialogue Between the Mistris And Her Aprentice

Come, John sit thee down, I have somewhat to say,
In my mind I have kept it this many a day,
Your Master you know is a Fool and a Sot,
And minds nothing else but the Pipe and the Pot.

Till twelve or till one he will never come home,
And then he's so drunk that he lies like a Mome:
 Such usage as this would make any one mad,
 But a woman will have it if 'tis to be had.

'Tis true forsooth mistris, the case is but hard,
That a woman should be of her pleasure debarred;
But 'tis the sad fate of a thousand beside,
Or else the whole City is fouly belied.
There is not a man among twenty that thrives,
Not ten in fifteen that lie with their Wives:
 Yet still you had better be merry than sad,
 And take it wherever it is to be had.

But, John, 'tis a difficult matter to find,
A man that is trusty and constantly kind:
An Inns-of-Court Gallant he cringes and bows,
He's presently known by his Oaths and his Vows,
And though both his clothes and his speeches be gay,
Yet he loves you but only a night and away:
 Such usage as this would make any one mad,
 Yet a woman will have it, if 'tis to be had.

What think you of one that belongs to the Court,
They say they are youthful, and given to sport:
He'll present you with bracelets, and jewels, and Rings,
With stones that are precious, and twenty fine things;
Or if you are not for the Court nor the Town,
What think you forsooth of a man with a Gown?
 You must have a gallant, a good or a bad,
 And take it where ever it is to be had.

No, John, I confess that not any of these,
Had ever the power my fancy to please;
I like no such blades for a trick that I know,
For as soon as they've trod they are given to crow;
Plain dealing is best, and I like a man well,
That when he has kiss'd will be hang'd ere he'll tell:
 My meaning is honest, and thou art the Lad,
 Then give it and take it where 'tis to be had.

Alas! my dear mistris, it never can be,
That you can affect such a fellow as me:
Yet heaven forbid, since I am but your man,
I should ever refuse to do all I can;
But then if my master should know what we've done,
We both shou'd be blown up as sure as a Gun:
> For after our joys, he would make us sad,
> For taking it where it ought not to be had.

But how shou'd he know it, thou scrupulous elf,
Do'st think I'm so silly to tell him myself?
If we are but so wise our own counsel to keep,
We may laugh and lie down while the sot is asleep:
Some hundreds I know in the city that use
To give to their men what their masters refuse:
> The man is the master, the Prentice the Dad,
> For women must take it where 'tis to be had.

Some prentices use it, forsooth, I allow,
But I am a novice and cannot tell how:
However, I hope that I shall not be blam'd,
For, to tell you the truth, I am somewhat asham'd;
I know how to carry your Bible to Church,
But to play with my mistris I'm left in the lurch;
> Yet if you can show me the way good or bad,
> I'll promise you all that there is to be had.

You quickly may learn it, my Johnny, for . . . Thus,
Before you proceed you begin with a buss;
And then you must clasp me about with your arm;
Nay, fear me not Johnny I'll do thee no harm;
Now I sigh, now I tremble, now backwards I lie,
And now dear Johnny, ah now I must die.
> Oh! who can resist such a mettlesome lad,
> And refuse such a pleasure when 'tis to be had.

Alas, pretty mistris, the pleasure is such,
We never can give one another too much:
If this be the business the way is so plain,
I think I can easily find it again:

'Twas thus we began; and . . . Thus we lie down,
And thus . . . Oh thus! that we fell in a swoun:
>   *Such sport to refuse who was ever so mad,*
>   *I'll take it where ever it is to be had.*

Now, Johnny, you talk like an ignorant mome,
You can have such pleasures no where but at home,
Here's fifty broad pieces for what you have done,
But see that you never a gadding do run:
For no new employment then trouble your brains,
For here when you work you'll be paid for your pains:
>   *But should you deceive me no woman so sad,*
>   *To lose all the pleasure that once she has had.*

A mistris so noble I never will leave,
'Twere a sin and a shame such a friend to deceive;
For my Master's shop no more will I care,
'Tis pleasanter handling my mistrisses ware:
A fig for Indentures, for now I am made
Free of a gentler and pleasanter trade:
>   *I know when I'm well, I was never so mad,*
>   *To forsake a good thing when 'tis to be had.*

⁓ ୬୧ ⌒

There Was a Knight

There was a knight and he was young,
A-riding along the way, sir,
And there he met a lady fair
Among the cocks of hay, sir,
Down, derry, down.

Quoth he, "Shall you and I, lady,
Among the grass lay down, O,
And I will take a special care
Of rumplin' of your gown, O,"
Down, derry down.

"If you go along with me
Unto my father's hall, sir,
You shall enjoy my maidenhead
And my estate and all, sir."
Down, derry, down.

375

He mounted her on a milk-white steed,
Himself upon another,
And then they rid upon the road
Like sister and like brother.
Down, derry, down.

And when she came to her father's house,
All moated round about, sir,
She stepped straight within the gate
And shut this young knight out, sir.
Down, derry, down.

"Here is a purse of gold," she said,
"Take it for your pains, sir,
And I will send my father's man
To go home with you again, sir."
Down, derry, down.

"And if you meet a lady fair
As you go through the town, sir,
You must not fear the dewy grass
Nor the rumplin' of her gown, sir."
Down, derry, down.

"And if you meet a lady gay
As you go by the hill, sir,
If you will not when you may,
You shall not when you will, sir."
Down, derry, down.

The Three Travelers

There was three travelers, travelers three,
(Hey down, ho down, lack a down derry)
And they would go travel the North Countree
Without ever a penny of money.

At length, by good fortune, they came to an inn
And they were as merry as e'er they had been
Without ever a penny of money.

A jolly young widow did smiling appear
Who gave them a banquet of delicate cheer
Without ever a penny of money.

They drank to their hostess a merry full bowl;
She pledged them in love, like a generous soul,
Without ever a penny of money.

The hostess, her maid and cousin, all three,
They kissed and was merry, as merry could be,
Without ever a penny of money.

When they had been merry good part of the day
They called their hostess to know what to pay,
Without ever a penny of money.

"There's thirty good shillings and sixpence," she cried.
They told her that she would be soon satisfied,
Without ever a penny of money.

The handsomest man of the three, up he got.
He laid her on her back and he paid her the shot
Without ever a penny of money.

The middlemost man to her cousin he went.
She being handsome, he gave her content
Without ever a penny of money.

The last man of all, he took up with the maid
And thus the whole shot, it was lovingly paid
Without ever a penny of money.

The hostess, the cousin and servant, we find,
Made curtsies and thanked them for being so kind
Without ever a penny of money.

Then, taking their leaves, they went merrily out.
They're gone for to travel the nation about
Without ever a penny of money.

Kit Hath Lost Her Key

Poor Kit hath lost her key
But I have one will fit
Her lock if she will try
And do me not deny—
I hope she hath more wit.

My key is bright, not rusty;
It is so oft applied
To locks that are not dusty
Of maidens that are lusty
And not too full with pride.

Then, Kit, be not too proud
But try my ready key
That oft hath been allowed
By ladies fair—a crowd!—
The best that e'er they see.

You can but try and then,
If it fits not, goodbye.
Go to some other man
And see if any can
Do better, Kit, than I.

But ne'er come back to me
When you have gone away,
For I shall keep my key
For others, not for thee;
So either go or stay.

'Tis But a Wanton Trick

If anyone long for a musical song
    Although that his hearing be thick,
The sound that it bears will ravish his ears—
    'Tis but a wanton trick.

A pleasant young maid on her instrument played
    That knew neither dot-note nor prick;

378

She had a good will to live by her skill—
    'Tis but a wanton trick.

A youth in that art well versed in his part,
    A lad named Darbyshire Dick,
Came as her suitor and would be her tutor—
    'Tis but a wanton trick.

The string of his viol she put to a trial
    Till she learned the full play of his stick;
Her white bellied lute she matched with his flute—
    'Tis but a wanton trick.

His viol string burst; her tutor she cursed,
    Rememb'ring the play of his stick.
From October to June she was quite out of tune—
    'Tis but a wanton trick.

All maids that make trial of lute or of viol,
    Take heed how you handle the stick.
If you like not this order, then try my recorder—
    'Tis but a wanton trick.

Love's Torment

Lady, why doth love torment you?
Cannot I your griefs remove?
Is there none that can content you
With the sweet delights of love?

If I grieve and you can ease me,
Will you be so fiercely bent?
Having wherewithal to please me
Must I still be discontent?

If I am your faithful servant
And my love doth still remain,
Will you think it ill-deserved
To be favored for my pain?

If I should but crave a favor
Which your lips invite me to,
Will you think it ill behavior
Thus to steal a kiss or two?

All amazing beauty's wonder,
May I presume your breast to touch?
Or to feel a little under
Will you think I do too much?

Once more, fairest, let me try thee;
Now my wish is fully sped.
If all night I would lie by thee,
Shall I be refused your bed?

The Frolicsome Farmer

'Tis of a brisk young Farmer, in Derbyshire did dwell;
He kept a buxom Dairy-maid, as I for truth do tell
She was both tall and handsome, and pleasing to his mind
Which made him to slight his wife, as you shall quickly find.

It happened on a certain time he did to market go,
But little did his wife think he meant to serve her so.
Twas near the hour of twelve that night, ere he went home again
When he found the buxom Dairy-maid waiting to let him in.

He said, charming Betsey, I'll tell unto thee this night
It's long I have admired thee, thy beauty so bright,
Here's half-a-crown, my pretty maid, I'll give unto thee,
Each market night when I come home, if you'll be kind to me.

Long time both master and dairy-maid kept up this game
Until at length his jealous wife suspected the same;
She said I'll find out their tricks, if the harlot she's play'd
To the devil I'll soon kick him and his fine Dairy-maid.

As it happen'd he to market went upon a certain day,
When night came the mistress unto her maid did say,
Now that your work is done you may go up to bed,
For your master's coming home I'll sit up in your stead.

About the hour of twelve that night unto the door he came,
The mistress thought, but nothing spoke, I'll find out same;
The kitchen being very dark, unto his wife he said,
My dear sit upon my knee, thinking it was the maid.

When that was past and over, he then without delay,
In his wife's hand slipt half-a-crown and to her did say,
Dear Betsey now go to bed, as fast as you can hie,
And at the fair a nice new gown for you I will buy.

Then the mistress to her room so quietly did creep,
When her husband came to bed she shammed fast asleep;
They laid, but never spoke until the morning came,
And when they at breakfast met, she began the game.

O Betsey, here's half-a-crown last night was giv'n for you;
Put it safe in your pocket, for I'm sure it's your due;
Besides your kind master, the first time he goes to town,
Did promise me last night he'd buy you a new gown.

Betsey then got discharged, and knew the reason why
The Farmer from his angry wife was forced to fly,
So all you cunning husbands that stay out late at night,
Be always sure when you come to choose the candle light.

The Jovial Tinker

It was a Lady of the North she lov'd a Gentleman,
And knew not well what course to take, to use him now and then.
Wherefore she writ a Letter, and seal'd it with her hand,
And bid him be a Tinker, to mend both pot and pan,
With a hey ho, hey, derry derry down; with hey trey,
   down down, derry.

And when the merry Gentleman the Letter he did read,
He got a budget on his back, and Apron with all speed,
His pretty shears and pincers, so well they did agree,
With a long pike staff upon his back, came tripping o'er the Lea.
With a hey ho, hey, derry derry down; with hey trey,
   down down, derry.

When he came to the Lady's house, he knocked at the gate,
Then answered this Lady gay, Who knocketh there so late?
'Tis I, Madam, the Tinker said, I work for gold and fee:
If you have any broken pots or pans, come bring them all to me.
With a hey ho, hey, derry derry down; with hey trey,
    down down, derry.

I am the bravest Tinker that lives beneath the Sun,
If you have any work to do, you shall have it well done;
I have brass within my budget, and punching under my Apron,
I'm come unto your Ladyship, and mean to mend your Cauldron.
With a hey ho, hey, derry derry down; with hey trey,
    down down, derry.

I prithee, said the Lady gay, bring now thy budget in
I have store of work for thee to do, if thou wilt once begin.
Now when the Tinker he came in that did the budget bear,
God bless, quoth he, your Ladyship! God save you, Madam fair.
With hey ho, hey, derry derry down; with hey trey,
    down down, derry.

But when the Lady knew his face, she then began to wink,
Haste, lusty Butler! then quoth she, to fetch the man some drink.
Give him such meat as we do eat, and drink as we do use,
It is not for a Tinker's Trade good liquor to refuse.
With hey ho, hey, derry derry down; with hey trey
    down down, derry.

But when that he had eat and drunk, the truth of all is so,
The Lady took him by the sleeve, her work to him to show,
Let up thy Tools, Tinker, quoth she, and see there be none lost,
And mend my Kettle handsomely, whate'er it doth me cost.
With hey ho, hey, derry derry down; with hey trey,
    down down, derry.

Your work, Madam, shall be well done, if you will pay me for't;
For every nail that I do drive, you shall give me a mark.
If I do not drive the nail to th'head, I'll have nothing for my pain,
And what I do receive of you shall be return'd again.
With hey ho, hey, derry derry down; with hey trey,
    down down, derry.

At last being come into the room, where he the work should do,
The Lady lay down on the bed, so did the Tinker too:
Although the Tinker knockt amain, the Lady was not offended,
But before that she rose from the bed, her Cauldron was well
  mended.
With hey ho, hey, derry derry down; with hey trey,
  down down, derry.

But when his work was at an end, which he did in the dark,
She put her hand into her purse and gave him twenty mark,
Here's money for thy work, said she, and I thank thee for thy pain,
And when my Cauldron mending lacks I'll send for thee again.
With hey ho, hey, derry derry down; with hey trey,
  down down, derry.

The Tinker he was well content for that which he had done,
So took his budget on his back, and quickly he was gone.
Then the Lady to her husband went, O my dear Lord, quoth she,
I have set the bravest Tinker at work that ever you did see.
With hey ho, hey, derry derry down; with hey trey,
  down down, derry.

No fault at all this Tinker hath, but he takes much for his work;
That little time that he wrought here it cost me twenty mark.
If you had been so wise, quoth he, for to have held your own,
Before you set him to this work the price you might have known.
With hey ho, hey, derry derry down; with hey trey,
  down down, derry.

Pray hold your peace, my Lord, quoth she, and think it not too
  dear.
If you could do't so well 'twould save you forty pound a year.
With that the Lord most lovingly, to make all things amends,
He kindly kist his Lady gay, and so they both were friends.
With hey ho, hey, derry derry down; with hey trey,
  down down, derry.

You merry Tinkers, every one, that hear this new-made Sonnet,
When as you do a Lady's work be sure you think upon it;
Drive home your nails to the very head, and do your work
  profoundly,

And then no doubt your Mistresses will pay you for it soundly.
With hey ho, hey, derry derry down; with hey trey,
   down down, derry.

A Ballad of All Trades

Oh the Miller, the dusty, musty Miller,
   The Miller, that beareth on his Back;
He never goes to Measure Meal,
   But his Maid, but his Maid, but his Maid holds ope the sack.

O the Barber, the neat and nimble Barber,
   The Baker that is so full of Sin;
He never heats his Oven hot,
   But he thrusts, but he thrusts, but he thrusts his Maiden in.

O the Brewer, the lusty, lusty Brewer,
   The Brewer that Brews Ale and Beer;
He never heats his Liquor hot,
   But he takes, but he takes, but he takes his Maid by the Geer.

O the Butcher, the bloody, bloody Butcher,
   The Butcher that sells both Beef and Bone;
He never grinds his Slaught'ring Knife,
   But his Maid, but his Maid, but his Maid must turn his Stone.

O the Weaver, the wicked, wicked Weaver,
   That followeth a weary Trade;
He never shoots his Shuttle right,
   But he shoots, but he shoots, but he shoots first at his Maid.

O the Barber, the neat and nimble Barber,
   Whose Trade is ne'er the worse;
He never goes to Wash and Shave,
   But he trims, but he trims, but he trims his Maiden first.

O the Taylor, the fine and frisking Taylor,
   The Taylor that gives no good regard;
He never goes to measure Lace,
   But his Maid, but his Maid, but his Maid holds out his Yard.

O the Blacksmith, the lusty, lusty Blacksmith,
　　The best of all good Fellows;
He never heats his Iron hot,
　　But his Maid, but his Maid, but his Maid must blow the
　　Bellows.

O the Tanner, the Merry, Merry Tanner,
　　The Tanner that draws good Hides into Leather;
He never strips himself to work,
　　But his Maid, but his Maid, but his Maid and he's together.

O the Tinker, the sturdy, sturdy Tinker,
　　The Tinker that deals all in Mettle;
He never clencheth home a Nail,
　　But his Trull, but his Trull, but his Trull holds up the Kettle.

The Jolly Driver

I am a jolly young fellow,
　　My fortune I wish to advance,
I first took up to London,
　　And I next took a tour to France,
I understand all kinds of servitude,
　　And every fashion so tight,
If you hire me as your coachman,
　　I am a safe driver by night.

Up came a lady of fashion,
　　And thus unto me did say,
If I hire you as my coachman,
　　You must drive by night and by day,
Ten guineas a month I will give you
　　Besides a bottle of wine,
If you keep me in plenty of drink,
　　I will drive you in a new fashion style.

She brought me into the kitchen,
　　Where she gave me liquors so quick,
She told me drink that in a hurry,
　　She wish'd to see my driving whip;

385

O when that she seen it
    She eyed it with a smile,
Saying, I know by the length of your lash,
    You can drive in a new fashion style.

She bid me get into her chaise box,
    And drive both mild and discreet,
And handle my whip with much judgment,
    And drive her quite through the street;
Three curls I gave to my cracker,
    And then I was up to her rig,
And the very first turn the wheel got,
    I broke the main-spring of her gig.

She brought me into the cellar,
    And gave me a bottle of wine,
She told me drink that in a hurry,
    As I had to drive her three miles;
She being a nice little young thing,
    And just in the height of her bloom,
And I being a dashing young fellow,
    I drove her nine times round the room.

My mistress being tired and weary,
    In order to take a rest,
She call'd for her waiting-maid, Sally,
    The maid that she loved best,
Saying, Sally, we've got a good coachman,
    That understands driving in style,
And while my gig wheel is repairing,
    I'll let him drive you for a mile.

So now to conclude and finish,
    Driving I mean to give o'er,
Carriages, cars, gigs, and coaches,
    I ne'er will drive any more;
When the Ladies of honor all heard it,
    The truth they did declare,
They ne'er could meet with a coachman,
    That understood driving so fair.

The Brisk Girl

There was a brisk girl both bonny and brown,
She'd courted her sweetheart here in our town.
She laid by her work, her wheel, and her yarn
To follow her love in the farmer's barn.
Quoth she, "If you'll be marrièd
We'll hie to the parson and then to bed;
My virgin treasure I'll give thee, Ned,
That is, to be plain, my maidenhead.

"You know that my love is a flame of fire
And burns when it cannot obtain its desire;
My beauty is now in its blooming time
And I cannot nor will not delay the time.
I long to taste those tender joys,
Those soft warm kisses and wanton toys
That every lass in her wedding enjoys,
While lads with young lasses get lusty boys.

"A garland of roses my love shall wear,
And I'll give him a lock of my coal-black hair;
At every wake my love I'll treat
And give him kind kisses as dream-boats sweet.
Thou'll be my buck and I'll be thy doe;
I shall mew and thou shalt mow;
I'll card and I'll spin whilst you harrow and sow,
And call upon Dobbin with, 'Hey, Gee, Ho!' "

Dabbling in the Dew

"Where are you going, my pretty little dear,
  With your bright blue eyes and your golden hair?"
"I'm going milking," she answered quick and clear,
  "For it's dabbling in the dew that keeps the milkmaids fair."

"Shall I carry your pail, my pretty little dear,
  With your bright blue eyes and your golden hair?"
"O no," she said,, "I can carry it from here,
  For it's dabbling in the dew that keeps the milkmaids fair."

"Supposing that I kiss you, my pretty little dear,
   With your bright blue eyes and your golden hair?"
"There would be no harm in that," she said, "so never fear,
   For it's dabbling in the dew that keeps the milkmaids fair."

"Supposing that I threw you down, my pretty little dear,
   With your bright blue eyes and your golden hair?"
"Why, then you'd pick me up again," she answered quick and clear,
   For it's dabbling in the dew that keeps the milkmaids fair."

"Supposing there's a baby, my pretty little dear,
   With your bright blue eyes and your golden hair?"
"Why, then you'd have to marry me before the end of the year,
   For it's dabbling in the dew that keeps the milkmaids fair."

"Suppose I ran away from you, my pretty little dear,
   With your bright blue eyes and your golden hair?"
"Why, then I'd run still faster and bring you back to here,
   For it's dabbling in the dew that keeps the milkmaids fair."

O, No, John

On yonder hill there stands a creature,
   Who she is I do not know.
I'll go court her for her beauty,
   Till she answer yes or no.
"O, no, John, no, John, no, John, no."

On her bosom there are flowers,
   On her breast sweet blossoms glow.
Should I put my hand upon them,
   She must answer yes or no.
"O, no, John, no, John, no, John, no."

"Madam in your face is beauty,
   On your lips red roses grow.
Will you take me for your lover?
   Madam, answer yes or no."
"O, no, John, no, John, no, John, no."

"My husband was a Spanish captain,
    Went to sea a year ago;
First he kissed me, then he left me,
    Bade me always answer no.
"So no, John, no, John, no, John, no."

"Madam, may I tie your garter
    Above your knee or a little below?
If my hand should slip a little,
    Would it hurt or vex you so?"
"O, no, John, no, John, no, John, no."

"Madam, since you are so cruel,
    And you keep me to and fro;
If I may not be your lover,
    Madam will you let me go?"
O, no, John, no, John, no, John, no!"

⁓୨୧⁓

Gently, Johnny My Jingalo

I put my hand upon her toe,
    Fair maid is a lily O;
I put my hand upon her toe,
Said she, "Young man, you've far to go.
    Come to me
    Quietly;
    Do not do me injury.
Gently, Johnny my Jingalo."

I put my hand upon her shin,
    Fair maid is a lily O;
I put my hand upon her shin.
Said she, "Young man, when you begin,
    Come to me
    Quietly
    Do not do me injury.
Gently, Johnny my Jingalo."

I put my hand upon her calf,
    Fair maid is a lily O;

389

I put my hand upon her calf.
Said she, "Young man, you're there by half;
    Come to me
    Quietly
    Do not do me injury.
Gently, Johnny, my Jingalo."

I put my hand upon her knee,
    Fair maid is a lily O;
I put my hand upon her knee.
Said she, "Young man, you're rather free.
    Come to me
    Quietly;
    Do not do me injury.
Gently, Johnny my Jingalo."

I put my hand upon her thigh,
    Fair maid is a lily O;
I put my hand upon her thigh.
Said she, "Young man, you're getting high;
    Come to me
    Quietly,
    Do not do me injury.
Gently, Johnny my Jingalo."

I put my hand as far as far,
    Fair maid is a lily O;
I put my hand as far as far.
Said she, "At last, now there you are,
    Come to me
    Quietly,
    Do not do me injury.
Gently, Johnny my Jingalo."

As I Walked in the Woods

As I walked in the woods one evening of late,
A lass was deploring her hapless estate;
In a languishing posture, poor maid, she appears,

All swelled with her sighs and flushed with her tears;
She cried and she sobbed, and I found it was all
For a little of that which Harry gave Doll.

At last she broke out, wretched, she said,
"Will not youth come succor a languishing maid
With what he with ease and pleasure may give,
Without which, alas, poor I cannot live!
Shall I never leave sighing and crying and call
For a little of that which Harry gave Doll?

"At first when I saw a young man in the place,
My color would fade and then flush in my face,
My breath it grew short and I shivered all o'er,
My breast never popped up and down so before,
I scarce knew for what, but now I find it was all
For a little of that which Harry gave Doll."

The Shepherd

A shepherd sat 'neath a tree one day
And as the shadows grew more long
Pull'd out his pipe and began to play
And sweet and merry was his song.

A country damsel from the town
With basket made of woven straw
Came gathering rushes on the down
And boldly smiled when she him saw.

The shepherd's pipe did gaily sound
As tempting on her back she lay
And when his quivering note she found
How sweetly then this lass could play.

She ne'er so much as blush'd at all
So sweetly play'd her shepherd swain
But e'er anon to him she'd call
To play her another double strain.

The shepherd again did tune his pipe
And play'd her a lesson loud and shrill.
The maid his face did often wipe
With many a thank for his good will.

She said, "I ne'er was so pleas'd before
And this is the first time that I knew thee.
Come play me this very tune once more
And never doubt that I'll dance to thee."

The shepherd, he said, "As I am a man,
I have kept playing from sun till moon.
Thou knowst I can do no more than I can,
My pipe is clearly out of tune."

"To ruin a shepherd, I'll not seek,"
She said as she kiss'd him 'neath the tree.
"I'll come again to the down next week
And thou shalt pipe and I'll come to thee."

The Nightingale

One morning, one morning, one morning in May
I met a fair couple a-making their way,
And one was a lady so neat and so fair,
The other a soldier, a brave volunteer.

"Good morning, good morning, good morning to thee,
O where are you going my pretty lady?"
"O I am a-going to the banks of the sea,
To see the waters a-gliding, hear the nightingale sing."

They hadn't been a-standing but one hour or two
When from his equipment a fiddle he drew,
The tune that he played made the valleys ring,
O see the waters a-gliding, hear the nightingale sing.

"Pretty lady, pretty lady, it's time to give o'er,"
"O no, pretty soldier, please play one tune more,
I'd rather hear your fiddle or the touch of one string
As see the waters a-gliding, hear the nightingale sing."

392

"Pretty soldier, pretty soldier, will you marry me?
"O no, pretty lady, that never can be;
I have a wife in London and children twice three:
Two wives in the army's too many for me."

"I'll go back to London and stay there one year
And often I'll think of you my little dear,
If ever I return, 'twill be in the spring
To see the waters a-gliding, hear the nightingale sing!"

What's Your Fancy

Would you have a young virgin of fifteen years;
You must tickle her fancy with sweets and dears,
Ever toying and playing and sweetly, sweetly,
Sing a love sonnet and charm her fears.
Wittily, prettily talk her down,
Chase her and praise her if fair or brown,
Soothe her and smooth her and tease her and please her,
And touch but her smicket and all's your own.

Do you fancy a widow well known in a man,
With a front of assurance come boldly on,
Let her rest not an hour but briskly, briskly,
Put her in mind how her time steals on;
Rattle and prattle although she grown,
Rouse her and towse her from morn 'til noon,
Show her some hour you're able to grapple,
Then get but her writings and all's your own.

Do you fancy a lass of a humor free,
That's kept by a fumbler of quality,
You must rail at her keeper and tell her, tell her,
Pleasure's best charm is variety;
Swear her more fairer than all the town,
Try her and ply her when cully's gone,
Dog her and jog her and meet her and treat her,
And kiss with two guineas, and all's your own.

Phillis

Phillis at first seemed much afraid,
Yet when I kissed, she soon repaid,
Could you but see, could you but see,
What I did more you'd envy me.

We then so sweetly were employed,
The height of pleasure we enjoyed,
Could you but see, could you but see,
You'd say so too, if you saw me.

She was so charming, kind and free,
None ever could more happy be;
Could you but see, could you but see,
Where I was then, you'd wish to be.

All the delights we did express,
Yet craving more still to possess,
Could you but see, could you but see,
You'd curse and say, "Why was't not me!"

Ladies, if how to love you'd know,
She can inform what we did do;
But could you see, but could you see,
You'd cry aloud, "The next is me!"

Tottingham Frolic

As I once came from Tottingham
Upon a market day,
'Twas there I met with a bonny lass
Clothed all in grey.
Her journey was to London,
With buttermilk and whey.
To come down, down . . . . .

And so he spoke to this fair lass.
"Sweetheart you're well o'ertook,"

With that she cast her head aside
And gave to him a look.
Then presently this young pair,
Both hands together shook.
To come down, down . . . . .

And as they rode along the way
Together side by side,
The maiden it so chanced
Her garter was untied;
For fear that she should lose it,
"Look here, sweetheart," he cried,
"Your garter is down, down . . . . ."

"Good sir," then quoth the maiden fair,
"I pray you take the pain,
To do a favor unto me
And take it up again."
With a right good will the young man spoke,
"When I come to yonder plain,
I will take you down, down . . . . ."

And when they came unto the place,
Upon the grass so green,
The maid she held her legs so wide,
The young man slipt between.
Such tying of a garter
You have but seldom seen.
To come down, down . . . . .

And thus sweet Tibb of Tottingham,
She lost her maidenhead,
But yet it is no matter for
It stood her in small stead;
For it did often trouble her
As she lay in her bed.
To come down, down . . . . .

You maidens, wives and widows,
That now do hear my song,
When young men proffer kindness

Pray take it short or long;
For there is no such comfort
As lying with a man.
To come down, down . . . . .

Up-Tails All

There hath a question been of late
Among the youthful sort;
What pastime is the pleasantest
And what the sweetest sport?
And it hath been adjudged,
As well by great and small,
That of all pastimes none is like
To up-tails all.

All bachelors will to this game
And marry'd men likewise;
Yea, wives and maids and widows
Will use it all their lives;
And old men that will have a go
Altho' their game's but small,
Yet these old colts will have a bout
At up-tails all.

It cannot be unwholesome,
Physicians do it use,
And if that it were noisome,
They would it then refuse:
But if it hurt the body,
Then sure their skill is small;
For why the best of these will play
At up-tails all.

All ladies love the pastime,
And do the pleasure crave,
And if it were a base thing,
Then it they would not have:
But yet the fairest women,

Will soonest for it call;
There is no one but that will play
At up-tails all.

And if it were a costly thing,
Then beggars could not buy it,
And if it were a loathsome thing
Then genteels would defy it:
But oh, it is a sweet thing,
And pleasing unto all;
There is no one but that will play
At up-tails all.

I'm Seventeen Come Sunday

As I walked out one May morning,
One May morning so early,
I overtook a handsome maid
Just as the sun was rising.

Her shoes were bright, her stockings white.
And her buckles shone like silver;
She had a black and a roving eye
And her hair hung down her shoulder.

How old are you my fair pretty maid?
How old are you my honey?
She answered me right cheerfully,
I'm seventeen come Sunday.

Can you love me, my fair pretty maid?
Will you marry me, my honey?
She answered me quite cheerfully,
I dare not for my Mummy.

If you'll come to my Mummy's house
When the moon is shining clearly,
I will come down and let you in,
And my Mummy shall not hear me.

I went down to her Mummy's house
When the moon was brightly shining;
She did come down and let me in,
And we lay with our arms entwining.

Now soldier will you marry me?
Now is your time or never;
For if you do not marry me,
I am undone for ever.

And now she is the soldier's wife,
And the soldier loves her dearly;
The drum and fife is her delight,
And a merry man in the morning.

One of the features of the early ballads is their deceptive in-genuousness. "Greensleeves," like Wither's "I Loved a Lass" (page 215), is not merely a plaintive love song but a resentful complaint of a lover who has been supporting an unfaithful mistress. "The Country Lovers" is a graphic picture of unashamed lovemaking, but time has tamed it into the nursery rhyme beginning "Lavender's blue, dilly, dilly." "Hares on the Mountain" scarcely troubles to disguise its quaint symbols of pleasure and pursuit, and the impli-cations in "Two Maids Went Milking" are no less suggestive for being about milking pails and birds.

Greensleeves

Alas, my love! ye do me wrong
    To cast me off discourteously;
And I have lovèd you so long,
    Delighting in your company.

Greensleeves was all my joy;
    Greensleeves was my delight;
Greensleeves was my heart of gold;
    And who but my Lady Greensleeves?

I have been ready at your hand,
    To grant whatever you would crave;
I have both wagèd life and land,
    Your love and goodwill for to have.

I bougnt thee kerchiefs for thy head,
That were wrought fine and gallantly;
I kept thee both at board and bed,
Which cost my purse well plentifully.

I bought thee petticoats of the best,
The cloth so fine as fine might be;
I gave thee jewels for thy chest,
And all this cost I spent on thee.

Thy gown was of the grassy green,
Thy sleeves of satin hanging by,
Which made thee be our harvest queen,
And yet thou wouldst not love me.

My gayest gelding I thee gave,
To ride wherever likèd thee;
No lady ever was so brave,
And yet thou wouldst not love me.

My men were clothèd all in green,
And they did ever wait on thee;
All this was gallant to be seen,
And yet thou wouldst not love me.

For every morning when thou rose,
I sent thee dainties orderly,
To cheer thy stomach from all woes,
And yet thou wouldst not love me.

Well, I will pray to God on high,
That thou my constancy mayst see,
And once again before I die,
Thou wilt vouchsafe to love me.

Greensleeves, now farewell! adieu!
God I pray to prosper thee;
For I am still thy lover true.
Come once again and love me.

Greensleeves was all my joy;
Greensleeves was my delight;
Greensleeves was my heart of gold;
And who but my Lady Greensleeves?

The Country Lovers

Lavender's blue, diddle diddle,
Lavender's green,
When I am king, diddle diddle,
You shall be queen.

Lavender's green, diddle diddle,
Lavender's blue,
You must love me, diddle diddle,
'Cause I love you.

Down in the vale, diddle diddle,
Where flowers grow,
And the birds sing, diddle diddle,
All in a row.

A brisk young man, diddle diddle,
Met with a maid,
And laid her down, diddle diddle,
Under the shade.

There they did play, diddle diddle,
And kiss and court,
All the fine day, diddle diddle,
Making good sport.

I've heard them say, diddle diddle,
Since I came hither
That you and I, diddle diddle,
Might lie together.

Therefore be kind, diddle diddle,
While here we lie,
And you will love, diddle diddle,
My dog and I.

For you and I, diddle diddle,
Now all are one,
And we will lie, diddle diddle,
No more alone.

Lavender's blue, diddle diddle,
Lavender's green,
Let me be king, diddle diddle,
You be the queen.

Hares on the Mountain

Young women, they run like hares on the mountain,
Young women, they run like hares on the mountain,
If I were a young man I'd soon go a-hunting.

Young women they sing like birds in the bushes,
Young women they sing like birds in the bushes,
If I were a young man I'd go bang those bushes.

Young women they swim like ducks in the water,
Young women they swim like ducks in the water,
If I were a young man I soon would swim after.

Young women are slender like rushes a-growing,
Young women are slender like rushes a-growing,
If I were a young man I'd soon go a-mowing.

Young women they blossom like buds that are buxom,
Young women they blossom like buds that are buxom,
If I were a young man I'd hurry and pluck some.

Two Maidens Went Milking

Two maidens went milking one day,
And the wind it did blow high,
And the wind it did blow low,
And it tossed their pails to and fro.

They met with a man they did know,
And they said "Have you the will?"
And they said "Have you the skill,
For to catch us a small bird or two?"

"Oh yes, I have excellent good skill,
If you will come along with me
Under yonder flowering tree,
I might catch you a small bird or two."

So they went and they sat 'neath a tree,
And the birds flew 'round about,
Pretty birds flew in and out,
And he caught them by one and by two.

Now my boys, let us drink down the sun,
Take your lady to the wood
If you really think you should,
You might catch her a small bird or two.

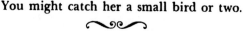

Many current favorites have their origin in ancient ballads but are so thoroughly revised as to be not only new versions but seemingly new tellings. "Pretty Polly" is based on the old Scottish ballad variously known as "May Colvin," "The Baffled Knight," and "The Lady's Policy," which acquired a local accent and was perfectly at home in the Kentucky mountains. "Bell-Bottomed Trousers" was once "Rosemary Lane"; in *The Idiom of the People* James Reeves prints two brisk old versions and calls attention to others. "The Foggy Dew" has had innumerable variations, two of which are reprinted here. The first is the more outspoken; in this version it is the girl who makes the advances. The second is the more refined treatment popularized in the United States as sung by Burl Ives and other ballad-singers.

Pretty Polly

"Get up, get up, pretty Polly," he says,
"And go along with me,
I'll take you away to Bowling Green,
And there we'll marry and stay."

She took fifty dollars of her father's gold,
And besides her mother's fee,
And two of the horses in the stall,
Where there were thirty and three.

She set herself on the bonny, bonny black
And him on the gelding gray;

402

They rode 'til they came to the high sea-side
One hour before it was day.

"Light down, light down, pretty Polly," he says,
"Light down, light down with me,"
This is the place I've drownèd six
And you the seventh shall be."

"Pull off, pull off, that costly gown
And lay it by yonder tree;
It never shall be said such costly wear
Shall rot in the salt, salt sea."

"O turn yourself around and about,
Your face toward the sea;
It never shall be said such a rascal as you
A naked lady for to see."

He turned himself around and about,
And his face toward the sea,
And with her little white tender arms
She shoved him into the sea.

"Lie there, lie there, you false-hearted man
Lie there instead of me,
If this be the place you drownèd six
The seventh you shall be."

She set herself on the bonny, bonny black
And she led the gelding gray;
She rode till she came to her father's house
One hour before it was day.

Bell-Bottomed Trousers

Once I was a serving maid who worked in Drury Lane,
My master he was kind to me, my mistress was the same.
Along came a sailor ashore on liberty,
And oh, to my woe, he took liberty with me.

Singing, "Bell-bottomed trousers, coat of Navy blue;
Let him climb the rigging like his daddy used to do."

As we were walking homeward I heard a neighbor say,
"There's a fair young maiden who's going to be led astray."
But heedless of the warning, I followed where he led,
And we stepped into the bedroom where he wished to test the bed.

He asked me for a candle to light his way to bed;
He asked me for a pillow to rest his weary head.
And I, a silly creature not meaning any harm,
I jumped right in beside him to keep the sailor warm.

Early next morning the sailor he awoke,
And from his trouser pocket he took a ten-bob note.
It was early in the morning, before the break of day,
A ten-bob note he gave to me, and these words he did say:

"Take this, my darling, for the damage I have done;
You may have a daughter, you may have a son.
If you have a daughter, bounce her on your knee;
If you have a son, send the bastard out to sea."

Listen, all you maidens, to my girlish plea,
Don't ever let a sailor get an inch above the knee.
Singing, "Bell-bottomed trousers, coat of Navy blue;
Let him climb the rigging like his daddy used to do."

The Joggy Dew: I

When I was a bachelor lively and young,
   I followed the weaving trade,
And all the harm ever I done,
   Was courting a servant maid.
I courted her the summer season,
   And part of the winter too,
And many a night I rolled her in my arms,
   Because of the foggy dew.

One night as I lay on my bed,
   As I laid fast asleep,
There came a pretty fair maid,

And most bitterly did weep.
She wept, she mourned, she tore her hair,
  Crying, alas what shall I do,
This night I'm resolved to come to bed with you
  For fear of the foggy dew.

It was in the first part of the night,
  We both did sport and play,
And in the latter part of the night,
  She slept in my arms till day.
When broad day-light did appear,
  She cried I am undone.
Hold your tongue you foolish girl,
  The foggy dew is gone.

Suppose that we should have a child;
  It would cause us to smile,
Suppose that we should have another;
  It would make us laugh awhile.
Suppose that we should have another,
  And another one too;
'Twould you leave off your foolish tricks
  And think no more of the foggy dew.

I love this young girl dearly,
  I love her as my life,
I took this girl and married her,
  And made her my lawful wife.
I never told her of her faults,
  Nor never intend to do,
But every time she winks or smiles,
  She thinks of the foggy dew.

The Foggy Dew: II

When I was a bachelor, I lived all alone,
I worked at the weaver's trade;
And the only, only thing I did that was wrong,
Was to woo a fair young maid.

I wooed her in the wintertime
And in the summer too;
And the only, only thing I did that was wrong,
Was to keep her from the foggy, foggy dew.

One night she knelt close by my side,
When I was fast asleep.
She threw her arms around my neck,
And then began to weep.
She wept, she cried, she tore her hair;
Ah me, would could I do?
So all night long I held her in my arms,
Just to keep her from the foggy, foggy dew.

Again I am a bachelor, I live with my son,
We work at the weaver's trade;
And every single time I look into his eyes
He reminds me of the fair young maid.
He reminds me of the wintertime
And of the summer too;
And the many, many times that I held her in my arms,
Just to keep her from the foggy, foggy dew.

It's the Same the Whole World Over

> She was poor but she was honest,
> Victim of a rich man's game;
> For she met the village squire,
> And she lost her maiden name.
>
> It's the same the whole world over;
> It's the poor as gets the blame;
> It's the rich as has the pleasure.
> Ain't it all a bleeding shame.
>
> So she hastened up to London
> For to hide her grief and pain;

There she met an army captain,
And she lost her name again.

See him riding in his carriage
Past the gutter where she stands;
He has made a stylish marriage
While she wrings her ringless hands.

See him in the House of Commons,
Passing laws to put down crime;
While the girl as he has ruined
Slinks away to hide her shame.

See him laugh at the theayter
In the front row with the best;
While the girl as he has ruined
Entertains a sordid guest.

In the little country village
Where her aged parents live,
Though they drink champagne she sends them,
Yet they never can forgive.

It's the same the whole world over;
It's the poor as gets the blame;
It's the rich as has the pleasure.
Ain't it all a bleeding shame.

Commenting on "Careless Love" in *Folk Song: U.S.A.*, John A. and Alan Lomax quote a rhyme saying that careless love can "make a good boy leave his happy home, make a grandmother marry her oldest son, make a preacher lay his Bible down, make a jack rabbit hug a hound." The following is one of countless versions of one of the most popular "blues."

∽ℴ∼

Careless Love

Love, O love, O careless love,
Love, O love, O careless love,
Love, O love, O careless love,
O, see what careless love has done.

It's gone and broke this heart of mine,
It's gone and broke this heart of mine,
It's gone and broke this heart of mine,
It'll break that heart of yours sometime.

When I wore my apron low,
When I wore my apron low,
When I wore my apron low,
You'd follow me through rain and snow.

Now I wear my apron high,
Now I wear my apron high,
Now I wear my apron high,
You won't come in but just pass by.

I cried last night and the night before,
I cried last night and the night before,
I cried last night and the night before,
Gonna cry tonight and evermore.

I love my mama and papa, too,
I love my mama and papa, too,
I love my mama and papa, too,
I'd leave them both for lovin' you.

A-Roving

In Plymouth Town there lived a maid,
  (Bless you, young women)
In Plymouth Town there lived a maid,
  (O, mind what I do say)
In Plymouth Town there lived a maid,
And she was mistress of her trade;
I'll go no more a-roving with you, fair maid.
  A-roving, a-roving,
  Since roving's been my ru-i-in,
I'll go no more a-roving with you, fair maid.

I took this fair maid for a walk
  (Bless you, young women)
I took this fair maid for a walk
  (O, mind what I do say)
I took this fair maid for a walk
And we had such a loving talk;
I'll go no more a-roving with you, fair maid.

And didn't I tell her stories too,
  (Bless you, young women)
And didn't I tell her stories too,
  (O, mind what I do say)
And didn't I tell her stories too
Of the gold I found in Timbuctoo!
I'll go no more a-roving with you, fair maid.

We only had one night, and yet
  (Bless you, young women)
We only had one night, and yet
  (O, mind what I do say)
We only had one night, and yet
She gave me something I won't forget.
I'll go no more a-roving with you, fair maid.
  A-roving, a-roving,
  Since roving's been my ru-i-in,
I'll go no more a-roving with you, fair maid.

A Handful of Foreign Folk Songs

This is a selection of folk songs from many lands and from many languages. All the renderings are by the editor and, with one exception, none has hitherto appeared in print.

─∾჋ჩ∾─

Spinning Song

(FROM THE GERMAN)

"Spin, oh my darling daughter, I'll give you a hat."
"Nay, oh my loving mother, I don't care for that.
   I'm through with my spinning;
   It hurts every finger
     And causes me pain."

"Spin, oh my darling daughter, I'll give you a shoe."
"Nay, oh my loving mother, what good would that do?
   I'm through with my spinning;
   It hurts every finger
     And cause me pain."

"Spin, oh my darling daughter, I'll give you a skirt."
"Nay, oh my loving mother, it won't help the hurt.
   I'm through with my spinning;
   It hurts every finger
     And causes me pain."

"Spin, oh my darling daughter, I'll give you a man!"
"Yes, oh my loving mother, as quick as you can.
   I'm off to my spinning,
   I'm eager and willing,
   My fingers are healing,
     The pain is all gone."

The Ripe Fruit

(FROM THE BRETON)

"Why are you sad, my darling daughter?
Why do you sigh the whole day through?
In all of France or across the water
There is none lovelier than you."

"What good is loveliness to me,
Mother, if you won't let me be
Free as the fruit upon the tree.

"There, as soon as the apple is red,
It must be plucked; if it hangs like lead
It rots and is ten times worse than dead.

"Apples that drop from the unplucked shoot
Wither and foul to the very root.
And what man cares for withered fruit?"

The Challenge

(FROM THE SPANISH)

Since, Señora, you torment me
    With each virtuous denial,
    Since my days are one long trial
For the boon you will not grant me,

Hear then, you who scoff at Venus,
    Death to friendship! I forswear that!
    From this moment I declare that
There is open war between us.

War! Grim war! O chaste supporter
    Of Diana—and of Circe.
    If I lose, I ask no mercy;
If I win, I grant no quarter.

Gird yourself in shining metal,
    For no truce will come to spare you
    Till my arms, triumphant, bear you
Blushing from the field of battle.

By Moonlight

(FROM THE FRENCH)

"In the moonlight evening,
 Neighbor, I must write;
Let me use your pencil,
 Let me use your light.
I am out of candles
 And you know I'm poor;
Be a helpful neighbor;
 Come, unbar the door."

In the moonlit evening
 Came the quick reply,
"Without light or pencil
 In the dark I lie.
But, oh, reverend father,
 If you are not loth,
Next door lives a widow;
 She, I know, has both."

In the moonlight evening
 Now our little priest
Goes and wakes the widow
 Till she cries, "You beast!
You disturb my slumber!
 Why make such a din?"
But he only answers,
 "Neighbor, let me in."

In the moonlit evening
 One can't see a-right,
Though one seeks a pencil,
 Though one looks for light.
What was found that evening?
 Who would tell of it?
This alone is certain:
 Not a light was lit.

The Fool of Love

(FROM THE RUSSIAN)

Beside the pool where shadows flit
Girls from the village like to sit.
Last night I heard the fairest say,
"Young man, what brings you out this way?"
"Your beauty brings me here; and I
Must have your body or I'll die."

Beside the pool she laughed and said,
"This stubble is no sort of bed.
Take horse and hound and ride to where
The army camps. Then steal from there
A thick, soft blanket; spread it wide
And I will lie down at your side."

Beside the pool we two found rest;
I slept upon her soothing breast.
But as I woke soon after dawn
The blanket, horse, and girl were gone.
I was alone. The sun above
Laughed down on me, the fool of love.

Interrupted Romance

(FROM THE RUSSIAN)

In the park I saw a stranger
    (Women always look at me);
Fond of deviltry and danger
    I came close to her, and she
Coyly dropped her heavy lashes,
    Nothing colder, nothing cruder—
Curling my perfumed mustaches,
    Naturally I pursued her.

She went on and I went after
    (Women have an eye for me),

413

Finally she turned with laughter,
    And that moment I could see
How my charms, so often hidden,
    Dazzled her. I glowed, I glistened,
As I talked of things forbidden,
    While she smiled at me and listened.

I grew bold; my blood was humming;
    (Women eye me lovingly).
"Tell my husband—see, he's coming—
    What," she said, "you want of me."
Up he came with fist extended,
    And his cane a lifted threat . . .
"I can't talk," I cried offended,
    "To a man I've never met."

The Merry Muses

Robert Burns

A ne'er-do-well Scottish farmer, son of a hard-luck peasant and an almost illiterate mother, Robert Burns (1759–1796) was also an earthborn poet who happened to write some of the world's purest as well as bawdiest stanzas. His schooling was brief; even as a child he had to help keep the farm going, and at fifteen he was the chief worker. The many labors were alleviated by lovemaking. Burns moved from place to place, but wherever he farmed he found young and eager girls. An entanglement in his mid-twenties resulted in the first of several illegitimate children. He never repudiated his by-blows; in this case, he dedicated a poem to his "bastard wean" and entitled it "A Poet's Welcome to His Love-Begotten Daughter." Not all of Burns's country sweethearts are known, but biographers have traced interludes with Alison Begbie ("Bonnie Peggy Alison"); Elizabeth Paton, mother of his first "love-begotten" child; Mary Campbell ("Highland Mary"), whom he promised to marry and who died in childbirth; Jean Armour, whom he finally did marry; and Anne Park, a good-looking barmaid who bore him a son nine days after Jean had delivered another boy. Jean accepted and brought up Anne's child. "Our Rob," she said calmly, "should hae twa wives."

At twenty-seven Burns got together a collection of random poems, including many which have since become his most famous, and had them printed in a small press at Kilmarnock. It was an unexpected success. Sophisticated critics felt they had discovered a hidden genius, a "heaven-taught plowman"; uncultured readers hailed the author as their natural voice. Suddenly the hapless farmer had become "Caledonia's Bard." He was not assured of a living, but he was certain of a place in literature.

Most of Burns's published poetry is his own, a spontaneous expression of a simple, forthright individuality. Much of it, however, is based on Scottish folk-stuff which he unearthed, adapted, and embellished. It is often difficult to tell (as in the case of the songs which he contributed to Johnson's *Scots Musical Museum*) where an old folk-song ends and where Burns begins.

This is especially true of Burns's private and, to a great extent, unpublished celebration of his enjoyment of the flesh, *The Merry Muses of Caledonia*. He knew the demands of the human animal, and, for the poor in particular, the one dependable and obtainable pleasure—"puir bodies hae naething but mow." He would have been amused at the efforts to transform him into an innocent chanter of rustic ditties. Such poems as "Godly Girzie," "The Lass that Made the Bed for Me," "Wha is that at My Bower-Door," and the more rowdy verses from *The Merry Muses of Caledonia* may be reprehensible to some, but they are the same hand and in the same voice that created "Anna," "Green Grow the Rashes," "Comin' Thro' the Rye," "I Once Was a Maid," and others which are part of the revered Burns canon and which are enshrined in the most respectable libraries.

Anna

Yestreen I had a pint o' wine,
  A place where body saw na;
Yestreen lay on this breast o' mine
  The gowden locks of Anna.

The hungry Jew in wilderness,
  Rejoicing o'er his manna,
Was naething to my hinnie[1] bliss
  Upon the lips of Anna.

Ye monarchs, take the East and West
  Frae Indus to Savannah;
Gie me, within my straining grasp,
  The melting form of Anna.

There I'll despise imperial charms,
  An empress or sultana,
While dying raptures in her arms
  I give and take wi' Anna!

Awa, thou flaunting God of Day!
  Awa, thou pale Diana!
Ilk star, gae hide thy twinkling ray,
  When I'm to meet my Anna!

Come, in thy raven plumage, night
  (Sun, moon, and stars, withdrawn a')
And bring an angel-pen to write
  My transports wi' my Anna!

The Kirk an' State may join, an' tell
  To do sic things I maunna:[2]
The Kirk an' State may gae to hell,
  And I'll gae to my Anna.

[1] Hinnie: honey. [2] Maunna: should not.

419

The Rigs O' Barley

IT was upon a Lammas night,
    When corn rigs[1] are bonie, O,
Beneath the moon's unclouded light
    I held awa to Annie, O;
The time flew by, wi' tentless[2] heed,
    Till 'tween the late and early,[3] O,
Wi' sma' persuasion she agreed,
    To see me thro' the barley, O.

Corn rigs, an' barley rigs,
    An' corn rigs are bonie, O,
O, I'll ne'er forget that happy night,
    Amang the rigs wi' Annie, O.

The sky was blue, the wind was still,
    The moon was shining clearly, O,
I set her down, wi' right good will,
    Amang the rigs o' barley, O:
I ken't[4] her heart was a' my ain;
    I lov'd her most sincerely, O:
I kiss'd her owre and owre again,
    Amang the rigs o' barley, O.

I lock'd her in my fond embrace;
    Her heart was beating rarely, O:
My blessings on that happy place,
    Amang the rigs o' barley, O!
But by the moon and stars so bright,
    That shone that night so clearly, O!
She ay shall bless that happy night,
    Amang the rigs o' barley, O!

I hae been blythe wi' comrades dear;
    I hae been merry drinking, O:
I hae been joyfu' gath'rin' gear;
    I hae been happy thinking, O:

[1] Rigs: ridges. [2] Tentless: careless. [3] Late and early: darkness and dawn. [4] Ken't: knew.

But a' the pleasures e'er I saw,
  Tho' three times doubl'd fairly, O,
That happy night was worth them a',
  Amang the rigs o' barley, O.

∽ઝ૯∾

Green Grow the Rashes, O

Green grow the rashes,[1] O;
  Green grow the rashes, O;
The sweetest hours that e'er I spend,
  Are spent among the lasses, O.

There's nought but care on ev'ry han',
  In every hour that passes, O:
What signifies the life o' man,
  An' 'twere na for the lass, O.

The war'ly[2] race may riches chase,
  An' riches still may fly them, O;
An' tho' at last they catch them fast,
  Their hearts can ne'er enjoy them, O;

But gie me a cannie[3] hour at e'en,
  My arms about my dearie, O,
An' war'ly cares an' war'ly men
  May a' gae tapsalteerie,[4] O!

For you sae douce,[5] ye sneer at this;
  Ye're nought but senseless asses, O:
The wisest man the warl' ere saw,
  He dearly lov'd the lasses, O.

Auld Nature swears, the lovely dears
  Her noblest work she classes, O:
Her prentice han' she try'd on man,
  An then she made the lasses, O.

[1] Rashes: rushes. [2] War'ly: worldly. [3] Cannie: quiet, easy. [4] Tapsalteerie: topsy-turvy.
[5] Douce: solemn.

Green grow the rashes, O;
Green grow the rashes, O;
The sweetest hours that e'er I spend,
Are spent among the lasses, O.

Whistle, and I'll Come To You, My Lad

O whistle, and I'll come to you, my lad,
O whistle, and I'll come to you, my lad,
Though father and mither and a' should gae mad,
O whistle, and I'll come to you, my lad,

But warily tent,[1] when ye come to court me,
And come na unless the back-yett be a-jee;[2]
Syne[3] up the back-stile, and let naebody see,
And come as ye were na comin to me.
    O whistle, etc.

At kirk, or at market, whene'er ye meet me,
Gang by me as though that ye cared nae a flie;[4]
But steal me a blink o' your bonie black e'e,
Yet look as ye were na lookin' at me.
    O whistle, etc.

Aye vow and protest that ye care na for me,
And whiles ye may lightly[5] my beauty a wee;
But court na anither, though jokin' ye be,
For fear that she wile your fancy frae me.
    O whistle, etc.

Comin' Thro' the Rye

Comin' thro' the rye, poor body,
    Comin' thro' the rye;
She draigl't[6] a' her petticoatie,
    Comin' thro' the rye.

---

[1] Warily tent: cautiously heed. [2] Back-yett be a-jee: back-gate be ajar. [3] Syne: then.
[4] Nae a flie: not a fly. [5] May lightly: think lightly of. [6] Draigl't: draggled.

Oh, Jenny's a' weet, poor body,
Jenny's seldom dry:
She draigl't a' her petticoatie,
Comin' thro' the rye.

Gin¹ a body meet a body
　Comin' thro' the rye;
Gin a body kiss a body,
　Need a body cry?
　　Oh, Jenny's a' weet, etc.

Gin a body meet a body
　Comin' thro' the glen;
Gin a body kiss a body,
　Need the warld ken?²
　　Oh, Jenny's a' weet, etc.

I'm Owre Young to Marry Yet

I am my mammie's ae bairn,³
　Wi' unco folk⁴ I weary, sir;
And lying, in a man's bed,
　I'm fley'd wad mak me eerie,⁵ sir.

I'm owre young, I'm owre young,
　I'm owre young to marry yet;
I'm owre young, 'twad be a sin
　To tak me frae my mammie yet.

My mammie coft⁶ me a new gown,
　The kirk maun hae⁷ the gracing o't;
Were I to lie wi' you, kind sir,
　I'm feared ye'd spoil the lacing o't.

Hallowmas is come and gane,
　The nights are lang in winter, sir;
And you an' I in ae bed,
　In truth I dare na venture, sir.

¹ Gin: should. ² Warld ken: world know. ³ Ae bairn: only child. ⁴ Unco folk: strangers.
⁵ I'm fley'd wad mak me eerie: I'm afraid it would frighten me. ⁶ Coft: bought. ⁷ The kirk
maun hae: the church may have.

Fu' loud and shrill the frosty wind
　　Blaws throu' the leafless timmer,[1] sir;
But if ye come this gate again,
　　I'll aulder be gin simmer,[2] sir.

◆◆◆

Godly Girzie

The night it was a holy night,
　The day had been a holy day;
Kilmarnock gleam'd wi' candle light,
　As Girzie hameward took her way,
A man of sin, ill may he thrive!
　And never holy meeting see!
With godly Girzie met belyve,[3]
　Among the Craigie hills sae hie.

The chiel'[4] was wight, the chiel' was stark,
　He was na wait to chat nor ca',
And she was fait wi' holy wark;
　She had no pith to say him na.
But ay she glowr'd up to the moon,
　And ay she sigh'd most piouslie,
"I trust my heart's in heaven aboon,
　"Whare'er your sinfu' pintle be."

◆◆◆

I Once was a Maid

(From *The Jolly Beggars*)
I once was a maid, tho' I cannot tell when,
An' still my delight is in proper young men;
Some one of a troop of dragoons was my daddie,
No wonder I'm fond of a sodger laddie.

The first of my loves was a swaggering blade,
To rattle the thundering drum was his trade;
His leg was so tight, and his cheek was so ruddy,
Transported I was with my sodger laddie.

[1] Timmer: timber; in this case, the woods. [2] Gin simmer: toward summer. [3] Belyve: by and by. [4] Chiel: lad.

But the godly old chaplain left him in the lurch,
The sword I forsook for sake of the church,
He ventured the soul, and I risk'd the body,
'Twas then I proved false to my sodger laddie.

Full soon I grew sick of my sanctified sot,
The regiment at large for a husband I got;
From the gilded spontoon to the life I was ready,
I asked no more but a sodger laddie.

But the peace it reduced me to beg in despair,
Till I met my old boy at a Cunningham fair;
His rags regimental they fluttered so gaudy,
My heart it rejoiced at my sodger laddie.

An' now I have lived—I know not how long,
An' still I can join in a cup or a song;
But whilst with both hands I can hold the glass steady,
Here's to thee, my hero, my sodger laddie.

~⁂~

Blooming Nelly

On a bank of flowers, in a summer-day,
    For summer lightly drest,
The youthful, blooming Nelly lay,
    With love and sleep opprest;
When Willie, wandering through the wood,
    Who for her favor oft had sued,
He gazed, he wished, he feared, he blushed,
    And trembled where he stood.

Her closèd eyes like weapons sheathed,
    Were sealed in soft repose;
Her lip, still as she fragrant breathed,
    It richer dyed the rose.
The springing lilies sweetly prest,
    Wild-wanton, kissed her rival breast;
He gazed, he wished, he feared, he blushed,
    His bosom ill at rest.

425

Her robes light waving in the breeze
  Her tender limbs embrace;
Her lovely form, her native ease,
  All harmony and grace:
Tumultuous tides his pulses roll,
  A faltering, ardent kiss he stole;
He gazed, he wished, he feared, he blushed,
  And sighed his very soul.

As flies the partridge from the brake
  On fear-inspired wings,
So Nelly starting, half awake,
  Away affrighted springs:
But Willie followed, as he should;
  He overtook her in in the wood.
He vowed, he prayed, he found the maid
  Forgiving all and good.

Wha is That at My Bower-Door?

Wha is that at my bower-door?
  O wha is it but Findlay.
Then gae your gate,[1] ye'se nae[2] be here!
  Indeed I must quo' Findlay.
What makes ye sae like a thief?
  O come and see, quo' Findlay;
Before the morn ye'll work mischief;
  Indeed will I, quo' Findlay.

Gif I rise an' let you in;
  Let me in, quo' Findlay;
Ye'll kep me waukin' wi' your din,
  Indeed will I, quo' Findlay.
In my bower, if you should stay?
  Let me stay, quo' Findlay;
I fear ye'll bide till break o' day;
  Indeed will I, quo' Findlay.

[1] Gae your gate: Go your way. [2] Ye'se nae: you should not.

Here this night, if ye remain,
　I'll remain, quo' Findlay;
I dread ye'll learn the gate again,
　Indeed will I, quo' Findlay.
What may pass within this bower,
　Let it pass, quo' Findlay;
Ye must conceal till your last hour;
　Indeed will I, quo' Findlay!

The Lass That Made the Bed for Me

When Januar' wind war blawin' cauld,
　As to the north I took my way
The mirksome night did me enfauld,
　I knew not where to lodge till day;
But by good luck a maid I met,
　Just in the middle o' my care,
And kindly she did me invite
　To walk into her chamber fair.

I bow'd fu' low unto this maid,
　And thanked her for her courtesy;
I bow'd fu' low unto this maid,
　An' bade her make a bed for me; .
She made the bed baith large and wide,
　Wi' twa white hands she spread it doun;
She put the cup to her rosy lips,
　And drank—"Young man, now sleep ye soun."

The bonnie lass made the bed to me,
　The braw[1] lass made the bed to me,
I'll ne'er forget till the day I die,
　The lass that made the bed for me.

She snatch'd the candle in her hand,
　And frae my chamber went wi' speed;
But I called her quickly back again,
　To lay some mair below my head;

---

[1] Braw: fine, lovely.

A cod[1] she laid below my head,
  And served me with due respect,
And, to salute her wi' a kiss,
  I put my arms about her neck.

"Haud off your hands, young man!" she said,
  "And dinna sae uncivil be:
Gif ye hae any love for me,
  O wrang na my virginitie."
Her hair was like the links of gowd,
  Her teeth were like the ivorie,
Her cheeks like lilies dipt in wine,
  The lass that made the bed for me.

Her bosom was the driven snaw,
  Twa drifted heaps sae fair to see;
Her limbs the polished marble stane,
  The lass that made the bed to me.
I kiss'd her o'er and o'er again,
  And ay she wist na what to say;
I laid her 'tween me and the wa',[2]
  The lassie thocht na lang till day.

Upon the morrow when we rose,
  I thanked her for her courtesy;
But aye she blushed and aye she sigh'd,
  And said, "Alas, ye've ruin'd m.."
I clasp'd her waist, and kiss'd her—
  While the tear stood twinkling in her e'e;
I said, "My lassie, dinna cry,
  For ye ay shall make the bed for me."

She took her mither's holland sheets,
  And made them a' in sarks[3] to me.
Blythe and merry may she be,
The lass that made the bed for me.

---

[1] Cod: pillow. [2] Wa': wall. [3] Sarks: shirts.

One of Burns's most cherished songs, "John Anderson, My Jo," is a heartwarming tribute to married bliss; but, before the poet turned it into its present form, it was an old wife's grievance about her husband's sexual incompetence. (See page 430.) Similarly the following verses are a startling contrast to the well-known, socially conscious "A Man's a Man for A' That." It has been questioned whether or not Burns wrote these lines as a wicked parody; some scholars doubt that he wrote them at all. However, the tone displays the characteristics of the Merry Muse summoned by the poet in one of his rambunctious moods.

For A' That an' A' That

The bonniest lass that ye meet neist,[1]
    Gie her a kiss an' a' that,
In spite o' ilka parish priest,
    Repentin' stool, an' a' that.
      For a' that an' a' that
        Their mim-mou'd sangs[2] an' a' that,
      In time and place convenient,
        They'll do't themselves for a' that.

Your patriarchs in days o' yore,
    Had their handmaids an' a' that;
O' bastard gets, some had a score,
    An' some had mair than a' that.
      For a' that an' a' that,
        Your Langsyne saunts[3], an' a' that,
      Were fonder o' a bonny lass
        Than you or I, for a' that.

King Davie, when he waxèd auld,
    An's bluid ran thin an' a' that,
An faund his cods were growin' cauld,
    Could not refrain for a' that.
      For a' that an' for a' that
        To keep him warm an' a' that,
      The daughters o' Jerusalem
        Were waled[4] for him, an' a' that.

[1] Neist: next. [2] Mim-mou'd sangs: mealy-mouthed songs. [3] Langsyne saunts: ancient or bygone saints. [4] Waled: chosen.

Wha wouldna pity thae sweet dames
 He fumbled at, an' a' that,
An' raised their bluid up into flames,
 He couldna drown for a' that.
  For a' that an' a' that,
   He wanted pith an' a' that;
  For, as to what we shall not name
   What could he do but claw that.

John Anderson, My Jo

John Anderson, my jo, John,
 I wonder what ye mean,
To lie sae lang i' the mornin',
 And sit sae late at e'en?
Ye'll bleer a' your een,[1] John,
 And why do ye so?
Come sooner to your bed at e'en,
 John Anderson, my jo.

John Anderson, my jo, John,
 When first that ye began,
Ye had as good a tail-tree
 As ony ither man;
But now it's waxen wan, John,
 And aft requires my helping hand,
And John Anderson, my jo.

When we were young and yauld, John,
 We've lain out'owre the dyke,
And O! it was a fine thing
 To see your hurdies fyke;[2]—
To see your hurdies fyke, John,
 And strike the risin' blow;
'Twas then I lik'd your chanter-pipe,
 John Anderson, my jo.

John Anderson, my jo, John,
 You're welcome when you please;

[1] Een: eyes. [2] Hurdies fyke: haunches move.

It's either in the warm bed,
  Or else aboon the claes.
Do ye your part aboon, John,
  And trust to me below;
I've twa gae-ups for your gae-down,
  John Anderson, my jo.

When ye come on before, John,
  See that ye do your best;
When I begin to haud ye,
  See that ye grip me fast;
See that ye grip me fast, John,
  Until that I cry "Oh!"
Your back shall crack, or I do that,
  John Anderson, my jo.

I'm backet like a salmon,
  I'm breastit like a swan;
My wyme is like a down-cod[3]
  My waist ye weel may span;
My skin frae tap to tae,[4] John,
  Is like the new fa'n snow,
And it's a' for your conveniency,
  John Anderson, my jo.

How Can I Keep My Maidenhead?

How can I keep my maidenhead,
My maidenhead, my maidenhead,
How can I keep my maidenhead
Among so many men?

The captain bid a guinea for it,
A guinea for it, a guinea for it,
The captain bid a guinea for it,
The colonel he bid ten.

[3] Down-cod: downy pillow. [4] Tap to tae: top to toe.

431

Oh, I'll do as my mother did,
My mother did, my mother did,
I'll do as my mother did
For silver I'll have none.

I'll give it to a bonnie lad,
A bonnie lad, a bonnie lad,
I'll give it to a bonnie lad
For just as good again.

How can I keep my maidenhead,
My maidenhead, my maidenhead,
How can I keep my maidenhead
Among so many men?

My Bonnie Highland Laddie

As I came o'er the Cairney Mount
And doon among the blooming heather,
The Highland laddie drew his dirk
And sheathed it in my wanton leather.

Oh, my bonnie Highland lad,
My handsome, charming, Highland laddie,
When I am sick and laid in bed
He'll roll me in his Highland plaiddie.

With me he played his warlike pranks,
On me boldly did adventure,
He did attack me on baith flanks
And pushed me fiercely in the center.

A furious battle then begun
With equal courage and desire,
Although he struck me three to one
I stood my ground and took his fire.

Our ammunition being spent
And we quite out of breath and sweating,
We did agree with one consent
To fight it out at the next meeting.

Oh, my bonnie Highland lad,
My handsome, charming, Highland laddie,
When I am sick and laid in bed
He'll roll me in his Highland plaiddie.

Could You Do That?

Guidwife when your guidman's from home
Might I but be sae bold,
As come into your bed-chamber
When the winter nights are cauld?
As come into your bed-chamber
When nights are cold and wet,
And lie down in your guidman's stead,
Guidwife, could you do that?

Young man if you should be so kind
When my guidman's from home,
As come into my bed-chamber
When I am laid alone,
And lie down in my guidman's stead,
Young man I'll tell you what:
He jigs me five times every nicht
Young man, could you do that?

The Plowman

I paid a man at Martinmas,
I gave good pennies three,
But all the fault I had wi' him
He couldna labor lea.[1]

1 Lea: a grassy field, a pasture.

So can you labor lea, young man,
Can you labor lea?
Go doon the road by which you came;
You ne'er shall scorn at me.

A stubble ridge is easy plowed,
And fallow land is free,
But what a silly fool is he
That canna labor lea.

In bonnie bush and grassy hill
The plowman points his plowshare,
He sheds the roughness, lays it by,
And boldly plows his day there.

The Nut-Gathering Lass

There was a lass and a bonnie lass
A-gathering nuts did gang,
And she pulled them high and she pulled them low,
And she pulled them where they hang.

Till tired at length she laid her doon
And slept the woods among,
When by there came three lusty lads,
Three lusty lads and strong.

Oh, the first did kiss her rosy lips,
He thought it wasna wrong;
The second unloosened her bodice fair
That was sewed wi' silk along.

And what the third did to the lass
Is no put in this song;
But the lassie wakened in a fright
And she says I have slept too long.

The Thrusting of It

Can you play me, Duncan Gray?
    Ha, ha, the thrusting of it;
Over the hills and far away,
    Ha, ha, the thrusting of it;
Duncan came our Meg to woo,
Meg was nice and wouldna do,
But like an ether puffed and blew,
    At offer o' the thrusting of it.

Duncan he came here again,
    Ha, ha, the thrusting of it;
All was oot and Meg alone,
    Ha, ha, the thrusting of it;
He kissed her here and there so sweet,
He banged a thing against her gate,
But yet it's name I willna state,
    I believe she got the thrusting of it.

She took him to the cellar then,
    Ha, ha, the thrusting of it;
To see if he could do it again,
    Ha, ha, the thrusting of it;
He kissed her once, he kissed her twice
Maybe Duncan kissed her thrice,
Till devil a more the thing would rise
    To give her the long thrusting of it.

But Duncan took her for his wife,
    Ha, ha, the thrusting of it;
To be the comfort of his life,
    Ha, ha, the thrusting of it;
Now she's cold both nicht and day
Except when Duncan's at the play,
And that's as seldom as he may,
He's weary o' the thrusting of it.

435

She'll Do It

Among our young lasses is Muirland Meg,
She'll beg you to do it, she'll beg and she'll beg,
At thirteen her maidenhead flew to the gate,
And the door of the cage it is wide open yet.

And for a sheepskin, she'll do it, she'll do it,
And for a sheepskin, she'll do it again,
And for a cow's horn, she'll do it all morn,
And merrily turn, and do it again.

Her kettle-black eyes want to tickle you through,
Her lips seem to say it, "Kiss me, please do,"
The curls and the links of her bonny black hair
Would put you in mind that the lassie has mair.

An armful of love is her bosom sae plump,
A span of delight is her middle and rump,
A taper white leg, and a stomach in style,
And a fiddle nearby you can play for a while.

For love's her delight, and kissing's her treasure,
She'll stick at no price and she'll give you good measure,
So take her warm hand, mon, or better, her leg,
And sing of the praises of Muirland Meg.

Suppertime[1]

Roseberry to his lady says,
    "My hinnie and my succor,
Now shall we do the thing ye ken?
    Or shall we have our supper?"

Wi' modest face sae fu' o' grace,
    Replied the bonnie lady.
"My noble lord, just as ye please.
    But supper is na ready."

[1] Compare these verses with a French version ("Hors d'Oeuvre") by Deems Taylor on page 523

The Lass and the Friar[1]

A lovely lass to a friar came
    To confess in the morning early.
"In what, my dear, are you to blame?
    Come, tell me most sincerely."
"I have done, sir, what I dare not name,
    With a lad that loves me dearly.

"The greatest fault in myself I know
    Is what I now discover."
"You for that fault to Rome must go
    Or discipline would suffer."
"Lack-a-day, sir, if it must be so,
    Pray send me with my lover."

"Oh, no, no, no, my dear, you dream;
    We'll have no double dealing.
But if with me you'll repeat the same
    I'll pardon your past failing."
"I own, sir, but I blush with shame,
    Your penance is prevailing."

[1] This poem has sometimes been credited to John Wilmot, Earl of Rochester (see page 305). It also appears in an edition of *The Merry Muses* under the title "The Fair Penitent" and was probably "retouched" by Burns.

437

Nineteenth Century Romantics

Nineteenth Century Romantics

The early part of the nineteenth century was suffused with lyric sensuousness. It was devoted to a romanticism which, though uplifted by spiritual vision, did not disdain sexual overtones. There are broad implications of incest in Byron and Shelley; Heine is outspoken about carnal appetite; in the midst of high seriousness the ponderous Browning and the mild Tennyson cannot quite conceal an involuntary, half-conscious sexuality. In general, the tone is elevated and often ecstatic.

Gradually the romantic mood gave way to an alternation of repressed puritanism and mild paganism. Fitzgerald's *Rubáiyát of Omar Khayyám* was a protest against smug Victorianism, a protest which brought about something like a poetic revolution. The Pre-Raphaelite writers and artists manifested a tendency to return to a directness of expression and an emphasis on sensation. As an organizer of the Pre-Raphaelites, Rossetti was attacked as the leader of the "fleshly school." Browning was among those who scorned the movement not because of its fleshliness but because of its affectations. "I hate the effeminacy of his [Rossetti's] school—the men that dress up like women—that use obsolete forms and archaic accentuations—I hate 'Love' as a lubberly naked young man putting his arms here and his wings there about a pair of lovers—a fellow they would kick away in the reality."

Nevertheless, with all their excesses, the romantics enlarged the range of poetic effects and made possible not only the experiments of their immediate successors but also the promise of modern poetry.

Francis Scott Key

It is doubtful that anyone who has ever reverently lifted his voice to the strains of "The Star Spangled Banner" would suspect that the author of our national anthem was also the author of a vividly erotic poem. Nevertheless, in 1816 Key (1780–1843) joined the Delphian Club of Baltimore; every Saturday night its members exchanged poems, puns, and toasts to their favorite Muses, mortal and immortal. Although he was a loving husband and devoted father, it is said that Key's "On a Young Lady's Going into a Shower Bath" was written to an altogether human Muse. The poem is in the proper classical vein, beginning with a quotation from Shakespeare, and is practically unknown.

On a Young Lady's
Going into a Shower Bath

"O that this too solid flesh would melt
Thaw and resolve itself" to water clear,
And pure as that which flows through flowery vales
Of Arcady, and stays its gentle wave
To kiss the budding blossoms on its brink,
Or to encircle in its fond embrace
Some trembling, blushing maid, who doubting stands,
And hopes and fears to trust the smiling stream!
Then, as the amorous rise of Gods and men
From Heav'n descended in a golden show'r
To Danaë's open arms, another heav'n
So from the bath, that o'er the shrinking charms
Of Sweet Nerea hung, would I more blest
Than rapturous love, upon a form more fair
Than Danaë's a silver show'r descends.
O then those charms of which the lighted touch
Would fire the frozen blood of apathy,
Each drop of me should touch, should eager run
Down her fair forehead, down her blushing cheek
To taste the more inviting sweets beneath,
Should trickle down her neck, should slowly wind,
In silver circles round those hills of snow,
Or lingering steal through the sweet vale between
And when at length perplex'd with the rich store
Of nature's varied, most luxuriant charms,
Amid the circling tendrils which entwine
An altar form'd for love's soft sacrifice,
Insinuating creep, there as a bee
In a fresh rosebud hid, a refuge find
From the rude napkin's sacrilegious touch.

443

George Gordon, Lord Byron

George Gordon, Lord Byron (1788-1824) was his own legend, and all his heroes—the wanderlusty but disenchanted Harold, the murderous but dignified Cain, the self-infatuated but scornful Don Juan—are himself. His was the spirit of revolt which, with the non-chalance of youth, mixed fantasy and reality, humor and despera-tion. The fluency of his poetry as well as his creation of the Byronic figure captivated not only the English-speaking countries but all Europe. His verse is both intellectual and conversational; he had a genius for improvisation pointed with surprise.

Byron's masterpiece, *Don Juan*, recounts the adventures of an aristocratic libertine, young, handsome, restless, and irresistible—a loving self-portrait of the author. There is also a background of bitter moodiness—which completes the likeness, for Byron thought of himself as a critic of hypocrisy and his work as an attack on so-called respectable society. The following excerpts from two of the Cantos emphasize the satirical as well as the ribald nature of Byron's wit.

From *Don Juan*

(CANTO I)

'Twas midnight—Donna Julia was in bed,
   Sleeping, most probably—when at her door
Arose a clatter might awake the dead,
   If they had never been awoke before,
And that they have been so we all have read,
   And are to be so, at the least, once more—
The door was fasten'd, but with voice and fist
First knocks were heard, then "Madam—Madam—hist!

"For God's sake, Madam—Madam—here's my master,
　　With more than half the city at his back—
Was ever heard of such a curst disaster!
　　'Tis not my fault—I kept good watch—Alack!
Do pray undo the bolt a little faster—
　　They're on the stair just now, and in a crack
Will all be here; perhaps he yet may fly—
Surely the window's not so *very* high!"

By this time Don Alfonso was arrived,
　　With torches, friends, and servants in great number,
The major part of them had long been wived,
　　And therefore paused not to disturb the slumber
Of any wicked woman, who contrived
　　By stealth her husband's temples to encumber:
Examples of this kind are so contagious,
Were *one* not punish'd, *all* would be outrageous.

I can't tell how, or why, or what suspicion
　　Could enter into Don Alfonso's head;
But for a cavalier of his condition
　　It surely was exceedingly ill-bred,
Without a word of previous admonition,
　　To hold a levee round his lady's bed,
And summon lackeys, armed with fire and sword,
To prove himself the thing he most abhorred!

Poor Donna Julia! starting as from sleep
　　(Mind—that I do not say—she had not slept),
Began at once to scream, and yawn, and weep;
　　Her maid, Antonia, who was an adept,
Contrived to fling the bed-clothes in a heap,
　　As if she had just now from out them crept;
I can't tell why she should take all this trouble
To prove her mistress had been sleeping double.

But Julia, mistress, and Antonia, maid,
　　Appeared'd like two poor harmless women, who
Of goblins, but still more of men afraid,
　　Had thought one man might be deterr'd by two,
And therefore side by side were gently laid,

445

Until the hours of absence should run through,
And truant husband should return, and say,
"My dear, I was the first who came away."

Now Julia found at length a voice, and cried,
   "In heaven's name, Don Alfonso, what d'ye mean?
Has madness seized you? Would that I had died
   Ere such a monster's victim I had been!
What may this midnight violence betide?
   A sudden fit of drunkenness or spleen?
Dare you suspect me, whom the thought would kill?"
Search then, the room!"—Alfonso said, "I will."

He search'd, *they* search'd, and rummaged everywhere,
   Closet and clothes-press, chest and window-seat,
And found much linen, lace, and several pair
   Of stockings, slippers, brushes, combs, complete,
Wth other articles, of ladies fair,
   To keep them beautiful, or leave them neat:
Arras they prick'd and curtains with their swords,
And wounded several shutters, and some boards.

Under the bed they search'd, and there they found—
   No matter what—it was not that they sought;
They open'd windows, gazing if the ground
   Had signs of footmarks, but the earth said nought;
And then they stared each other's faces round:
   'Tis odd, not one of all these seekers thought,
And seems to me almost a sort of blunder,
Of looking *in* the bed as well as under.

During this inquisition Julia's tongue
   Was not asleep—"Yes, search and search," she cried,
"Insult on insult heap, and wrong on wrong!
   It was for this that I became a bride!
For this in silence I have suffered long
   A husband like Alfonso at my side;
But now I'll bear no more, nor here remain,
If there be law or lawyers, in all Spain.
"Yes, Don Alfonso! husband now no more,
   If ever you indeed deserved the name,

446

Is't worthy of your years?—you have threescore—
 Fifty, or sixty, it is all the same—
Is't wise or fitting, causeless to explore
 For facts against a virtuous woman's fame?
Ungrateful, perjured, barbarous Don Alfonso,
How dare you think your lady would go on so? . . .

"There is the closet, there the toilet, there
 The antechamber—search them under, over;
There is the sofa, there the great arm-chair,
 The chimney—which would really hold a lover.
I wish to sleep, and beg you will take care
 And make no further noise, till you discover
The secret cavern of this lurking treasure—
And when 'tis found, let me, too, have that pleasure.

"And now, Hidalgo! now that you have thrown
 Doubt upon me, confusion over all,
Pray have the courtesy to make it known
 Who is the man you search for? How d'ye call
Him? what's his lineage? let him but be shown—
 I hope he's young and handsome—is he tall?
Tell me—and be assured, that since you stain
Mine honor thus, it shall not be in vain."

She ceased, and turn'd upon her pillow; pale
 She lay, her dark eyes flashing through their tears,
Like skies that rain and lighten; as a veil,
 Waved and o'ershadowing her wan cheek, appears
Her streaming hair; the black curls strive, but fail,
 To hide the glossy shoulder, which uprears
Its snow through all—her soft lips lie apart,
And louder than her breathing beats her heart.

But Don Alfonso stood with downcast looks,
 And, truth to say, he made a foolish figure;
When, after searching in five hundred nooks,
 And treating a young wife with so much rigor,
He gain'd no point, except some self-rebukes,
 Added to those his lady with such vigor
Had pour'd upon him for the last half hour,
Quick, thick, and heavy—as a thunder-shower.

447

He stood in act to speak, or rather stammer,
　　But sage Antonia cut him short before
The anvil of his speech received the hammer,
　　With "Pray, sir, leave the room, and say no more,
Or madam dies."—Alfonso mutter'd, "D—n her."
　　But nothing else; the time of words was o'er.
He cast a rueful look or two, and did,
He knew not wherefore, that which he was bid.

With him retired his *"posse comitatus,"*
　　The attorney last, who linger'd near the door
Reluctantly, still tarrying there as late as
　　Antonia let him—not a little sore
At this most strange and unexplain'd *"hiatus"*
　　In Don Alfonso's facts, which just now wore
An awkward look; as he revolved the case,
The door was fasten'd in his legal face.

No sooner was it bolted, than—Oh shame!
　　Oh sin! Oh sorrow! and Oh womankind!
How can you do such things and keep your fame,
　　Unless this world, and t'other too, be blind?
Nothing so dear as an unfilch'd good name!
　　But to proceed—for there is more behind:
With much heartfelt reluctance be it said,
Young Juan slipp'd, half-smother'd, from the bed.

He had been hid—I don't pretend to say
　　How, nor can I indeed describe the where—
Young, slender, and pack'd easily, he lay,
　　No doubt, in little compass, round or square;
But pity him I neither must nor may
　　His suffocation by that pretty pair;
'Twere better, sure, to die so, than be shut
With maudlin Clarence in his Malmsey butt.

And, secondly, I pity not, because
　　He had no business to commit a sin,
Forbid by heavenly, fined by human laws,
　　At least 'twas rather early to begin;
But at sixteen the conscience rarely gnaws
　　So much as when we call our old debts in

448

At sixty years, and draw the accompts of evil,
And find a deuced balance with the devil.

Of his position I can give no notion:
  'Tis written in the Hebrew Chronicle,
How the physicians, leaving pill and potion,
  Prescribed, by way of blister, a young belle,
When old King David's blood grew dull in motion,
  And that the medicine answer'd very well;
Perhaps 'twas in a different way applied,
For David lived, but Juan nearly died.

From *Don Juan*

(CANTO III)

In her first passion woman loves her lover,
  In all the others all she loves is love,
Which grows a habit she can ne'er get over,
  And fits her closely, like an easy glove,
As you may find, whene'er you like to prove her:
  One man alone at first her heart can move;
She then prefers him in the plural number,
Not finding that the additions much encumber.

I know not if the fault be men's or theirs;
  But one thing's pretty sure: a woman planted
(Unless at once she plunge for life in prayers)
  After a decent time must be gallanted;
Although, no doubt, her first of love affairs
  Is that to which her heart is wholly granted.
Yet there are some, they say, who have had none;
But those who have, ne'er end with only one.

'Tis melancholy, and a fearful sign
  Of human frailty, folly, also crime,
That love and marriage rarely can combine,
  Although they both are born in the same clime;
Marriage from love, like vinegar from wine—
  A sad, sour, sober beverage—by time
Is sharpened from its high celestial flavor
Down to a very homely household savor.

449

There's something of antipathy, as 'twere,
  Between their present and their future state;
A kind of flattery that's hardly fair
  Is used until the truth arrives too late—
Yet what can people do, except despair?
  The same things change their names at such a rate;
For instance—passion in a lover's glorious,
But in a husband is pronounced uxorious.

Men grow ashamed of being so very fond;
  They sometimes also get a little tired
(But that, of course, is rare), and then despond:
  The same things cannot always be admired,
Yet 'tis "so nominated in the bond,"
  That both are tied till one shall have expired.
Sad thought! to lose the spouse that was adorning
Our days, and put one's servants into mourning.

There's doubtless something in domestic doings
  Which forms, in fact, true love's antithesis;
Romances paint at full length people's wooings,
  But only give a bust of marriages;
For no one cares for matrimonial cooings,
  There's nothing wrong in a connubial kiss:
Think you, if Laura had been Petrarch's wife,
He would have written sonnets all his life?

Shelley and Keats

One does not think of Shelley and Keats as erotic poets, yet far from disdaining the note of passion they exulted in it. Percy Bysshe Shelley (1792–1822) used it constantly with efflorescence and lush effects. John Keats (1795–1821) trifled with it in his lighter moments, such as "Where Be You Going, You Devon Maid," but his major poems have the deep sensual response that shows Keats's delight in all the senses. Sometimes his passion breaks the bonds of control, as in the sonnet "To Fanny." Here, instead of the expected smoothly molded pattern, is a violent outcry. It falters, rushes on, and falters again in an effort to express the lover's anguish, his desire not only for the beloved's hands, eyes, the "sweet minor zest of love, your kiss," and her "warm, white, lucent, million-pleasured breast," but for every "atom's atom," ' the impossible fulfillment. Never has there been a swifter and more painfully sensuous outpouring.

Love's Philosophy

The fountains mingle with the river
And the rivers with the ocean,
The winds of heaven mix for ever
With a sweet emotion;
Nothing in the world is single,
All things by a law divine
In one another's being mingle—
Why not I with thine?

See the mountains kiss high heaven,
And the waves clasp one another;
No sister-flower would be forgiven
If it disdained its brother:
And the sunlight clasps the earth,
And the moon beams kiss the sea—
What are all these kissings worth,
If thou kiss not me?

PERCY BYSSHE SHELLEY

The Indian Serenade

I arise from dreams of thee
    In the first sweet sleep of night,
When the winds are breathing low,
    And the stars are shining bright.
I arise from dreams of thee,
    And a spirit in my feet
Hath led me—who knows how?
    To thy chamber window, Sweet!

The wandering airs they faint
    On the dark, the silent stream—
The champak odors fail
    Like sweet thoughts in a dream;
The nightingale's complaint,
    It dies upon her heart,
As I must on thine,
    O beloved as thou art!

O lift me from the grass!
    I die! I faint! I fail!
Let thy love in kisses rain
    On my lips and eyelids pale.
My cheek is cold and white, alas!
    My heart beats loud and fast:
O press it to thine own again,
    Where it will break at last!

PERCY BYSSHE SHELLEY

To Janny

I cry your mercy—pity—love!—aye, love!
    Merciful love that tantalizes not,
One-thoughted, never-wandering, guileless love,
    Unmasked, and being seen—without a blot!
O! let me have thee whole—all—all—be mine!
    That shape, that fairness, that sweet minor zest
Of love, your kiss—those hands, those eyes divine,
    That warm, white, lucent, million-pleasured breast—
Yourself—your soul—in pity give me all,
    Withhold no atom's atom or I die,
Or living on perhaps, your wretched thrall,
    Forget, in the mist of idle misery,
Life's purposes—the palate of my mind
Losing its gust, and my ambition blind!

               JOHN KEATS

Where Be You Going, You Devon Maid

Where be you going, you Devon maid?
    And what have ye there in the basket?
Ye tight little fairy, just fresh from the dairy,
Will ye give me some cream if I ask it?

I love your hills and I love your dales,
    And I love your flocks a-bleating;
But oh, on the heather to lie together,
    With both our hearts a-beating!

I'll put your basket all safe in a nook;
    Your shawl I'll hang on a willow;
And we will sigh in the daisy's eye,
    And kiss on a grass-green pillow.

               JOHN KEATS

Heinrich Heine

Nineteenth century poets sounded the extremes of romanticism and ironism. Heinrich Heine (1797–1856) combined both. His life, like his work, was a continual paradox. The poet who wrote rapturously of roses, moonlight, and nightingales was the same man who sarcastically remarked, "We praise the poet, the preacher, and the actor who move us to tears—a talent they share with the common onion." Born a Jew, he became a Protestant so that he might be admitted to the bar, then abjured both Christianity and the law. Exiled from his native Germany, he earned a living as a French journalist but, while mocking German philistinism, was always in love with his homeland. He acquired a Catholic mistress, was casually unfaithful, made fun of her ignorance but, so that she might have legal rights as a widow, finally married her. A finicky stylist, he used the idiom of the people and gave German poetry a new and flexible language.

Like his subject matter, Heine's diction is alternately delicate and coarse. His bittersweet voice is heard not only in the countless songs set to music by Schumann, Schubert, Mendelssohn, and practically every other composer of the nineteenth century, but also in his less popular lyrics, the half-sensual, half-cynical verses to a variety of women in *Verschiedene,* and the mocking eroticism of the later poems.

All the translations are by the editor.

The Song of Songs

Woman's white body is a song,
    And God Himself's the author;
In the eternal Book of Life
    He put the lines together.

It was a thrilling hour; the Lord
    Felt suddenly inspired;
Within his brain the stubborn stuff
    Was mastered, fused, and fired.

Truly, the Song of Songs is this,
    The greatest of his trophies:
This living poem where white limbs
    Are a rare pair of strophes.

Oh, what a heavenly masterpiece
    That neck and its relation
To the fair head, like an idea
    Crowned with imagination.

In pointed epigrams, the breasts
    Rise under teasing rallies;
And a caesura lies between,
    The loveliest of valleys.

He published the sweet parallel
    Of thighs—what joy to be there!
The fig-leaf grotto joining them
    Is not a bad place either.

It is no cold, conceptual verse,
    No patterned abstract study.
This poem sings with rhyming lips,
    With sweet bones and warm body.

Here breathes the deepest poetry!
    Beauty in every motion,
Upon its brow it bears the stamp
    Of His complete devotion.

Here in the dust, I praise Thee, Lord.
    We are—and well I know it—
Rank amateurs, compared to Thee:
    Heaven's first major poet!

I'll dedicate myself to learn
    This song, the lyric body;
With ardor and with energy
    All day—and night—I'll study.

Yes, day and night, I'll never lack
    For constant application;
And though the task may break my back
    I'll ask for no vacation!

Song of the Vivandière [1]

The gay hussars—I love them all—
    They are such splendid fellows;
The thin and small, the large and tall,
    The blue ones and the yellows.

And then I love the musketeers—
    I love them without penance;
The shy recruits, the grizzled boots,
    The privates and lieutenants.

The cavalry and the infantry
    Have furnished many a lover,
And often the old artillery
    Has kept me under cover.

I love the Welsh, I love the Dutch,
    The Swedes, the French, the Germans;
I serve them all whate'er befall
    Th'upstanding and infirm 'uns.

I do not care what flag they bear;
    Whether they're poor or wealthy;
I do not care what faith they swear,
    As long as they are healthy.

Faith and the Fatherland! These are
    The shreds of outworn clothing!
Without his clothes a woman knows
    If man's a man—or nothing.

Woman and man are greater than
    Religion and its raiment!
So strip and be at one with me—
    Forget about the payment.

Laughter and youth surround my booth;
    Heaven declares good weather;
The *Malvoisie* today is free.
    Come, let's be drunk together!

[1] For another treatment of this theme, see Burns's "I Once Was a Maid" on page 424.

457

The Beating Heart

We laugh and we are troubled
    Whene'er our fingers touch,
That hearts can love so greatly
    And minds can doubt so much.

Do you not feel, my darling,
    My heart beat through the gloom?
She nods her head, and murmurs,
    "It beats—God knows for whom!"

Three Sweethearts

It makes a man feel happy,
    It drains him to the dregs,
When he has three fair sweethearts
    And just one pair of legs.

I visit the first in the morning;
    I seek the second at night;
The third does not wait, but comes to me
    At noon in a blaze of light.

Farewell, my three fair sweethearts,
    Two legs are all I've got;
I'll go and make love to Nature
    In some more quiet spot.

Healing the Wound

With kisses my lips were wounded by you,
    So kiss them well again;
And if by evening you are not through,
    You need not hurry then.

For you have still the whole, long night,
    Darling, to comfort me.
And what long kisses and what delight
    In such a night may be!

Your Snow-White Shoulder

Upon your snow-white shoulder
    My weary head's at rest,
And I can hear the longing
    That stirs within your breast.

The blue Hussars come bugling,
    Come riding past your door;
And tomorrow, my love, you'll leave me
    And I shall see you no more.

But though you will leave me tomorrow,
    Today you are wholly mine,
Today you shall bless me doubly;
    Closer your arms shall twine.

Precaution

Do not fear, my love; no danger
    Ever will approach us here;
Fear no thief or any stranger.
    See, I lock the door, my dear.

Do not fear the wind that's quarreling,
    For these walls are strong and stout;
To prevent a fire, my darling,
    See, I blow the candle out.

Let my arms fold close and thickly
    Here about your neck and all—
One can catch a cold so quickly
    In the absence of a shawl.

I Close Her Eyes

I close her eyes, and keep them tight
    Whene'er we come to kiss;
Her laughter, curious and bright,
    Asks me the cause of this.

From early morn till late at night
  She questions why it is
I close her eyes, and keep them tight
  Whene'er we come to kiss.

I do not even know—not quite,
  What my own reason is.
I close her eyes, and keep them tight
  Whene'er we come to kiss.

Katharine

I spent the day in a heavenly way;
  Evening still found me elated.
We dined and we wined; Kitty was kind;
  And love remained unsated.

Her red lips warmed and pleaded and stormed;
  Hot and wild were her hands;
The brown eyes yearned; the bosom burned
  With ever-increasing demands.

She held me fast, and only at last
  I slipped the amorous tether.
In the living snare of her own bright hair
  I tied her hands together.

This White and Slender Body

I love this white and slender body,
  These limbs that answer love's caresses,
Passionate eyes, and forehead covered
  With a wave of thick, black tresses.

You are the very one I've searched for
  In many lands, in every weather.
You are my sort; you understand me;
  As equals we can talk together.

460

In me you've found the man you care for.
　And, for a while, you'll richly pay me
With kindness, kisses, and endearments—
　And then, as usual, you'll betray me.

The Morning After

The bottles are empty; the breakfast was good;
　The ladies are gay as at night.
They pull off their corsets—I knew that they would—
　I think they are just a bit tight.

The shoulders—how white! The young breasts—how neat!
　I look, the most favored of lovers.
They throw themselves down on the bed's snowy sheet
　And, giggling, dive under the covers.

They draw the bed-curtains; I watch them prepare
　To shed the last stitch of their clothing.
And there, like the fool of the world, I just stare
　At the foot of the bed, and do nothing.

The Brownings

Although the romance of Elizabeth Barrett Browning (1806–1861) and Robert Browning (1812–1889) has been told, dramatized, and analyzed innumerable times, it is sometimes forgotten that both poets were prodigies—Elizabeth composed an epic, *The Battle of Marathon*, at fourteen; Robert's first published poem, The confessional *Pauline*, was written at nineteen—and that he was six years younger than the invalid who was forty years old when he married her. Her *Sonnets from the Portuguese* (so called because her olive complexion suggested her husband's pet name for her, "my little Portuguese") are the unashamedly sentimental record of conjugal love, of promise and fulfillment. In return, Browning prefaced his *Men and Women* with a touching and humble dedication to her. "She was the poet," he told a friend after her death. "In comparison I was merely a clever person." Theirs was an unmatched mutual admiration and unwavering love.

The first of the next five poems is by Elizabeth Barrett Browning; the other four are by Robert Browning.

Inclusions

Oh, wilt thou have my hand, Dear, to lie along in thine?
As a little stone in a running stream, it seems to lie and pine.
Now drop the poor pale hand, Dear, unfit to plight with thine.

Oh, wilt thou have my cheek, Dear, drawn closer to thine own?
My cheek is white, my cheek is worn, by many a tear run down.
Now leave a little space, Dear, lest it should wet thine own.

Oh, must thou have my soul, Dear, commingled with thy soul?—
Red grows the cheek, and warm the hand; the part is in the whole.
Nor hands nor cheeks keep separate, when soul is joined to soul.

The Moment Eternal

Out of your whole life give but a moment!
All of your life that has gone before,
All to come after it—so you ignore,
So you make perfect the present—condense,
In a rapture of rage, for perfection's endowment,
Thought and feeling and soul and sense—
Merged in a moment which gives me at last
You around me for once, you beneath me, above me—
Me—sure that despite of time future, time past,
This tick of our life-time's moment you love me!
How long such suspension may linger? Ah, sweet—
The moment eternal—just that and no more—
When ecstasy's utmost we clutch at the core
While cheeks burn, arms open, eyes shut, and lips meet!

From A Blot in the 'Scutcheon

There's a woman like a dew-drop, she's so purer than the purest;
And her noble heart's the noblest, yes, and her sure faith's the surest.
And her eyes are dark and humid, like the depth on depth of luster
Hid i' the harebell, while her tresses, sunnier than the wild-grape
    cluster,
Gush in golden-tinted plenty down her neck's rose-misted marble:
Then her voice's music . . call it the well's bubbling, the bird's
    warble!

And this woman says, "My days were sunless and my nights were
    moonless,
"Parched the pleasant April herbage, and the lark's heart's outbreak
    tuneless,

"If you loved me not!" And I who— (ah, for words of flame!) adore
    her!
Who am mad to lay my spirit prostrate palpably before her—
I may enter at her portal soon, as now her lattice takes me,
And by noontide as by midnight make her mine, as hers she makes
    me!

From *In a Gondola*

The moth's kiss, first!
Kiss me as if you made believe
You were not sure, this eve,
How my face, your flower, had pursed
Its petals up; so, here and there,
You brush it, till I grow aware
Who wants me, and wide ope I burst.

The bee's kiss, now!
Kiss me as if you entered gay
My heart at some noonday,
A bud that dares not disallow
The claim, so all is rendered up,
And passively its shattered cup
Over your head to sleep I bow.

A Woman's Last Word

Let's contend no more, Love,
    Strive nor weep;
All be as before, Love,
    —Only sleep!

What so wild as words are?
    I and thou
In debate, as birds are,
    Hawk on bough!

See the creature stalking
    While we speak!
Hush and hide the talking,
    Cheek on cheek!

What so false as truth is,
    False to thee?
Where the serpent's tooth is
    Shun the tree—

Where the apple reddens
    Never pry—
Lest we lose our Edens,
    Eve and I.

Be a god and hold me
    With a charm!
Be a man and fold me
    With thine arm!

Teach me, only teach, Love!
    As I ought
I will speak thy speech, Love,
    Think thy thought—

Meet, if thou require it,
    Both demands,
Laying flesh and spirit
    In thy hands.

That shall be tomorrow
    Not tonight:
I must bury sorrow
    Out of sight.

—Must a little weep, Love,
    (Foolish me!)
And so fall asleep, Love,
    Loved by thee.

Alfred, Lord Tennyson

Less than a hundred years ago Lord Alfred Tennyson (1809–1892) was praised (and, one suspects, knighted) for having held "the proud honor of never uttering a single line which an English mother could wish unwritten or an English girl would wish unread." Nevertheless such a poem as "Fatima" must have brought a blush to many a Victorian cheek, while the devices that express desire in "The Miller's Daughter" circumvented the repressions of the period.

Now Sleeps The Crimson Petal

Now sleeps the crimson petal, now the white;
Nor waves the cypress in the palace walk;
Nor winks the gold fin in the porphyry font:
The firefly wakens: waken thou with me.

Now droops the milk-white peacock like a ghost,
And like a ghost she glimmers on to me.

Now lies the earth all Danaë to the stars,
And all thy heart lies open unto me.

Now slides the silent meteor on, and leaves
A shining furrow, as thy thoughts in me.

Now folds the lily all her sweetness up,
And slips into the bosom of the lake:
So fold thyself, my dearest, thou, and slip
Into my bosom and be lost in me.

Ask Me No More

Ask me no more: the moon may draw the sea;
    The cloud may stoop from heaven and take the shape
    With fold to fold, of mountains or of cape;
But O too fond, when have I answer'd thee?
        Ask me no more.

Ask me no more: what answer should I give?
    I love not hollow cheek or faded eye:
    Yet, O my friend, I will not have thee die!
Ask me no more, lest I should bid thee live;
        Ask me no more.

Ask me no more: thy fate and mine are seal'd:
    I strove against the stream and all in vain:
    Let the great river take me to the main:
No more, dear love, for at a touch I yield.
        Ask me no more.

Fatima

    O Love, Love, Love! O withering might!
    A sun, that from thy noonday height
    Shudderest when I strain my sight,
    Throbbing thro' all thy heat and light,
        Lo, falling from my constant mind,
        Lo, parched and withered, deaf and blind,
        I whirl like leaves in roaring wind.

    Last night I wasted hateful hours
    Below the city's eastern towers:
    I thirsted for the brooks, the showers:
    I rolled among the tender flowers:
        I crushed them on my breast, my mouth:
        I looked athwart the burning drouth
        Of that long desert to the south.

467

Last night, when some one spoke his name,
From my swift blood that went and came
A thousand little shafts of flame
Were shivered in my narrow frame
    O Love, O fire! once he drew
    With one long kiss my whole soul thro'
    My lips, as sunlight drinketh dew.

Before he mounts the hill, I know
He cometh quickly; from below
Sweet gales, as from deep gardens, blow
Before him, striking on my brow.
    In my dry brain my spirit soon,
    Down-deepening from swoon to swoon,
    Faints like a dazzled morning moon.

The wind sounds like a silver wire,
And from beyond the noon a fire
Is poured upon the hills, and nigher
The skies stoop down in their desire;
    And, isled in sudden seas of light,
    My heart, pierced thro' with fierce delight,
    Bursts into blossom in his sight.

My whole soul waiting silently,
All naked in a sultry sky,
Droops blinded with his shining eye:
I *will* possess him or will die.
    I will grow round him in his place,
    Grow, live, die looking on his face,
    Die, dying clasped in his embrace.

The Miller's Daughter

It is the miller's daughter,
    And she is grown so dear, so dear,
That I would be the jewel
    That trembles at her ear:
For hid in ringlets day and night,
I'd touch her neck so warm and white.

And I would be the girdle
    About her dainty, dainty waist,
And her heart would beat against me,
    In sorrow and in rest:
And I should know if it beat right,
I'd clasp it round so close and tight.

And I would be the necklace,
    And all day long to fall and rise
Upon her balmy bosom
    With her laughter or her sighs:
And I would lie so light, so light,
I scarce should be unclasped at night.

Sir Samuel Ferguson

Like many other poets, Sir Samuel Ferguson (1810-1886) was called to the bar but devoted himself to literature rather than law. In his mid-twenties he was appointed deputy-keeper of Irish Records; later he became president of the Royal Irish Academy. *Lays of the Western Gael* contains many lively pages; his epic *Congal* celebrates the last stand of Irish paganism against conquering Christianity.

Dear Dark Head

Put your head, darling, darling, darling,
    Your darling black head on my heart above;
Oh, mouth of honey with thyme for fragrance,
    Who, with heart in breast, could deny you love?

Oh, many and many a young girl for me is pining,
    Letting her locks of gold to the cold wind free,
For me, the foremost of our gay young fellows;
    But I'd leave a hundred, pure love, for thee!

Then put your head, darling, darling, darling,
    Your darling black head my heart above;
Oh mouth of honey with thyme for fragrance,
    Who with heart in breast could deny you love?

John Godfrey Saxe

The Vermont-born John Godfrey Saxe (1816-1887) was a lawyer, lecturer, school superintendent, collector of customs, journalist, politician, and poet. His reputation as a writer of light verse was widespread; his collected *Poems* went through more than fifty editions in less than twelve years. His witty "The Blind Men and the Elephant" continues to be quoted; it never fails to appear in humorous anthologies and instructive textbooks.

"To Lesbia" is one more variation on the famous poem by Catullus. Versions by George Lamb and Ben Jonson are on pages 44 and 45.

471

To Lesbia

Give me kisses! Do not stay,
Counting in that careful way.
All the coins your lips can print
Never will exhaust the mint.
      Kiss me, then,
Every moment—and again!

Give me kisses! Do not stop,
Measuring nectar by the drop.
Though to millions they amount,
They will never drain the fount.
      Kiss me, then,
Every moment—and again!

Give me kisses! All is waste
Save the luxury we taste;
And for kissing,—kisses live
Only when we take or give.
      Kiss me, then,
Every moment—and again!

Give me kisses! Though their worth
Far exceeds the gems of earth,
Never pearls so rich and pure
Cost so little, I am sure.
      Kiss me, then,
Every moment—and again!

Give me kisses! Nay, 'tis true
I am just as rich as you;
And for every kiss I owe,
I can pay you back, you know,
      Kiss me, then,
Every moment—and again!

Dante Gabriel Rossetti

When, with a few others, Dante Gabriel Rossetti (1828-1882) founded the Pre-Raphaelite Brotherhood, the group was attacked as "sacrilegious" and Rossetti was particularly scored for his "fleshly mysticism." He did not reply to the indictment. Instead he went on uniting his talents as poet and painter, found the perfect Pre-Raphaelite model in a red-haired, seventeen-year-old milliner's assistant, made her his mistress, and, after ten years, married her. When she died, Rossetti buried all his unpublished poems in her coffin. Nine years later, he dug them up and had them published. "What Smouldering Senses" is one of the most fervid of the love sonnets.

What Smouldering Senses

What smouldering senses in death's sick delay,
Or seizure of malign vicissitude,
Can rob this body of honor, or denude
This soul of wedding-raiment worn to-day?
For lo! even now my lady's lips did play
With these my lips such consonant interlude
As laureled Orpheus longed for when he wooed
The half-drawn hungering face with that last lay.

I was a child beneath her touch—a man
When breast to breast we clung, even I and she—
A spirit when her spirit looked through me—
A god when all our life-breath met to fan
Our life-blood, till love's emulous ardors ran
Fire within fire, desire in deity.

473

George Meredith

Even in his maturity, author of some fifteen novels, George Meredith (1828-1909) insisted that he was the illegitimate son of high-born parents—he hated to admit that one of his grandfathers was an innkeeper and the other a tailor. Actually Melchizedek Meredith was the head of a large tailoring establishment, and he was accepted in county society; one of his granddaughters became a marquise.

Society preoccupied George Meredith, society and sex. His first wife had deserted him, and he turned against women; he even had a male nurse for his son. *Modern Love* is a series of semi-sonnets which centers on tragic incompatibility. "Love in the Valley" is an early work—Tennyson loved it and said he could not forget any of its exquisite lines.

<hr/>

From *Love in the Valley*

Under yonder beech-tree single on the greensward,
    Couched with her arms behind her golden head,
Knees and tresses folded to slip and ripple idly,
    Lies my young love sleeping in the shade.
Had I the heart to slide an arm beneath her,
    Press her parting lips as her waist I gather slow,
Waking in amazement she could not but embrace me:
    Then would she hold me and never let me go?

Shy as the squirrel and wayward as the swallow,
    Swift as the swallow along the river's light
Circleting the surface to meet his mirror'd winglets,
    Fleeter she seems in her stay than in her flight.
Shy as the squirrel that leaps among the pine-tops,
    Wayward as the swallow overhead at set of sun,

She whom I love is hard to catch and conquer,
    Hard, but O the glory of the winning were she won!
        . . . . .
Happy happy time, when the white star hovers
    Low over dim fields fresh with bloomy dew,
Near the face of dawn, that draws athwart the darkness,
    Threading it with color, like yewberries the yew.
Thicker crowd the shades as the grave East deepens
    Glowing, and with crimson a long cloud swells,
Maiden still the morn is; and strange she is, and secret;
    Strange her eyes; her cheeks are cold as cold sea-shells.

Hither she comes; she comes to me; she lingers,
    Deepens her brown eyebrows, while in new surprise
High rise the lashes in wonder of a stranger;
    Yet am I the light and living of her eyes.
Something friends have told her fills her heart to brimming,
    Nets her in her blushes, and wounds her, and tames.—
Sure of her haven, O like a dove alighting,
    Arms up, she dropp'd: our souls were in our names!

Rana Mukerji

Little is known of Rana Mukerji. The name is a pseudonym for an author and artist who spent many years in India and Ceylon.

Spring Night

With the spring moon's first beams
You enter my dreams.
Is it you or a moonbeam that lies
On my forehead brushing my eyes?
Is it you or a light that lingers
With invisible fingers
Teasing my lips, my mouth, my cheeks
For what so subtly it seeks?
A shy yet shameless warmth caresses my breasts
And nests
Where the young rosebuds rise.
Then over smooth and sloping sides
A light hand glides,
Sliding between soft hills until it turns
Into a half-hidden valley of ferns.
There, in the glowing center,
The moonlight gathers and gleams
And burns
Till all my lips open, and you enter
All my dreams.

A Sampler of German Love Sayings

Vita Brevis

Though pain and care are everywhere,
  Give freely, lass; live fully, lover.
For death's a rather long affair,
  And when we die, we die all over.

Recipe

Keep love a-boiling; keep soup in the pot.
Both are enjoyable only when hot.

All for Love

What a man may do for love
Even the angels must approve.
What a man for love has done
That, after all, concerns no one.

Look to the Leaf

When the leaf is tight and gray
Bid your love good day.

When the leaf unfolds its wing
Tell your love it's spring.

When the leaf inclines to fall
She will give you all.

When the leaf decides to fly
Kiss your love goodbye.

Love's Torment

Love is a torment, there's no question,
Almost as great as indigestion.

Constancies

Woman's love, April weather,
Man's honor, birds of a feather,
Good fortune, blessings beyond price,
Are constant—as the fall of dice.

Birds and Bees

Robins wait for early worms; bees will find their clover;
Girls believe and men deceive the whole world over.

Pleasure

Pleasure could be carried to
The very end of life
If a man were married to
Anyone but his wife.

Woman

A comfort but a queer companion
Who prods and puzzles, goads and whips,
Woman is something like an onion.
We weep, and curse, and smack our lips.

Caution

Listen, lass, if you would be
    Safe from every sort of scourge in
This life-long uncertainty,
    Keep your head. Remain a virgin.

Boastful Husbandman

The foolish man who boasts that he is able
    To manage a horse or a woman without a bit,
Will never get a mare inside of his stable,
    And as for his bed—he'll sleep alone in it.

The Right Time

Presents of money, furs, and pearls
    For a long time should be refused.
Diplomats and clever girls
    Know when to be seduced.

Advice to Bachelors

Alike from love and marriage hurry;
    Run while you can from your desire.
The cooked goose has no time to worry
    Whether it's frying-pan or fire.

Age and Youth

A fine old wine and a fair young wife
Will keep you dizzy most of your life.

Advice to Country Girls

An innocent country girl going to town
Should keep her head up and her skirts down.

Heaven

Heaven is closed, proclaims the preacher,
To any weak or wayward creature.
But if we were alone one minute
I'd show you a good way to get in it.

PARAPHRASED BY LOUIS UNTERMEYER

The Modern World

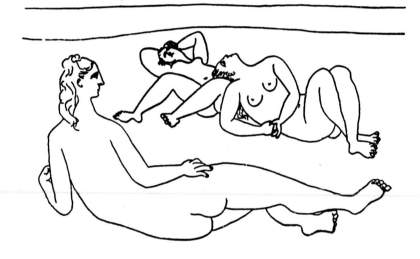

The Modern World

Apart from its other characteristics, modern writing is marked by a renewed liberty of thought and full freedom of phrase. It presents a vivid contrast to the restraints of the prim advocates of "sweetness and light" and recalls the license as well as the naturalism of the eighteenth century poets.

The aestheticism of the Pre-Raphaelites developed into the daring of such disciples as Algernon Charles Swinburne, Oscar Wilde, Arthur Symons, and Ernest Dowson—poets who surpassed Dante Gabriel Rossetti, founder of the movement, in an impulse to shock the reader out of his complacence. Max Beerbohm wittily exposed some of the foibles of the group, particularly its special interpretation of Beauty and the use of it as a slogan by Oscar Wilde. "Beauty," wrote Beerbohm, "had existed long before 1880. It was Oscar Wilde who managed her debut. To study the period is to admit that to him was due no small part of the social vogue that Beauty began to enjoy." Other critics were more savage than Beerbohm; the sensational young writers and artists were labeled "decadents" and reviled for their audacity, which was considered the same as immorality. To this Wilde replied: "There is no such thing as a moral or immoral book. Books are well written or badly written. That is all."

Wilde's precept summarizes the modern attitude to works of the creative imagination. Today a work of art is seldom appraised as something which is either moral or immoral; it is judged as either good art or bad art. This is especially true of the poetry of our times, a poetry which includes, among many others, such original and variously expressive poets as D. H. Lawrence, E. E. Cummings, Stanley Kunitz, A. D. Hope, Theodore Roethke, and Alex Comfort. Here is a poetry which is both passionate and tender, romantic and realistic, witty, honest, sometimes provoking, often penetrating, and always persuasive.

Emily Dickinson

America's (and possibly the world's) greatest woman poet, Emily Dickinson (1830-1886) wrote more than 1700 poems in secrecy, of which only seven were published during her lifetime. Her unique mind and manner focused on a few major concerns: love, nature, the meaning of life and death. A New England spinster denied the fulfillment of passion, she reveals wishful dreams in the repressed but intense emotion of such poems as "Come Slowly, Eden!" and "Wild Nights!"

Come Slowly, Eden

Come slowly, Eden!
Lips unused to thee,
Bashful, sip thy jasmines,
As the fainting bee,
Reaching late his flower,
Round her chamber hums,
Counts his nectars—enters,
And is lost in balms!

Wild Nights!

Wild nights! Wild nights!
Were I with thee,
Wild nights should be
Our luxury!

Futile the winds
To a heart in port—
Done with the compass
Done with the chart.

Rowing in Eden.
Ah! the sea!
Might I but moor
Tonight in thee!

Algernon Charles Swinburne

During the first half of his life Algernon Charles Swinburne (1837–1909) led the life of a determined bohemian; famous at twenty-eight, he outdid his fellow eccentrics in drinking, attitudinizing, and general recklessness. His sexual preoccupations were peculiar if not perverse. As an undergraduate he had been frequently flogged, a punishment he enjoyed to such an extent that his poems are full of fantasies of flagellation. Expressions of algolagnia, the sexual pleasure derived from suffering, are heard in many masochistic-sadistic poems which play continual variations on the theme of pleasure in pain and pain in pleasure.

Unable to stand the strain of living up to his reputation, Swinburne broke down and spent the last sterile thirty years of his life in seclusion under the spinsterly care of his friend Theodore Watts-Dunton—Max Beerbohm's "No. 2 The Pines" is a cruelly accurate picture of those dull, declining days.

Swinburne's theatrical style has gone out of fashion, but readers encountering him for the first time are fascinated by his excess, his inexhaustible alliteration, his rolling rhythms and rushing rhymes. He has been called, with alliterative mockery, the Poet Prince of Puberty. Nevertheless, there still is a kind of intoxication in his romantic lavishness, his singing rhetoric, and his richly erotic suggestiveness.

For a Swinburnian rendering of a medieval poem see "In the Orchard" on page 106.

Fragoletta

O Love! what shall be said of thee?
The son of grief begot by joy?
Being sightless, wilt thou see?
Being sexless, wilt thou be
Maiden or boy?

I dreamed of strange lips yesterday
And cheeks wherein the ambiguous blood
Was like a rose's—yea,
A rose's when it lay
Within the bud.

What fields have bred thee, or what groves
Concealed thee, O mysterious flower,
O double rose of Love's,
With leaves that lure the doves
From bud to bower?

I dare not kiss it, lest my lip
Press harder than an indrawn breath,
And all the sweet life slip
Forth, and the sweet leaves drip,
Bloodlike, in death.

O sole desire of my delight!
O sole delight of my desire!
Mine eyelids and eyesight
Feed on thee day and night
Like lips of fire.

Lean back thy throat of carven pearl,
Lest thy mouth murmur like the dove's;
Say, Venus hath no girl,
No front of female curl,
Among her Loves.

Thy sweet low bosom, thy close hair,
Thy straight soft flanks and slenderer feet,
Thy virginal strange air,
Are these not over fair
For Love to greet?

How should he greet thee? what new name,
Fit to move all men's hearts, could move
Thee, deaf to love or shame,
Love's sister, by the same
Mother as Love?

Ah sweet, the maiden's mouth is cold,
Her breast-blossoms are simply red,
Her hair mere brown or gold,
Fold over simple fold
Binding her head.

Thy mouth is made of fire and wine,
Thy barren bosom takes my kiss
And turns my soul to thine
And turns thy lip to mine,
And mine it is.

Thou hast a serpent in thine hair,
In all the curls that close and cling;
And ah, thy breast-flower!
Ah love, thy mouth too fair
To kiss and sting!

Cleave to me, love me, kiss mine eyes,
Satiate thy lips with loving me;
Nay, for thou shalt not rise;
Lie still as Love that dies
For love of thee.

Mine arms are close about thine head,
My lips are fervent on thy face,
And where my kiss hath fed
Thy flower-like blood leaps red
To the kissed place.

O bitterness of things too sweet
O broken singing of the dove!
Love's wings are over fleet,
And like the panther's feet
The feet of Love.

Love and Sleep

Lying asleep between the strokes of night
  I saw my love lean over my sad bed,
  Pale as the duskiest lily's leaf or head,
Smooth-skinned and dark, with bare throat made to bite,
Too wan for blushing and too warm for white,
  But perfect-colored without white or red.
  And her lips opened amorously, and said—
I wist not what, saving one word: Delight.
And all her face was honey to my mouth,
  And all her body pasture to mine eyes;
  The long lithe arms and hotter hands than fire,
The quivering flanks, hair smelling of the south,
The bright light feet, the splendid supple thighs
  And glittering eyelids of my soul's desire.

Faustine

Lean back, and get some minutes' peace;
  Let your head lean
Back to the shoulder with its fleece
  Of locks, Faustine.

490

The shapely silver shoulder stoops,
   Weighed over clean
With state of splendid hair that droops
   Each side, Faustine.

Let me go over your good gifts
   That crown you queen;
A queen whose kingdom ebbs and shifts
   Each week, Faustine.

Bright heavy brows well gathered up:
   White gloss and sheen;
Carved lips that make my lips a cup
   To drink, Faustine.

Wine and rank poison, milk and blood,
   Being mixed therein
Since first the devil threw dice with God
   For you, Faustine.

Your naked new-born soul, their stake,
   Stood blind between;
God said "let him that wins her take
   And keep Faustine."

But this time Satan throve, no doubt:
   Long since, I ween,
God's part in you was battered out;
   Long since, Faustine.

The die rang sideways as it fell,
   Rang cracked and thin,
Like a man's laughter heard in hell
   Far down, Faustine.

A shadow of laughter like a sigh,
   Dead sorrow's kin;
So rang, thrown down, the devil's die
   That won Faustine.

A suckling of his breed you were,
  One hard to wean;
But God, who lost you, left you fair,
  We see, Faustine.

You have the face that suits a woman
  For her soul's screen—
The sort of beauty that's called human
  In hell, Faustine.

You could do all things but be good
  Or chaste of mien;
And that you would not if you could,
  We know, Faustine.

Even he who cast seven devils out
  Of Magdalene
Could hardly do as much, I doubt,
  For you, Faustine.

Did Satan make you to spite God?
  Or did God mean
To scourge with scorpions for a rod
  Our sins, Faustine?

I know what queen at first you were,
  As though I had seen
Red gold and black imperious hair
  Twice crown Faustine.

As if your fed sarcophagus
  Spared flesh and skin,
You come back face to face with us
  The same Faustine.

She loved the games men played with death,
  Where death must win;
As though the slain man's blood and breath
  Revived Faustine.

Nets caught the pike, pikes tore the net;
  Lithe limbs and lean
From drained-out pores dripped thick red sweat
  To soothe Faustine.

She drank the steaming drift and dust
  Blown off the scene;
Blood could not ease the bitter lust
  That galled Faustine. . . .

         . . . .

A star upon your birthday burned,
  Whose fierce serene
Red pulseless planet never yearned
  In heaven, Faustine.

Stray breaths of Sapphic song that blew
  Through Mitylene
Shook the fierce quivering blood in you
  By night, Faustine.

The shameless nameless love that makes
  Hell's iron gin
Shut on you like a trap that breaks
  The soul, Faustine.

And when your veins were void and dead,
  What ghosts unclean
Swarmed round the straitened barren bed
  That hid Faustine?

What sterile growths of sexless root
  Or epicene?
What flower of kisses without fruit
  Of love, Faustine?

What adders came to shed their coats?
  What coiled obscene

493

Small serpents with soft stretching throats
    Caressed Faustine?

But the time came of famished hours,
    Maimed loves and mean,
This ghastly thin-faced time of ours,
    To spoil Faustine.

You seem a thing that hinges hold,
    A love-machine
With clockwork joints of supple gold
    No more, Faustine.

Not godless, for you serve one God,
    The Lampsacene,
Who metes the gardens with his rod;
    Your lord, Faustine.

If one should love you with real love
    (Such things have been,
Things your fair face knows nothing of,
    It seems, Faustine) ;

That clear hair heavily bound back,
    The lights wherein
Shift from dead blue to burnt-up black;
    Your throat, Faustine,

Strong, heavy, throwing out the face
    And hard bright chin
And shameful scornful lips that grace
    Their shame, Faustine,

Curled lips, long since half kissed away,
    Still sweet and keen;
You'd give him—poison shall we say?
    Or what, Faustine?

From *Dolores*

We shift and bedeck and bedrape us,
  Thou art noble and nude and antique;
Libitina thy mother, Priapus
  Thy father, a Tuscan and Greek.
We play with light loves in the portal,
  And wince and relent and refrain;
Loves die, and we know thee immortal,
  Our Lady of Pain.

Fruits fail and love dies and time ranges;
  Thou art fed with perpetual breath,
And alive after infinite changes,
  And fresh from the kisses of death;
Of languors rekindled and rallied,
  Of barren delights and unclean,
Things monstrous and fruitless, a pallid
  And poisonous queen.

Could you hurt me, sweet lips, though I hurt you?
  Men touch them, and change in a trice
The lilies and languors of virtue
  For the raptures and roses of vice;
Those lie where thy foot on the floor is,
  These crown and caress thee and chain,
O splendid and sterile Dolores,
  Our Lady of Pain.

There are sins it may be to discover,
  There are deeds it may be to delight.
What new work wilt thou find for thy lover,
  What new passions for daytime or night?
What spells that they know not a word of
  Whose lives are as leaves overblown?
What tortures undreamt of, unheard of,
  Unwritten, unknown?

Ah beautiful passionate body
  That never has ached with a heart!
On thy mouth though the kisses are bloody,

Though they sting till it shudder and smart,
More kind than the love we adore is,
  They hurt not the heart or the brain,
O bitter and tender Dolores,
  Our Lady of Pain.

As our kisses relax and redouble,
  From the lips and the foam and the fangs
Shall no new sin be born for men's trouble,
  No dream of impossible pangs?
With the sweet of the sins of old ages
  Wilt thou satiate thy soul as of yore?
Too sweet is the rind, say the sages,
  Too bitter the core.

Hast thou told all thy secrets the last time,
  And bared all thy beauties to one?
Ah, where shall we go then for pastime,
  If the worst that can be has been done?
But sweet as the rind was the core is;
  We are fain of thee still, we are fain,
O sanguine and subtle Dolores,
  Our Lady of Pain.

By the hunger of change and emotion,
  By the thirst of unbearable things,
By despair, the twin-born of devotion,
  By the pleasure that winces and stings,
The delight that consumes the desire,
  The desire that outruns the delight,
By the cruelty deaf as a fire
  And blind as the night,

By the ravenous teeth that have smitten
  Through the kisses that blossom and bud,
By the lips intertwisted and bitten
  Till the foam has a savor of blood,
By the pulse as it rises and falters,
  By the hands as they slacken and strain,
I adjure thee, respond from thine altars,
  Our Lady of Pain.

496

Wilt thou smile as a woman disdaining
  The light fire in the veins of a boy?
But he comes to thee sad, without feigning,
  Who has wearied of sorrow and joy;
Less careful of labor and glory
  Than the elders whose hair has uncurled;
And young, but with fancies as hoary
  _And gray as the world.

I have passed from the outermost portal
  To the shrine where a sin is a prayer;
What care though the service be mortal?
  O our Lady of Torture, what care?
All thine the last wine that I pour is,
  The last in the chalice we drain,
O fierce and luxurious Dolores,
  Our Lady of Pain.

All thine the new wine of desire,
  The fruit of four lips as they clung
Till the hair and the eyelids took fire,
  The foam of a serpentine tongue,
The froth of the serpents of pleasure,
  More salt than the foam of the sea,
Now felt as a flame, now at leisure
  As wine shed for me.

          .   .   .   .   .

Love listens, and paler than ashes,
  Through his curls as the crown on them slips,
Lifts languid wet eyelids and lashes,
  And laughs with insatiable lips.
Thou shalt hush him with heavy caresses,
  With music that scares the profane;
Thou shalt darken his eyes with thy tresses,
  Our Lady of Pain.

Thou shalt blind his bright eyes though he wrestle,
  Thou shalt chain his light limbs though he strive;
In his lips all thy serpents shall nestle,
  In his hands all thy cruelties thrive.
In the daytime thy voice shall go through him,
  In his dreams he shall feel thee and ache;

Thou shalt kindle by night and subdue him
   Asleep and awake.

Thou shalt touch and make redder his roses
   With juice not of fruit nor of bud;
When the sense in the spirit reposes,
   Thou shalt quicken the soul through the blood.
Thine, thine the one grace we implore is,
   Who would live and not languish or feign,
O sleepless and deadly Dolores,
   Our Lady of Pain.

Paul Verlaine

One of the Parnassian poets who, opposed to formless roman-
ticizing, championed art for art's sake, Paul Verlaine (1844–1896)
inspired the moderns with his adjuration: "Take rhetoric and wring
its neck." His was a career which began on the heights and ended
in utter degradation. The turning point came when Verlaine, mar-
ried and father of a son, fell in love with a seventeen-year-old poet,
Arthur Rimbaud. The homosexual involvement ended in a shoot-
ing and a prison sentence. After Verlaine was released he sank into
poverty, debauchery, and misery. Some of his fellow-writers com-
pared him to Villon.

The following translation is by the editor.

I Hate to See You Clad

In your silk robe I hate to see you clad;
Your filmiest veil is just as bad;
  It clouds your eyes,
  My dearest skies.
Your bustle I abominate; its size
Distorts the contour of your sumptuous thighs.

I am the enemy of each and every dress
Which hides your shining nakedness.
  Dazzled, I dote
  On your white throat,
On your bright shoulders and, below, the pair
Of tender sorceries that nestle there.

Fie on a woman overdressed! You please
Me best, my dear, in your chemise,
  That bit of gauze
  Which never was
An obstacle, but a pure symbol of
And prelude to the endless rites of love.

George Moore

Famous for his novels, plays, memoirs, historical reconstructions, autobiographical confessions and conversations, George Moore (1852–1933) is seldom mentioned as a poet. Yet his first two books, significantly entitled *Flowers of Passion* and *Pagan Poems*, were those of a promising poet. He shocked the Victorians with these and with the subsequent prose fiction of *A Mummer's Wife* and *Esther Waters*. The later *Heloise and Abelard* and *Aphrodite in Aulis* are stylistically distinguished; they have the pitch as well as the polish of poetry.

Rondo

Did I love thee? I only did desire
To hold thy body unto mine,
And smite it with strange fire
Of kisses burning as a wine,
And catch thy odorous hair, and twine
It thro' my fingers amorously.
    Did I love thee?

Did I love thee? I only did desire
To watch thine eyelids lilywise
Closed down, and thy warm breath respire
As it came through the thickening sighs,
And speak my love in such fair guise
Of passion's sobbing agony.
    Did I love thee?

Did I love thee? I only did desire
To drink the perfume of thy blood
In vision, and thy senses tire
Seeing them shift from ebb to flood
In consonant sweet interlude.
And if love such a thing not be,
    I loved not thee.

Oscar Wilde

Like Verlaine's, the brilliant career of Oscar Wilde (1854–1900) was ruined by a homosexual attachment, a term in prison *(The Ballad of Reading Gaol),* and subsequent self-exile. Leader of the Aesthetic Movement, influenced by the French Parnassians, until his collapse Wilde both amused and provoked his generation with plays and whiplash epigrams and by mocking the conventions. His "Hélas" synthesizes his attitude in a single sonnet; it is an excuse as well as an outcry.

From *The Sphinx*

How subtle-secret is your smile! Did you love none
      then? Nay, I know
Great Ammon was your bedfellow! He lay with you
      beside the Nile!

The river-horses in the slime trumpeted when they saw him
      come
Odorous with Syrian galbanum and smeared with spikenard
      and with thyme.

He came along the river bank like some tall galley argent-
      sailed,
He strolled across the waters, mailed in beauty, and the
      waters sank.

He strode across the desert sand: he reached the valley
      where you lay:
He waited till the dawn of day: then touched your black
      breasts with his hand.

You kissed his mouth with mouths of flame: you made
    the hornèd god your own:
You stood behind him on his throne: you called him by
    his secret name.

You whispered monstrous oracles into the caverns of his
    ears:
With blood of goats and blood of steers you taught him
    monstrous miracles.

White Ammon was your bedfellow! Your chamber was
    the steaming Nile!
And with your curved archaic smile you watched his
    passion come and go.

La Bella Donna Della Mia Mente

My limbs are wasted with a flame,
    My feet are sore with traveling;
For calling on my Lady's name
    My lips have now forgot to sing.

O Linnet in the wild-rose brake
    Strain for my Love thy melody,
O Lark sing louder for love's sake,
    My gentle Lady passeth by.

She is too fair for any man
    To see or hold his heart's delight,
Fairer than Queen or courtezan
    Or moon-lit water in the night.

Her hair is bound with myrtle leaves,
    (Green leaves upon her golden hair!)
Green grasses through the yellow sheaves
    Of autumn corn are not more fair.

Her little lips, more made to kiss
   Than to cry bitterly for pain,
Are tremulous as brookwater is,
   Or roses after evening rain.

Her neck is like white melilote
   Flushing for pleasure of the sun,
The throbbing of the linnet's throat
   Is not so sweet to look upon.

As a pomegranate, cut in twain,
   White-seeded, is her crimson mouth,
Her cheeks are as the fading stain
   Where the peach reddens to the south.

O twining hands! O delicate
   White body made for love and pain!
O House of love! O desolate
   Pale flower beaten by the rain!

Hélas

To drift with every passion till my soul
Is a stringed lute on which all winds can play,
Is it for this that I have given away
Mine ancient wisdom, and austere control?
Methinks my life is a twice-written scroll
Scrawled over on some boyish holiday
With idle songs for pipe and virelay,
Which do but mar the secret of the whole.
Surely there was a time I might have trod
The sunlit heights, and from life's dissonance
Struck one clear chord to reach the ears of God:
Is that time dead? lo! with a little rod
I did but touch the honey of romance—
And must I lose a soul's inheritance?

A. E. Housman

A. E. Housman (1859–1936) was an irascible Latin scholar who believed in short bursts of song rather than sustained flights of thought; within its limitations, his poetry attains an almost classic brevity. The alternately blithe and bitter stanzas in *A Shropshire Lad* have been called the best Latin lyrics ever written in English.

❧

Along the Field as We Came By

Along the field as we came by
A year ago, my love and I,
The aspen over stile and stone
Was talking to itself alone.
"Oh, who are these that kiss and pass?
A country lover and his lass;
Two lovers looking to be wed;
And time shall put them both to bed,
But she shall lie with earth above,
And he beside another love."

And sure enough beneath the tree
There walks another love with me,
And overhead the aspen heaves
Its rainy-sounding silver leaves;
And I spell nothing in their stir,
But now perhaps they speak to her,
And plain for her to understand
They talk about a time at hand
When I shall sleep with clover clad,
And she beside another lad.

504

Arthur Symons

A leader of the Symbolist movement, Arthur Symons (1863–1945) brought back with him to England the spirit of some of the French literature then in fashion. His own work was strongly influenced by Verlaine and Baudelaire. Although much of his own poetry is heavily scented with the fragrance of hot-house blossoms and suggestions of what has been called the Deadly Nightshade flowering of verse, it has a growth of its own. The best of his lyrics and monologues blend sophistication with sensuousness. Even when the romanticism is unrestrained, Symons excels in nuances of sensation; the technique is disciplined and the touch is precise.

Escalade

Tenderly as a bee that sips,
Your kisses settle on my lips,
And your soft cheek begins to creep
Like the downy wing of Sleep
Along my cheek, and nestles smiling,
As if Love's truth were but beguiling,
Too utterly content to move,
Only to smile, only to love.

But if, to tease you, as I use,
I feign, unthankful, to refuse
Your dear caresses, and turn cold,
Then the shy lips, waxing bold,
Advance to vanquish my resistance,
And, with a passionate persistence,

Clinging closer, fold on fold,
They suck my lips into their hold.

And, if, still feigning, I resist,
Fondly feigning to be kissed,
They wax still bolder and begin
Hungrily to fasten in
Upon my neck, as they would gloat
On the protesting veins that tingle
As they and your deep kisses mingle,
Your kisses burning in my throat.

But ah! if, lastly, I should hear
Your sudden lips upon my ear
Set my brain singing and my blood
Dancing the measure of your mood,
And pouring over me and under
Scented billows of soft thunder,
I yield, I'll love you, lest it be
I die of you ere you of me!

Leves Amores

Your kisses, and the way you curl,
Delicious and distracting girl,
Into one's arms, and round about,
Inextricably in and out,
Twining luxuriously, as twine
The clasping tangles of the vine;
So loving to be loved, so gay
And greedy for our holiday;
Strong to embrace and long to kiss,
And strenuous for the sharper bliss,
A little tossing sea of sighs,
Till the slow calm seal up your eyes.
And then how prettily you sleep!
You nestle close and let me keep
My straying fingers in the nest
Of your warm comfortable breast;

And as I dream, lying awake,
Of sleep well wasted for your sake,
I feel the very pulse and heat
Of your young life-blood beat, and beat
With mine; and you are mine; my sweet!

Envoi

All that remains for me,
In this world, after this,
Is, but to take a kiss
For what a kiss should be;

To stake one's heart to win,
Yet have no heart to lose:
Now I am free to choose,
Now, let the game begin!

If my hand shakes and swerves
A little as I play,
Well, such a yesterday
Was trying for one's nerves.

But I am wary, see!
I know the game at last.
I know the past is past,
And what remains for me:

To play a lighter stake,
Nor lay one's heart above,
And to have done with love
For ever, for your sake.

Ecstasy

What is this reverence in extreme delight
That waits upon my kisses as they storm,
Vehemently, this height
Of steep and inaccessible delight;
And seems with newer ecstasy to warm
Their slackening ardor, and invite,
From nearer heaven, the swarm
Of hiving stars with mortal sweetness down?
Never before
Have I endured an exaltation
So exquisite in anguish, and so sore
In promise and possession of full peace.
Cease not, O nevermore
Cease,
To lift my joy, as upon windy wings,
Into that infinite ascension, where,
In baths of glittering air,
It finds a heaven and like an angel sings.
Heaven waits above,
There where the clouds and fastnesses of love
Lift earth into the skies;
And I have seen the glimmer of the gates,
And twice or thrice
Climbed half the difficult way,
Only to say
Heaven waits,
Only to fall away from paradise.
But now, O what is this
Mysterious and uncapturable bliss
That I have never known, yet seems to be
Simple as breath, and easy as a smile,
And older than the earth?
Now but a little while

This ultimate ecstasy
Has parted from its birth,
Now but a little while been wholly mine,
Yet am I utterly possessed
By the delicious tyrant and divine
Child, this importunate guest.

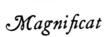

Magnificat

Praise God, who wrought for you and me
Your subtle body made for love;
God, who from all eternity
Willed our divided ways should move
Together, and our love should be.

I wandered all these years among
A world of women, seeking you.
Ah, when our fingers met and clung,
The pulses of our bodies knew
Each other: our hearts leapt and sung.

It was not any word of mine,
It was not any look of yours;
Only we knew, and knew for sign
Of Love that comes, Love that endures,
Our veins the chalice of his wine.

Because God willed for us and planned
One perfect love, excelling speech
To tell, or thought to understand,
He made our bodies each for each,
Then put your hand into my hand.

Bianca

Her cheeks are hot, her cheeks are white;
The white girl hardly breathes tonight,
So faint the pulses come and go,
That waken to a smouldering glow
The morbid faintness of her white.

What drowsing heats of sense, desire
Longing and languorous, the fire
Of what white ashes, subtly mesh
The fascinations of her flesh
Into a breathing web of fire?

Only her eyes, only her mouth,
Live, in the agony of drouth,
Athirst for that which may not be:
The desert of virginity
Aches in the hotness of her mouth.

I take her hands into my hands,
Silently, and she understands;
I set my lips upon her lips;
Shuddering to her finger tips
She strains my hands within her hands.

I set my lips on hers; they close
Into a false and phantom rose;
Upon her thirsting lips I rain
A flood of kisses, and in vain;
Her lips inexorably close.

Through her closed lips that cling to mine,
Her hands that hold me and entwine,
Her body that abandoned lies,
Rigid with sterile ecstasies,
A shiver knits her flesh to mine.

Life sucks into a mist remote
Her fainting lips, her throbbing throat;
Her lips that open to my lips,
And, hot against my finger-tips,
The pulses leaping in her throat.

Ernest Dowson

Ernest Dowson (1867–1900) came from a most respectable family; his uncle was onetime Prime Minister of New Zealand, his father owned a London drydock. Dowson, one of the more precious products of the Eighteen Nineties, spent most of his short life in France. There he fell in love with a café proprietor's daughter—she became the "Cynara" of his famous poem—and paid court to her until she left him for a waiter. After that he sank rapidly in health—he was already suffering from tuberculosis—and drank himself to death.

More of a French decadent than an English poet, Dowson was, said William Butler Yeats, "gentle, affectionate, drifting." He was fascinated both by religion and the irresponsible life, wavering between his devotion to the Virgin and his adoration of Venus.

Cynara

Last night, ah, yesternight, betwixt her lips and mine
There fell thy shadow, Cynara! thy breath was shed
Upon my soul between the kisses and the wine;
And I was desolate and sick of an old passion,
    Yea, I was desolate and bowed my head:
I have been faithful to thee, Cynara! in my fashion.

All night upon mine heart I felt her warm heart beat,
Night-long within mine arms in love and sleep she lay;
Surely the kisses of her bought red mouth were sweet;
But I was desolate and sick of an old passion,
    When I awoke and found the dawn was grey:
I have been faithful to thee, Cynara! in my fashion.

I have forgot much, Cynara! gone with the wind,
Flung roses, roses riotously with the throng,
Dancing, to put thy pale, lost lilies out of mind;
But I was desolate and sick of an old passion,
    Yea, all the time, because the dance was long:
I have been faithful to thee, Cynara! In my fashion.

I cried for madder music and for stronger wine,
But when the feast is finished and the lamps expire,
Then falls thy shadow, Cynara! the night is thine;
And I am desolate and sick of an old passion,
    Yea, hungry for the lips of my desire:
I have been faithful to thee, Cynara! in my fashion.

Your Hands

I was always a lover of ladies' hands!
    Or ever mine heart came here to tryst,
For the sake of your carved white hands' commands;
    The tapering fingers, the dainty wrist;
    The hands of a girl were what I kissed.

I remember a hand like a fleur-de-lys
    When it slid from its silken sheath, her glove;
With its odors passing ambergris:
    And that was the empty husk of a love.
    Oh, how shall I kiss your hands enough?

They are pale with the pallor of ivories;
    But they blush to the tips like a curled seashell:
What treasure, in kingly treasuries,
    Of gold, and spice for the thurible,
    Is sweet as your hands to hoard and tell?

I know not the way from your finger-tips,
    Nor how I shall gain the higher lands,
The citadel of your sacred lips:
    I am captive still of my pleasant bands,
    The hands of a girl, and most, your hands.

The Royal Love Scene

(Adapted From Voltaire's *La Pucelle*)

Our good King Charles within his youthful prime
His revels kept at Tours, at Eastertime,
Where at a ball (for well he loved to dance)
It so fell out, that for the good of France
He met a maid who beggared all compare,
Named Agnes Sorel (Love had framed the fair).
Let your warm fancy youthful Flora trace,
Of Venus add her most enchanting grace,
The wood-nymph's stature and bewitching guise,

With Love's seductive air and brilliant eyes,
Arachne's art, the Syren's dulcet song—
All these were hers and she could lead along
Kings, Heroes, Sages in her captive chain.
To see her, love her, feel the increasing pain,
Of young Desire, its growing warmth to prove,
With faltering utterance to speak of Love;
To tremble and regard with dove-like eyes,
To strive and speak and utter nought but sighs,
Her hand, with a caressing hand to hold,
Till panting all the flames her breast enfold;
By turns each other's tender pains impart,
And own the luscious thrill that sways the heart;
To please, in short, is just a day's affair,
For Kings in love are swift and debonnaire.
Agnes was fain—she knew the art to please
To deck the thing in garb of mysteries,
Veils of thin gauze, through which will always pry,
The envious courtier's keen, malignant eye.
To mask this business, that none might know
The King made choice of Councillor Bonneau;
A trusty man of Tours, skilled in device
Who filled a post that is not over nice,
Which, though the court, that always seeks to lend
Beauty to all things, calls the Prince's friend,
The vulgar town and every rustic imp
Are grossly apt to designate a Pimp.
Upon Loire's banks thus worthy Sieur Bonneau
Stood seigneur of an elegant château,
Whither one day, about the time of shade,
In a light skiff fair Agnes was conveyed,
There the same night King Charles would fain recline
And there they supped, while Bonneau poured the wine.
State was dismissed, though all was served with care,
Banquets of gods could not with this compare!
Our Lovers their delight and joy confessed,
Desire inflamed and transport filled each breast,
Supremely formed by sprightly wit to please
Eager they listen and alternate gaze;
While their discourse, without indecence, free,
Gave their impatience fresh vivacity.

514

The ardent prince's eyes her charms devoured,
While in her ear soft tales of love he poured,
And with his knee her gentle knees deflowered.
The supper over, music played awhile,
Italian music—the chromatic style.
Flutes, hautboys, viols softly breathed around,
While three melodious voices swelled the sound;
They sang historic allegories, their strain
Told of those heroes mighty Love had slain,
And those they sang, who some proud Fair to please,
Quit fields of glory for inglorious ease.
In a recess this skilful band was set
Hard by the chamber where the good king ate;
As yet they sought their secret joys to screen
And Agnes fair enjoyed the whole unseen.
The moon upon the sky begins to glower;
Midnight has struck; it is Love's magic hour;
In an alcove begilt with art most sure,
Not lit too much and yet not too obscure,
Between two sheets of finest Holland made
The lovely Agnes' glowing charms were laid.
Here did Dame Alix leave her to repose;
But, cunning Abigail forgot to close
The private door that ope'd an easy way
To eager Charles, impatient of delay.
Perfumes most exquisite, with timely care
Are poured already on his braided hair;
And ye, who best have loved, can tell the rest
The anxious throbbings of our monarch's breast;
The sanctuary gained which shrines her charms,
In bed he clasps her naked to his arms,
Moment of ecstasy! propitious night!
Their hearts responsive beat with fond delight.
Love's brightest roses glow on Agnes' cheek;
In the warm blush, her fears and wishes speak.
But maiden fears in transport melt away,
And Love triumphant rules with sovran sway.
The ardent Prince now pressed her to his breast,
His eyes surveyed, his eager hands caressed,
Beauties enough which had been given her
To make a hermit an idolater.

Beneath a neck, whose dazzling whiteness shone
Pure and resplendent as the Parian stone,
With gentlest swell two breasts serenely move,
Severed and moulded by the hand of Love.
Each crowned with vermeil bud of damask rose,
Enchanting nipples, which ne'er know repose,
Yet seemed the gaze and pressure to invite,
And wooed the longing lips to seek delight.
Ever complying with my reader's taste,
I meant to paint as low as Agnes' waist;
To show that symmetry, devoid of blot,
Where Argus' self could not discern a spot;
But Virtue, which the world good manners calls,
Stops short my hand—and lo! the pencil falls.
In Agnes all was beauty, all was fair;
Voluptuousness, whereof she had her share,
Spurred every sense which instant took the alarm,
Adding new grace to every brilliant charm
It animated: Love can use disguise,
And pleasure heightens beauty in our eyes.

Pierre Louÿs

Famous as a French poet and novelist, Pierre Louÿs (1870–1925) was born in Ghent, Belgium. After going to France he founded a review whose contributors included Paul Valéry, Henri de Régnier, and André Gide. He was twenty-four when he published *Scenes from the Life of the Courtesans* and *The Songs of Bilitis.* The latter was a sensational success; his approximation of the Greek manner was hailed as masterful; and his passionate lyrics were widely reprinted. At twenty-six Louÿs issued an equally provocative work, the lurid novel *Aphrodite.*

The translations from *Les Chansons de Bilitis* are by Horace M. Brown.

From *The Songs of Bilitis*

REMORSE

At first I would not reply, and my shame showed upon my cheeks, and the beating of my heart brought pain to my breasts.

Then I resisted, I told him "No! No!"—I turned my head away, and his kiss did not open my lips—nor love, my tight-closed knees.

Then he begged me to forgive him, kissed my hair, I felt his burning breath, and he went away. . . . Now I am alone.

I gaze upon the empty place, the deserted wood, the trampled earth. And I bite my fingers until they bleed, and I stifle my sobs in the grass.

THE LITTLE HOUSE

The little house in which is his bed is the prettiest in all the world. It is made with the branches of trees, four walls of dried earth, and a roof of thatch.

I love it, for, since the nights have grown cold, we have slept there together: and the cooler the nights are the longer are they also. When I rise with the coming of the day, even I find myself weary.

The mattress is upon the ground: two coverlets of black wool cover our bodies, which warm each other. His body presses against my breasts. My heart throbs.

He presses me so closely that he will crush me, poor little girl that
I am. But when he is within me, I know nothing more in the
world, and they might cut off my limbs without recalling me
from my ecstasy.

ENDEARMENTS

Close softly thine arms about me like a girdle. Oh, touch, touch
my skin thus! Neither water, nor the breath of the south
wind are softer than thy hand.

Today endear me, little sister, it is thy turn. Remember thou the
endearments that I taught thee last night, and kneel thou near
to me who am fatigued; kneel thou in silence.

Thy lips descend upon my lips. All thine undone hair follows
them, as a caress follows a kiss. Thy locks glide upon my left
breast; they hide thine eyes.

Give me thy hand, it is hot! Press mine and leave it not. Hands
better than lips unite, and their passion is equalled by
nothing.

DESIRE

She entered, and passionately, the eyes half closed, she fixed her
lips to mine, and our tongues touched each other. . . . Never
in my life have I had a kiss like that one.

She stood erect against me, full of love and consentment. One of
my knees, little by little, mounted between her hot thighs,
which gave way as though to a lover.

My wandering hand upon her tunic sought to divine the naked
body, which softly bent like waves, or arching, stiffened itself
with shiverings of the skin.

With her eyes in delirium she signs toward the bed: but we have
not the right to indulge our love before the ceremony of the
wedding, and brusquely we separate.

THE KISS

I would kiss the whole length of the rich black locks that grace thy neck like wings; oh! sweet bird, oh! captured dove, whose passion-filled heart beats under my hand.

I would take thy lips between mine own, as a babe takes the breast of its mother. Tremble!—Thrill! Sweet one—my kisses reach far, and should satisfy thy love.

Lightly will I touch thy breasts and arms with my tongue and lips, and behind thine ears, and upon thy neck I will leave the marks of my kisses; and while I kiss thee my hands shall stray in mad delight over the ivory nakedness of thy sensitive body, trembling under the touch of my nails.

Listen, Mnasidika! Hear the murmuring of my love in thine ears like the wild humming of the sea. Mnasidika, thy look drives me mad; I will close thy burning eyes with a kiss, as if they were thy lips.

THE DESPAIRING EMBRACE

Love me, not with smiles, or with flutes, or with the plaited flowers, but with thy heart and with thy tears, even as I love thee with my sorrowing breast, and my moans.

When thy breasts alternate with my breasts, when I feel thy life touch my life, when thy knees stand up behind me, then my panting mouth knows not more how to join itself to thine.

Press me to thee as I press thee to me! See, the lamp has died down, the darkness is upon us; but I press thy moving body, and I hear thy perpetual plaint.

Moan! Moan! oh, woman! Eros leads us in sorrow. Thou shalt suffer less when thou liest upon a bed to bring a child into the world than when thou givest birth to thy love.

ABSENCE

She has gone out, she is far from me, but I see her, for all things in the room, all pertain to her, and I, like all the rest.

This bed still warm, over which I let my lips wander, is disordered with the imprint of her form. Upon this soft cushion has lain her little head enveloped in its wealth of hair.

This basin is that in which she hath bathed; this comb has penetrated the knots of her tangled locks. These slippers beg for her naked feet. These pockets of gauze contained her breasts.

But what I dare not touch, is the mirror in which she gazed upon her hot bruises, and where perhaps remains still the reflection of her moist lips.

BILITIS

One woman may robe herself in a tunic of white wool. Another dress in a garment of silk and gold. Another. covers herself with flowers, with leaves and grapes.

As for me, I take no joy of life except when naked. My lover takes me just as I am; without robes, or jewels, or sandals. Behold me, Bilitis, naked, alone.

My hair is black with its own blackness, my lips are red with their own color. My locks float about me free and round, like feathers.

Take me as my mother made me in a night of love long past; and if I please you thus, forget not to tell me.

Deems Taylor

Composer of cantatas, operas, suites, and symphonic poems, Deems Taylor, born in 1885 in New York City, is also a critic and an accomplished writer of light verse. His *The One-Track Mind* consists of more than fifty modernizations of seventeenth and eighteenth century French love poems. Taylor succeeded in deftly turning versions which are as neat as they are naughty.

Proof Positive

Alice, for whom my love is deep,
  I swear—and on my honor, too—
  That just the very sight of you
So moves me that I cannot sleep.

But if, desipte what I protest
In reference to my troubled rest,

You still believe that I pretend,
  This evening come with me to bed;
And you will learn, my skeptic friend,
  The truthfulness of what I've said.

Hors d'Oeuvre

Cerylas, jesting, called his pretty jade,
  Said to her, "Shall we sup, or—you know what?"
"Just as you wish, of course," replied the maid,
  "But—supper, darling, still is in the pot."

Turn to the Left

When I hold you in the night,
Kiss your breast upon the right,

Then you say: "My love, beware!
That one is my husband's share.
Take the left one, lover bold;
That is yours, to have and hold.

Yours is much the better part,
For it lies above my heart."

Concerning Mme. Robert

Everything you own, Robert,[1]
    Meadows, orchards, cattle, sheep—
    All of that is yours to keep;
No one gets a tiny share.

Yours the food that's in your poke;
We can't even cadge a smoke.

Your cellar's costly wines—taboo.
    In fact, of all that you possess,
    Your wife's the only thing, I guess,
That all of us have shared with you.

---

[1] Since Robert is French, the name is pronounced "Robare."

D. H. Lawrence

Those who know the son of a miner and a school-teacher, D. H. Lawrence (1885–1930), only as the author of the overly publicized, much pirated, and often censored *Lady Chatterley's Lover* know little of the man who wrote the sensitive *Sons and Lovers* and nothing of the poet of *Love Poems* and *Look! We Have Come Through*. Because of his belief in instinct, "the hot blood's blindfold art" as opposed to cold reason, he was accused of sensationalism, preoccupation with sex, and downright pornography. Today he is acknowledged as a great visionary and one of the strongest influences on contemporary writing.

Lightning

I felt the lurch and halt of her heart
  Next my breast, where my own heart was beating;
And I laughed to feel it plunge and bound,
And strange in my blood-swept ears was the sound
  Of the words I kept repeating,
Repeating with tightened arms, and the hot blood's
  blindfold art.

Her breath flew warm aginst my neck,
  Warm as a flame in the close night air;
And the sense of her clinging flesh was sweet
Where her arms and my neck's blood-surge could meet.
  Holding her thus, did I care
That the black night hid her from me, blotted out every
  speck?

I leaned me forward to find her lips,
  And claim her utterly in a kiss,
When the lightning flew across her face,
And I saw her for the flaring space
  Of a second, afraid of the clips
Of my arms, inert with dread, wilted in fear of my kiss.

A moment, like a wavering spark,
  Her face lay there before my breast,
Pale love lost in a snow of fear,
And guarded by a glittering tear,
  And lips apart with dumb cries;
A moment, and she was taken again in the merciful dark.

I heard the thunder, and felt the rain,
  And my arms fell loose, and I was dumb.
Almost I hated her, she was so good,
Hated myself, and the place, and my blood,
  Which burned with rage, as I bade her come
Home, away home, ere the lightning floated forth again.

Louis Untermeyer

Unwilling (or unable) to acquire a formal education, Louis Untermeyer educated himself by indiscriminate reading, travel, and a variety of ways of earning a living. Born in New York City in 1885, he was, at different periods, a designer of jewelry, factory manager, book reviewer, publisher's advisor, editor of a large record company, lecturer, radio and television performer, anthologist, critic, and Consultant in Poetry at the Library of Congress. By the time he was seventy he had written and compiled more than seventy volumes of fact and fiction, prose and verse. His collections of American and English poetry became standard textbooks in the universities.

A poet, he also translated poetry from several languages. His versions of poems from *The Greek Anthology*. Horace, Petronius, Heine, and Verlaine appear in the sections beginning with pages 23, 50, 72, 454 and 499.

Equals

You child, how can you dare complain
That you and I may be mismated
Because, you say, you lack a brain
And I'm so highly educated.

The body is the greater thing;
And you are greatly gifted when
You have such hands and breasts that bring
More peace than all the words of men.

Take pride in this, your beauty; drink
The wine it offers for our love.
Be glad you do not have to think.
One thoughtful lover is enough!

We're equal partners, that is plain;
Our life cannot grow dull or shoddy.
While I have such a lovely brain
And you have such a lively body.

Hair-Dressing

Before the prim old mirror
That stands so stiffly there,
With puritan precision
You rearrange your hair.

Knitting your childlike forehead,
As, with a whimsical pout,

527

Your fingers, brisk and busy,
    Bring order out of rout.

But here a coil escapes you,
    And there a bright strand shakes
Over your neck and shoulder
    In little yellow snakes.

Serious and ensnaring,
    Each skillful hand begins
To make an artful pattern
    Woven with puffs and pins.

You pause to turn and ask me
    How this appears, or that,
Till all is smoothed and finished
    With a last, careful pat.

My pretty, proper darling,
    With not one hair amiss,
Who turns, like some calm duty,
    One powdered cheek to kiss.

Are you the same wild creature
    I held last night, and found
Sleeping upon my shoulder
    With all her hair unbound?

The Dream and the Blood

Go back, dark blood, to the springs from which you came.
    Go back, though each mutinous drop swells upward in flood.
What! Am I nothing more now than a wave of onrushing flame?
    Nothing but sport of my pulse? Back, back, dark blood!

Am I not master here in my own house of flesh?
    Cease roaring and rising. Be still, I tell you, be still.

I have work that calls for cool evenings; I have stuff of the mind
    to thresh.
  Must you pit your unreasoning hunger against my inflexible
    will?

I tell you this body for which we are always contending
  Is more than mere fuel for you to be turned into ash.
It was shaped by white visions of leaving its bones, of extending
  Itself into realms where your heat would be less than a flash.

What! Will you not even listen? I hear you, O hater
  Of all that I plan. I hear how the thud
In my veins beats your victory. . . . Later, then, later;
  Give me myself for an hour. Go back, dark blood.

Appeal to the Phoenix

Phoenix, phoenix in the blood,
Will you always beat and flash
Through the mind's unwilling mood,
Even to the ash?

Phoenix, phoenix without end,
Though you set the body free
You are not the body's friend,
But the enemy.

Barricades are broken through,
Strength and solitude are vain,
While the body burns with you
And you rise again.

Phoenix, you have fed enough
On the flesh that terrifies;
Turn to me at last with love,
Not with agonies.

Not as ravisher but guest,
With one clasp, one shattering cry,
Come, and in this glowing nest,
Phoenix, learn to die.

Summer Storm

We lay together in the sultry night.
A feeble light
From some invisible street-lamp crept
Into the corner where you slept,
Fingered your cheeks, flew softly round your hair,
Then dipped in the sweet valley of your breasts
And fluttered, like a bird between two nests,
Till it lay quiet there.
My eyes were closing and I may have dreamed—
At least it seemed
That you and I
Had ceased to be but were somehow
As earth and sky . . .

The night grew closer still, and now
Heat-lightnings played between us, and warm thrills
Ran through the cool sides of the trembling hills.
Then darkness and a tension in the black
Hush like a breath held back;
A rippling through the ground, a windless breeze
That reached down to the sensitive roots of trees;
A tremor like the pulse of muffled knocks,
Or like the silent opening of locks.
There was a rising of unfettered seas
With great tides pulling at the stars and rocks
As though to draw them all together.
Then in a burst of blinding weather,
The lightnings flung
Long, passionate arms about the earth that clung
To her wild lover.
Suddenly above her
The whole sky tumbled in a sweeping blaze,
Gathering earth in one tight-locked embrace,
Drenching her in a flood of silver flame.
Hot thunders came;
And still the storm kept plunging, seeking ever
The furthest cranny, till the faraway
Streams felt each penetrating quiver

And the most hidden river
Rose and became released.

At last the stabbings ceased,
The thunders died.
But still they lay
Side by side,
While moonbeams crept
Into the heavenly corner where earth slept;
Dipping among her rosy hills, lighting above
Her curved and sloping hollows, till
She too was still.
Beloved and blest,
His cloudy head lay, seeking rest
In the sweet-smelling valley of her breast,
And each was huddled in each other's love—
Or so it seemed.
My eyes were closing and I may have dreamed.

Earnest Albert Hooton

Born in Clemansville, Wisconsin, in 1887, Earnest Albert Hooton was a Rhodes scholar at Oxford, taught many years at Harvard, and was curator at the Peabody Museum when he died in 1954. One of the foremost anthropologists of his day, he diverted himself with the occasional composition of light-hearted rhymes.

In a foreword to a privately printed collection entitled *Subverse*, Hooton wrote: "The author acknowledges to the reader, the reviewer (if any), and to himself that this little book is not a contribution to letters nor to art nor to science. It has been a contribution to the author's own amusement in hours of idleness, voluntary and unforced."

To Chloe

Her Bust

Chloe, the contours of your bust
Fill me with wonder and distrust—
Beneath your neck a bare plateau,
Then rising suddenly below
The line at which your gown commences
Twin formidable eminences.
This anatomic disconformity
Strikes me as being an enormity.
The poet may interrogate;
The scientist investigate;
Shall I inquire with utmost tact
Whether your breasts are artifact,
Or boldly seek the explanation
By firm and vigorous palpation?

Her Waist

Chloe, whenever I've embraced
The sweet constriction of your waist,
My questing hand seems to discover
That you have a synthetic cover.
Tell me, how far your form is plastic
Beneath that girdle of elastic?
Does it roll down your adiposities
To pad your ischial callosities?
Is it a stringent wall that checks
A front inclined to be convex?
Or perhaps your method of prevention
Against intestinal distention?
For woman 'tis an evil omen
To straiten thus a round abdomen.
The more I puzzle o'er this riddle,
The less I want to squeeze your middle.

Mark Van Doren

A beloved teacher, a provocative essayist, and a self-effacing fighter for unpopular causes, Mark Van Doren (1894–   ) won the Pulitzer Prize in 1939 for his *Collected Poems*. His later works include a play, *The Last Days of Abraham Lincoln*, an autobiography, and a book of new poems, *Morning Worship*.

The Whisperer

Be extra careful by this door,
No least, least sound, she said.
It is my brother Oliver's,
And he would strike you dead.

Come on. It is the top step now,
And carpet all the way.
But wide enough for only one,
Unless you carry me.

I love your face as hot as this.
Put me down, though, and creep.
My father! He would strangle you,
I think, like any sheep.

Now take me up again, again:
We're at the landing post.
You hear her saying Hush, and Hush?
It is my mother's ghost.

She would have loved you, loving me.
She had a voice as fine—
I love you more for such a kiss,
And here is mine, is mine.

And one for her—Oh, quick the door!
I cannot bear it so.
The vestibule, and out; for now
Who passes that would know?

Here we could stand all night and let
Strange people smile and stare.
But you must go, and I must lie
Alone up there, up there.

Remember? But I understand.
More with a kiss is said.
And do not mind it if I cry,
Passing my mother's bed.

e. e. cummings

The unorthodox verbal devices and odd typographical arrangements invented by E (dward) E (stlin) Cummings, (1894–1962) tended to overshadow his accomplishments as a creative writer. Filling his lines with surprising effects, he wrote in contrasting and often contradictory manners. He was, by turns, an ultra-romantic and unflinchingly realistic poet, a penetrating satirist as well as a tender amorist. In every mood he was unique. His *Poems: 1923–1954* contains almost 500 highly individualistic and sharply compressed pages. It received the National Book Award for 1955.

From *SONNETS—REALITIES*

my girl's tall with hard long eyes
as she stands, with her long hard hands keeping
silence on her dress, good for sleeping
is her long hard body filled with surprise
like a white shocking wire, when she smiles
a hard long smile it sometimes makes
gaily go clean through me tickling aches,
and the weak noise of her eyes easily files
my impatience to an edge—my girl's tall
and taut, with thin legs just like a vine
that's spent all of its life on a garden-wall,
and is going to die. When we grimly go to bed
with these legs she begins to heave and twine
about me, and to kiss my face and head.

From *SONNETS—ACTUALITIES*

i like my body when it is with your
body. It is so quite new a thing.
Muscles better and nerves more.
i like your body. i like what it does,
i like its hows. i like to feel the spine
of your body and its bones, and the trembling
-firm-smooth ness and which i will
again and again and again
kiss, i like kissing this and that of you,
i like, slowly stroking the, shocking fuzz
of your electric fur, and what-is-it comes
over parting flesh . . . . And eyes big love-crumbs,

and possibly i like the thrill

of under me you so quite new

537

From *no thanks*

may i feel said he

may i feel said he
(i'll squeal said she
just once said he)
it's fun said she

(may i touch said he
how much said she
a lot said he)
why not said she

(let's go said he
not too far said she
what's too far said he
where you are said she)

may i stay said he
(which way said she
like this said he
if you kiss said she

may i move said he
is it love said she)
if you're willing said he
(but you're killing said she

but it's life said he
but your wife said she
now said he)
ow said she

(tiptop said he
don't stop said she
oh no said he)
go slow said she

(cccome?said he
ummm said she)

you're divine!said he
(you are Mine said she)

From *is 5*

she being Brand

she being Brand

-new;and you
know consequently a
little stiff i was
careful of her and (having

thoroughly oiled the universal
joint tested my gas felt of
her radiator made sure her springs were O.

K.) i went right to it flooded-the-carburetor cranked her

up,slipped the
clutch (and then somehow got into reverse she
kicked what
the hell) next
minute i was back in neutral tried and

again slo-wly;bare,ly nudg.   ing (my

lev-er Right-
oh and her gears being in
A 1 shape passed
from low through
second-in-to-high like
greasedlightning just as we turned the corner of Divinity

avenue i touched the accelerator and give

her the juice,good

                    (it
was the first ride and believe i we was
happy to see how nice she acted right up to
the last minute coming back down by the Public
Gardens i slammed on
the

internalexpanding
&
externalcontracting
brakes Bothatonce and

brought allofher tremB
-ling
to a:dead.

stand-
;Still)

Stanley Kunitz

Stanley Kunitz was born in Worcester, Massachusetts, in 1905, was graduated from Harvard, where he was awarded the Garrison Medal for Poetry, engaged on a long series of biographical volumes—*American Authors: 1600–1900, Twentieth Century Authors,* etc.—which have become invaluable reference books, taught at Bennington College and at literary workshops throughout the country, and continued to write poetry appreciated by the few. Five publishers declined to issue his *Selected Poems* which, upon its appearance in 1958, won the Pulitzer Prize. Suddenly the author who had been neglected as well as rejected was established. In his fifty-fourth year he received long-deferred recognition, an award from the National Institute of Arts and Letters, and a grant from the Ford Foundation.

The Science of the Night

I touch you in the night, whose gift was you,
My careless sprawler,
And I touch you cold, unstirring, star-bemused,
That are become the land of your self-strangeness.
What long seduction of the bone has led you
Down the imploring roads I cannot take
Into the arms of ghosts I never knew,
Leaving my manhood on a rumpled field
To guard you where you lie so deep
In absent-mindedness,
Caught in the calcium snows of sleep?

And even should I track you to your birth
Through all the cities of your mortal trial,
As in my jealous thought I try to do,
You would escape me—from the brink of earth
Take off to where the lawless auroras run,
You with your wild and metaphysic heart.
My touch is on you, who are light-years gone.
We are not souls but systems, and we move
In clouds of our unknowing
                              like great nebulae.
Our very motives swirl and have their start
With father lion and with mother crab.

Dreamer, my own lost rib,
Whose planetary dust is blowing
Past archipelagoes of myth and light,
What far Magellans are you mistress of
To whom you speed the pleasure of your art?
As through a glass that magnifies my loss
I see the lines of your spectrum shifting red,
The universe expanding, thinning out,
Our worlds flying, oh flying, fast apart.

From hooded powers and from abstract flight
I summon you, your person and your pride.
Fall to me now from outer space,
Still fastened desperately to my side;
Through gulfs of streaming air
Bring me the mornings of the milky ways
Down to my threshold in your drowsy eyes;
And by the virtue of your honeyed word
Restore the liquid language of the moon,
That in gold mines of secrecy you delve.
Awake!
        My whirling hands stay at the noon,
Each cell within my body holds a heart
And all my hearts in unison strike twelve.

Lovers Relentlessly

Lovers relentlessly contend to be
Superior in their identity:

The compass of the ego is designed
To circumscribe intact a lesser mind

With definition; tender though would wrest
Each clean protective secret from the breast;

Affection's eyes go deep, make morbid lesion
In pride's tissue, are ferocious with possession;

Love's active hands are desperate to own
The subtly reasoned flesh on branching bone;

Lovers regard the simple moon that spills
White magic in a garden, bend their wills

Obliquely on each other; lovers eat
The small ecstatic heart to be complete;

Engaged in complicate analysis
Of passionate destruction, lovers kiss;

In furious involvement they would make
A double meaning single. Some must break

Upon the wheel of love, but not the strange,
The secret lords, whom only death can change.

Walter Benton

Born in Austria of Russian parents in 1907, Walter Benton found a wide variety of jobs in America, including that of steel-worker, farmer, window-washer, salesman, social investigator, and captain in the United States Army. He was thirty-six when he published his first volume, *This Is My Beloved,* a kind of rhapsodic diary. The book was an immediate success but, unlike most sudden phenomena, survived its initial popularity. Nineteen years after its publication it went into its thirty-fourth printing.

From *This is My Beloved*

ENTRY AUGUST 27

The white full moon like a great beautiful whore
solicits over the city, eggs the lovers on—
the haves . . . walking in twos to their beds and to their mating.

I walk alone. Slowly. No hurry. Nobody's waiting.
My love who loved me (she said) is gone. My love is gone.

And I walk alone. It's goodnight time . . . the haves are everywhere,
in parked cars and passing taxis—
the still, abstracted figures pressed against walls and niched
in dark doorways . . . each two arm-hooped into one body rigid with
joy.

A lighted window holds me like high voltage. I see . . .
cupped in the bed's white palm, the haves—O she is beautiful, her
breasts are white dogwood and her thighs
barked poplars growing out of the dark-matted jungle of her crotch.

He is kissing her, interminably her mouth . . . and one by one each
breast is carried to the lips with tender violence.
Now he lays his hand to her secret body. Her frantic thighs invite
invasion. He covers her, enters . . . turns god—and my eyelids fall.

ENTRY AUGUST 29

It was like something done in fever, when nothing fits,
mind into mind nor body into body . . . when nothing
meets or equals—when dimensions lie and perceptions go haywire.

With what an alien sense my fingers curved about her breasts
and searched the tangled dark where love lay hiding!
I closed my eyes better to imagine you—
but the rehearsed body would not ratify the mind's deception.

The kisses of her mouth, the rhythm natural to love—and the exciting
musk with which love haloes itself . . . these thwarted my imagination.
Her love, too, was centered and intent,

it did not reach her eyes and forehead, or light her throat
as your love did—
it did not fill the room . . . or spread all over the ceiling of the sky.
It did not span the years and miles and hold hands with beast
and God.

Nor did her thighs rise with that splendid grade I stroked from
memory. Her body met me unlike your body
and I entered the heaven of her uneasily . . . and could not stay—
for my heart being yours released no blood to make ready for love.

545

I saw autumn today . . . incipiently, on the sunset
and the leaf—in the spontaneous whitecaps shingling the bay
and the window-displayed chrysanthemums and asters.
I saw its night's water color leavings on the cottonwood and the
maple—and heard its voice
in the locust's high powered chatter in the camouflaged somewhere.

Ah! Fierce exhilaration flows through me like dry current.
Soon we shall walk on the sunny side of the street . . . hold hands,
mingle in bed for warmth. Autumn is our season—yours and mine.

See, I have lain naked and long in the sun to match your body.
We shall look beautiful lying side by side.
The stain of the season is rich upon you, only your breasts are white
as the winter grouse . . . you have not shown them to the sun—
nor the low of your belly where you are white, soft and
dark-feathered

A. D. Hope

Born in Cooma, New South Wales, in 1907, A. D. Hope waited until he was almost fifty before publishing his first volume, *Poems.* With it, critics agreed, Australian poetry had come of age. One commentator compared Hope to Yeats; another said he wrote "with a fierceness seldom felt in English literature since Swift."

Using the traditional forms, Hope intensifies them with stripped power, strange but exact images, and bitter passions. "Imperial Adam" retells the story from Genesis with new vividness and an unexpectedly violent conclusion. "The Gateway" and "Chorale" are two particularly candid and altogether lovely erotic lyrics in a book full of surprises.

547

Imperial Adam

Imperial Adam, naked in the dew,
Felt his brown flanks and found the rib was gone.
Puzzled he turned and saw where, two and two,
The mighty spoor of Jahweh marked the lawn.

Then he remembered through mysterious sleep
The surgeon fingers probing at the bone,
The voice so far away, so rich and deep:
"It is not good for him to live alone."

Turning once more he found Man's counterpart
In tender parody breathing at his side.
He knew her at first sight, he knew by heart
Her allegory of sense unsatisfied.

The pawpaw drooped its golden breasts above
Less generous than the honey of her flesh;
The innocent sunlight showed the place of love;
The dew on its dark hairs winked crisp and fresh.

This plump gourd severed from his virile root,
She promised on the turf of Paradise
Delicious pulp of the forbidden fruit;
Sly as the snake she loosed her sinuous thighs,

And waking, smiled up at him from the grass;
Her breasts rose softly and he heard her sigh—
From all the beasts whose pleasant task it was
In Eden to increase and multiply

Adam had learned the jolly deed of kind:
He took her in his arms and there and then,
Like the clean beasts, embracing from behind,
Began in joy to found the breed of men.

Then from the spurt of seed within her broke
Her terrible and triumphant female cry,
Split upward by the sexual lightning stroke.
It was the beasts now who stood watching by:

The gravid elephant, the calving hind,
The breeding bitch, the she-ape big with young
Were the first gentle midwives of mankind;
The teeming lioness rasped her with her tongue;

The proud vicuña nuzzled her as she slept
Lax on the grass; and Adam watching too
Saw how her dumb breasts at their ripening wept,
The great pod of her belly swelled and grew,

And saw its water break, and saw, in fear,
Its quaking muscles in the act of birth,
Between her legs a pigmy face appear,
And the first murderer lay upon the earth.

The Gateway

Now the heart sings with all its thousand voices
To hear this city of cells, my body, sing.
The tree through the stiff clay at long last forces
Its thin strong roots and taps the secret spring.

And the sweet waters without intermission
Climb to the tips of its green tenement;
The breasts have borne the grace of their possession,
The lips have felt the pressure of content.

Here I come home: in this expected country
They know my name and speak it with delight.
I am the dream and you my gates of entry,
The means by which I waken into light.

Chorale

Often had I found her fair;
Most when to my bed she came,
Naked as the moving air,
Slender, walking like a flame.
In that grace I sink and drown:
Opening like the liquid wave
To my touch she laid her down,
Drew me to her crystal cave.
  Love me ever, love me long—
  Was the burden of her song.

All divisions vanish there;
Now her eyes grow dark and still;
Now I feel the living air
With contending thunder fill;
Hear the shuddering cry begin,
Feel the heart leap in her breast,
And her moving loins within
Clasp their strong, rejoicing guest.
  Love me now, O now, O long!
  Is the burden of her song.

Now the wave recedes and dies;
Dancing fires descend the hill;
Blessed spirits from our eyes
Gaze in wonder and are still.
Yet our wondering spirits come
From their timeless anguish freed:
Yet within they hear the womb
Sighing for the wasted seed.
  Love may not delay too long
  Is the burden of their song.

Theodore Roethke

Readers are fascinated by the fresh and always surprising creativeness of Theodore Roethke. Born in 1908 in Saginaw, Michigan, Roethke taught at various colleges ranging from Bennington in Vermont to the University of Washington. His volume, *The Waking,* received the Pulitzer Prize in 1953; six years later his collection, *Words for the Wind,* brought three more prizes, including the National Book Award. Roethke excelled in a kind of controlled wildness which his fellow-poets were quick to appreciate. One of them, Stanley Kunitz (see page 541), wrote: "The ferocity of his imagination makes most contemporary poetry seem pale and tepid by comparison."

The Mistake

He left his pants upon a chair;
She was a widow, so she said;
But he was apprehended, bare,
By one who rose up from the dead.

I Knew a Woman

I knew a woman, lovely in her bones,
When small birds sighed, she would sigh back at them;
Ah, when she moved, she moved more ways than one:
The shapes a bright container can contain!
Of her choice virtues only gods should speak,
Or English poets who grew up on Greek
(I'd have them sing in chorus, cheek to cheek).

How well her wishes went! She stroked my chin,
She taught me Turn, and Counter-turn, and Stand;
She taught me Touch, that undulant white skin;
I nibbled meekly from her proffered hand;
She was the sickle; I, poor I, the rake,
Coming behind her for her pretty sake
(But what prodigious mowing we did make).

Love likes a gander, and adores a goose:
Her full lips pursed, the errant note to seize;
She played it quick, she played it light and loose;
My eyes, they dazzled at her flowing knees;
Her several parts could keep a pure repose,
Or one hip quiver with a mobile nose
(She moved in circles, and those circles moved).

Let seed be grass, and grass turn into hay:
I'm martyr to a motion not my own;
What's freedom for? To know eternity.
I swear she cast a shadow white as stone.
But who would count eternity in days?
These old bones live to learn her wanton ways:
(I measure time by how a body sways).

The Sensualist

"There is no place to turn," she said,
  "You have me pinned so close;
My hair's all tangled on your head,
  My back is just one bruise;
I feel we're breathing with the dead;
  O angel, let me loose!"

And she was right, for there beside
  The gin and cigarettes,
A woman stood, pure as a bride,
  Affrighted from her wits,
And breathing hard, as that man rode
  Between those lovely tits.

"My shoulder's bitten from your teeth;
  What's that peculiar smell?
No matter which one is beneath,
  Each is an animal,"—
The ghostly figure sucked its breath,
  And shuddered toward the wall;
Wrapped in the tattered robe of death,
  It tiptoed down the hall.

"The bed itself begins to quake,
  I hate this sensual pen;
My neck, if not my heart, will break
  If we do this again,"—
Then each fell back, limp as a sack,
  Into the world of men.

Light Listened

O what could be more nice
Than her ways with a man?
She kissed me more than twice
Once we were left alone.
Who'd look when he could feel?
She'd more sides than a seal.

The close air faintly stirred.
Light deepened to a bell,
The love-beat of a bird.
She kept her body still
And watched the weather flow.
We live by what we do.

All's known, all, all around:
The shape of things to be;
A green thing loves the green
And loves the living ground.
The deep shade gathers night;
She changed with changing light.

We met to leave again
The time we broke from time;
A cold air brought its rain,
The singing of a stem.
She sang a final song;
Light listened when she sang.

Michael Lewis

Pseudonym of a well-known writer, the name Michael Lewis has appeared under poems for children and has also been signed to translations and occasional verse.

Broken Monologue

(From the German)

And you believed that I would do it so?
  Oh!
That you could touch and set me all aglow?
  No!
Do I refuse one intimate caress?
  Yes.
What! You expected, warm with kissing, we'd—
  Indeed!
Other young girls have done it without blame?
  Shame!
Leave me. I hate you. Now you know.
  Go!
You will? You'll go to Gladys 'cross the way?
  Stay.

Cherry Blossoms

(*After the Chinese*)

REMEMBERING

All night I lie awake and hear
    The storm's wild ruthlessness;
I feel half pleasure and half fear,
As when my lover, coming near.
    Tears at my flimsy dress.

LONGING

How long until the war's end sets you free?
    How long until the end of cruel weather?
How long until they send you back to me
    So we can snuff the candle out together?

CURSING AND BLESSING

I used to curse the wind and rain
    That trampled on my roof all day;
But, worst of all, I would complain
    Because they kept my love away.

But then she came, and now I bless
    The rain that, blowing cold and damp,
Made her take off her dripping dress
    While the good wind blew out the lamp.

LEAVING

Dawn is here. Now I must go.
Move your head a little; so
I would see you and remember
All that happened in this chamber
All last night, contain it all
In my heart and mind, recall

556

Each caress and every kiss
Wilder than the last one. This
Is for a keepsake; turn your face
And receive one more embrace,
One more promise to invite
One more moment of delight.
So farewell—until tonight.

LIVING AND DYING

You are loveliness and all desire;
  Your body bends toward mine like drooping laurel;
Your eyes light up with ever-eager fire;
  Your breasts grow hard with little points of coral.
Your whispering wine-and-honey lips incite me;
  Your limbs grow soft; you drop your robe and sigh;
You give your secret treasure to delight me;
  And when I take it I both live and die.

J. V. Cunningham

James Vincent Cunningham was born in 1911 in Maryland, grew up in Montana, was graduated from Stanford University, taught in Virginia, Hawaii, and Massachusetts, where he became chairman of the English Department at Brandeis University. Nearing fifty he put together three previous volumes in *The Exclusions of a Rhyme,* a collection which is sharpened with unfettered wit and unsuppressed ribaldry. Cunningham's epigrams express and expose the natural (and unnatural) pleasures of human nature.

It Was in Vegas

It was in Vegas. Celibate and able
I left the silver dollars on the table
And tried the show. Aloha, baggy pants,
Of course, and then this answer to romance:
Her ass twitching as if it had the fits,
Her gold crotch grinding, her athletic tits,
One clock-, the other counter-clockwise twirling.
It was enough to stop a man from girling.

Five Epigrams

1

Bride loved old words, and found her pleasure marred
On the first night, her expectations jarred,
And thirty inches short of being a yard.

2

Career was feminine, resourceful, clever.
You'd never guess to see her she felt ever
By a male world oppressed. How much they weigh!
Even her hand disturbed her as she lay.

3

Lip was a man who used his head.
He used it when he went to bed
With his friend's wife, and with his friend,
With either sex at either end.

4

And now you're ready who while she was here
Hung like a flag in a calm. Friend, though you stand
Erect and eager, in your eye a tear,
I will not pity you, or lend a hand.

5

Naked I came, naked I leave the scene,
And naked was my pastime in between.

The Pick-Up

The soft lights, the companionship, the beers,
The night promises everything you lacked.
The short drive, the unmade bed, and night in tears
Hysteric in the elemental act.

Eve Merriam

After graduating from the University of Pennsylvania, Eve Merriam—born in Philadelphia, July 19, 1916—became a copywriter, editor, teacher, free-lance writer, and lecturer. Her first book, *Family Circle,* awarded the Yale Series of Younger Poets prize, was followed by various volumes of prose and verse, including the controversial *Figleaf: The Business of Fashion. The Double Bed* explores the intricate relations between the sexes; the writing is both candid and delicate, frank in its sensuous descriptions, and always authentic in feeling. Essentially a woman's book, it is both idealistic and disillusioned. Ambivalent about the pleasures of love and the difficulty of being a woman, it discloses the mixed emotions not only of the double bed but also the double mind.

⌒◦⌒

Ballad of the Double Bed

The time has come for a wench to wed:
Now how shall I make my marriage bed?

"No plain cot like mine," my worn mother pled,
"With birthpains and bloodstains and halfalivedead.
May a lace canopy and a hood overhead
Shield you from strife in your marriage bed.
Go wed with a man who is richly kind,
And if he's rich enough, you won't mind."

My father murdered his meat with his knife:
"You're too young to think about married life.
Play home with your dolls and your trinkets and toys,
Stay dear to me and forget about boys.
But if you insist upon living life free,
Be sure that you mate with the image of me."

560

The minister prayed his hand on my head:
"Go narrow to your marriage bed.
Eyes closed as a virgin, eyes closed as a bride,
Well-groomed for a virgin—open not wide.
Keep the covers up high, the bolsters tucked tight,
And the sheets pulled taut to ward off all light."

My brother winked his eye and laughed:
"Give him both barrels—fore and aft.
It doesn't last long, it's quickest fled,
So corner the market of the marriage bed.
For fancy will roam, and freshness stale;
Prime is the male, betime the female."

My sister sighed for me in dread:
"Don't worry, you'll soon have a baby's bed.
A soft smooth hairless loving all round,
Not unshaven and rough and clomping the ground.
Alas, the coupling of woman with man
Is a needed—but you needn't like it—span."

Teacher tapped me with her rule:
"Hide your questions, play smart the fool.
Roll with the mattress as best you can;
The bed is paid for by the man.
'Money is evil' intone the preachers:
There are fewer women preachers than teachers."

"Relax yourself," the doctor said.
"Take tranquilizers to your bed.
Lie back as on a couch of dreams,
And tread your reals to all your seems.
Dust to must, ash to tray,
And fly with a movie star far away."

"Come love with me and be my life!"
My lover pressed me for his wife.
"You shall be my queen of night,
My shield against the glaring light;
As I shall strive to be your goal,
Your world entire, your world made whole."
So marrily to life's house I sped:
And herein shape our double bed.

The Moment Before Conception

In the fleece of your flesh
I sink and rise:
here in my garment, my raiment of gold.

In the sweet clover of your flesh
I pace all desire
and never move from this grassy meadow.

Through the treetops of your flesh
I prance like a cat
and silken stroke the sky.

In the secrets of your flesh
I make myself words
to be read by you alone.

I curve myself as a sickle moon
for you to hammer flat and silver
under your pillow of night.

In your cartons and burdens of day
I am the twining rope
to bind up your proud bulky portage.

Carve me into a talisman
small and shaped as a seaworn stone
to fit the palm of your hand,
tracing the lines of your hand in mind,
embracing our lives together.

Oh deepening image of my unsleeping dream,
whatever your finger;
work paper tool cup pen:

touch me constantly!

The Love-Making: His and Hers

(The roaring masted forest becomes a park with little trees for
shade planted at intervals; with benches to sit straight up on; with
wastebaskets for trash; with pigeons to feed crumbs to and scatter.
They make love: removing their gloves, as is only to be expected
in a model Mr. and Mrs.)

—And was it good for you this time?
  Please, let me help you take off your gloves.

—Thank you. Very good.
    Of course, I can see, we are both trying to strip them off,
      only the dye of the cloth seems to be stained into my flesh.
Ah where has my lover gone
gone before dawn   gone before dark?
gone with no lark

gone like a ghost before I could heraldhymn my host
before I could wreathe him
before I could breathe upon his stranger's face

his perfect stranger face   his changeling grace
no one I've known   so like my own
nightly his errant pace I race and never meet

I trace him so clearly behind my closed eyes
when will he slake me for his bride?
Will he never come calling falling climbing careless dareful
rising spreading me wide
when will he rage foaming roaming the tunneling stair
to fling me high up beside him where
the saddle shines damp with darkbright desire
by rosebush aflame with thorny desire
on softest fire   on sharpest fire
love's steed bestride   together to ride
Ah gallop oh gallop hoh gallop us clear!
slow, whoa . . . hohum again here
so home to the stable the sugar the sniff
down to the plain from the sheermounting cliff

tamely samely round bridle-rein trot
but do not suppose my gaping's forgot

steeped in the dark I paw, I rage
scratching deep into clipped-claw age!

—And was it good for you?
      Here, let me touch your hand.
—Oh very. Of course, it always is.
      Only my hands are encased too.
Ah where has she vanished who never came yet?
My Venus My Venice I cannot forget
my lake of desire I dip my oar

Monogamania

Lure me with lovers,
I'll eunuch them all:
For I am the queen
Of monogamy's ball.

Spoke me as wheel,
I go round one road;
Goad me as burro,
I balk but one load.

As I am no lady
I swear by one lord
That he is my coming
And I am his toward.

Go sow your wild oats
And reap as you will;
I hoe in one furrow
And heap all my fill.

Direct Song

High cockalorum diddledum!
But crook your finger and I come.

Thus I pander to your taste:
I will make your heat my haste —

Or dalliance suit your delay . . .
At midnight meet the rising day.

Am I then subservient?
That may, beloved, be your intent;

If so, you'll have to vie again
In vain and vie in vain again.
You must face up to the facts of love,
That I hold no higher law above,

That of tribute or honors I pay naught as due;
In short, I scarcely think of you —

But cut my cloth straight to this unit of measure:
The more I give you gives me the more pleasure.

Judson Crews

Judson Crews was born in Waco, Texas, in 1917, received his A.B. in sociology at Baylor University and, returning there after the Second World War to obtain his M.A., did post-graduate work in fine arts. At thirty he moved to Taos, New Mexico, married, and made a living as a printer.

Oh Beach Love Blossom

Oh beach love blossom half blooming
the sand like love in my hands
the sundered hour glass of your breasts
the bell long knell of your bosom
for there are reeds in the sand

Reeds in sand by the reach of waves
I kiss the palm of your hand
the linger of fish-bone white as your spine
the sand dune flow of your thighs
submerged in the kiss of the sand

The tips of your breasts emerging
like buds of roses from the sand
the cry of the waves brittle as reeds
I lose the dream from my hand

The hours are gone, how white how white
the bones left by the sands
I reach I reach for the rose buds
twinned near the darkened reeds
and I kiss but a mouthful of sand

Declaration at Forty

I have loved so many violent loves
without disturbing a single hair

I have broken no marriages
nor healed any. When I love again

May her complacency be shattered
the lawn cluttered with underthings

Her hair mussed and her heart pounding
and may she remember forever

That for one moment she at least
was not utterly alone

Love Poem

Oh, your thighs
are numbered:

Two

But they are
as the poles of the earth

And all
that there is

Is

Between them

William Jay Smith

William Jay Smith is more indigenously American than most American writers. His father's family helped found Winfield, Louisiana, where Smith was born, April 22, 1918; on his mother's side he is one-sixteenth Cherokee. He has been a politician as well as a poet—he was a member of the Vermont House of Representatives—a teacher as well as the author of books for children and designer of typographical diversions.

The Voyages of Captain Cock

You, sad Captain, big-knobbed staff of life,
You should be mountaineering with a wife —
Off probing that crevasse few husbands reach —
Not panting here, upended in the breech.

Cerise Farallon was born Lena Johnston in Fort Worth, Texas, in 1919. She and her husband, also a poet, write intermittently and publish occasionally. The following pair are the first of her poems to be anthologized.

~ঔে~

The Serpent of God

Our bodies were sunlit spattered
with bright leaves dropping
here and there about us

A great one banked and swirled
and settled squarely
upon my immodest exposure

You are Eve, you are Eve
you laughed, heaping others upon me

Yes, Eve. But not Eve
in her bitterness, but Eve
in the fullness of love

For this serpent I met
was not of the devil
and he spoke with action
not words

This serpent I met was not subtle
but very direct, and oh
he was strong and of God!

Pride and Hesitation

I would not meek in dire rebuttal
to route the bulls of gong
but my thighs would flex
to slightest love
if love were slightest shown
My hatred is holy
but less holy than lust
I curse you as I pray

I file my teeth like savage
and chant a curdling song
but my heart would bedded clover become
to blossom beneath your form

John Press

Poet, critic, and essayist, John Press was born at Norwich, Norfolk, England, January 11, 1920. He attended Corpus Christi College, Cambridge, before and after the Second World War, during which he served in the Royal Artillery. After 1946 his work as member of the British Council brought him to Greece, India, Ceylon, and the United States, where he delivered a series of penetrating lectures. *The Chequer'd Shade* is a set of "Reflections on Obscurity in Poetry," and *Uncertainties* contains some of his most personal poems.

Narcissus

The scarlet poppy smouldering in the fields
Blazes and coruscates with my desire.
The molten mirror of the sunset yields
A pale and troubled image of my fire.

What is all music but the echoing
Of the great leaping themes within my veins?
And when the stricken heavens are thundering
What is it but my heart that cracks and strains?

I am the sap that creeps within the trees;
My deep unpastured questioning expands
Into the tossing of the unquiet seas;
My loneliness pervades the level sands.

And even when desire has mastered me,
Breast strained on breast, taut thighs on loosening thighs,
I cannot lose myself, but still must see
My own reflection in wide-opened eyes.

Alex Comfort

Alexander Comfort was born in London, February 10, 1920, and became a doctor, biologist, sociologist, pacifist, and philosophical anarchist. As Alex Comfort he is the author of half a dozen novels, several books of non-fiction, and seven volumes of poetry. *Haste to the Wedding*, published in 1962, is the most uninhibited of these. It combines the witty sensuality of the seventeenth century—the theme of love as play—with the candor of our own times.

Sublimation

The proud who never loved
the shy man or the slow
make a woman of words:
why should I do so?

Catullus and John Donne —
did they enjoy, or lack?
The cock-bird dances on
for the hen who turns her back.

The songs that stand are sung
chiefly by hungry men.
With better things in hand
no one would dip a pen:

the written word provides
a form of exercise —
the gist of poetry
you have between your thighs.

Bird and fish bequeathed
aesthetics to their race

to drive us into bed;
all other arts digress —

Those serve to fill the space
between meeting and meeting —
this is the eloquent thing
that they are celebrating,

and nothing that we write
myself or any other
matches the fine content
of what we do together.

⌒◟◞◝⌒

After You, Madam

There are no upper hands in love
though one is under, one above:
  the man who said so lied —
it is a choice for human mates
lacking in other vertebrates
  that you or I should ride.

Adam, that Freudian figurehead,
considered his prestige in bed —
  taking their cure from that
the Moslem schoolmen who believe
in the delinquency of Eve
  extend her like a mat:

The casuists of the Vatican
in placing woman under man
  take Paul *au pied de la lettre*.[1]
Before the mediaeval *conte*
made it a source of *mauvaise honte*,[2]
  Petronius knew better.

Lady, the whimsical restraints
imposed by inexperienced saints
  on modes of procreation
have little interest for us.
We share the honors without fuss
  by frequent alternation.

[1] *Au pied de la lettre*: to the letter, literally. [2] *Mauvaise honte*: false shame.

Helga Sandburg

Daughter of a famous poet, Helga Sandburg is also a poet as well as a folklorist, lecturer, and novelist. Born in 1922 she began her career typing manuscripts for her father in a loft room in Michigan. Recipient of several grants, she went abroad on cultural and educational missions for the State Department. Her third novel, *The Owl's Roost,* published in 1962, was compared to the work of Ellen Glasgow.

Cantata for Two Lovers

This is the way the ladies are
They are always washing and drying their hair
They are always walking into spring
And exclaiming at how long it's been
Since last year and how they've forgot the names
Of birds and flowers and other things
They are always attending to a gentleman who begs
To kneel again between their legs
And they lift their hands and put back their hair
For this is the way the ladies are

This is the way the gentlemen are
They are always in love with their mother
They are always hoping to make themselves free
And they carry swords in company
With other gentlemen who feel the same
(Though begetting sons on wives is a recognized aim)
They are always seeking to fit their hand
On a thigh which explodes above a stocking
To protect themselves from ladies they must have war
For this is the way the gentlemen are

X. J. Kennedy

Born August 21, 1929, in Dover, New Jersey, X. J. Kennedy received his M.A. from Columbia University, served for four years in the U. S. Navy, and, after his discharge, attended the Sorbonne in Paris for a year. Returning to the United States he became an Instructor of English at the University of Michigan shortly before his *Nude Descending a Staircase* was chosen as the Lamont Poetry Selection by the Academy of American Poets in 1961. His poems, said another poet, W. D. Snodgrass, "clearly intend to delight the reader, and they do. No one around is wittier or pokes more delicious fun at our foolishness."

Lilith

Adam's first wife had soft lips but no soul:
He looked her in the eye, back looked a hole.
Her small ear lay, a dry well so profound
No word he pebbled in it drew a sound.

Could he complete what God had left half-wrought?
He practiced in a looking lake, he taught
Stray rudiments of wriggle, where to stand
Her liltless feet. She handed him her hand.

Her breasts stood up but in them seemed to rise
No need for man. He roamed lone in her thighs
And inmost touching, most knew solitude.
In vacant rooms, on whom can one intrude?

O let down mercy on a poor man who clings
To echoes, beds him with imaginings!
Sweet Lord, he prayed, *with what shade do I lie?*
Second came she whom he begot us by.

575

In A Prominent Bar in Secaucus

In a prominent bar in Secaucus one day
Rose a lady in skunk with a topheavy sway,
Raised a knobby red finger—all turned from their beer—
While with eyes bright as snowcrust she sang high and clear:

"Now who of you'd think from an eyeload of me
That I once was a lady as proud as could be?
Oh I'd never sit down by a tumbledown drunk
If it wasn't, my dears, for the high cost of junk.

"All the gents used to swear that the white of my calf
Beat the down of the swan by a length and a half.
In the kerchief of linen I caught to my nose
Ah, there never fell snot, but a little gold rose.

"I had seven gold teeth and a toothpick of gold,
My Virginia cheroot was a leaf of it rolled
And I'd light it each time with a thousand in cash—
Why the bums used to fight if I flicked them an ash.

"Once the toast of the Biltmore, the belle of the Taft,
I would drink bottle beer at the Drake, never draft,
And dine at the Astor on Salisbury steak
With a clean tablecloth for each bite I did take.

"In a car like the Roxy I'd roll to the track,
A steel-guitar trio, a bar in the back,
And the wheels made no noise, they turned over so fast,
Still it took you ten minutes to see me go past.

"When the horses bowed down to me that I might choose,
I bet on them all, for I hated to lose.
Now I'm saddled each night for my butter and eggs
And the broken threads race down the backs of my legs.

"Let you hold in mind, girls, that your beauty must pass
Like a lovely white clover that rusts with its grass.
Keep your bottoms off barstools and marry you young
Or be left—an old barrel with many a bung.

"For when time takes you out for a spin in his car
You'll be hard-pressed to stop him from going too far
And be left by the roadside, for all your good deeds,
Two toadstools for tits and a face full of weeds."

All the house raised a cheer, but the man at the bar
Made a phonecall and up pulled a red patrol car
And she blew us a kiss as they copped her away
From that prominent bar in Secaucus, N.J.

Robert Bagg

A true representative of the young men of the mid-fifties, Robert Bagg was born in New Jersey in 1935. Before he was graduated from Amherst College he had won several prizes, including a fellowship for a year's study in Europe. A Prix de Rome followed, and a National Defense Fellowship on which Bagg did graduate work at the University of Connecticut. His first rich and delicately perceptive collection of poems, *Madonna of the Cello,* was published when he was twenty-six.

Soft Answers

Her wraithful turnings and her soft answers head
   · Me off. The easiest allusion of her hips,
No matter how well spoken for, soon slips
   Her mind. I ask her long blonde braids where they lead,

Hold them over her head, and let them fall.
   Even her breasts' tactfully gathered favor
Can't hold my hand's attention forever.
   Lazy as her love is, I have my hands full

With her, letting every beauty she owns
   Slip through my tongue and fingers, still hoping
For the whole of her, soon closing and opening
   Like a giant heart toying with my bones.

A Selected Bibliography

Books

The Roxburghe Ballads. 4 parts. 1540-1790.

The Roxburghe Ballads, reprinted by The Ballad Society of London. 8 vols. 1869-80.

A Handefull of Pleasant Delites. 1584. Edited by H. E. Rollins, Cambridge, U.S.A., 1924.

Love's Garland. 1624.

The Crumbs of Comfort. 1628.

The Female Glory. 1634.

Wits' Recreations. 1640.

Wits' Recreations Refined. 1645.

Catch That Catch Can. 1652.

The Card of Courtship. 1653.

Wit & Drollery, Jovial Poems. 1656.

Cupid's Posies. 1683.

The True Lover's New Academy. 1688.

Joyful Cuckoldom. 1690.

Venus' Looking-Glass. 1700.

Wit & Mirth: or, Pills to Purge Melancholy. 4 vols. 1707-09.

The Merry Muses of Caledonia, collected by Robert Burns. c. 1800.

A Pedlar's Pack of Ballads and Songs. Edited by W. H. Logan. 1869.

English and Scottish Popular Ballads. Edited by Francis James Child. 5 vols. 1882-98.

Modern Street Ballads. Edited by John Ashton. 1888.

Merry Songs and Ballads. Edited by J. S. Farmer. 5 vols. 1897.

The Common Muse. Edited by Pinto and Rodway. 1957.

The Idiom of the People. Edited by James Reeves. 1958.

Folk Songs of England, Ireland, Scotland & Wales. Edited by William Cole. 1961.

The Ballad-Mongers. By Oscar Brand. 1962.

Records

Merry Muses of Caledonia. Sung by Paul Clayton. Elektra 155.

Songs of Robert Burns. Sung by Betty Sanders. Riverside RLP 12-823.

When Dalliance Was in Flower. 3 albums. Sung by Ed McCurdy. Elektra 110, 140, 160.

Son of Dalliance. Sung by Ed McCurdy. Elektra 170.

Bawdy Songs and Backroom Ballads. 5 albums. Edited and sung by Oscar Brand. AF 1840-47.

Index to Authors

580

Printed in the United States
1493100003B/77-85